MAN
AND THE
ENVIRONMENT

DISCARDED

MAN
AND THE
ENVIRONMENT

Wes Jackson

Kansas Weslayan

Foreword by Paul Ehrlich

WM. C. BROWN COMPANY PUBLISHERS
Dubuque, Iowa

BIOLOGY SERIES

Consulting Editor
 E. Peter Volpe
 Tulane University

Copyright © 1971 by
Wm. C. Brown Company Publishers

Library of Congress Catalog Card Number: 74-135421

ISBN 0–697–04666–4

Printed in the United States of America

to LAURA, SCOTT and SARA

CONTENTS

xi

FOREWORD

Unless we radically change our national life style within the next two years, we might as well begin preparing ourselves for the eco-catastrophies which are certain to be upon us before the end of the decade. For years most of our public officials have failed to recognize the impending environmental disasters parading before their very eyes and have continued to wallow in the bipartisan swamp of American optimism. Since these irresponsible officials have proved time and again that they are crisis-oriented, it may well take a massive die-off from a killer smog, an epidemic, or starvation to convince our politicians to institute even the most obvious reforms.

The present population of the United States is already two or more times larger than any possible optimum figure for the country. Every additional birth merely increases the pressures on our life-support systems and further decreases the likelihood of our survival. Even if every American couple limited themselves to two natural children starting tomorrow, the population of the United States would not level off until the year 2020—at a figure of almost *300 million.* But, at the present rate of environmental destruction, it may not matter by that time anyway.

Considering our per capita level of affluence and the lag time of population limitation programs, we must move to a simpler life ethic based on inner security, rather than on the acquisition and conspicuous consumption of material things. We must reduce our population growth to zero as rapidly as possible; we must reduce and control our military-industrial complex; we must move to the low consumption recycling philosophy of a "spaceman" economy. And, we must move quickly, if not immediately. Technology will help but it is not the entire answer. Attitude change is the key.

As the readings in this book will show, we must seek to improve the quality of life for all Americans, rather than to increase the quantity of junk consumed by a privileged few. People pollute, and more people consuming more things will continue to foul the environment even more—environmental deterioration feeds on itself. Just as technology is not the sole solution to the environmental crisis, neither is population limitation the entire answer, but at least reducing our population will give us a chance to solve some of our critical problems: war, racism, pollution, hunger, crime and disease. And, if we moved to a simpler existence, life might even be joyous again.

PAUL R. EHRLICH

PREFACE

February 1, 1967 was the beginning of my conversion. Just fresh out of graduate school and into undergraduate teaching, one of my responsibilities was to teach an introductory biology course with a large enrollment of non-biology majors "working off their general education requirement."

As the semester progressed, it soon became obvious that the Krebs cycle, a waltz through the phyla, and even protein synthesis, were not relevant to these students, at least as far as they could tell. Consequently, I pledged to sacrifice some of the more classical information and to weave in as much "relevance" as possible the next time around. During the 1967-68 academic year I clipped, tore, xeroxed, and filed. By the end of the 1968 summer session, Man and the Environment had supplanted Introductory Biology in nearly every way, except by catalog description and title.

This monstrously growing accumulation of readings consisted of well over one thousand units. Shakedown by topic and within topic became necessary. It was here that the complete conversion occurred, for two central but intertwined threads emerged: the *population-food problem* and *environmental destruction*.

Concern emerging from my conversion and that of my fellow faculty members eventually became translated into the establishment of a Survival Studies Program and a major offered in that area at Kansas Wesleyan. Thirty-one of my fellow faculty members from seventeen disciplines are now joined in this interdisciplinary effort. It would be difficult to single out their specific contributions to this collection.

I am grateful to my survival-activist wife, Dana, and my one-too-many children for their numerous contributions in the development of the course, the new program and this collection.

In various stages of preparation, Miss Rachel Stucky, Miss Joan Foss and Miss Teresa Grier, survival-active undergraduate students, graciously typed and proofread materials. In addition, my friend Mr. Robert Hill was kind enough to read the manuscript and make suggestions. This help is appreciated.

Miss Martha Bieri patiently put up with my ever-changing mind as to what was to be included, rejected or modified. She took whatever time was necessary every week to send nearly all permission forms and follow-up letters to authors and publishers, run the Xerox machine and generally manage things.

Finally, I wish to acknowledge the contribution of my students, especially those who are naive enough to think that the world can avoid catastrophe. Although I am doubtful, I am also hopeful.

ACKNOWLEDGEMENTS

1. Reprinted with permission of The Macmillan Co. from *Collected Poems* by William Butler Yeats. Copyright 1934 by The Macmillan Co., renewed 1962 by Bertha Georgia Yeats.

2. A letter by Ralph A. Lewin in *BioScience* 19:584. July 1969. Copyright 1969 by the American Institute of Biological Sciences.

3. Copyright 1966 by George Gaylord Simpson. Reprinted from his volume, *Biology and Man*, by permission of Harcourt, Brace & World, Inc.

4. Bible, Genesis 1:26.

* From the advertisement "Now Is the Time for All Good Men to Come to the Aid of Their Planet" by Leo Burnett Co., Inc. Copyright 1969 by Leo Burnett Co., Inc.

5. "The Historical Roots of Our Ecological Crisis" by Lynn White, Jr. *Science* 155:1203-1207. 10 March 1967. Copyright 1967 by the American Association for the Advancement of Science.

6. From "The Attitude Lag," an editorial by Eugene P. Odum. *BioScience* 19:403. May 1969. Copyright 1969 by the American Institute of Biological Sciences.

7. "Man and the Air" by LaMont C. Cole. *Population Bulletin* 24:103-113. December 1968. Copyright 1968 by the Population Reference Bureau, Inc.

8. From "Evolution of the Earth's Atmosphere" by S.I. Rasool. *Science* 157:1466-1467. 22 September 1967. Copyright 1967 by the American Association for the Advancement of Science.

9. From "The Atmospheres of Mars and Venus" by Von R. Eshleman. Copyright 1969 by Scientific American, Inc. All rights reserved.

10. "Perhaps Pollution Ruined Venus" by Jeffrey D. Alderman, Associated Press Writer. Copyright by the Associated Press.

11. From "Winds, Pollution, and the Wilderness" by Lester Machta. *The Living Wilderness* 33:3-8. Summer 1969. Copyright 1969 by The Wilderness Society.

12. From "Automobile Engines: Pollution and Power" by Israel Katz. *Science* 162:1221-1222. 13 December 1968. Copyright 1968 by the American Association for the Advancement of Science.

13. "The Car: An Electric Challenge." *Time* 94:55. 14 November 1969. Copyright 1969 by Time, Inc.

14. From "Steam Automobiles: Advocates Seek Government Support for Research" by Andrew Jamison. *Science* 161:27-29. 5 July 1968. Copyright 1968 by the American Association for the Advancement of Science.

15. From "Methanol: A New Fuel?" by Ronald G. Minet. *Science* 157:1373-1374. 22 September 1967. Copyright 1967 by the American Association for the Advancement of Science.

16. From "Diminishing the Role of Sulfur Oxides in Air Pollution," an editoral by Philip H. Abelson. Science 157:1265. 15 September 1967. Copyright 1967 by the American Association for the Advancement of Science.

17. Senate Report on the Air Quality Act of 1967.

18. From "Pollution: The Wake of the 'Torrey Canyon' " by John Walsh. *Science* 160:167-169. 12 April 1968. Copyright 1968 by the American Association for the Advancement of Science.

19. "Oil in the Ecosystem" by Robert W. Holcomb. *Science* 166:204-206. 10 October 1969. Copyright 1969 by the American Association for the Advancement of Science.

20. From "Oil Spills—An Old Story" by S.W.A. Gunn, a letter to *Science* 165:967. 5 September 1969. Copyright 1969 by the American Association for the Advancement of Science.

21. "The Oil Pollution Threat." *The Wilderness Report* 6: No. 2. 15 September 1969. Copyright 1969 by the Wilderness Society.

22. "Thermal Pollution" by LeMont C. Cole. *BioScience* 19:989-992. November 1969. Copyright 1969 by the American Institute of Biological Sciences.

23. From "Thermal Addition: One Step from Thermal Pollution" by Sharon Friedman. *BioScience* 19:60-61. January 1969. Copyright 1969 by the American Institute of Biological Science.

24. Executive Order 11288, Section 7.

25. "The Effects of Pesticides" by William A. Niering. *BioScience* 18:869-875. September 1968. Copyright 1968 by the American Institute of Biological Sciences.

26. From "Battle of Coral Sea." *Newsweek* 74:53. 14 July 1969. Copyright 1969 by Newsweek, Inc.

27. "Monitoring Pesticide Pollution" by Philip A. Butler. *BioScience* 19:889-891. October 1969. Copyright 1969 by the American Institute of Biological Sciences.

28. From ."Pesticide Pollution Control" by H. Page Nicholson. *Science* 158:371-376. 17 November 1967. Copyright 1967 by the American Association for the Advancement of Science.

29. From a letter by Robert Van den Basch in *Science* 164:497. 2 May 1969. Copyright 1969 by the American Association for the Advancement of Science.

30. From a letter by Yosiaki Itô, et al. in *Science* 162:513-514. 1 November 1968. Copyright 1968 by the American Association for the Advancement of Science.

31. From "Gardening Without DDT." *Time* 94:41. 8 August 1969. Copyright 1969 by Time, Inc.

32. From a letter by David E. Elrick in *Science* 154:1275. 6 December 1966. Copyright 1966 by the American Association for the Advancement of Science.

33. A letter by Edward S. Deevey, Jr. in *Science* 154:68. 7 October 1966. Copyright 1966 by the American Association for the Advancement of Science.

34. Reprinted by permission from *The Christian Science Monitor.* Copyright 1969 by The Christian Science Publishing Society. All rights reserved.

35. "Shock at Sea." *Time* 94:40. 15 August 1969. Copyright 1969 by Time, Inc.

36. From "Radioiodine Fallout Over the Midwest in May" by Lester Machta. *Science* 160:64-66. 5 April 1968. Copyright 1968 by the American Association for the Advancement of Science.

37. From "Nerve Gas: Dugway Accident Linked to Utah Sheep Kill" by Philip M. Boffey. *Science* 162: 1460-1464. 27 December 1968. Copyright 1968 by the American Association for the Advancement of Science.

38. "Academy Charges Army Gas Dump Plan," an editorial by Philip M. Boffey. *Science* 165:45. 4 July 1969. Copyright 1969 by the American Association for the Advancement of Science.

* From *The Sound of Mountain Water* by Wallace Stegner. Copyright 1969 by Wallace Stegner. Reprinted by permission of Doubleday & Co., Inc.

39. Lee Merriman Talbot from *Wildlands in Our Civilization,* ed. David Brower. Copyright 1964 by the Sierra Club.

40. From *Deserts on the March,* by Paul B. Sears. Copyright 1935 by the University of Oklahoma Press.

41. From "California's Natural Land and Water Reserve System" by Kenneth S. Norris. *BioScience* 18:415-417. May 1968. Copyright 1968 by the American Institute of Biological Sciences.

42. "A Letter from the Arctic" by Samuel Wright. *The Living Wilderness* 33:5-6. Spring 1969. Copyright 1969 by The Wilderness Society.

43. From "National Parks: Traffic Jams Turn Attention to Roads" by Luther J. Carter. *Science* 161:770-772. 23 August 1968. Copyright 1968 by the American Association for the Advancement of Science.

44. "We Must Earn Again for Ourselves What We Have Inherited: A Lesson in Wilderness Economics" by Garrett Hardin, from *Wilderness: The Edge of Knowledge.* Copyright 1970 by the Sierra Club.

45. From "Animals from the Amazon Basin" a letter by Paul Gregory Heltne. *Science* 157:134. 14 July 1967. Copyright 1967 by the American Association for the Advancement of Science.

46. "Whales: Decline Continues Despite Limitations on Catch" by John Walsh. *Science* 157:-1024-1025. 1 September 1967. Copyright 1967 by the American Association for the Advancement of Science.

47. From the advertisement "I'm All Lathered Up About the Poor Whale" by Ralph Taylor. Copyright 1969 by the Caswell-Massey Co., Ltd.

48. From "The Tortoise and the Jet" an editorial by Dael Wolfle. *Science* 157:255. 21 July 1967. Copyright 1967 by the American Association for the Advancement of Science.

49. From "California's Natural Land and Water Reserve System" by Kenneth S. Norris. *BioScience* 18:415-417. May 1968. Copyright 1968 by the American Institute of Biological Sciences.

50. A letter by Edward C. Stone and Richard B. Vassey in *Science* 160:836-837, and a letter by Bestor Robinson in *Science* 160:833-836. 24 May 1968. Copyright 1968 by the American Association for the Advancement of Science.

51. From "Forest Fires: Suppression Policy Has Its Ecological Drawbacks" by Mark Oberle. *Science* 165:568-571. 8 August 1969. Copyright 1969 by the American Association for the Advancement of Science.

52. From a letter by Amédeé A. Peugnet in *Science* 158:205. 13 October 1967. Copyright 1967 by the American Association for the Advancement of Science.

53. "Eco-catastrophe!" by Paul Ehrlich. *Ramparts* 8:24-28. September 1969. Copyright 1969 by Ramparts Magazine, Inc. By permission of the editors.

54. From "The Resolution of Conflicts in Conservation through Adult Education" by Charles A. Dambach. *BioScience* 18:864-868. September 1968. Copyright 1968 by the American Institute of Biological Sciences.

55. From "Action by State Departments of Conservation" by Charles H. W. Foster. *BioScience* 18:418-420. May 1968. Copyright 1968 by the American Institute of Biological Sciences.

56. "The Population Crisis Is Here *Now*" by Walter E. Howard. *BioScience* 19:779-784. September 1969. Copyright 1969 by the American Institute of Biological Sciences.

57. From *The Population Bomb* by Paul R. Ehrlich. Copyright 1968 by Paul R. Ehrlich. Published by Ballantine Books, Inc.

58. "The Social Consequences of Population Growth" by Benjamin Viel. *PRB Selection,* No. 30. October 1969. Copyright 1969 by The Population Reference Bureau, Inc.

59. "Birth Control for Economic Development" by Stephen Enke. *Science* 164: 798-802. 16 May 1969. Copyright 1969 by the American Association for the Advancement of Science.

60. "Population Policy: Will Current Programs Succeed?" by Kingsley Davis. *Science* 158:730-739. 10 November 1967. Copyright 1967 by the American Association for the Advancement of Science.

61. From "Soviet Population Theory," an editorial by Dael Wolfle. *Science* 158:999. 24 November 1967. Copyright 1967 by the American Association for the Advancement of Science.

62. "Do Roman Catholic Countries Have the Highest Birth Rates?" *Population Profile,* July 1968. Copyright 1968 by the Population Reference Bureau, Inc.

63. "Population Control, Sterilization, and Ignorance" an editorial by Thomas Eisner, Ari van Tienhoven, and Frank Rosenblatt. *Science* 167:337. 23 January 1970. Copyright 1970 by the American Association for the Advancement of Science.

64. From a book review of *Abortion in the United States* (edited by Mary Steichen Calderone) by James R. Newman in *Scientific American* 200:149-154. January 1959. Copyright 1959 by Scientific American, Inc. All rights reserved.

65. A letter by Ashley Montagu in *Science* 163:1271. 10 January 1969. A letter by Kiffin A. Rockwell in *Science* 164:770. 16 May 1969. Copyright 1969 by the American Association for the Advancement of Science.

66. "Abortion—or Compulsory Pregnancy?" by Garrett Hardin. *Journal of Marriage and the Family* 30:246-251. May 1968. Copyright 1968 by the National Council on Family Relations.

67. "Coping with Contraceptive Failure" by Garrett Hardin. *Perspectives in Biology and Medicine,* August 1966. Copyright 1966 by the University of Chicago Press.

68. "The Explosive Desire for Children" *Time* 94:57. 22 August 1969. Copyright 1969 by Time, Inc.

69. "The Tragedy of the Commons" by Garrett Hardin. *Science* 162:1243-1248. 13 December 1968. Copyright 1968 by the American Association for the Advancement of Science.

70. "The Tragedy of the Commons Revisited" by Beryl L. Crowe. *Science* 166:1103-1107. 28 November 1969. Copyright 1969 by the American Association for the Advancement of Science.

71. From the *Journals of Lewis and Clark* by Meriwether Lewis. Used with the permission of the American Philosophical Society.

72. From "Food Production in Prehistoric Europe" by H. T. Waterbolk. *Science* 162: 1093-1101. 6 December 1968. Copyright 1968 by the American Association for the Advancement of Science.

73. From "Digging Up Prehistoric America" by Robert Claiborne. *Harper's Magazine* 232:69-74. April 1966. Copyright 1966 by Harper's Magazine, Inc. Permission granted by the Julian Bach, Jr., Literary Agency.

74. "Japan: A Crowded Nation Wants to Boost Its Birthrate" by Philip M. Boffey. *Science* 167:-960-962. 13 February 1970. Copyright 1970 by the American Association for the Advancement of Science.

75. Bible, Revelation 6:5,6.

76. From *Famine—1975!* by William and Paul Paddock. Copyright 1967 by Little, Brown and Co.

77. State of the Union Message, 10 January 1967.

78. By James Bonner from *The Next Ninety Years.* Copyright 1967 by California Institute of Technology.

79. "The Dual Challenge of Health and Hunger—A Global Crisis" by Georg A. Borgstrom. *PRB Selection,* No. 31. January 1970. Copyright 1970 by the Population Reference Bureau, Inc.

80. "Agricultural Production in the Developing Countries" by G. F. Sprague. *Science* 157:774-778. 18 August 1967. Copyright 1967 by the American Association for the Advancement of Science.

81. From "Can We Prepare for Famine? A Social Scientist's View" by E. James Archer. *BioScience* 18:685-690. July 1968. Copyright 1968 by the American Institute of Biological Sciences.

82. From "Paying the Piper" by Paul R. Ehrlich. *New Scientist* 36:652-655. 14 December 1967. Copyright 1967 by Cromwell House.

83. From a letter by Jean Mayer in *Science* 152:291. 15 April 1966. Copyright 1966 by the American Association for the Advancement of Science.

84. From "Malnutrition, Learning, and Behavior," an editorial by Philip H. Abelson. *Science* 164:17. 4 April 1969. Copyright 1969 by the American Association for the Advancement of Science.

85. From a book review of *Famine—1975!* (William and Paul Paddock) by James Bonner in *Science* 157:914-915. 25 August 1967. Copyright 1967 by the American Association for the Advancement of Science.

86. Concurrent Resolution of the Senate, 22 January 1969.

87. "Dry Lands and Desalted Water" by Gale Young. *Science* 167:339-343. 23 January 1970. Copyright 1970 by the American Association for the Advancement of Science.

88. From "Water Importation into Arid Lands" by Jay M. Bagley. *Science* 162:478. 25 October 1968. Copyright 1968 by the American Association for the Advancement of Science.

89. From "The Use of Arid Lands," an editorial by Dael Wolfle in *Science* 164: 1345. 20 June 1969. Copyright 1969 by the American Association for the Advancement of Science.

90. From "Dams and Wild Rivers: Looking Beyond the Pork Barrel" by Luther J. Carter. *Science* 158:233-242. 13 October 1967. Copyright 1967 by the American Association for the Advancement of Science.

91. "Aquatic Weeds" by L. G. Holm, L. W. Weldon, and R. D. Blackburn. *Science* 166: 699-709. 7 November 1969. Copyright 1969 by the American Association for the Advancement of Science.

92. From "Think Big (An Open Letter to the Secretary of the Interior)" by Bruce Stewart. *Harper's Magazine* 231:62-63. August 1965. Copyright 1965 by Harper's Magazine, Inc. Reprinted by permission of the author.

93. "The Myth of Fertility Dooms Development Plans" by Darryl G. Cole. *The National Observer* 7:10. 22 April 1968. Copyright 1968 by Dow Jones and Co., Inc.

94. From "Brazil: A Prodigy of Growth" by William E. Moran, Jr. *Population Bulletin* 25:89-90. September 1969. Copyright 1969 by the Population Reference Bureau, Inc.

95. From "Human Food from Ocean and Land" by K. O. Emery and C. O'D. Iselin. *Science* 157:1279-1281. 15 September 1967. Copyright 1967 by the American Association for the Advancement of Science.

96. From "Milk Production of Cows on Protein-Free Feed" by Artturi I. Virtanen. *Science* 153:-1603-1614. 30 September 1966. Copyright 1966 by the American Association for the Advancement of Science.

97. By Howard T. Odum from *The World Food Problem.* Vol. III by the President's Science Advisory Committee. U.S. Government Printing Office, 1967.

HUMAN BEHAVIOR

Man's numbers are exploding, his oceans are dying and his cities threaten to strangle him. Nuclear threat lurks in the background. We know that all of the major problems facing man are the result of his own behavior. Much of this behavior is obviously destructive. Why does man have such a strong tendency to destroy? Does the answer lie in how man existed on the African savannahs more than two million years ago, and later in the valleys of Europe and Asia? Is the answer simply that usually when man destroyed, he ate and survived? If so, this violent behavior has a strong genetic component. In those days, human numbers were low and man was not armed with technology. Behavior that was formerly adaptive now threatens our species.

To avert catastrophe we must alter some of our behavior. The birth rate must come to equal the death rate, and eventually the death rate must exceed the birth rate. Is this possible? What will be the psychological effects on society at large with only two, one or zero children in a family? The destruction of the biosphere must be stopped. Does this mean that we *not* do all that we are capable of doing technologically? I think so!

Despite his frequent anthropocentric ego-trips, man is not a self-sufficient demigod who stands arrogantly astride a prostrate and alien natural world. Man is a finite part of Nature. As a result of mutation and selection he has an animal brain. His glandular system is likely to be more at home in a paleolithic cliff dwelling than in a steel and concrete cliff of midtown Manhattan.

Professor Simpson's paper provides a baseline for an understanding of man in a total evolutionary context. It is from such an understanding of man that we must begin if we are to solve the population-environment-resource problems of this planet.

The Four Ages of Man 1

WILLIAM BUTLER YEATS

He with body waged a fight,
But body won; it walks upright.
Then he struggled with the heart;
Innocence and peace depart.
Then he struggled with the mind;
His proud heart he left behind.
Now his wars on God begin;
At stroke of midnight God shall win.

Human Nature 2

RALPH A. LEWIN

Everything I like is either illegal or immoral, pollutes the environment, or increases the population.

The Biological Nature of Man 3

The answer to the ancient question "What is man?"
must be based first on man's biological character.

GEORGE GAYLORD SIMPSON

It has often and confidently been asserted, that man's origin can never be known: but ignorance more frequently begets confidence than does knowledge: it is those who know little, and not those who know much, who so positively assert that this or that problem will never be solved by science. (1)

Those words were written by Charles Darwin nearly 100 years ago and were published in 1871 in the introduction to his book on *The Descent of Man.* In his even better known work on *The Origin of Species* (2), which had appeared 12 years earlier, he had been content to say (somewhat coyly) that by that work "light would be thrown on the origin of man and his history." Others soon indicated the nature of that light. Thomas Henry Huxley's classic *Man's Place in Nature (3)* was published in 1863, and by 1871 numerous other naturalists of the first rank had already accepted the evolutionary origin of the human species. Darwin's own contribution to the problem of man's origin firmly established two points: first, *Homo sapiens,* like all other organisms, has evolved from prior, extremely different species by natural means and under the directive influence of natural selection; and second, man is the descendant of apes or monkeys of the Old World.

Darwin's first point, that man is the product of evolution involving natural selection, has been attacked on emotional grounds, but it was not and is not now honestly questionable on strictly scientific grounds and by anyone really familiar with the facts. The second point, of man's descent from an Old World ape or monkey, was for some time more open to scientific dispute. However, here, too, the debate was often more emotional than objective. In some pedagogic circles it became usual to maintain that man is not descended from an ape but from a common ancestor neither man nor ape nor, if one cared to go still further afield, monkey. Some went so far as to attempt to enlist Darwin posthumously in their own pussyfooting ranks by saying that he never maintained that man arose from an ape but only from a common ancestor . . . and so forth. In fact, although Darwin was slow to enter the dispute, when he did so he was more honest than those supposed defenders. He flatly said, "We must conclude, however much the conclusion may revolt our pride, that our early progenitors would have been properly . . . designated (as apes or monkeys)." The unscientific and really un-called-for remark on pride does little to modify the forthrightness of the conclusion.

Darwin's conclusions in 1871 already covered what is most vital for consideration of man's biological status. Subsequent discovery and study have fully corroborated Darwin and have added an enormous amount of detail. That is interesting and important, and most of what I have to say here concerns it. At this point, however, the essential thing is that Darwin put the whole subject of the nature of man on a new and sound footing. To be sure, in the introduction of *The Descent of Man,* from which I have already quoted, Darwin went on to say that, "The conclusion that man is the codescendant with other species of some ancient, lower, and extinct form, is not in any degree new." He then cited Lamarck, Wallace, Huxley, Lyell, Vogt, Lubbock, Büchner, Rolle, Haeckel, Canestrini, and Barrago as "having taken the same side of the question." In fact, as regards this particular point, Darwin was doing too much honor to those worthies, some still famous and some now forgotten. It is true that they had all discussed the descent of man before Darwin himself did so in an explicit way, but with the sole exception of Lamarck they had done so after publication of *The Origin of Species* and on the basis of that work by Darwin. As for the few who really had postulated an evolutionary origin for man before *The Origin of Species,* their views were largely philosophical speculations inadequately or not at all supported by objective evidence and sometimes, as in the case of Lamarck, reaching a conclusion only approximately correct on grounds that were flatly wrong (4).

What Is Man?

The question "What is man?" is probably the most profound that can be asked by man. It has always been central to any system of philosophy or of theology. We know that it was being asked by the most learned humans 2000 years ago, and it is just possible that it was being asked by the most brilliant australopithecines 2 million years ago. The point I want to make now is that all attempts to answer that question before 1859 are worthless and that we will be better off if we ignore them completely. The reason is that no answer had a solid, objective base until it was recognized that man is the product of evolution from primeval apes and before that through billions of years of gradual but protean change from some spontaneously, that is, naturally, generated primordial monad.

It is the biological nature of man, both in his evolutionary history and in his present condition, that presents us with our only fixed point of departure. These are the facts we can find out for ourselves, in great, ever-increasing detail and soundness, open to all of us in irrefutable observations. Their interpretation is in some respects ambiguous and disputable, but interpretation at a given point becomes increasingly clear and undisputed as time goes on. Doubtfulness moves outward with the expanding frontier of knowledge.

I do not mean to say that the biological study of man or even that the scientific study of man in terms broader than biological can here and now—if ever—provide a satisfactorily complete answer to the question "What is man?" The other, older approaches through metaphysics, theology, art, and other nonbiological, nonscientific fields can still contribute, or can now contribute anew. But unless they accept, by specification or by implication, the nature of man as a biological organism, they are merely fictional fancies or falsities, however interesting they may be in those nonfactual categories. I am here concerned with man's biological nature in a rather broad sense, on the grounds that this is a necessary, even though it is not a completely sufficient, approach to comprehension of man's nature.

Already in Darwin's day it was clearly established that among living animals the great apes are anatomically most similar to man. Some anatomists, reluctant to acknowledge their poor relatives, stressed differences between man and any apes: the larger human brain, obviously; the longer and less divergent first toe of man; the absence or, more commonly, the only-sporadic presence in us of certain apish muscles and other structures. Such discussions completely missed the point. Of course men and apes differ. In itself, that means only that we belong to different species. The point at issue is not whether we differ, but in what way and how closely the different species are related.

All later study has corroborated the special relationship between men and apes and has made knowledge of it more precise. The evidence has lately been greatly increased in extent, in detail, and in its basic character. It now includes such fundamental points as the numbers and shapes of chromosomes, the exact molecular structure of hemoglobins, the resemblances and differences of serum proteins, and many others (5). All the evidence agrees and the conclusion is unequivocal. Man is not identical with apes in these or other respects. However, he is clearly related to the apes, and among the apes he is most particularly related to chimpanzees and gorillas, which are closely related between themselves. A necessary inference from this evidence is that the common ancestor of apes and men was itself a member of the ape family. Not only that; we had a common ancestor with gorilla and chimpanzee after their ancestry had become distinct from that of the other living apes (orangutan and gibbons). Our relationships to gorilla and to chimpanzee are about equal, although gorillas may have become somewhat more specialized with respect to the common ancestry.

Evidence from Fossils

More precise evidence as to relationships and as to the course of anatomical change in the human ancestry must come from fossils. There are special reasons why pertinent fossils are comparatively uncommon: Crucial stages apparently occurred in the tropics, where preservation and discovery of fossils are difficult and where exploration has generally lagged; populations of apes and of pre-humans were always small, not at all comparable with the great herds of grazing animals, for example, common as fossils; and the habits and abilities of apes and pre-humans were such as to reduce chances of natural burial and preservation as fossils.

Nevertheless, a great many fossils have been recovered and discovery is active at present. We are far from having the whole story, but parts of it are increasingly clear.

In Darwin's time only one really distinctive kind of fossil ape *(Dryopithecus)* and only one really distinctive kind of fossil man (Neanderthal) were known. From the former, Darwin correctly inferred that by late Miocene, at least, the lineages of apes and monkeys had separated. He was not clear as to the possible implications for separation of the strictly human lineage, which he thought might have occurred much earlier. As regards Neanderthal man Darwin could only express surprise that in spite of their antiquity the Neanderthals had brain capacities probably greater than the average for modern man.

Now it is known that apes more or less similar to *Dryopithecus* were widespread and, as apes go, numerous through the Miocene and Pliocene of Europe, Asia, and Africa (6). Present estimates place the beginning of the Miocene at approximately 25 million years ago (7). The divergence of apes and Old World monkeys is thus at least that old. There is, in fact, some evidence that this divergence occurred in the Oligocene, which preceded the Miocene and began some 10 million years earlier. Divergence of apes and monkeys was identical with divergence of the human ancestry and monkeys, because the earliest apes were also ancestral to man. The time of the final split of the specifically prehuman lineage from that leading to gorilla and chimpanzee has not yet been closely determined. On present evidence it seems most likely to have occurred during the

Miocene, that is, quite roughly between 10 and 25 million years ago. The earliest known forms that may be definitely on a prehuman line as distinct from a pre-gorilla-chimpanzee line are *Ramapithecus* from India and the closely similar, indeed probably identical supposed genus *Kenyapithecus* from Africa (8). Unfortunately those animals are known only from teeth and fragments of jaws, so that their affinities are somewhat uncertain and the anatomy of their skulls and skeletons is entirely unknown. The known specimens are approximately 10 million years old, give or take a few million.

The next significant group of fossils is that of the australopithecines, literally "southern monkeys" although they almost certainly were not exclusively southern and with complete certainty were not monkeys. They are surely and comparatively well known from East and South Africa, doubtfully and, at best, poorly known from elsewhere in Africa and from Eurasia. In Africa they are clearly divisible into two distinct groups. There is dispute as to whether those groups should not be subdivided still further and whether they should be called species or genera. Although the specialists can become enraged over those questions, they have no real importance for others, the important fact being simply that the two separate groups did exist, a point on which even the specialists now agree. Both groups resemble apes much more than we do now, but both are more nearly related to us than to the apes—another point on which the specialists have finally agreed after years of wrangling. They definitely belong to the human family, Hominidae.

One group, typified by *Australopithecus robustus* or, as it is also often called, *Paranthropus robustus,* retained some particularly primitive (more or less ape-like) features and yet became somewhat aberrantly specialized. It cannot have been directly ancestral to modern man. The other group, typified by *Australopithecus africanus,* although also primitive within the human family, more closely resembles our own genus, *Homo.* Both groups are now believed to have appeared at least 2 million years ago. For a long time, perhaps 1-1/2 million years, there were at least two distinct lineages of the human family living in Africa and probably throughout the warmer parts of the Old World. One, more primitive and aberrant, showed little progress and finally became extinct. The other, more progressive, evolved into *Homo.* A matter still under sharp dispute is whether the latter lineage included *Australopithecus africanus* as our direct ancestor, or whether for a time there were not actually three distinct lines: the two kinds of australopithecines and still another more directly related to *Homo.* The latter suggestion arises from Leakey's discovery of what he calls *Homo habilis* (9). However, some authorities believe that supposed species not to be on a distinct lineage but to belong to the line leading from *Australopithecus africanus* eventually to *Homo sapiens.*

That dispute is interesting and we hope it may soon be settled, but it is far less important than the fact that our ancestry passed through a stage closely similar to *Australopithecus africanus* if it was not that group itself. Our ancestors were then fully bipedal, ground-living animals, using their hands for manipulation as we do but perhaps not quite so skillfully. Their teeth were so like ours as to be hard to distinguish, but their brains were little larger than those of apes, and if we could see them alive their physiognomy, while distinctive, would probably strike us as more apelike than manlike.

By a time probably not later than 500,000 years ago and perhaps earlier, gradual evolution from australopithecines had reached a stage that was human in a more restricted sense, belonging not only to the human family, Hominidae, but also to the same genus as ourselves, *Homo.* Doting and ambitious discoverers have given many different names to such early fossil men, including *Pithecanthropus* and *Sinanthropus,* but most of them are now usually placed in a single species, *Homo erectus.* Bodily anatomy and even physiognomy were now almost fully human, but to our eyes there was still a coarse or brutish cast of countenance because of heavy brow ridges over the eyes and a low, small brain case. The brain size was neatly intermediate between australopithecines (or modern apes) and modern man.

Finally, and still gradually, our own species, *Homo sapiens,* emerged. Although not entirely certain, it is now the usual opinion that the quite varied fossils known collectively as Neanderthal men belonged to *Homo sapiens* and only represent ancient races that were at first primitive (not so far removed from *Homo erectus*) and later somewhat aberrant. The more aberrant late Neanderthals became extinct as such, although it is probable that some of their genes survive.

So much for more or less direct knowledge of man's physical, anatomical origin. The main points are these:

1. Man evolved from apes also ancestral to chimpanzees and gorillas, but less specialized than the latter.

2. The divergence of man's ancestry from the apes was early marked by bipedalism and upright posture, with extensive correlations and implications in anatomy, habits, and capabilities.

3. Also early was divergent dental evolution, again with other implications, for example as to diet and means of defense. It is not known whether posture and dentition diverged from the apes simultaneously or in which order.

4. Only after evolution of human posture and dentition was essentially complete did man's brain begin to enlarge beyond that of the apes. (Intelligence depends not only on size of the brain but also on its internal anatomy, and we do not know the internal anatomy of our fossil ancestors' brains. However, it is fairly certain that a species with average brain size as in apes could not be as intellegent as *Homo sapiens.*)

Systematics of Modern Man

Now let us briefly consider the taxonomic, biological systematic nature of mankind as it exists today. First and most important is the fact that mankind *is* a kind, a definite and single species. A biological species is an evolutionary unit composed of continuing populations that regularly interchange genes by interbreeding and that do not or cannot have such regular interchange with other species (10). The definition clearly applies to mankind: all human populations can and, as opportunity occurs, do interbreed, producing fertile offspring and thus continuing the species and keeping it bound together as a unit. It is unlikely that, for example, a Greenland Eskimo has ever interbred with a South African Bushman, but since all intervening populations can and do interbreed they are nevertheless members of the same species. That species, *Homo sapiens,* is not connected with any other species by interbreeding.

Comparison of Eskimo and Bushman brings up the obvious (although occasionally denied) fact that the human species includes quite diverse races. A race is simply a population (or group of populations) that is genetically distinguished from others. The distinction is not absolute. It is unlikely that Negroes, for example, have any genes that do not occur in some white populations, or that whites have any genes absent in all Negro populations. The usual situation is that a race has certain genes and gene combinations that are more frequent in it than elsewhere, and therefore typical in that sense, but not confined to the race. Races always grade into each other without definite boundaries. There is not now and never has been such a thing as a pure race, biologically speaking. Any two human populations, no matter how small or how large, differ in some respects, so that there is no fixed number of races. One could count thousands or two, and no matter how many are counted, there will be some populations and many individuals that do not clearly fit into one or another. Moreover, races are evanescent in the course of evolution. A given race may change, disappear by fusion with others, or die out altogether while the species as a whole simply continues its evolutionary course (11).

Races of man have, or perhaps one should say "had," exactly the same biological significance as the subspecies of other species of mammals. Widespread animals have local populations that live under diverse conditions and that may become temporarily and in part isolated from each other. They may then more or less accidentally have different proportions of genes (in stricter technical language, of alleles) from other such populations, and if the situation continues long enough, they will almost inevitably evolve somewhat different adaptations to local conditions. Primitive men were relatively few in number and relatively immobile, but they spread over enormous areas—the whole land area of the earth except for Antarctica and a few small islands. They evolved into races or, in better biological terms, into subspecies exactly as any other animal would have under those circumstances. Racial differentiation in man was originally geographic and, for the most part, adaptive.

That was the original biological significance of race. One must say that Negroes were biologically superior to whites, if reference is to prehistoric times, when the races were originating, and to African conditions, to which Negroes were biologically adapted and whites were not. At the present time race has virtually no strictly biological significance because of two crucial changes. First, human adaptation to different environments is now mostly cultural and is directly biological only in lesser part, so that the prehistoric biological adaptations have lost much of their importance. Second, tremendous increases in population size, in mobility, and in environmental changes brought about by man himself have the result that extremely few men are now living under the conditions to which their ancestors were racially adapted.

Evolution does not necessarily proceed at the same rate in different populations, so that among many groups of animals it is possible to find some species that have evolved more slowly, hence are now more primitive, as regards some particular trait or even over-all. It is natural to ask—as many have asked—whether among human races there may not similarly be some that are more primitive in one way or another or in general. It is indeed possible to find single characteristics that are probably more advanced or more primitive in one race than in another. For example, the full lips and kinky hair of some Negroes are almost certainly progressive traits in comparison with the more primitive, decidedly apelike thin lips and straight hair of most whites. However, that does not mean that whites in general are more primitive than Negroes or otherwise inferior to them. Overall primitiveness and progressiveness in comparison of different groups of animals is practically confined to cases in which the groups are of different species, so that genes of the more rapidly evolving species cannot be transferred to the lagging species. Human races all belong to the same species and have generally had enough interbreeding so that genetic progress, as distinct from local adaptation, could and evidently did spread through the entire species. Only if some race entirely ceased to interbreed with any other would it be likely for it to fall behind and become definitely inferior. Let us hope that will not happen.

Resemblances, Anatomical and Psychological

Regardless of the diversity of races, it is obvious that all men resemble one another much more than any of them differ from each other. They all share the basic qualities, anatomical, physiological and psychological, that make us human, *Homo sapiens,* and no other species that is or ever was. Something has already been said of anatomical peculiarities of *Homo sapiens* with respect to living apes and human ancestors. Here are some of the most striking human anatomical traits:

Normal posture is upright.

Legs are longer than arms.

Toes are short, the first toe frequently longest and not divergent.

The vertebral column has an *S* curve.

The hands are prehensile, with a large and strongly opposable thumb.

Most of the body is bare or has only short, sparse, inconspicuous hair.

The joint for the neck is in the middle of the base of the skull.

The brain is uniquely large in proportion to the body and has a particularly large and complex cerebrum.

The face is short, almost vertical under the front of the brain.

The jaws are short, with a rounded dental arch.

The canine teeth are usually no larger than the premolars, and there are normally no gaps in front of or behind the canines.

The first lower premolar is like the second, and the structure of the teeth in general is somewhat distinctive.

Given those characteristics, a museum curator could readily identify any specimen of *Homo sapiens* that was added to the collections, or that happened to walk into his office. However, we who are pondering the question "What is man?" must feel that these anatomical features, fully diagnostic as they are, yet do not amount to an answer adequate for our purposes. Even if we were defining, say, a species of mouse, the anatomical definition would not take us far toward understanding "What is mouse?" or, better, "What is mouseness?" unless we related the bodily mouse to the behaving mouse and the thinking mouse. Even thus, human anatomy reflects truly essential man-ness or human nature only to the extent that it is related to human activities and psychology. Already in *The Descent of Man* (1) Darwin discussed such traits in which man appears to be most distinctive. His points, here greatly abbreviated and paraphrased, were as follows:

In proportion with his higher intelligence, man's behavior is more flexible, less reflex or instinctive.

Man shares such complex factors as curiosity, imitation, attention, memory, and imagination with other relatively advanced animals, but has them in higher degree and applies them in more intricate ways.

More, at least, than other animals, man reasons and improves the adaptive nature of his behavior in rational ways.

Man regularly both uses and makes tools in great variety.

Man is self-conscious; he reflects on his past, future, life, death, and so forth.

Man makes mental abstractions and develops a related symbolism; the most essential and complexly developed outcome of these capacities is language.

Some men have a sense of beauty.

Most men have a religious sense, taking that term broadly to include awe, superstition, belief in the animistic, supernatural, or spiritual.

Normal men have a moral sense; in later terms, man ethicizes.

Man is a cultural and social animal and has developed cultures and societies unique in kind and in complexity.

The last point, which some students now consider the most important of all, was least emphasized by Darwin, who was here mainly concerned with the relationship of social evolution to the origin of the moral sense. Darwin's general purpose was not to characterize *Homo sapiens* as the unique species that he is. The purpose was to show that the characteristics that make him unique are nevertheless foreshadowed in other animals, and that the evolution of man from other, earlier, quite distinct species is therefore plausible. We are no longer concerned with *whether* man evolved, because we know that he did. We are still very much concerned with *how* he evolved, with what is most characteristically human about him and how those characteristics arose. The list of traits discussed by Darwin is still valid from this somewhat different point of view.

That list should not be taken as involving so many separate and distinct things. These are aspects of the behavior, capacities, and accomplishments of a species that is characterized by all of them together and not by each or any one separately. They interact and interlock not only with each other but also with the previously mentioned physical or anatomical characteristics of man. For example, complex human societies, especially the modern industrial civilization rapidly spreading to the whole world, require specialization of activities by different members of society further involving manipulation of complex machines. Such specialization, which is nongenetic, requires individual flexibility and could not occur in a mainly instinctive animal. The machines are tools and could only have been devised by a reasoning, toolmaking animal. Invention also required manual deftness, which was provided by (and which also gave selective value to) the structure of the human hand, which required upright posture and could not have been acquired by a quadruped. Further evolution of the early cultural adaptations that led eventually to modern industry also had increased intelligence as a necessary concomitant, and that eventually required larger brains, which in turn involved change in skull structure and in stance—and so on. Even the changing pattern of the teeth can be related to this unitary complex.

The Major Evolutionary Changes

Because all the specifically human traits are integrated within the whole that is human, and because each of the traits as well as their integration must have arisen gradually, it is somewhat questionable to speak of definite milestones or even of particular critical phases in the evolution of man. Yet there are three among these slow and coordinated changes that seem particularly basic for the concept of human-ness. The most crucial single anatomical point is acquisition of upright posture and strictly bipedal locomotion. Most of the other main peculiarities of human anatomy either follow from that or are coadapted with it. The other two major factors are cultural, but are no less biological since both represent attainment and maintenance of biological adaptation by cultural means. They are tool making and language.

Extremely crude but unmistakable stone tools are found in the oldest rock strata containing indisputable members of the human family, nearly, if not quite, 2 million years old. It will be difficult to authenticate still older and more primitive stone tools, because they must have consisted of natural pebbles or rock fragments picked up and used with little or no modification. It has long been maintained that deliberate manufacture of a tool is the distinctive human trait, since many other animals, even including some insects, use natural objects as tools but do not make tools. Now it has been found that chimpanzees may trim and shorten twigs or straws for use as tools (12), and although that simple behavior is almost too primitive to be called tool making, it sufficiently demonstrates that the capacity for tool making is biologically ancient and prehuman. If one wants a more diagnostic statement, it probably is true that man is the only living animal that uses tools to make tools. However, that trait would follow soon and inevitably once tool making really got under way. A stone used to knock flakes off an incipient stone ax is already a machine tool.

Ancient tools more perishable than stone are rarely preserved. Nevertheless, the course of increasing diversity and complication of tools can be followed well enough to demonstrate the gradual and inconstant but generally continual progress through prehistory. The tremendously accelerated progress in historic times is very well documented and is familiar to all of us in general outline, at least. The whole sweep from stone axes to electronic computers is a natural and comprehensible extension of the biological capacities of an unusual species. It is uniquely wonderful, and yet, lest we stand too much in awe of our own products, let us remember that a digital computer is merely a rapid and automated tool for what amounts to counting on fingers.

As posture is focal for consideration of man's anatomical nature and tools are for consideration of his material culture, so is language focal for his mental nature and his non-material culture (13). Language is also the most diagnostic single trait of man: all normal men have language; no other now-living organisms do. That real, incomparably important, and absolute distinction has been blurred by imprecise use of the word "language" not only in popular speech but also by some scientists who should know better, speaking, for example, of the "language of the bees" (14).

In any animal societies, and indeed in still simpler forms of aggregation among animals, there must be some kind of communication in the very broadest sense. One animal must receive some kind of information about another animal. That information may be conveyed by specific signals, which may be of extremely diverse kinds both as to form and as to modality, that is, the sensory mode by which it is received. The odor of an ant, the movements of a bee, the color pattern of a bird, the howl of a wolf, and many thousands of others are all signals that convey information to other animals and that, in these and many other examples, are essential adaptations for behavioral integration in the species involved.

Human language is also a system of interpersonal communication and a behavioral adaptation essential for the human form of socialization. Yet human language is absolutely distinct from any system of communication in other animals. That is made most clear by comparison with other animal utterances, which most nearly resemble human speech and are most often called "speech." Nonhuman vocables are, in effect, interjections. They reflect the individual's physical or, more frequently, emotional state. They do not, as true language does, name, discuss, abstract, or symbolize. They are what the psychologists call affective; such purely affective so-called languages are systems of emotional signals and not discourse. The difference between animal interjection and human language is the difference between saying "Ouch!" and saying "Fire is hot."

That example shows that the nonlanguage of animal interjection is still present in man. In us it is in effect not a part of language, but the negative of language, something we use in place of speech. In part we even use the same signals as do the apes, a fact already explored to some depth by Darwin in another of his basic works, *The Expression of the Emotions in Man and Animals* (15). Much more is now known about such expressions in animals, and particularly in our closer relatives the apes and monkeys, and it is not surprising to find that the non-linguistic, affective system is particularly complicated in them and has not progressed but may even have retrogressed in man. Still we do retain that older system along with our wholly new and wholly distinct system of true language. It is amusing that the human affective interjectional reaction to a bad smell is practically the same as in all other primates, down even to the most primitive.

Attempts To Trace Language

Darwin's study and many later studies sought to trace the evolutionary origin of language from a prehuman source. They have not been successful. As a recent expert in the field (16) has said, "The more that is known about it (that is, communication in monkeys and apes), the less these systems seem to help in the understanding of human language."

Many other attempts have been made to determine the evolutionary origin of language, and all have failed. Because language is so important for any concept of man and because this is an interesting example of methodology and limitations, it is worthwhile to consider some of these futile attempts. One, fairly obvious once the idea of linguistic evolution had arisen, was by comparison of living languages. One result was a supposed genetic sequence: (i) isolating languages, like Chinese, which string together invariable word roots; (ii) agglutinating languages, like Mongolian, which modify roots by tacking on prefixes and suffixes; and (iii) flexional languages, like Latin, which modify by (partly) internal changes in words. The trouble is that these categories are not really distinct and, especially, that they did not historically occur in this sequence. For example, Chinese was probably flexional at one time and is now becoming agglutinating with a possibility of becoming flexional again. English was flexional until quite recently and is now mostly isolating with a strong dash of agglutination. Moreover at the present time no languages are primitive in the sense of being significantly close to the origin of language. Even the peoples with least complex cultures have highly sophisticated languages, with complex grammar and large vocabularies, capable of naming and discussing anything that occurs in the sphere occupied by their speakers. Tales of tribal natives who cannot count beyond 4 and who have vocabularies of only two or three hundred words betray the shortcomings of gullible travelers, not of the natives (17).

Another approach is to follow back directly historical records, which cover several thousand years for some European, Asiatic, and north African languages. It is then possible to project still further and to reconstruct, for example, a proto-Indo-European anterior to Sanskrit. But this still leaves us tens or hundreds of thousands of years—perhaps even more—from the origin of language. The oldest language that can reasonably be reconstructed is already modern, sophisticated, complete from an evolutionary point of view.

Still another attempt, which now seems very naive, is through the ontogeny of language, that is, the acquisition of language by children. This relies on the famous but, as it happens, quite erroneous saying that ontogeny repeats phylogeny. In fact the child is not evolving or inventing primitive language but is learning a particular modern language, already complete and unrecognizably different from any possible primitive language. Moreover, the child is doing this with a modern brain already genetically constructed (through the long, long action of natural selection) for the use of complete, wholly nonprimitive language.

It is a tempting hypothesis that the time, at least, of the origin of language might be determined by structural characteristics in fossils. One rather elaborate attempt departed from the fact that all linguistic phonetic systems, varied as they are, depend in part on the shape of the lower jaw and the hard palate, anatomi-cally quite different in typical members of the human and the ape families. It was postulated that speech began when these anatomical parts reached human form, which was in the australopithecines or somewhat earlier. But the postulate is clearly wrong. Audible signals capable of expressing language do not require any particular phonetic apparatus, but only the ability to produce sound, any sound at all. Almost all mammals and a great number of other animals can do that. Moreover, a number of animals, not only birds but also some mammals, can produce sounds recognizably similar to those of human language, and yet their jaws and palates are radically nonhuman. A parrot is capable of articulating a human word but is completely incapable of understanding what the word means.

Given any method of sound production, the capacity for language depends not on characteristics of the sound apparatus but on the central nervous system. Speech is particularly connected with the left temporal lobe of the human brain, as shown, for example, by the fact that ability to speak is generally lost if that lobe is severely damaged. The gross development of the lobe can be seen in plaster casts of the insides of fossil skulls, and that, too, has been proposed as a means of determining whether or not a given fossil individual could speak. But all mammals have left temporal lobes, some smaller and some larger. Those with smaller lobes do not speak just a little and those with larger lobes more. There is no graded sequence: normal men speak completely; other animals, whatever the relative size of their temporal lobes, do not speak at all.

The essential anatomical and physiological basis of speech is nevertheless in the structure and function of the brain (18). That basis is not fully known, but it evidently involves not just a language center, such as might be localized in the temporal lobe, but an intricate and widespread system of associative connections throughout much of the brain. (The nature or presence of these connections cannot be determined in fossils.) Thus sensations of any kind derived from an external object or event can be generalized according to similarities with others. Each kind can then be associated with a distinctive symbol, which does not resemble the object or event at all but which arbitrarily stands for it. That symbol, a supreme element in the nature of man, is the word, and it is not surprising that words meaning "word," abstraction and symbolization on still another level, have acquired such mystical and philosophical overtones. (Λόγος!)

It is still possible but it is unlikely that we will ever know just when and how our ancestors began to speak. Yet it is certain that this ability depends on physical, structural, and chemical characteristics of the nervous system which evolved from our nonspeaking ancestors under the force of natural selection. The capacity for this unique kind of symbolization is quite general. It does not determine what symbol will be used for a given concept, but that any symbol can be associated with any concept. Thus we are all using exactly the same genetic capacity and symbolizing the same concept when various of us say "woman," "Weib," "femme," "mujer," "zhenshchina," or "imra," depending on whether we happen to have been raised in England, Germany, France, Spain, Russia, or Egypt. The words do not resemble each other and even less resemble the concept they stand for. Moreover, they can be written in different ways, as in Latin,

Arabic, or Chinese characters, that do not resemble each other and that have no physical resemblance to the spoken words. They can even be associated with some symbol that is not verbal at all, as in this example with the simplified representation of Venus's mirror that biologists use to designate females: ♀.

Conclusion

Language has become far more than a means of communication in man. It is also one of the principal (although far from the only) means of thought, memory, introspection, problem-solving, and all other mental activities. The uniqueness and generality of human symbolization have given our mental activities not only a scope but also a quality far outside the range of other animals. It keeps us aware, to greater extent than can otherwise be, of past and future, of the continuity of existence and its extension beyond what is immediately sensed. Along with other peculiarly human capacities, it is involved in what I consider the most important human characteristic from an ethical point of view: foresight. It is the capacity to predict the outcome of our own actions that makes us responsible for them and that therefore makes ethical judgement of them both possible and necessary (19).

Above the individual level, language and related powers of symbolization make possible the acquisition, sharing, and preserving of knowledge far beyond what would be possible for any single individual. That is an indispensable element in all forms of human social organization and cultural accomplishment, even the most primitive.

It is obvious that I have by no means touched on all aspects of the biological nature of man. That would be impossible in one essay by one author. Those familiar with recent developments in biology may particularly miss reference to molecular biology and especially to the compound called DNA, now known to be largely involved in heredity and also in control of biochemical activities in cells. Those subjects are extremely fascinating at present and may be portentous for the future. However, in my opinion nothing that has so far been learned about DNA has helped significantly to understand the nature of man or of any other whole organism. It certainly is necessary for such understanding to examine what is inherited, how it is expressed in the developing individual, how it evolves in populations, and so on. Up to now the triumphs of DNA research have had virtually no effect on our understanding of those subjects. In due course molecular biology will undoubtedly become more firmly connected with the biology of whole organisms and with evolution, and then it will become of greater concern for those more interested in the nature of man than in the nature of molecules.

Finally, it should be pointed out that although man is a unique animal and although we properly consider his nature in the light of his peculiarities, he also has many non-peculiarities. Man is not *merely* an animal, that is, his essence is not simply in his shared animality. Nevertheless he *is* an animal and the nature of man includes and has arisen from the nature of all animals. Indeed if all the material characteristics of man could be enumerated, it would surely be found that the vast majority of them also occur in other animals. In fact at the level of molecular structure and interaction, information storage and transfer, energy transactions, and other defining characteristics of life, man is hardly significantly different from a bacterium—another illustration of the fact that that level of study is not particularly useful in considering the nature of man.

Like other animals, man develops, is born, grows, reproduces, and dies. Like other animals, he eats, digests, eliminates, respires, locomotes. He bends the qualities of nature to his own ends, but he is as fully subject to nature's laws as is any other animal and is no more capable of changing them. He lives in biological communities and has a niche and an ecology, just as do robins and earthworms. Let us not forget those aspects of man's nature. But let us also remember that man stands upright, builds and makes as never was built or wrought before, speaks and may speak truth or a lie, worships and may worship honestly or falsely, looks to the stars and into the mud, remembers his past and predicts his future, and writes (perhaps at too great length) about his own nature.

REFERENCES AND NOTES

1. C. Darwin, *The Descent of Man, and Selection in Relation to Sex* (Murray, London, 1871).
2. ———, *On the Origin of Species by Means of Natural Selection, or The Preservation of Favoured Races in the Struggle for Life* (Murray, London, 1859).
3. T. H. Huxley, *Evidence as to Man's Place in Nature* (Williams and Norgate, London, 1863).
4. Lamarck's view (unknown to most Neo-Lamarckians) was that *all* organisms are evolving toward and will eventually become human, after which they will degenerate through the inorganic world and eventually be spontaneously generated as lowly organisms and start again on the path to man. Today's amoeba is tomorrow's man, day after tomorrow's mineral, and still another day's amoeba once more. In the state of knowledge and philosophy of Lamarck's day it would perhaps be too strong to label his views as absurd, but they were certainly less sensible and less progressive than has often been claimed.
5. These new data are well exemplified in S. L. Washburn, Ed., *Classification and Human Evolution* (Aldine, Chicago, 1963).
6. E. L. Simons and D. R. Pilbeam, *Folia Primatol.* No. 46 (1965).
7. On this and other absolute (year) dates see D. E. Savage, J. F. Evernden. G. H. Curtis, G. T. James, *Am. J. Sci.* 262, 145 (1964).
8. E. L. Simons, *Postilla* (Yale Peabody Museum) No. 57 (1961); *Proc. Nat. Acad. Sci. U.S.* 51, 528 (1964).
9. L. S. B. Leakey, P. V. Tobias, M. D. Leakey, J. R. Napier, *Nature* 202, 3 (1964); P. V. Tobias, *Science* 149, 22 (1965). For discussion and dissent see P. L. DeVore, Ed., *The Origin of Man* (transcript of a symposium, Wenner-Gren Foundation, New York, 1965).
10. Age-long argument on the definition of species is perhaps sufficiently summarized in G. G. Simpson, *Principles of Animal Taxonomy* (Columbia Univ. Press, New York, 1961) and E. Mayr, *Animal Species and Evolution* (Harvard Univ. Press, Cambridge, 1963).
11. On animal races see especially Mayr (10). On the perennial, knotty problem of human races, a sensible general statement with many references is in Th. Dobzhansky, *Mankind Evolving* (Yale Univ. Press, New Haven, 1962).
12. J. Goodall, in *Primate Behavior,* I. DeVore, Ed. (Holt, Rinehart and Winston, New York, 1965). p. 425.
13. The literature on human culture and linguistics is as voluminous as that of any field of science. Some recent studies especially pertinent to my text are: A. L. Bryan, *Current Anthropol.* 4, 297 (1965); M. Critchley, in *Evolution after Darwin,* S. Tax, Ed. (Univ. of Chicago Press, Chicago, 1960), vol. 2, p. 289; A. S. Diamond, *The History and Origin of Language* (Philosophical Library, New York, 1959); E. L. DuBrul, *Evolution of the Speech Apparatus* (Thomas, Springfield, Ill., 1958); B. R. Fink, *Perspectives Biol. Med.* 7, 85 (1963); C. F. Hockett, in *The Evolution of Man's Capacity for Culture,* J. N. Spuhler, Ed. (Wayne State Univ. Press, Detroit, 1959), p. 32; C. F. Hockett and R. Ascher, *Current Anthropol.* 5, 135 (1964); A. Kortlandt, *ibid.* 6, 320 (1965). See also works cited in 16.

14. Misuses of the term "language" are too widely exemplified to need citation. The distinction is discussed by several of the authors cited in *13*, also (among other places) in J. B. S. Haldane and H. Spurway, *Insectes Sociaux* 1, 247 (1954) and J. B. S. Haldane, *Sci. Progr.* No. 171, 385 (1955).
15. C. Darwin, *The Expression of the Emotions in Man and Animals* (Murray, London, 1872).
16. J. B. Lancaster, in *The Origin of Man*, P. L. DeVore, Ed. (transcript of a symposium, Wenner-Gren Foundation, New York, 1965). See also discussions by A. R. Diebold, Jr., T. A. Sebeok, D. Slobin in the same volume, and bibliography on pp. 149-150.
17. I first began to appreciate the richness and complexity of "primitive" languages when I visited the Kamarakotos of Venezuela in 1939, and I commented on it in G. G. Simpson, *Los Indios Kamarakotos* (Ministerio de Fomento, Caracas, 1940).
18. N. Geschwind, *Brain* 88, 237 (1965).
19. G. G. Simpson, *Am. Psychologist* 21, 27 (1966).
20. During 1965 varying versions of this essay were presented as lectures at Randolph Macon College, the University of Paris, and the University of Washington. I have profited by discussions on those occasions.

THE ENVIRONMENT

What we don't know—or refuse to recognize—is that modern man has been altering his total environment so swiftly that the whole "great chain of life" on this planet is endangered.

All of us live on a tiny space-ship which is hurtling through the universe at a speed 600 times faster than the fastest jet plane—carrying with it its own limited resources for sustaining life.

What we have now is all that we will ever have to keep us alive. Having already set foot on the lifeless moon, we shall presumably find that we are the only creatures in our solar system. As lonely astronauts on our own ceaseless journey through space, what do we have as our basic equipment for survival?

Above us, a narrow band of usable atmosphere, no more than seven miles high, with no "new" air available to us.

Beneath us, a thin crust of land with only one-eighth of the surface hospitable to human life.

And around us, a finite supply of "usable" water that we must perpetually cleanse and re-use.

These are the elements of man's physical environment. This is the "envelope" in which our planet is eternally sealed.

Together, and left alone, land, air, and water work well as an "ecosystem" to maintain the great chain of life, and the delicate balance of nature, from ocean depth to mountain top.

But man, since he first rose up on two legs, has been tampering with this system. He cannot help it. Everything we do alters our environment: the ways we grow food and build shelter and create what we call "culture" and "civilization."

Now, entering the last three decades of the 20th century, we face the shocking realization that we have gone too far too fast and too heedlessly—and now we are forced to cope with some of the consequences of our "progress" as a species.

For, increasingly, all over the world scientists and statesmen and specialists in many fields are coming to agree on the pressing paradoxes of our modern age:

As societies grow richer, their environments grow poorer.

As the array of objects expands, the vigor of life declines.

As we acquire more leisure to enjoy our surroundings, we find less around us to enjoy.

Man's Perspective

The Ainu on Hokkaido, the large north island of Japan, practice a religion which centers around Nature. The high point of their ritual is the sacrifice of the bear. Past generations of Ainu, heavily dependent upon the bear for food and warmth, placated his spirit before taking his life. It is doubtful if there was ever wanton destruction of bears among the Ainu. Judaeo-Christian groups, on the other hand, were not so respectful of Nature.

There is a view that much of the ecologic crisis may be attributed to the Judaeo-Christian influence (reading 5). Although it is dangerous to pull from context passages which support a particular point of view—especially from the Bible, where so many conflicting passages exist—Genesis 1:26 (reading 4) may provide a clue to—and cue for Western man's behavior.

Before new ways can be implemented, attitudes—which are notoriously recalcitrant (reading 6)—must change. A willingness to survey objectively the earth's resources and systems, past and present, can give us some hint of what we must do to secure a viable future.

Genesis 1:26   4

Let us make man in our image, after our likeness: and let them have dominion over the fish of the sea, and over the fowl of the air, and over the cattle, and over every creeping thing that creepeth upon the earth.

5   The Historical Roots Of Our Ecologic Crisis

LYNN WHITE, JR.

A conversation with Aldous Huxley not infrequently put one at the receiving end of an unforgettable monologue. About a year before his lamented death he was discoursing on a favorite topic: man's unnatural treatment of nature and its sad results. To illustrate his point he told how, during the previous summer, he had returned to a little valley in England where he had spent many happy months as a child. Once it had been composed of delightful grassy glades; now it was becoming overgrown with unsightly brush because the rabbits that formerly kept such growth under control had largely succumbed to a disease, myxamatosis, that was deliberately introduced by the local farmers to reduce the rabbits' destruction of crops. Being something of a Philistine, I could be silent no longer, even in the interests of great rhetoric. I interrupted to point out that the rabbit itself had been brought as a domestic animal to England in 1176, presumably to improve the protein diet of the peasantry.

All forms of life modify their contexts. The most spectacular and benign instance is doubtless the coral polyp. By serving its own ends, it had created a vast undersea world favorable to thousands of other kinds of animals and plants. Ever since man became a numerous species he has affected his environment notably. The hypothesis that his fire-drive method of hunting created the world's great grasslands and helped to exterminate the monster mammals of the Pleistocene from much of the globe is plausible, if not proved. For 6 millennia at least, the banks of the lower Nile have been a human artifact rather than the swampy African jungle which nature, apart from man, would have made it. The Aswan Dam, flooding 5000 square miles, is only the latest stage in a long process. In many regions terracing or irrigation, overgrazing, the cutting of forests by Romans to build ships to fight Carthaginians or by Crusaders to solve the logistics problems of their expeditions, have profoundly changed some ecologies. Observation that the French landscape falls into two basic types, the open fields of the north and the *bocage* of the south and west, inspired Marc Bloch to undertake his classic study of medieval agricultural methods. Quite unintentionally, changes in human ways often affect nonhuman nature. It has been noted, for example, that the advent of the automobile eliminated huge flocks of sparrows that once fed on the horse manure littering every street.

The history of ecologic change is still so rudimentary that we know little about what really happened, or what the results were. The extinction of the European aurochs as late as 1627 would seem to have been a simple case of overenthusiastic hunting. On more intricate matters it often is impossible to find solid information. For a thousand years or more the Frisians and Hollanders have been pushing back the North Sea, and the process is culminating in our own time in the reclamation of the Zuider Zee. What, if any, species of animals, birds, fish, shore life, or plants have died out in the process? In their epic combat with Neptune have the Netherlanders overlooked ecological values in such a way that the quality of human life in the Netherlands has suffered? I cannot discover that the questions have ever been asked, much less answered.

People, then, have often been a dynamic element in their own environment, but in the present state of historical scholarship we usually do not know exactly when, where, or with what effects man-induced changes came. As we enter the last third of the 20th century, however, concern for the problem of ecologic backlash is mounting feverishly. Natural science, conceived as the effort to understand the nature of things, had flourished in several eras and among several peoples. Similarly there had been an age-old accumulation of technological skills, sometimes growing rapidly, sometimes slowly. But it was not until about four generations ago that Western Europe and North America arranged a marriage between science and technology, a union of the theoretical and the empirical approaches to our natural environment. The emergence in widespread practice of the Baconian creed that scientific knowledge means technological power over nature can scarcely be dated before about 1850, save in the chemical industries, where it is anticipated in the 18th century. Its acceptance as a normal pattern of action may mark the greatest event in human history since the invention of agriculture, and perhaps in nonhuman terrestrial history as well.

Almost at once the new situation forced the crystallization of the novel concept of ecology; indeed, the word *ecology* first appeared in the English language in 1873. Today, less than a century later, the impact of our race upon the environment has so increased in force that it has changed in essence. When the first cannons were fired, in the early 14th century, they affected ecology by sending workers scrambling to the forests and mountains for more potash, sulfur, iron ore, and charcoal, with some resulting erosion and deforestation. Hydrogen bombs are of a different order: a war fought with them might alter the genetics of all life on this planet. By 1285 London had a smog problem arising from the burning of soft coal, but our present combustion of fossil fuels threatens to change the chemistry of the globe's atmosphere as a whole, with consequences which we are only beginning to guess. With the population explosion, the carcinoma of planless urbanism, the now geological deposits of sewage and garbage; surely no creature other than man has ever managed to foul its nest in such a short order.

There are many calls to action, but specific proposals, however worthy as individual items, seem too partial, palliative, negative: ban the bomb, tear down the billboards, give the Hindus contraceptives and tell them to eat their sacred cows. The simplest solution to any suspect change is, of course, to stop it, or, better yet, to revert to a romanticized past: make those ugly gasoline stations look like Anne Hathaway's cottage or (in the Far West) like ghost-town saloons. The "wilderness area" mentality invariably advocates deep-freezing an ecology, whether San Gimignano or the High Sierra, as it was before the first Kleenex was dropped. But neither atavism nor prettification will cope with the ecologic crisis of our time.

What shall we do? No one yet knows. Unless we think about fundamentals, our specific measures may produce new backlashes more serious than those they are designed to remedy.

As a beginning we should try to clarify our thinking by looking, in some historical depth, at the presuppositions that underlie modern technology and science. Science was traditionally aristocratic, speculative, intellectual in intent; technology was lower-class, empirical, action-oriented. The quite sudden fusion of these two, towards the middle of the 19th century, is surely related to the slightly prior and contemporary democratic revolutions which, by reducing social barriers, tended to assert a functional unity of brain and hand. Our ecologic crisis is the product of an emerging, entirely novel, democratic culture. The issue is whether a democratized world can survive its own implications. Presumably we cannot unless we rethink our axioms.

The Western Traditions of Technology and Science

One thing is so certain that it seems stupid to verbalize it: both modern technology and modern science are distinctly *Occidental.* Our technology has absorbed elements from all over the world, notably from China; yet everywhere today, whether in Japan or in Nigeria, successful technology is Western. Our science is the heir to all the sciences of the past, especially perhaps to the work of the great Islamic scientists of the Middle Ages, who so often outdid the ancient Greeks in skill and perspicacity: al-Razi in medicine, for example; or Ibn al-Haytham in optics; or Omar Khayyam in mathematics. Indeed, not a few works of such geniuses seem to have vanished in the original Arabic and to survive only in medieval Latin translations that helped to lay the foundations for later Western developments. Today, around the globe, all significant science is Western in style and method, whatever the pigmentation or language of the scientists.

A second pair of facts is less well recognized because they result from quite recent historical scholarship. The leadership of the West, both in technology and in science, is far older than the so-called Scientific Revolution of the 17th century or the so-called Industrial Revolution of the 18th century. These terms are in fact outmoded and obscure the true nature of what they try to describe—significant stages in two long and separate developments. By A.D. 1000 at the latest—and perhaps, feebly, as much as 200 years earlier—the West began to apply water power to industrial processes other than milling grain. This was followed in the late 12th century by the harnessing of wind power. From simple beginnings, but with remarkable consistency of style, the West rapidly expanded its skills in the development of power machinery, labor-saving devices, and automation. Those who doubt should contemplate that most monumental achievement in the history of automation: the weight-driven mechanical clock, which appeared in two forms in the early 14th century. Not in craftsmanship but in basic technological capacity, the Latin West of the later Middle Ages far outstripped its elaborate, sophisticated, and esthetically magnificent sister cultures, Byzantium and Islam. In 1444 a great Greek ecclesiastic, Bessarion, who had gone to Italy, wrote a letter to a prince in Greece. He is amazed by the superiority of Western ships, arms, textiles, glass. But above all he is astonished by the spectacle of waterwheels sawing timbers and pumping the bellows of blast furnaces. Clearly, he had seen nothing of the sort in the Near East.

By the end of the 15th century the technological superiority of Europe was such that its small, mutually hostile nations could spill out over all the rest of the world, conquering, looting, and colonizing. The symbol of this technological superiority is the fact that Portugal, one of the weakest states of the Occident, was able to become, and to remain for a century, mistress of the East Indies. And we must remember that the technology of Vasco da Gama and Albuquerque was built by pure empiricism, drawing remarkably little support or inspiration from science.

In the present-day vernacular understanding, modern science is supposed to have begun in 1543, when both Copernicus and Vesalius published their great works. It is no derogation of their accomplishments, however, to point out that such structures as the *Fabrica* and the *De revolutionibus* do not appear overnight. The distinctive Western tradition of science, in fact, began in the late 11th century with a massive movement of translation of Arabic and Greek scientific works into Latin. A few notable books—Theophrastus, for example—escaped the West's avid new appetite for science, but within less than 200 years effectively the entire corpus of Greek and Muslim science was available in Latin, and was being eagerly read and criticized in the new European universities. Out of criticism arose new observation, speculation, and increasing distrust of ancient authorities. By the late 13th century Europe had seized global scientific leadership from the faltering hands of Islam. It would be as absurd to deny the profound originality of Newton, Galileo, or Copernicus as to deny that of the 14th century scholastic scientists like Buridan or Oresme on whose work they built. Before the 11th century, science scarcely existed in the Latin West, even in Roman times. From the 11th century onward, the scientific sector of Occidental culture has increased in a steady crescendo.

Since both our technological and our scientific movements got their start, acquired their character, and achieved world dominance in the Middle Ages, it would seem that we cannot understand their nature or their present impact upon ecology without examining fundamental medieval assumptions and developments.

Medieval View of Man and Nature

Until recently, agriculture has been the chief occupation even in "advanced" societies; hence, any change in methods of tillage has much importance. Early plows, drawn by two oxen, did not normally turn the sod but merely scratched it. Thus, cross-plowing was needed and fields tended to be squarish. In the fairly light soils and semiarid climates of the Near East and Mediterranean, this worked well. But such a plow was inappropriate to the wet climate and often sticky soils of northern Europe. By the latter part of the 7th century after Christ, however, following obscure beginnings, certain northern peasants were using an entirely new kind of plow, equipped with a vertical knife to cut the line of the furrow, a horizontal share to slice under the sod, and a moldboard to turn it over. The friction of this plow with the soil was so great that it normally required not two but eight oxen. It attacked the land with such violence that cross-plowing was not needed, and fields tended to be shaped in long strips.

In the days of the scratch-plow, fields were distributed generally in units capable of supporting a single family. Subsistence farming was the presupposition. But no peasant owned eight oxen: to use the new and more efficient plow, peasants pooled their oxen to form large plow-teams, originally receiving (it would appear) plowed strips in proportion to their contribution. Thus, distribution of land was based no longer on the needs of a family but, rather, on the capacity of a power machine to till the earth. Man's relation to the soil was profoundly changed. Formerly man had been part of nature; now he was the exploiter of nature. Nowhere else in the world did farmers develop any analogous agricultural implement. Is it coincidence that modern technology, with its ruthlessness toward nature, has so largely been produced by descendants of these peasants of northern Europe?

This same exploitive attitude appears slightly before A.D. 830 in Western illustrated calendars. In older calendars the months were shown as passive personifications. The new Frankish calendars, which set the style for the Middle Ages, are very different: they show men coercing the world around them—plowing, harvesting, chopping trees, butchering pigs. Man and nature are two things, and man is master.

These novelties seem to be in harmony with larger intellectual patterns. What people do about their ecology depends on what they think about themselves in relation to things around them. Human ecology is deeply conditioned by beliefs about our nature and destiny—that is, by religion. To Western eyes this is very evident in, say, India or Ceylon. It is equally true of ourselves and of our medieval ancestors.

The victory of Christianity over paganism was the greatest psychic revolution in the history of our culture. It has become fashionable today to say that, for better or worse, we live in "the post-Christian age." Certainly the forms of our thinking and language have largely ceased to be Christian, but to my eye the substance often remains amazingly akin to that of the past. Our daily habits of action, for example, are dominated by an implicit faith in perpetual progress which was unknown either to Greco-Roman antiquity or to the Orient. It is rooted in, and is indefensible apart from, Judeo-Christian teleology. The fact that Communists share it merely helps to show what can be demonstrated on many other grounds: that Marxism, like Islam, is a Judeo-Christian heresy. We continue today to live, as we have lived for about 1700 years, very largely in a context of Christian axioms.

What did Christianity tell people about their relations with the environment?

While many of the world's mythologies provide stories of creation, Greco-Roman mythology was singularly incoherent in this respect. Like Aristotle, the intellectuals of the ancient West denied that the visible world had had a beginning. Indeed, the idea of a beginning was impossible in the framework of their cyclical notion of time. In sharp contrast, Christianity inherited from Judaism not only a concept of time as nonrepetitive and linear but also a striking story of creation. By gradual stages a loving and all-powerful God had created light and darkness, the heavenly bodies, the earth and all its plants, animals, birds, and fishes. Finally, God had created Adam and, as an afterthought, Eve to keep man from being lonely. Man named all the animals, thus establishing his dominance over them. God planned all of this explicitly for man's benefit and rule: no item in the physical creation had any purpose save to serve man's purposes. And, although man's body is made of clay, he is not simply part of nature: he is made in God's image.

Especially in its Western form, Christianity is the most anthropocentric religion the world has seen. As early as the second century both Tertullian and Saint Irenaeus of Lyons were insisting that when God shaped Adam he was foreshadowing the image of the incarnate Christ, the Second Adam. Man shares, in great measure, God's transcendence of nature. Christianity, in absolute contrast to ancient paganism and Asia's religions (except, perhaps, Zoroastrianism), not only established a dualism of man and nature but also insisted that it is God's will that man exploit nature for his proper ends.

At the level of the common people this worked out in an interesting way. In antiquity every tree, every spring, every stream, every hill had its own *genius loci,* its guardian spirit. These spirits were accessible to men, but were very unlike men; centaurs, fauns, and mermaids show their ambivalence. Before one cut a tree, mined a mountain, or dammed a brook, it was important to placate the spirit in charge of that particular institution, and to keep it placated. By destroying pagan animism, Christianity made it possible to exploit nature in a mood of indifference to the feelings of natural objects.

It is often said that for animism the Church substituted the cult of saints. True; but the cult of saints is functionally quite different from animism. The saint is not *in* natural objects; he may have special shrines, but his citizenship is in heaven. Moreover, a saint is entirely a man; he can be approached in human terms. In addition to saints, Christianity of course also had angels and demons inherited from Judaism and perhaps, at one remove, from Zoroastrianism. But these were all as mobile as the saints themselves. The spirits *in* natural objects, which formerly had protected nature from man, evaporated. Man's effective monopoly on spirit in this world was confirmed, and the old inhibitions to the exploitation of nature crumbled.

When one speaks in such sweeping terms, a note of caution is in order. Christianity is a complex faith, and its consequences differ in differing contexts. What I have said may well apply to the medieval West, where in fact technology made spectacular advances. But the Greek East, a highly civilized realm of equal Christian devotion, seems to have produced no marked technological innovation after the late 7th century, when Greek fire was invented. The key to the contrast may perhaps be found in a difference in the tonality of piety and thought which students of comparative theology find between the Greek and the Latin Churches. The Greeks believed that sin was intellectual blindness, and that salvation was found in illumination, orthodoxy—that is, clear thinking. The Latins, on the other hand, felt that sin was moral evil, and that salvation was to be found in right conduct. Eastern theology has been intellectualist. Western theology has been voluntarist. The Greek saint contemplates; the Western saint acts. The implications of Christianity for the conquest of nature would emerge more easily in the Western atmosphere.

The Christian dogma of creation, which is found in the first clause of all the Creeds, has another meaning for our comprehension of today's ecologic crisis. By revelation, God had given man the Bible, the Book of Scripture. But since God had made nature, nature also must reveal the divine mentality. The religious study of nature for the better understanding of God was known as natural theology. In the early Church, and always in the Greek East, nature was conceived primarily as a symbolic system through which God speaks to men: the ant is a sermon to sluggards; rising flames are the symbol of the soul's aspiration. This view of nature was essentially artistic rather than scientific. While Byzantium preserved and copied great numbers of ancient Greek scientific texts, science as we conceive it could scarcely flourish in such an ambience.

However, in the Latin West by the early 13th century natural theology was following a very different bent. It was ceasing to be the decoding of the physical symbols of God's communication with man and was becoming the effort to understand God's mind by discovering how his creation operates. The rainbow was no longer simply a symbol of hope first sent to Noah after the Deluge: Robert Grosseteste, Friar Roger Bacon, and Theodoric of Freiberg produced startlingly sophisticated work on the optics of the rainbow, but they did it as a venture in religious understanding. From the 13th century onward, up to and including Leibnitz and Newton, every major scientist, in effect, explained his motivations in religious terms. Indeed, if Galileo had not been so expert an amateur theologian he would have got into far less trouble: the professionals resented his intrusion. And Newton seems to have regarded himself more as a theologian than as a scientist. It was not until the late 18th century that the hypothesis of God became unnecessary to many scientists.

It is often hard for the historian to judge, when men explain why they are doing what they want to do, whether they are offering real reasons or merely culturally acceptable reasons. The consistency with which scientists during the long formative centuries of Western science said that the task and the reward of the scientist was "to think God's thoughts after him" leads one to believe that this was their real motivation. If so, then modern Western science was cast in a matrix of Christian theology. The dynamism of religious devotion, shaped by the Judeo-Christian dogma of creation, gave it impetus.

An Alternative Christian View

We would seem to be headed toward conclusions unpalatable to many Christians. Since both *science* and *technology* are blessed words in our contemporary vocabulary, some may be happy at the notions, first, that, viewed historically, modern science is an extrapolation of natural theology and, second, that modern technology is at least partly to be explained as an Occidental, voluntarist realization of the Christian dogma of man's transcendence of, and rightful mastery over, nature. But, as we now recognize, somewhat over a century ago science and technology—hitherto quite separate activities—joined to give mankind powers which, to judge by many of the ecologic effects, are out of control. If so, Christianity bears a huge burden of guilt.

I personally doubt that disastrous ecologic backlash can be avoided simply by applying to our problems more science and more technology. Our science and technology have grown out of Christian attitudes toward man's relation to nature which are almost universally held not only by Christians and neo-Christians but also by those who fondly regard themselves as post-Christians. Despite Copernicus, all the cosmos rotates around our little globe. Despite Darwin, we are *not,* in our hearts, part of the natural process. We are superior to nature, contemptuous of it, willing to use it for our slightest whim. The newly elected Governor of California, like myself a churchman but less troubled than I, spoke for the Christian tradition when he said (as is alleged), "when you've seen one redwood tree, you've seen them all." To a Christian a tree can be no more than a physical fact. The whole concept of the sacred grove is alien to Christianity and to the ethos of the West. For nearly two millennia Christian missionaries have been chopping down sacred groves, which are idolatrous because they assume spirit in nature.

What we do about ecology depends on our ideas of the man-nature relationship. More science and more technology are not going to get us out of the present ecologic crisis until we find a new religion, or re-think our old one. The beatniks, who are the basic revolutionaries of our time, show a sound instinct in their affinity for Zen Buddhism, which conceives of the man-nature relationship as very nearly the mirror image of the Christian view. Zen, however, is as deeply conditioned by Asian history as Christianity is by the experience of the West, and I am dubious of its viability among us.

Possibly we should ponder the greatest radical in Christian history since Christ: Saint Francis of Assisi. The prime miracle of Saint Francis is the fact that he did not end at the stake, as many of his left-wing followers did. He was so clearly heretical that a General of the Franciscan Order, Saint Bonaventure, a great and perceptive Christian, tried to suppress the early accounts of Franciscanism. The key to an understanding of Francis is his belief in the virtue of humility —not merely for the individual but for man as a species. Francis tried to depose man from his monarchy over creation and set up a democracy of all God's creatures. With him the ant is no longer simply a homily for the lazy, flame a sign of the thrust of the soul toward union with God; now they are Brother Ant and Sister Fire, praising the Creator in their own ways as Brother Man does in his.

Later commentators have said that Francis preached to the birds as a rebuke to men who would not listen. The records do not read so: he urged the little birds to praise God, and in spiritual ecstasy they flapped their wings and chirped rejoicing. Legends of saints, especially the Irish saints, had long told of their dealings with animals but always, I believe, to show their human dominance over creatures. With Francis it is different. The land around Gubbio in the Apennines was being ravaged by a fierce wolf. Saint Francis, says the legend, talked to the wolf and persuaded him of the error of his ways. The wolf repented, died in the odor of sanctity, and was buried in consecrated ground.

What Sir Steven Ruciman calls "the Franciscan doctrine of the animal soul" was quickly stamped out. Quite possibly it was in part inspired, consciously or unconsciously, by the belief in reincarnation held by the Cathar heretics who at that time teemed in Italy and southern France, and who presumably had got it originally from India. It is significant that at just the same moment, about 1200, traces of metapsychosis are found also in western Judaism, in the Provencal *Cabbala*. But Francis held neither to transmigration of souls nor to pantheism. His view of nature and of man rested on a unique sort of pan-psychism of all things animate and inanimate, designed for the glorification of their transcendent Creator, who, in the ultimate gesture of cosmic humility, assumed flesh, lay helpless in a manger, and hung dying on a scaffold.

I am not suggesting that many contemporary Americans who are concerned about our ecologic crisis will be either able or willing to counsel with wolves or exhort birds. However, the present increasing disruption of the global environment is the product of a dynamic technology and science which were originating in the Western medieval world against which Saint Francis was rebelling in so original a way. Their growth cannot be understood historically apart from distinctive attitudes toward nature which are deeply grounded in Christian dogma. The fact that most people do not think of these attitudes as Christian is irrelevant. No new set of basic values has been accepted in our society to displace those of Christianity. Hence we shall continue to have a worsening ecologic crisis until we reject the Christian axiom that nature has no reason for existence save to serve man.

The greatest spiritual revolutionary in Western history, Saint Francis, proposed what he thought was an alternative Christian view of nature and man's relation to it: he tried to substitute the idea of the equality of all creatures, including man, for the idea of man's limitless rule of creation. He failed. Both our present science and our present technology are so tinctured with orthodox Christian arrogance toward nature that no solution for our ecologic crisis can be expected from them alone. Since the roots of our trouble are so largely religious, whether we call it that or not, we must rethink and refeel our nature and destiny. The profoundly religious, but heretical, sense of the primitive Franciscans for the spiritual autonomy of all parts of nature may point a direction. I propose Francis as a patron saint for ecologists.

6   The Attitude Lag

EUGENE P. ODUM

In the 1920's sociologist William F. Ogburn introduced the concept of "cultural lag" to indicate that man's social customs and attitudes change more slowly than his technical culture. My father, the late Howard W. Odum, also a sociologist, preferred to think of this tendency in the more positive sense of an "achievement lag." Certainly, cultural or achievement lags often contribute to malfunctions in society. Furthermore, as an ecologist I am convinced that what might be termed an "attitude lag" is at the root of much of the current maladjustment between man and his environment.

As man begins to tax the limits of the biosphere his basic attitude and strategy toward the environment must undergo an about-face, or at least a basic reorientation of goals becomes necessary, if high quality rather than mere quantity of human existence is to be the primary motivation for human society. In cybernetic language we are faced with the problem of going from the positive transient state, when everything is growing and expanding at a great rate, to the steady state when growth rates approach zero and enough is enough, so to speak. We are also talking about avoiding a negative transient state of declining numbers and resources! Sooner or later transition from youth to maturity must be faced by all kinds of life, and by life at all levels of organization whether it be cell, teenager, or ecosystem. What is good, desirable, or adaptive—howsoever one wishes to express it—in the youthful stage is oftentimes bad, undesirable, or unadaptive in the mature system. Thus, in the pioneer society as in the early successional ecosystem high birth rates, rapid growth, and exploitation of accessible and unused resources are advantageous. As human beings we can be justly proud of the fact that we have succeeded in modifying and controlling our natural environment to our very great collective advantage. An aggressive or war-like approach to nature is a perfectly natural and desirable drive during the establishment and growth phases of societal systems. However, as the saturation level is approached this drive becomes increasingly unadaptive, and must be shifted to the opposite pole as, for example, to considerations of birth control, recycling of resources, territoriality (i.e., regulation of land use) and symbiosis (i.e., peaceful co-existence of man and nature). The danger is not so much that man may not adapt to the equilibrium state, but he may not apply the brakes fast enough to avoid the serious overshoots and severe, perhaps disastrous, oscillations that befall any system capable of rapid change but which lacks adequate feedback control.

Air

Most of life could not exist on Earth without the atmosphere as it is now constituted. This atmosphere is in intimate contact with nearly every living cell on the surface of our planet. What is the composition of the atmosphere and how did it get that way (reading 8)? How much stress can the atmosphere sustain before it will no longer support life? How does the Earth's atmosphere compare with that of other planets in our solar system (reading 9)? Is there a chance the atmosphere of the Earth will some day resemble that of Mars or Venus (readings 9 and 10)?

7   # Man And The Air

Atmospheric elements and living organisms are linked together in cycles which may be highly vulnerable to the impact of technology.

LAMONT C. COLE

Man is changing the world environment. He has been doing this almost from the time of his appearance as a new species a million or so years ago, but now he has become so numerous and technologically adept that there is a real danger he may destroy the ability of the earth to support life.

Early man subsisted by gathering wild foods and by hunting and fishing. At some point he discovered that he could use fire to drive game animals, and this was the start of man-made air pollution and soil erosion. However, early man was incredibly lucky. In many places the forests he burned were replaced by grasslands which supported increasing populations of grazing mammals, and these grasslands—including our North American prairies—developed soils that would eventually place them among the world's most valuable lands for agriculture. Although the evidence is lost in the past, man's first use of grasslands was probably for the grazing of domestic animals, and this grazing probably helped to inhibit the regeneration of forests.

Early agricultural man would have found it virtually impossible to cope with the heavy sod of grasslands, and so he confined his efforts to the flood plains of rivers where the soil was fertile, well watered and easy to cultivate with simple tools. He learned to store food so that the produce of the growing season could support him and his domestic animals throughout the year. Then he started to build towns and cities and to expand his numbers, and he felt the need for more agricultural land and year-round agriculture. These needs were satisfied by building dams and canals for irrigation. Great civilizations grew up in the valleys of rivers such as the Tigris, Euphrates, Nile, and Indus, and their human populations multiplied.

There were, however, side effects. The very crowding of people into towns and cities exposed them to frequent epidemics, and these, together with wars and famines, took a frightful toll of human life. The smoke from man-made fires polluted the atmosphere, and the erosion of soil from burned-over and overgrazed slopes polluted bodies of water and sometimes blocked streams to create swamps and marshes with attendant health hazards such as malaria. At this stage man could not anticipate the disasters that his own activities were bound to create. Without adequate drainage, for instance, his irrigation works would cause water to move upward through the soil, where it would evaporate and deposit a fertility-destroying layer of salts on the surface.

The Ravaging of Resources

As soils were rendered lifeless by salts and as irrigation systems filled with silt, great civilizations vanished. Pliny tells of the farmers of the great Babylonian Empire, dating from before 2000 B.C., who harvested two annual crops of grain and grazed sheep on the land between crops. But by the twelfth century Otto of Freising could write in his *Chronicon:* "But what now is Babylon . . . ? A shrine of sirens, a home of lizards and ostriches, a den of serpents." Today less than 20 percent of the land in modern Iraq is cultivated and more than half of the national income is from oil. The landscape is dotted with mounds representing forgotten towns, the old irrigation works are filled with silt (the end product of soil erosion), and the ancient seaport of Ur is now 150 miles from the sea with its buildings buried under silt as deep as 35 feet.

We hear a great deal today about the "underdeveloped" and "developing" nations but, as in the case of Iraq, many of them could more accurately be described as *overdeveloped* nations. Modern Iran was once the seat of the great Persian Empire where Darius I was the "King of Kings" 2400 years ago. Ancient Greece had forested hills, ample water and productive soils, and it is clear from Plato's *Critias* (or *Atlanticus)* that he knew that deforestation and overgrazing could cause soil erosion and the drying up of springs. Apparently nobody listened to his warnings.

The glories of ancient Mali and Ghana in west Africa were legends in medieval Europe. In the land that once exported the cedars of Lebanon to Egypt, the erosion-proof Roman roads and the soil beneath them now stand several feet above the rock desert. But about 1940, Dr. Walter Loudermilk of the U. S. Soil Erosion Service found the cedars to be flourishing as of old in a churchyard where the soil had remained and where the grazing of goats had been prevented for 300 years. In China and India, ancient irrigation systems stand abandoned and filled with silt. When the British assumed the rule of India two centuries ago, the population was about 60 million. Today it is over 500 million and most of its land problems have been created in the past century through deforestation and plowing and the resulting erosion and siltation, all stemming from efforts to support such fantastic population growth.

Everyone knows about the wonders of ancient Egypt. The annual spring flood of the Nile watered and fertilized the soil, and crops could be grown for seven months each year. Extensive irrigation systems were established before 2000 B.C. The country was the granary of the Roman Empire, and agriculture flourished for 4000 years or more. But in 1902 a dam was built at Aswan to prevent the spring flood and permit year-round irrigation. Now the soils are deteriorating from salinization, and a higher Aswan Dam is being built to bring more land under cultivation. Meanwhile, population growth has virtually destroyed any possibility that the new agricultural land can significantly raise the per capita level of nutrition.

In various parts of South America and Africa, modern aerial reconnaissance has revealed ancient ridged fields on flood plains. These are the remnants, according to J. J. Parsons and W. M. Denevan, of "a specialized system of agriculture that physically reshaped large parts of the South American continent." In many parts of Mexico towns that were originally located to take advantage of superior springs now must carry in water from distant sites. And in Guatemala and Yucatan the ruins of the Mayan civilization stand as stark evidence of what the land was once capable of supporting.

In our own young country thousands of acres of agricultural land have been lost to erosion and gullying, and thousands more to strip mining. The inherent fertility of our best agricultural land is declining so that yields can only be maintained or increased by massive programs of fertilization. In our irrigated lands of the West there is the constant danger of salinization, while from Long Island to southern California we have lowered water tables so greatly that in coastal regions salt water is seeping into the aquifers. Meanwhile, an estimated 2000 irrigation dams in the United States are now useless impoundments of silt, sand, and gravel, and a conservatively estimated million acres of land per year are being sacrificed to paving, building, and other manifestations of "progress."

This is what man has done to the land. In the last 300 years, moreover, he has been able to *accelerate* his destructive processes by obtaining energy from the fossil fuels—coal, peat, natural gas, and petroleum. Several recent surveys have found that modern "progressive" farmers expend more calories running their machinery than they remove from the land in crops. Now, quite suddenly, man has come to realize that these fuels will soon be exhausted—various estimates of the timetable give us anywhere from 20 years to a half-dozen generations. By then, present thinking holds, we shall have converted to nuclear energy. But uranium and thorium are also exhaustible resources, and modern reactors convert less than one percent of the energy in their fuel into electricity—as compared with some 40 percent for conventional plants burning fossil fuels. Indeed, the nuclear age threatens us with a wholly new magnitude of global contamination.

To fully appreciate modern man's impact on his environment, we must consider how the earth's atmosphere and hydrosphere (the surface waters) have reached their present state. They are made up of an exquisite "mix" of elements and are related to one another through biochemical mechanisms which are dangerously vulnerable to the influence of man.

How the Atmosphere Evolved

Modern geological experts are pretty well agreed that the primitive earth did not have an atmosphere of the gases now present. Degassing of rocks in the earth's interior, by volcanic activity and other processes, produced both a gaseous atmosphere and the water vapor that eventually gave rise to the hydrosphere. Whatever the composition of this original atmosphere, it was very different from the present one, which is of biological origin.

Neglecting contaminants, our atmosphere at sea level now consists by volume of about 78 percent nitrogen, 21 percent oxygen, 0.03 percent carbon dioxide, and minor amounts of other gases. This is a very curious composition in view of the fact that nitrogen is a scarce element on earth and is not among the 18 chemical elements that account for 99.9 percent of the mass of all known terrestrial matter. Also curious is the fact that oxygen, although abundant, is highly reactive chemically and almost never occurs in an uncombined state outside of the atmosphere. Both of these gases occur in the atmosphere only because living organisms keep putting them there.

The earth's atmosphere could not have contained more than traces of free oxygen before the origin of photosyntheis—the process by which green plants take in water and carbon dioxide and, with the aid of energy from sunlight, combine them to produce organic matter and liberate oxygen as a by-product. Gradually, through perhaps two billion years since the origin of photosynthesis, some of the organic matter in the bodies of living things has become buried— mostly in marine sediments—and so has been prevented from recombining with oxygen. It is this process which has produced the large reservoir of oxygen in the atmosphere as well as the stores of fossil fuels that we are now extracting and burning to keep our economy going. The amount of oxygen in the atmosphere probably has not undergone significant change since the end of the Carboniferous period some 300 million years ago, and we should not expect it to change so long as photosynthesis can keep up with oxidation.

The oxygen cycle which I have just sketched is linked to the equally delicate biochemical cycles of other elements such as carbon, sulfur and nitrogen. Let us briefly consider the third of these elements.

All living things require nitrogen because the main structural components of their bodies are nitrogen compounds called proteins. Since animals and most microorganisms make their proteins directly or indirectly from the constituents of plant proteins, we must again focus on green plants to understand how the composition of the atmosphere is maintained. Higher plants cannot build proteins directly from the atmosphere's molecular nitrogen. Certain types of bacteria and blue-green algae must first convert the molecular nitrogen to ammonia and nitrate, in which forms it can be used by higher plants and passed on as proteins to animals, including man. When plants and animals die, other bacteria known as "decomposers" break down their proteins and inert nitrogen compounds, and additional bacteria called "dentrifiers" release a fresh supply of molecular nitrogen into the air. It is only because of these bacteria that plants and animals have not long ago extracted all of the nitrogen from the atmosphere—thereby making further plant plant and animal life impossible on most of the earth. I am terrified to recall that I have twice heard prominent chemists say, and have once read in a textbook, that it would be desirable to find a way to *block* dentrification because ammonia and nitrate are so important to agriculture!

These and other complex interconnections equally essential for life have thus far assured the constancy of our atmosphere, and they have done so despite the fact that photosynthesis stops in darkness, at low temperatures, and when other requirements of living things are not met. The crucial point in all of this is that neither man nor other familiar living things could survive without the photosynthesis of plants—most of which are in the oceans—or without a host of microorganisms whose very existence is unknown to most persons. Today, through our various forms of pollution, we are thoughtlessly putting these very organisms in jeopardy!

The Growth of Pollution

Like soil erosion and deforestation, man-made pollution has an ancient history. Neolithic man started polluting the environment with his fires, though the major resulting pollutants—smoke, soot, silt—also existed without man. But many new pollutants appeared as civilization advanced. The Romans mined lead in Britain and smelted it there, and it is said that the sites of these old smelting operations can still be recognized by the improverished vegetation growing on the poisoned soil. In Rome the lead went into paints, water pipes, and the lining of vessels in which wine was stored. Recent studies of Roman bones have shown concentrations of lead which indicate that many members of the upper classes must have suffered from lead poisoning; it has even been suggested that this may have contributed to the decline of the Empire.

As cities grew they began to concentrate materials produced over a wide area into a small space, and these materials gave rise to wastes, pollution problems arose. Otto's *Chronicon* tells us that when Frederick Barbarossa's army arrived in Rome in the summer of 1167 ". . . the ponds, caverns, and ruinous places around the city were exhaling poisonous vapors, and the air in the entire vicinity had become densely laden with pestilence and death." Waters were also polluted. The name "Rhine" was supposedly derived from the German word for "pure," but by the 13th century St. Hildegard wrote that the Rhine's waters, if drunk unboiled, would "produce noxious blue fluids in the body."

Man added a whole new dimension to environmental pollution when he started burning fossil fuels for energy. In the year 1306 a citizen of London was tried and executed for burning coal in the city, but three centuries later coal combustion was a way of life and London had a smog problem. This new source of energy made it possible for many more people simultaneously to inhabit the earth than ever before, and the resulting colonization and exploitation of new lands further aggravated environmental deterioration. With the start of the 20th century, petroleum assumed a growing role as a source of energy. The internal combustion engine and a huge, diverse chemical industry have released into the environment countless new materials to which the world's living things have never before had to adapt. Miraculously, man's run of dumb luck has continued —and the biogeochemical cycle on which his life depends have kept on functioning. But since World War II man-made stresses on the environment have so intensified that it would be incredible if such luck long continued.

The pollution problem, of course, is not limited to the by-products of our commercial activities. Waste matter is also a major culprit. We have continued to dispose of our wastes as of old—largely by dumping them into the atmosphere and hydrosphere—and human populations are now so dense that it is difficult to see how we can ever reclaim a clean environment. As Dean Charles Bradley of Montana State College wrote in 1962: "If river-disposal of waste were suddenly denied the city of St. Louis, the city fathers would have to decide what else to do with the daily discharge of 200,000 gallons of urine and 400 tons of solid body-wastes, to say nothing of all the industrial wastes."

Because of these biological wastes and other pollutants, it has been estimated by the U. S. Food and Drug Administration that we are now exposing ourselves and our environment to over a half-million man-made substances, and that this number is growing by 400-500 new chemicals per year. Just in the period since World War II we have asked the environment to cope with such unprecedented classes of materials as synthetic pesticides, plastics, antibiotics, radioisotopes and detergents. The end of our production of novel chemicals is not in sight. No more than a minute fraction of these substances, singly or in combination, has been tested for toxicity to the marine diatoms that produce some 70 percent of the earth's annual supply of oxygen. Nor have they been tested for toxicity to the equally vital forms involved in the cycles of nitrogen and other essential elements.

For the 48 coterminous United States I have attempted some calculations of the oxygen balance. I took the figures for production and imports of fossil fuels for the year 1966, corrected these for exports and non-combustible residues, and calculated the amount of oxygen that would be required for their combustion. Then I made what I believe to be a good estimate of the amount of oxygen produced by photosynthesis within our borders that year. The amount of oxygen produced turned out to be not quite 60 percent of the amount consumed.

The implication is clear: we are absolutely dependent on oxygen which is produced outside our borders—mostly in the Pacific Ocean and brought in by atmospheric circulation. If we should inadvertently kill enough marine diatoms or the organisms they depend on for fixed nitrogen, we would start running out of oxygen to breathe. Yet these organisms are now being exposed to our half-million chemicals. There is evidence that the insecticide DDT can suppress photosynthesis in bodies of water, and this chemical has not become world-wide in distribution. More frightening yet to me are the herbicides or "weed killers" —chemicals specifically designed to be poisonous to plants. At present the military is taking most of our production of these chemicals and shipping it to

Vietnam to kill rice and defoliate jungle vegetation. What will happen if a few tankers loaded with concentrated herbicides are sunk in the Pacific? The fate of Lake Erie and many lesser bodies of water has shown that man is indeed capable of blocking the oxygen cycle through sheer carelessness.

Our Contaminated Air

Earlier I described the atmosphere as it would exist if it were free of contaminants. In our actual atmosphere, however, more than 3,000 foreign chemicals have been identified. The air of our cities is rich in solid matter such as soot, fly ash, particles of rubber from tires and asbestos from brake linings—all of which have implications for public health. Our smoke stacks and exhaust pipes pour forth carbon monoxide, sulfur dioxide and various oxides of nitrogen; these chemicals can affect health and, in the case of the sulfur and nitrogen oxides, they are capable of corroding metal and concrete. Ethyl gasoline causes our automobiles to release so much lead to the atmosphere that snow near the North Pole contains 300 percent more lead than it did in 1940. And, to increase agricultural output, we have processed phosphate rock into fertilizer, releasing as a by-product poisonous fluorine which ironically sometimes kills vegetation and livestock in the vicinity of the fertilizer plants. Ironically also, our biodegradable detergents are compounds of phosphorus, and we are discarding this precious element so recklessly that it has become one of our most significant water pollutants.

What about our ever-increasing use of fossil fuels? We are burning them at a rate which is putting carbon dioxide into the atmosphere more rapidly than the oceans can assimilate it. Carbon dioxide is quite transparent to solar radiation but quite opaque to the longwave heat radiation from earth to space. In other words it acts as a heat trap which has the potential for altering the earth's climates. The precise form that such changes might take are still very controversial and uncertain, but the combustion of fossil fuels is one more example of the way we are playing Russian roulette with our environment. Nevertheless, our leaders are determined in the name of progress to see industry expand to build more, larger, and higher-flying airplanes that will pollute the upper atmosphere, and to take more land out of photosynthetic production for housing and other "good things."

People are grasping at straws for ways to keep our economy growing. We are told that bacteria, fungi and yeasts will convert fossil fuels directly into food for man. Not only are the fossil fuels exhaustible, but, unfortunately, this proposed new type of food production will not generate any oxygen. We are told that nuclear energy will provide the answer to air pollution.

This may be the cruelest hoax of all. Before the controlled release of atomic energy, the total amount of radioactivity under human control consisted of about 10 curies, in the form of about 10 grams of radium divided among the world's hospitals and laboratories. Great concern and publicity arose whenever a few millicuries were lost or misplaced. Those who can recall this concern will not take lightly the news that a nuclear power plant now being constructed on the shores of Lake Ontario near Oswego, New York, will, by the company's own estimate, release 130 curies per day into the atmosphere. This plant is actually to be a small one in terms of present dreams. It represents only about 2 percent of the generating capacity for which nuclear plant permits were sought from the Atomic Energy Commission in 1967.

Present-day reactors produce prodigious quantities of extremely hazardous and long-lived radioisotopes such as Strontium^{90} and Cesium^{137} which, everyone agrees, should be stored for at least 600 years before being released into the environment. Yet one Atomic Energy Commission found that about 5 percent of the underground storage tanks were leaking after only about 20 years.

In all of the foregoing instances of pollution, the fundamental problem as I see it, is our fetish for equating growth with progress. Economists state that companies must grow to survive. We take pride in a gross national product growing at between 4 and 5 percent per year, and we try to ignore the fact that our per capita production of trash is growing at about the same rate. We are told that our electrical generating capacity must increase by 10 percent per year, but we forget that all of that energy must eventually be imposed on the environment as heat; I don't believe that there is any way short of repealing the laws of thermodynamics to sustain such growth without bringing disaster to our environment.

In a related field, growing populations are viewed by many planners simply as expanding markets—and here we come to a fundamental problem. There must be *some* level of human population that the earth could support indefinitely without undergoing deterioration, but we don't know what that level is. Through the first million or so years of man's existence, his population probably doubled no more often than once in every 50,000 years. During the summer of 1968 the human population passed the 3.5 billion mark, and, if present trends should continue, this population would double again every 35 years! There is no possibility that the earth's environment can long sustain such pressure; in fact I consider it very improbable that the earth could continually support, on a nondestructive basis, a population as large as the *present* one. We shall have to decide, and soon, what quality of life we want for ourselves and what steps in pollution and population control are necessary to get it.

Unfortunately, our big decisions are made on economic grounds. Factories burning fossil fuels don't *have* to release particulates and sulfur and nitrogen oxides into the atmosphere; nor do nuclear plants, barring accidents, *have* to release radioisotopes into the environment. They do these things because it would cost money not to. Pollution by automobiles could surely be controlled at some expense and perhaps with some loss of performance. There are valuable raw materials in wornout automobile bodies; if economics made the mining of fresh ore as expensive as reclaiming used metals, our auto graveyards would vanish. No-return glass bottles are the thing today, and Federal law even prohibits the re-use of liquor bottles—thereby adding to the burden of trash. Even tin cans could have salvage value, as they did for a while during the tin shortage of World War II. The organic matter in garbage and sewage could be converted to fertilizers, but not at present competitive costs. Other wastes could be burned in smoke-less incinerators and the heat could be made to do useful work, as is being done on a small scale in Europe.

Who Should Pay for Pollution?

Influencing all the foregoing choices we might make is the question: *Who should pay for pollution?* Our system now allows the public utility, the manufac-turer, the chemical company and the incinerating firm to dump pollutants into the air at little or no cost. Other people pay the bill: the city government which must repair its roads and bridges and replace its trees far too often, and the emphysema sufferer who must frequent a doctor's office. If the bills for pollution were handed back to the *sources* of pollution, we might see some surprising improvements in the quality of our air. But such a system of social accounting, I hasten to point out, involves political and ethical decisions rather than purely technological ones.

Meanwhile, we are on a collision course with disaster. It is encouraging to know that we already have, or can develop, the technology to reverse our course. But it is disturbing to realize that we have not yet applied this technology in an effective way. We know how to regulate population size and how to do it economi-cally. We could control pollution and even do a great deal to clean up our filthy and deteriorating environment—provided, of course, that we have not already made disaster inevitable by dooming some species on which the continuation of life depends or by burdening ourselves with a load of defective genes that will make future human generations inviable. Surely, man faces no more urgent problem than the need to save his environment. What will be required is intense collaboration by the best minds among biologists, physical scientists, sociologists, economists, political scientists, and policy makers!

Origin and Evolution of the Air

8

Evolution of the Earth's Atmosphere

S. I. RASOOL

We living things are a late outgrowth of the metabolism of our Galaxy. The carbon that enters so importantly into our composition was cooked in the remote past in a dying star. From it at lower temperatures nitrogen and oxygen were formed. These, our indispensable elements, were spewed out into space in the exhalations of red giants and such stellar catastrophes as super-novae, there to be mixed with hydrogen, to form eventually the substance of the sun and the planets, and ourselves. The waters of ancient seas set the pattern of ions in our blood. The ancient atmospheres molded our metabolism.

George Wald

The present composition of the earth's atmosphere is 78 percent nitrogen, 21 percent oxygen, and 1 percent argon, with traces of carbon dioxide, water vapor, and ozone. The atmospheres of Mars and Venus, on the other hand, are predominately composed of carbon dioxide, while those of Jupiter and Saturn contain mainly hydrogen, helium, methane, and ammonia. Such a wide variety in the composition of the atmospheres of the planets appears most intriguing when one considers that all nine planets were probably formed at the same time and out of the same chemically homogeneous mixture of gas and dust; that is, the primitive solar nebula.

The most likely explanation for this diversity in composition seems to be that the planetary atmospheres have undergone important evolutionary changes during their long history of about 4.5 billion years. On the earth, the evidence for such changes is manifold. Ever since Louis Pasteur demonstrated that spontaneous generation of life does not take place at the present time, it has become obvious that if life originated on the earth, as it probably did, the atmospheric conditions in the early history of the planet must have been quite different in order for the chemical evolution to have taken place. Also, it appears that relative to the sun, the earth is deficient by several orders of magnitude, not only in hydrogen and helium, which being the lightest can be assumed to have escaped from the gravitational field of the earth, but also in carbon, nitrogen, and the cosmically abundant rare gases (neon, argon-36, krypton, and xenon). A comparison of the deficiency factors of these elements with those of nonvolatiles such as sodium, magnesium, aluminum, and silicon, strongly suggests that the earth lost all elements which could have been gaseous at temperatures of a few hundred degrees during the very early history of the planet. The relatively small amounts of carbon, hydrogen, nitrogen, and oxygen now present in the crust, hydrosphere, and atmosphere were probably outgassed from the interior and accumulated slowly during the lifetime of the earth.

Both biochemical arguments and geological evidence, therefore, strongly suggest that the atmosphere of the earth has undergone major evolutionary changes during its long history. Whether the atmospheres of Mars and Venus have also gone through similar stages of evolution is a question which cannot be answered without more knowledge about their composition. Future *in situ* exploration of these planets and a search for the rare gases, especially neon which is deficient on earth by a factor of 10^{10}, will provide important clues to the origin of these atmospheres.

For the earth there is convincing evidence that the present atmosphere and hydrosphere arose largely from the interior by volcanic emanations. But the sequence of events which led to present-day composition of N_2 and O_2 has yet to be established. What is the history of volatiles now present at the surface of the earth? Has the carbon, nitrogen, oxygen, and hydrogen always been in the form of CO_2, N_2, H_2O, and H_2, or did carbon and nitrogen combine with hydrogen early in the earth's history to form CH_4 and NH_3? Under what atmospheric conditions did life originate on earth and how did the appearance of life change the atmosphere? These are some of the basic questions which must be answered in order to paint a coherent picture of the evolution of the earth's atmosphere. Opinions on these questions are many and varied. Sometimes they are almost diametrically opposed. The Oparin-Urey theory of the origin of life on the earth, supported by the laboratory experiments of Miller and, more recently, of Ponnamperuma, suggest a primitive atmosphere composed mainly of CH_4 with small amounts of NH_3, H_2, and H_2O vapor. On the other hand, the school of thought led by Abelson, and supported also by laboratory experiments on the synthesis of amino acids, holds that the early atmosphere of the earth was made up of CO_2, CO, H_2, N_2, and H_2O vapor.

Geologists are also divided on the subject. Holland has presented a model for the evolution of the atmosphere in which, during the very early stage after the formation of the earth and at the commencement of outgassing, the dominant gases could have been CH_4 and H_2, provided free hydrogen did not "escape" as rapidly as it does today. Rubey, on the other hand, believes that the early atmosphere was probably made of CO_2 and N_2 because not enough hydrogen was available to keep CH_4 from converting into CO_2. Holland's model is supported by the calculations of Rasool and McGovern, who have investigated the thermal properties of model primitive atmospheres of the earth. They find that in an atmosphere with a ratio percent of 99 CH_4 to 1 percent H_2 the average exospheric temperature may be as low as $650^{\circ}K$ (compared with the present-day value of $1500^{\circ}K$), thus making the escape of hydrogen a relatively slow phenomenon. However, Abelson has argued that if methane were abundant in the primitive atmosphere, the earliest rocks should contain unusual amounts of organic matter, which apparently is not the case.

Despite the disagreement over the composition of the primitive atmosphere, it is almost certain that it was devoid of free oxygen. How and when did free oxygen then become a major constituent of the atmosphere? The late Lloyd V. Berkner and L. C. Marshall have presented detailed calculations of the photochemistry of H_2O, indicating that free oxygen was limited to about 0.1 percent of the present atmospheric level during the entire prebiological history and accumulated slowly to the present amount since the start of photosynthesis about 800 million years ago. This theory is probably the most widely accepted explanation for the growth of oxygen in the earth's atmosphere. However, difficulties arise when one attempts to construct an evolutionary model of the atmosphere which would be consistent from the prebiological period to the present. For example, it is not well understood whether the small amount of O_2 suggested to be present in the primitive atmosphere would not be sufficient to rapidly oxidize CH_4 and NH_3 into CO_2 and N_2. It may be that the production of even this small amount of free oxygen in the upper atmosphere by the photodissociation of water vapor was inhibited by the presence of NH_3 itself.

The Atmospheres of Mars and Venus   9

VON R. ESHLEMAN

The atmosphere of Venus is hot and dense and the atmosphere of Mars is cold and thin.

Venus, the earth and Mars are within a factor or two of being the same distance from the sun and the same size. All three planets were doubtless formed from the same primordial source of matter at the same time. The atmospheres of all three appear to have been created after the initial supplies of light gases (hydrogen and helium) were largely lost to space. It is generally thought that these secondary atmospheres represent gases "exhaled" from the main body of the planet, with atmospheric evolution proceeeding for aeons to produce the markedly different conditions we find on the three planets today.

It has recently been suggested that if all life on the earth were destroyed, the atmosphere would slowly begin to change and eventually would resemble the atmosphere of either Venus or Mars.

The space probes to Mars and Venus have emphasized, I think, that biological processes themselves may play a more central role in the characteristics of planetary atmospheres than we have thought.

It would seem that our relative ignorance of the possible global effects of small changes in the composition and temperature of the earth's atmosphere should give us serious and immediate concern about man's use of the atmosphere as a garbage dump. In the past 100 years the percentage of atmospheric carbon dioxide has increased 15 percent, primarily owing to man's burning of fossil fuels. This same activity now uses 15 percent of the biological production of oxygen and in the future could become the major sink. Smog, jet contrails, deforestation and pollution of the earth's waters may affect the constituents and temperature of the atmosphere by only minute amounts, yet they may nonetheless have far-reaching consequences. Let us hope that continuing studies of the earth and its planetary neighbors will lead rapidly to a fuller understanding of planetary atmospheres in general. At the same time it behooves us to take strong steps to eliminate the known harmful effects of man's activities and to minimize those effects that are not yet fully understood. Whatever else we may wish to know, we hardly wish to test whether a lifeless earth would become like Mars or like Venus.

10   Perhaps Pollution Ruined Venus

JEFFREY D. ALDERMAN

When Apollo 132 lands on Venus in the year, say, 2,000, what will man find?
The duller members of the scientific community say he will find a lifeless
planet shrouded in lethal gases such as carbon monoxide.

Carbon monoxide? Yep, the very same stuff that billows from every automobile exhaust pipe here on earth.

And this coincidence has not gone unnoticed by some of the more imagina-
tive scientists. These men theorize that Venus may once have had life but that
it was done in by a gigantic case of air polution.

Could it be, as these learned men suggest, that the noxious fumes weren't
always there? Was the air there once as fresh as it is here on earth?

Perhaps when man sets foot on Venus he will find the remains of a society
that perished in an atmosphere that strangled life.

Perhaps he'll see Venusian streets littered with skeletons, their bony hands
either clutching at their throats or reaching hopelessly toward gasmasks they
carried with them.

He may see a 400-mile traffic jam that never unjammed, with dead drivers
behind each steering wheel and air conditioners switched to "on" position.

An inspection of the Venusian congress may reveal a bill which died in
committee, to outlaw gas-powered vehicles in favor of electric ones. Another bill
passed over might be one for control of water pollution, industrial wastes and
sewage. Still another might have preserved the planet's only forest—at the end,
only two scrub pines and a weeping willow.

The Venusian monetary system undoubtedly would have been based on the
most precious element on the planet, oxygen. Venusian alchemists would have
spent all their time trying to turn soot into either oxygen or the planet's second
most precious element, water. Only the rich could have afforded the ultimate
Venusian vacation—two weeks in an oxygen tent.

Perhaps an old political campaign banner saying "A chicken in every pot and
a gasmask on every face," would be found.

The planet would have one garbage dump, stretching over half the Venusian
surface. The other half would be a large, crowded city.

The weather forecast in the final edition of the Venus Times would read:
"Temperature inversion will raise thermometer to record 515 degrees. Four-foot
soot-fall expected overnight."

And will man, as he surveys the wreck that was Venus, feel contempt for
the Venusians much as he does now for the departed dinosaur?

Probably.

And perhaps another writer at another time, looking down on earth from
a planet circling a distant star, will wonder about the noxious fumes obscuring
earth and speculate whether there was once life here.

Effects on Wilderness

A classic example of the effect of polluted air on wilderness is the 1,300,000 ponderosa pine trees dead or dying from Los Angeles smog. Before that time the public had considered air pollution a city problem and something that you escape from when you enter the wilderness. Dr. Machta (reading 11) dispels that myth.

Winds, Pollution, and the Wilderness   11

LESTER MACHTA

Wilderness stands as a splendid sanctuary from human encroachment on the ground, but no barriers can exclude wind-borne pollution. Man can clean up the atmosphere if he is willing to pay the price, but we foresee no way of modifying the winds to spare a favored region.

The concentrations of air pollutants are almost always smaller far from a city, as in a wilderness, than nearby. But this absolute level of contamination is only one measure of comparison of urban to wilderness harm. Society accepts urban pollution and the use of pesticides because these grew slowly and seem inextricably bound to a higher standard of living. Some of the modern technology, such as pesticides, have been used in the wilderness. But, in contrast to the city dweller, man-made air-borne pollutants from afar yield very few benefits to balance their cost to those enjoying a wilderness.

It is often not appreciated that gaseous and fine particulate matter injected into the atmosphere remains there until scavenging processes or chemical reactions remove it. Proof of the pervasiveness of air-borne pollution as a global problem was dramatically illustrated by radioactive fallout over every part of the earth, land and sea, pole to pole, from nuclear tests exploded at very few locations. Most commonly, pollutants are washed out of the air in rain and snow, but this contaminates soil, lakes, and rivers, usually remote from the source of pollution. The reason some imagine that the atmosphere can be used as a boundless sewer is its tremendous volume, which swallows the pollutants and usually dilutes them to acceptable levels. The atmosphere is indeed enormous, containing about five million trillion tons of air. But as we have discovered in the past few decades, even this vast envelope of air is insufficient to cope with man's ability to produce ever larger amounts of pollutants.

Our early atmosphere contained virtually no oxygen, but much more carbon dioxide than now exists. Green life converted carbon dioxide to its "waste," oxygen, producing the present 20 per cent oxygen. But man, particularly during the past 80 years of industrialization, has now reversed the process. His burning of fossil fuels—coal and oil—stored from the past has now raised the present carbon dioxide content of the air over 10 percent since the end of the last century.

Each year the clean atmosphere increases its carbon dioxide content by about one-quarter of a percent, according to records at Mauna Loa, Hawaii, and at Antarctica. This growth rate is only half the estimated release rate from burning of fuels; the remaining half of the output is absorbed mainly by the oceans. More carbon dioxide in the air is not necessarily detrimental; trees and other plants can grow faster in the presence of higher concentrations.

There is special concern about the growth of carbon dioxide in the air because of its vital importance in establishing the heat balance of the atmosphere. As the carbon dioxide increases so should the temperature in the lower atmosphere, by blanketing outgoing radiation from the earth—the "greenhouse" effect. Fortunately, recent calculations suggest that the warming from increased carbon dioxide should be very small. During the first half of the twentieth century, there has been, in fact, a gradual small warming, but this trend has been replaced over the past twenty years by a slight cooling. It is speculated that this latter effect may also be attributed to pollution in the form of increased dustiness which, by reflecting and scattering sunlight back to space, cools the lower atmosphere. The greater dustiness may have counteracted the warming due to increased carbon dioxide. Some observations in non-urban environments show increases with time in atmospheric turbidity or dustiness; similar measurements in urban regions reveal higher turbidity than nearby rural areas. One must be cautious in necessarily blaming climatic trends on human activities; there have also been climatic fluctuations before 1900 when human intervention was less likely.

The more important aspect of air pollution to a wilderness comes from sources immediately upwind, rather than undergoing global dilution. Certain topographic and weather features might provide some protection for the wilderness, but in general, there is little to impede the air-borne plume from a factory chimney or a DDT aerial spray blowing to an otherwise inaccessible region. The wind speeds in the lower atmosphere typically blow 5 to 25 miles per hour. Thus wilderness areas many tens of miles from a city or farm can be affected by wind-borne pollution within a few hours. During this travel time, the pollutants are diluted and often depleted. Dilution is accompanied by both horizontal and vertical mixing. Horizontal mixing reduces concentrations near a plume center, but a wider area contains low concentrations. Vertical mixing of contaminants from low altitude sources carries pollution aloft and is always beneficial in reducing ground level concentrations. The wind direction is variable. Thus, pollution from a single source may reach a wilderness only infrequently. But as industrialization grows, pesticide usage increases, and new roads ring the wilderness, the frequency of successively higher levels of pollution can be expected, since winds from many directions will bring pollution to the wilderness.

Topographic barriers such as mountains and special weather patterns frequently impede atmospheric mixing. It is clear that the air within a valley cannot mix horizontally beyond the valley walls. This is evident to aircraft passengers observing smoke from chimneys meander within the natural terrain channels, like river beds. Some of the more infamous air pollution episodes have occurred within or downwind of industrialized valleys: The Donora, Pennsylvania, and the Trail, British Columbia, cases, for example.

But of greater significance, because it changes, is the lid that nature can impose to impede vertical mixing. Normally, the temperature decreases with altitude; the greater the decrease the more vigorous the up-and-down mixing. But under certain weather situations one finds a temperature increase with height (called an inversion), sometimes at the ground but more often aloft, lasting for many days. This inversion inhibits upward mixing through it. When the mixing lid lies below about 5,000 feet, the pollution from many of the current massive sources cannot be diluted adequately to maintain acceptable air quality levels at the ground. This latter circumstance is common to the California coastal area and is one of the prime reasons why Los Angeles smog is so notorious.

There is a world-wide "lid" to up-down mixing called the tropopause, located at about 35,000 feet over the United States. About 75 per cent of the mass of the atmosphere lies below 35,000 feet. Pollutants released to the air take a few days to a few weeks to mix up to the tropopause, and in that time the horizontal winds keep the air in roughly the same band of latitudes as it started in. This is unfortunate because both the maximum industrialization and population lie in the temperate latitudes, say between 25^0 and 60^{0}N. Air pollutants may stay in the same latitudinal band blowing around the world from west to east, mixing with three-quarters of the depth of air for up to a few months. For these meteorological reasons, not all of the atmospheric volume is available to dilute wastes released during the preceding few months.

The combination of channelling within valleys and imperfect vertical mixing produces particularly undesirable air pollution conditions. It has been found that some of the oxidants, components of smog created photochemically in the Los Angeles basin and contained below the mixing lid, channel through the Rim Forest of the San Bernardino Pass. Here one finds ponderosa pine with burned tips identical to those produced from controlled exposure to observed oxidant levels. The Rim Forest lies 4,400 feet above and four miles north of the city of San Bernardino, and over fifty miles from downtown Los Angeles. As another example, scientists at La Jolla, California, note a marked increase in carbon dioxide as a murky pall approaches from the north, capped below the mixing lid and sliding along the coastal mountain range. The source of the pollution again is the Los Angeles Basin, eighty miles to the north.

While the weather and the temperature inversions along the California coast are somewhat unique, other meteorological patterns can create persistent inversions over almost any part of the United States. The slow moving, light wind, high pressure weather system has been recognized as an air pollution culprit over both the eastern and western United States. In the east it is most common in the southern Appalachian Mountains, over the Great Smoky Mountains, in fact, and in the west over the Great Basin. The Smoky Mountains were named in colonial times because of the blue haze produced by atmospheric reactions involving turpenes from the trees. Nowadays, man's wastes add to those of nature. The prevalence of reduced visibility due to either source is a consequence of weather conditions in the southern Appalachian Mountains. The eastern high pressure systems or anticyclones are most frequent in October. Before the advent of pollution, man would eagerly look forward to their onset in October as beautiful

Indian summers. Today, the sluggish anticyclones can be recognized by the air traveler by a layer of dirty air with a sharp top covering many thousands of square miles for several days. Since there are usually few clouds associated with an anticyclone, the abundant sunshine may produce photochemical smog of the Los Angeles variety to add to other pollutants. The light winds drift about aimlessly rather than follow the prevailing flow. A wilderness may be covered by air with attendant pollution from many diverse sources tens to hundreds of miles away.

The downwind decrease of pollutant concentration results from chemical reactions as well as from dilution. These atmospheric reactions which transform a given pollutant to another substance are complex and, by and large, imperfectly understood. Lest one imagine that such reactions are necessarily beneficial, one ought quickly to note at least two which are not. The photochemical oxidants of the Los Angeles smog start out as oxides of nitrogen, hydrocarbons, and other compounds, none of which are necessarily as toxic as the ozone, and other oxidants which they and sunlight produce. Sulfur dioxide oxidizes and its products react with water to form sulfuric acid. In many ways, the acid is more deleterious than the original gaseous sulfur dioxide and water.

The prime means by which the atmosphere cleanses itself is through precipitation scavenging—the removal of impurities by rain and snow. The deposition of pollutants in rainwater can cause damage far from the source. For example, in southern Sweden, during the past ten years, the rainwater and the lakes and rivers which it feeds have exhibited a dramatic increase of acidity. The once prosperous salmon industry is now almost extinct and there is concern over ancient stone monuments. The cause is thought to be sulfuric acid in rainwater from sulfur dioxide coming from heavily industrialized northwest Europe, probably over 100 miles away. Certain contaminants, like sulfates and artificial radioactivity, are observed in rainwater all over the world. They and others have been changed from an air to a soil or water contaminant and can enter humans and animals via food rather than inhalation. A second and largely unexplored mode of removal of dust from the atmosphere is filtration of air passing through forests. Conifers with their sticky needles are especially effective filters.

The details of the mechanism of washout of contaminants have been, and continue to be, a lively subject of research.

It may be surprising that some gases are also removed by falling water droplets. After pollutants have mixed vertically through many thousands of feet, it is found that, on the average, the lifetime of a typical pollutant particle is about two to four weeks. Within this time, if you will recall, the pollution from the industrialized temperate latitudes can remain in the same geographical band. Thus, the wastes from man's activities both contaminate the air and fall back to earth in the same general band of latitude in which they started.

The transport of pollution to a living wilderness is not purely theoretical; living things will respond, most often unfavorably, to such intrusion. The varied response of flora and fauna to pollution could occupy many pages in this journal; for our purposes, a few examples may be cited.

Michael Treshow in the August 1968 volume of *Phytopathology* states:

The historical record, as well as our own studies, have demonstrated how air pollution can entirely destroy vast acreages of sensitive vegetation. One classic illustration of devastation wrought by air pollutants is in the Copper Basin area of Tennessee, where about 7,000 acres of once rich deciduous forest were completely denuded and another 17,000 acres replaced with grassland species following the destruction of the native forest species. Gully erosion stripped away the soil, and even the climate was altered. The mean monthly maximum air temperature was up to 3.5 F higher, and rainfall nearly 10 per cent less, in the bare area. Timber and watersheds were similarly decimated in areas surrounding the town of Trail, B.C.; in Ontario, Canada; and in Anaconda, Mont., where sulfur oxides again were present in concentrations lethal to dominant conifers. In another incident, fluorides were reported to have been responsible for the needle burning and death of ponderosa pine over a 50-square-mile area near Spokane, Wash. Pine was eliminated as a dominant species in the immediate vicinity of the operations.

Sometimes the identification of pollution as the subtle damaging agent requires detective work. Dochinger reports that a white pine disease called chlorotic dwarf in the Northeast, Central, and Lake States has puzzled pathologists for the past 60 years. Certain trees in a stand appear to be congenital runts; the disease has been attributed to fungi, unfavorable soil, and a virus. Only recently has he demonstrated the damage to be due to air pollution.

Examples of the damage to fauna are equally numerous. In this case, it is not only the effluents from urbanization and industrialization but the pesticides and herbicides which are equally if not more at fault. Many animals and birds are capable of concentrating certain pollutants found in low concentrations in the environment. The widespread grazing habits of reindeer have introduced far more cesium-137, a product of nuclear testing, into their muscle tissue than was expected. Dead and dying robins had between three and twenty times more DDT in the residues of their brains as in the leaves that formed the source of food for the earthworms that, in turn, were eaten by the robins.

A Government report, "Restoring the Quality of Our Environment," states: "Such herbicides, though providing beneficial effects in agricultural regions, may produce serious adverse effects in natural communities, in state and national parks, and other areas dedicated to recreational purposes."

The tale of destruction from air pollution can continue almost endlessly. But it must be recognized that in the foreseeable future the solution lies in pollution control, not weather control. One cannot erect fences around the wilderness to restrain the winds. The cure for air pollution in the wilderness is the same as elsewhere: limit the emissions at the sources.

Smog and the Automobile

Although the word *smog* was coined in London, this clammy mix of fog, smoke and poisonous chemicals is now most characteristic of Los Angeles, California. To make predictions about the control of polluted air in cities we could look at Los Angeles as the model of a city which happens to be "running hard and standing still." In our search for solutions to air pollution we must choose to have fewer petroleum-powered automobiles, stricter emission standards, or both. Among approaches currently under consideration are: (1) control the conventional engine (reading 12); (2) permit only electric cars (reading 13) and control pollution where the electricity is generated; (3) introduce a steam-mobile (reading 14); or (4) employ methanol as a fuel (reading 15). Each of these solutions has its own inherent problems.

12   Automobile Engines: Pollution and Power

ISRAEL KATZ

Almost everything that was done over the past 40 years to improve engine performance, such as increasing the power-volume ratio, raising the compression ratio, extending the valve overlap, increasing the crankshaft speed, and improving the resistance of engine parts to high combustion temperatures, has also contributed to contamination. Yet, I believe that we would be unwilling to compromise the present performance, reliability, and speed flexibility of the automotive engine to reduce the atmospheric pollutants issuing from the engine's exhaust. Despite the numerous gadgets proposed to cope with the problem, about the only thing that would really do the trick without penalizing performance is to go back to much larger engines with lower compression ratios and deliberately design them to run at about one-half present peak mean effective pressures and crankshaft speeds. Of course, this solution would currently be as unacceptable on economic grounds as the automotive diesel refined to eliminate its characteristic noise and roughness during acceleration.

About 20 years ago some of the then latest turbosupercharged aircraft piston engines utilizing internal cooling, direct injection, and dual valve timing (such as in the Lycoming 7755) as a function of load had the sophistication required to offset the degrading effects of high compression ratios and high piston speeds on incomplete combustion, but the amounts of tetraethyl lead to suppress knock and sodium di-bromide useful in the fuel to get rid of the metallic lead deposits in the combustion space made the exhaust efflux lethal. The problem in those days was to build an engine that would operate reliably in the Berlin airlift rather than keep the atmosphere clean. In the late 40's I ran some large turbo-compound engines of this kind at Cornell as well as at Pratt & Whitney Aircraft and found surprisingly low level of carbon monoxide in the exhaust during operation below 80 percent of full load at all speeds. In the early 50's, I witnessed the "Texaco Combustion Process" engine, which seemed unusually indifferent to octane rating. The engine ran on almost anything. My recollection is that I wasn't particularly impressed with the combustion chamber design and privately predicted nothing would come of it. Nevertheless, I recall that the design permitted a form of air-fuel mixing that promoted detonation resistance and might be worth another look from the standpoint of lowering atmospheric contamination from fuel additives, but I doubt whether the CO level would be reduced. Virtually every method for reducing pollution would introduce serious performance penalties.

I do not think that the automotive steam engine (even if somehow run condensing) would be especially attractive either in terms of economy or the instant response required of characteristic stop-and-go driving as well as of sudden accelerations as in high speed passing. Therefore, I doubt whether there is a truly practical solution to the pollution problem without inordinate costs to the car operator.

The Car: An Electric Challenge   13

TIME MAGAZINE

Silent, exhaust-free and otherwise kind to the environment. Powered by an simple motor that is 90% efficient. Easy to handle. Inexpensive to maintain.

Does this description fit some future vehicle that is still beyond man's technological grasp? It does not. [In 1969,] twelve shiny versions of this ideal car were lined up for public inspection at the first International Electric Vehicle Symposium in Phoenix, Ariz. Some of the models were familiar Volkswagens and Renaults, converted to run on battery power. Others were brand new and strange looking. General Electric unveiled its squat, three-door "Delta," which looks like a stylized descendant of the Jeep. Not to be outdone, Westinghouse showed off a sleek "Lotus Europa" sports car. Ford had a streamlined "Lead Wedge" that has whirred across Utah's salt flats at 138 m.p.h. Two Japanese electric cars were on display along with a British minicar costing about $1,000 and already in production.

The new era in transporation that such vehicles promise will be somewhat delayed. The one obstacle that keeps the electric car little more than a conversation piece and unable to compete with conventional automobiles is not the motor but the battery. As many as 16 expensive, low-energy-density batteries are needed to make an electric car go. Together they weigh the car down and completely fill what is now trunk space. More serious, no electric car can cruise much farther than 80 miles or longer than a few hours without having to stop to be recharged.

To create a new battery that would enable the electrics to match the performance of conventional cars, says Dr. J.H.B. George of Arthur D. Little, Inc., would take "hundreds of millions of dollars in a crash research program, or 50 to 100 years." As an alternate solution, G.E.'s Bruce Laumeister reckons, it is now possible to recharge today's batteries in a few minutes—but only with heavy-duty circuits and chargers that cost far more than the car itself.

Such glum speculation about electric cars is brightly optimistic compared with the realistic analysis of Economist Bruce C. Netschert, director of National Economic Research Associates. He bluntly points out that the U.S. economy is geared directly to the mighty internal-combustion engine. Conversion of the nation's 101 million vehicles to electricity, even if possible, would cause nothing less than an economic trauma.

The automobile industry could probably adapt to electric cars, but it would be a painful and costly process. For one thing, since electric cars tend to be extremely durable, "planned obsolescence" would itself become obsolete. For another, the new cars, to minimize the drain on their batteries, would have to be light, small and free of many of today's high-profit accessories. As for the oil industry, Netschert figures that it would lose fully half its market.

Does the combination of technical and economic problems mean that the electric passenger car will never come to be? Manufacturers do not seem to be discouraged. They are trying to develop better batteries while producing more and more electric golf carts, lift trucks, minibuses, industrial sweepers and postal delivery vans.

Meanwhile, the advantages of electric vehicles are being gradually recognized. Even better, the oil and automobile industries, aware of the rising tide of anti-pollution sentiment, and hearing the gentle sound of electric motors (and possibly steam engines) in the future, have already started projects to stay ahead of the competition. Ironically, by the time the electric car becomes competitive, the conventional car will probably be silent, fumeless, durable, small and less harmful to the environment.

14   Steam Automobiles: Advocates Seek Government Support for Research

ANDREW JAMISON

In May, [1968,] the Senate Committee on Commerce and the Public Works Committee's Subcommittee on Air and Water Pollution held joint hearings on the steam car. The hearings generally concentrated on one point: should the government subsidize research and development in an industry that traditionally has financed its own activities. Representatives from the automobile companies said such action would be undesirable and unnecessary. Proponents of steam cars said that in the interests of cleaner air, government support was essential.

So far the government has shown an unwillingness to subsidize research and development of steam cars, electric cars, or any other low-pollutant vehicles. Its position, as expressed by a Department of Transportation spokesman, has been to "leave it all to private enterprise." And private enterprise's position, as expressed by Henry Ford II and others, has been all but to ignore steam-powered vehicles because, as auto company spokesmen have candidly stated, they have a huge investment in the internal combustion engine. Ford and General Motors are conducting research on steam cars, but, as attested to at the Senate hearings, they feel that their most advantageous approach to pollution problems is the development of better emission controls for internal combustion engines.

The steam proponents testified, however, that internal combustion engines could never reach the low emission levels of steam engines without impractical and cumbersome controls. Charles and Calvin Williams, two steam engine manufacturers who have spent over 20 years developing steam vehicles, took Senator Edmund S. Muskie (D—Me.) and Senator Howard H. Baker (R—Tenn.) for a ride in their steam car. They said that their car had been tested for emissions of pollutants after 25,000 miles. It had produced a hydrocarbon level of 20 parts per million, a carbon monoxide level of 0.3 percent, and a nitrogen oxides level of 35 ppm. By comparison, the standards recently set for 1970 vehicles by the Department of Health, Education, and Welfare are 275 ppm for hydrocarbons, 1.5 percent for carbon monoxide, and 1500 ppm for nitrogen oxides. Even the Ford representative said that he found it difficult to envision a way to reduce the internal combustion engine emissions to the level already reached by steam cars. "Low emission is not an option with steam power," Charles Williams told the senators, "it is built in, requiring no 'clean air packages,' expensive catalytic mufflers, or other devices whose complexity requires tuning and maintenance."

This testimony led Muskie, chairman of the Subcommittee for Air and Water Pollution, to take a fairly critical view of the pleas the auto manufacturers made in behalf of the internal combustion engine. Muskie contended that the commitment to the standard engine was based on investment, consumer acceptance, and consumer familiarity, rather than on any actual superiority. "Doesn't all this," Muskie concluded, "add to the momentum of the status quo in a way that may run counter to the public interest?"

By their own admission the automotive companies have not expended the same time, energy, and commitment to steam car research that the "other side" —the steam car advocates—have. The companies' research has been minimal, and it has been heavily biased against steam cars. Ford and GM representatives contend that boiler explosions occur frequently in steam cars. They told the Senate Committee that steam vehicles would also be more cumbersome, expensive, and less efficient than the internal combustion vehicles. The proponents of steam presented an opposite picture. They said that their cars would be cheaper, less complicated mechanically, and safer. Not only were boiler explosions a thing of the past, they said, but the steam car's need for less fuel and less flammable fuels at that, make it safer than an internal combustion vehicle. In addition, they argued, the steam car would produce practically no pollutants, and would be relatively silent. The Williams brothers said that, with some financial support, their cars could compete favorably in terms of performance with the present internal combustion vehicles.

Steam cars have come a long way since the days of the old Stanley Steamer. The Williams car, for example, can reach speeds of up to 100 miles per hour, and takes less than 30 seconds to start up in any weather. It does away with many of the parts of the internal combustion vehicles, having no need for a carburetor, muffler, distributor, or air-pollution control equipment. It also employs a much simpler transmission and starter. However, steam cars have components that the internal combustion engine does not need, such as a boiler and combustion controls. Many of the basic components are the same for both, however—such as the pistons, cylinders, crankcase, and valves—so that, on a mass scale, there should not be a great deal of difference in price between the two; steam proponents actually claim that theirs would be significantly cheaper to produce. The Williams car can use any distillate fuel to heat the water, although kerosene has been standard. It averages about 30 miles per gallon of kerosene, and can go about 500 miles on 10 gallons of water; seepage causes the need for refilling. Although the Williams brothers claim that they use regular tap water and have had success with it, they admit that distilled water is, in the long run, better for the engine.

However, without government support, steam cars face difficulty. Lloyd D. Orr, professor of economics at Indiana University, told the senators that economic factors, such as resistance to change and so-called barriers to entry, including the high capital commitment necessary to establish a new automotive corporation, all play a part in keeping the steam producers from successfully competing with the internal combustion manufacturers. Theodore Johnson, executive vice president of Thermo Electron Corporation, a company that has tried to work with the motor companies in producing steam engines possibly for boats and golf carts, raised another point. He said that "consumers today do not perceive freedom from pollution in the exhaust of a vehicle as a desirable feature for which they are willing to pay very much."

In the past, Congress has generously provided money for projects considered necessary to the defense of the country. This is why the government took such an active role in the development of the aircraft industry. Congress has been much more wary of supporting projects that are not defense oriented. There have been exceptions, prominent among them being agriculture and health-related activities. But, in most nondefense cases, the government has not been in direct competition with corporations conducting research along similar lines, as it would be if it supported steam car research and development.

Methanol: A New Fuel?   **15**

RONALD G. MINET

The chemical process used to convert fuel gas, petroleum fractions, or even coal to methanol is essentially the same as the process used for production of ammonia. In both, the original raw material is converted to a mixture of carbon monoxide and hydrogen which is then further processed to produce the desired final product. The efficiency of conversion is approximately the same in both cases, and a substantial fraction of the carbon originally present in the fossil fuel disappears from the system as carbon dioxide. In the case of ammonia, all of the carbon is separated in this manner; with methanol, about two-thirds is removed.

The cost of erected facilities for the production of ammonia or methanol are roughly comparable. Once very large plants are designed for producing methanol, the relative simplicity possible in handling the product as compared with the requirements for liquifying and pressurizing the ammonia product will probably result in an advantage in the overall investment cost. Methanol can be stored at atmospheric pressure under all normal conditions and can be readily shipped by pipeline, by normal tank car, or tank truck. Because of its very low freezing point and low viscosity, it can be used easily for all conventional fuel requirements.

It is interesting to note that, with some adjustment to the carburetor, methanol can be used as a fuel in ordinary internal combustion engines. It is a completely clean fuel requiring no additives, lead, or other constituents which tend to aggravate atmospheric pollution problems. Of course, it would be essential that the internal combustion engine be adjusted properly to avoid formation of oxygenated hydrocarbon compounds in the exhaust gases.

Of even more interest is the possibility of utilizing methanol directly as a fuel for a direct conversion fuel cell. Substantial work in this direction has been carried out at Institute Francais du Petrole where demonstration cells have already been built and operated for many thousands of hours. Use of methanol in this manner would permit a ready transition from hydrocarbon fuels inside of city areas with a gradual replacement of internal combustion engines by electric motors powered by fuel cells.

Production of methanol could be taken over completely by large energy companies currently refining petroleum and distributing hydrocarbon fuels. The investment required to produce enough methanol to replace all existing fuels would certainly be extremely high, but may not be out of proportion to that required for producing low-sulfur conventional fuels such as is being required by legislation currently being enacted throughout the country.

Sulfur Pollution

16 Diminishing the Role of Sulfur Oxides in Air Pollution

PHILIP H. ABELSON

Each year, in the United States, more than 20 million tons of sulfur are discharged into the atmosphere, most of it in the form of SO_2. This gas is slowly converted into sulfuric acid, which is corrosive to many materials, including metals, building stones, and clothing. The toxicity of SO_2 and H_2SO_4 to plants and animals is controversial, as is the effect of these compounds when they are inhaled along with other components of smog. Because of the complexities of long-term and synergistic effects, many years must elapse before precise conclusions can be reached concerning the role of the sulfur compounds. In the meantime, the public is becoming impatient with slow progress made in overcoming air pollution. Already, in various cities restrictions are being placed on the amount of sulfur fuel may contain.

Principal targets for such restrictions are electric power generating plants. These are a major source of air pollutants when they use coal or residual oil as fuel. Coal, the principal fuel, contains various quantities of sulfur; a typical amount is 3 percent. Concern about air pollution has been a factor in the sudden acceptance of nuclear energy. Unless the pollution problems attending the use of coal are solved, the coal industry will face a gloomy future, caused in part by regulation, in part by competition from other energy sources.

Five means of meeting the sulfur pollution problem seem feasible. One is to use fuel containing only small amounts of sulfur. A second is to discharge the fumes from tall smokestacks (more than 200 meters high). If stacks are tall enough to pierce the inversion layer, the pollutants are thoroughly diluted before reaching the ground. A third method is to add a material such as powdered limestone to the flue-gas stream, following combustion, to convert the gaseous sulfur oxides into a solid form. A fourth is to convert the coal to gas and to remove the sulfur from the gas prior to combustion. A fifth method, which seems very interesting, is to pass the flue gases through a chemical processing plant, the sulfur being recovered in elemental form or as H_2SO_4. A number of variants of this method are under investigation.

Both sulfur and the H_2SO_4 are consumed on a large scale. The price of sulfur has advanced sharply during the last year and is currently quoted at close to $50 a ton. With present technology the value of the sulfur recovered from coal-fired power plants would about offset the cost of investment and operation of the processing plants. A combination of better technology with a higher price for sulfur may eventually convert a nuisance into a valued asset.

Legislation

Has our air improved in quality since the much-ballyhooed legislation of 1967? Worsened in quality? "Held its own"? How many major industries have been or are now involved in lawsuits arising out of their refusal to stop vandalizing the atmosphere? What are some of the fines being paid? Are they substantial enough to convince potential offenders that pollution is a bad investment? Can we expect a marked improvement in our air? When? Ever? How?

Air Quality Act of 1967   **17**

SENATE REPORT

"The Air Quality Act of 1967 ... serves notice that no one has the right to use the atmosphere as a garbage dump, and that there will be no haven for polluters anywhere in the country."

OIL IN THE ECOSYSTEM

The running aground of the tanker "Torrey Canyon" and the Santa Barbara blowout demonstrate—and through their notoriety have come to symbolize—the two major ways oil enters an ecosystem and some of the cruel consequences which follow. Tankers are getting larger and tanker traffic is increasing. Since 1954 some 8,000 oil wells have been drilled in offshore waters. At this writing, approximately 17 gas and 8 oil blowouts have occurred. The Oil Spill Panel has pointed out that if drilling continues at the present rate, by 1980 there will be 3,000 to 5,000 new offshore wells each year and a major pollution incident will occur annually. The blowout in the Santa Barbara channel alone spilled from one to three million gallons of oil into the ecosystem. With the recent oil discovery in Alaska, even the Arctic tundra is in danger of pollution by oil (reading 21).

18   Pollution: The Wake of the "Torrey Canyon"

JOHN WALSH

London. When the tanker *Torrey Canyon* ran aground near the southwest tip of England, it gave its name to a new kind of maritime disaster, the cost of which is counted not in human life but in widespread economic and ecological damage. This in part accounts for the special efforts subsequently made to assess the implications of the accident.

The government was criticized, for example, for waiting a full 10 days before ordering an attempt by aerial bombing to burn oil still left in the tanker. First the government hoped the ship might be refloated or the oil might be transferred. Then there were doubts that the oil could be effectively released by bombing, ignited, and kept alight. And Britain, as a major maritime nation, was reluctant to take a step such as bombing while the salvagers held out hopes and so many questions about responsibility were unanswered.

Pollution of the English coast by oil is a perennial problem. What was unprecedented was the scale of pollution threatened by the *Torrey Canyon,* loaded with 117,000 tons of Kuwait crude oil. Exposed to the threat were the beaches of the southern coasts of England, Britain's principal holiday area. Very heavy pressure was immediately exerted to "save the beaches."

With first priority given to safeguarding coastal amenities, the reflex action was to employ measures developed by the Navy in dealing with oil spills in harbors. This meant using detergents to emulsify and disperse the oil. Some 10,000 tons (2 million gallons) of detergents were used to treat 13,000 tons of oil on Cornish beaches, and another half million gallons were sprayed at sea.

In its effects on marine life this detergent "cure" proved much more damaging than the oil itself. The chief conclusion of the Plymouth Laboratory study is that, except for serious effects on some species of sea birds, the oil was not lethal to flora and fauna. Detergents used to disperse the oil, on the other hand, were highly toxic to marine life, most conspicuously to intertidal life such as limpets and barnacles. In the open sea, detergents in quantities as small as one part detergent per million parts of seawater proved lethal to planktonic growth.

Toxic Effects

Detergents used in spraying operations are mixtures of several compounds —a surfactant (or surface-active agent), an organic solvent, and a stabilizer. A stable emulsion of oil and water was necessary if the oil was to be dispersed. Solvents which enable the surfactants to mix with oil to form an emulsion contain a high proportion of aromatic hydrocarbons. Research indicated that the detergents with the highest proportion of aromatics are the best emulsifiers, and also the most toxic to flora and fauna.

Spraying of a half-million gallons of such detergent could be expected to have a devastating effect on plankton living near the surface of the water. Biologists reported surprisingly little damage to planktonic organisms in the spraying area. The explanation, they suggest, is that toxic aromatics evaporate very rapidly from the surface of seawater. Otherwise, as the report puts it, "the biological consequences in the English Channel would have been vastly worse than they were."

The worst sufferers from the oil were sea birds; the heaviest casualties were suffered by diving birds—guillemots, razorbills, cormorants, and shags. Gulls seem to have learned to avoid oil, and very few were affected. Ornithologists have reported a decline in the number of auks and other diving birds breeding on southern British coasts in the last 30 years and have attributed it to oil pollution. Total casualties of the *Torrey Canyon* oil were estimated at 20,000 guillemots and 5000 razorbills. A sad aspect of the oil fouling of sea birds was the failure of rescue operations. The British are unrivaled bird lovers, and a big effort at cleaning birds was made by the government and by voluntary agencies and individuals. But of nearly 8000 birds recorded as treated, only 450 were alive by mid-April and only about 1 percent of the birds treated were expected to be returned to the sea.

Little Effect on Seals

Contrary to some predictions, effects on offshore fisheries seem to have been negligible. The seal population does not appear to be seriously affected, although some breeding caves were badly polluted by oil and scientists suggest that ill effects may become apparent later. No commercial shellfish ground was affected by oil, as such grounds were in France, and care was taken not to spray detergent near such beds.

France's battle with *Torrey Canyon* oil was different from Britain's, in part because the French had more time and perhaps because they profited from the British experience. The main difference was that the French shunned detergents. Oil came ashore on the coast of Brittany in higher concentrations than in most parts of Cornwall, but the French relied on mechanical means of removal and such natural effects as waves, tides, and bacterial degradation. Oil did do considerable damage to Breton shellfish beds, but these are expected to recover. At sea, a big patch of oil in the Bay of Biscay was successfully treated with powdered chalk. The chalk binds the oil into particles which sink to the bottom. The French estimate that 3000 tons of chalk will sink 20,000 tons of oil.

The two British reports give the impression that, after the accident, luck was with the defenders. A northerly wind blew for nearly 2 months afterward, at a time of year when the wind normally blows from the southwest. Under normal conditions much more oil would have come ashore, instead of being blown out to sea. It even appears that if the bombing and the burning of oil aboard the *Torrey Canyon* had been done earlier, a lot of unburned residue would have ended up on the beaches. The immediate costs of the wreck to Britain (estimated at £ 3 million), the setback to the tourist industry, and the damage to coastal ecology all could have been devastatingly increased if even half the oil in the *Torrey Canyon's* tanks had come ashore.

Research Needed

The Zuckerman committee asks that better means be developed for transferring cargo from disabled tankers and for destroying or dispersing oil at sea. Detergents should be used judiciously, and less toxic detergents should be developed, both reports agree. And more research needs to be done on the neglected questions of the effects of pollution on marine life and ways of minimizing these effects.

And the odds are that there will be other *Torrey Canyon*s. Some 10 percent of the world's shipping accidents occur in Britain's heavily trafficked coastal waters. And tankers are getting bigger. The 210,000-ton Japanese supertanker *Idemitsu Maru,* for example, dwarfs the *Torrey Canyon.* And within a few years tankers of a half-million tons deadweight may be plying the seas.

The Plymouth Laboratories scientists say in summing up, "We are progressively making a slum of nature and may eventually find that we are enjoying the benefit of science and industry under conditions which no civilized society should tolerate."

Oil in the Ecosystem 19

ROBERT W. HOLCOMB

Oil pollution has been a human problem for most of this century, but it took the grounding of the tanker *Torrey Canyon* and the blowout of the well off the coast of Santa Barbara to draw public attention to the major problems that can arise in the production and shipping of petroleum. A five-fold increase in oil production is expected by 1980, and the potential for large-scale pollution can increase even faster because of changes in drilling location and shipping practice. Knowledge of how oil affects the environment is fragmentary and gives only dim clues about what to expect in the future.

The problems involved in oil studies are complex. Crude oil is not a single chemical but a collection of hundreds of substances of widely different properties and toxicities. Paul Galtsoff of the Bureau of Commercial Fisheries at Woods Hole, Massachusetts, stated recently that "oil in sea water should be regarded not as an ordinary pollutant but as a dynamic system actively reacting with the environment."

Viewing the problem of oil this way, one finds that biologists present an essentially unified account of how oil came to be an important part of the environment and that they can give a rough outline of the way oil interacts with the rest of the ecological system. However, it is still impossible to predict the behavior of specific oil spills, and little is known about the long-term effects of oil in the marine environment.

Most current research is directed toward the immediate problem of handling oil spills. There is little prospect that detailed ecological studies will increase dramatically in the near future, but plans are being considered for the establishment of broad-based environmental-monitoring programs.

Oil at Sea

In 1966, 700 million tons of oil—about half the world's total ocean tonnage —were shipped in 3281 tankers. In the best of worlds, this oil would remain in that part of the "ecological" system of interest only to humans—wells, tankers, refineries, and, finally, furnaces and machines. It is difficult to estimate just how far short we are of living in the best of worlds, but Max Blumer of Woods Hole Oceanographic Institute estimates that somewhere between 1 million and 100 million tons of oil are added to our oceans each year.

The major sources of this oil are handling errors, leaks from natural deposits, tanker and barge accidents, and illegal tanker bilge washings. Normal techniques of transferring oil to small coastal tankers, barges, and shore facilities result in a chronic source of coastal oil. The total amount of oil from this source is unknown, but the Massachusetts Division of Natural Resources says that, in Boston Harbor alone, a spill involving several tons of oil can be expected every third week. Less frequent, but more spectacular, are leaks from offshore deposits.

These can occur naturally, but they have been associated with drilling operations since the 1930's, when fields in the Gulf of Mexico were opened. The biggest loss associated with the more than 9000 offshore wells was the million-gallon blowout early this year off the California coast near Santa Barbara. Tanker accidents are similar to well blowouts in that an occasional major catastrophe highlights a constant source of contamination. The grounding of the *Torrey Canyon* off the southwest coast of England in March 1967 was simply the most dramatic example of a type of accident that, on a worldwide basis, occurs more than once a week. Finally, deliberate dumping of bilge washings adds a considerable, but unknown, amount of oil to the oceanic environment. In 1962 Shell Oil Company developed a method to separate oil from such washings, and there is a tacit international agreement to use the method; however, shipmasters find the procedure inconvenient, and the dumping practice continues.

Although our oil resources are not unlimited, a quick look to the future indicates that pumping and shipping operations will continue to expand for the next few decades. The continental shelves of North and South America, Africa, and Australia all have oil. Seismic profiling has indicated the probable presence of oil in the North Sea, Persian Gulf, and Indonesia, and large deposits have been discovered in Alaska and Canada.

Oil from these new sources will be transported through pipelines and by gigantic tankers. Construction has already begun on a road that will be used to build the 800-mile, 48-inch, 900-million dollar pipeline from Alaska's North Slope to Valdez Bay, an ice-free port on the Gulf of Alaska. The large United States merchant vessel S.S. *Manhattan* was specially strengthened for travel in ice and fought her way through the Canadian Arctic in September. If such trial runs are judged successful, a fleet of six, quarter-million-ton vessels will be built for year-round service. (The *Torrey Canyon,* considered a large ship at the time of her grounding, had a displacement of 127,000 tons.)

The proposed drilling activities will involve greater risks of major losses because work must be done at sea or in inhospitable northern latitudes. The use of large tankers will reduce the probability of collisions and groundings, but there are few port facilities for these giants, so the possibility of spills during transfers to smaller tankers or barges will be increased. Major accidents, of course, will be of colossal proportions.

Behavior in Water

After coming in contact with water, crude oil rapidly spreads into a thin layer and the lighter fractions evaporate. In protected areas the oil often becomes adsorbed on particulate matter and sinks, but in open sea it tends to remain on the surface where wind and wave action aid in further evaporation. Some oil dissolves in seawater and some is oxidized but the hundreds of species of bacteria, yeasts, and molds that attack different fractions of hydrocarbons under a variety of physical conditions are primarily responsible for oil degradation.

Bacteria found in open seas tend to degrade only straight-chain hydrocarbons of moderate molecular weight, so branched-chain hydrocarbons of high molecular weight in the form of tarry chunks may persist for a long time. In still waters, a series of complex events results in almost complete degradation. In 1950, Soviet microbiologists showed that, after the lighter fractions of oil spilled on the Moskva River evaporated, the remaining oil was adsorbed by particles and sank. Bottom-dwelling microorganisms produced a new mixture of organic substances that were carried to the surface with bubbles of methane and other light gases. The new compounds again were adsorbed, sank, and the cycle was repeated. A number of cycles, repeated over several months, were necessary to degrade most of the oil.

Studies on the thoroughness of degradation have produced conflicting results. Research at Terrebonne Bay, Louisiana, in 1966 showed that essentially complete degradation occurs within a period of several months. Oil has been a consistent pollutant in the Bay since the 1930's, but analysis of bottom mud showed that significant concentrations of petrochemicals could be found only in areas that had received oil relatively recently. However, studies in the French Mediterranean, which will be discussed later, indicate that important chemicals are persistent in bottom sediments.

There is now a considerable body of literature on the interactions of microorganisms and petroleum products, most of it based on laboratory studies and much of it dating back to Soviet work in the 1930's and American work in the 1940's. However, these studies are scarcely past the descriptive stage, and, even when combined with field studies, they are not adequate for predicting the course of degradation of an oil spill.

Oil and Marine Life

The most visible victims of ocean oil are sea birds. It is impossible to even guess how many are killed each year, and about the only thing known for sure is that, once oiled, very few birds survive. After the *Torrey Canyon* disaster, 5711 oiled birds were cleaned off; apparently 150 of them returned to health and were released, but banding counts of these indicate that at least 37 died within the first month after release. Similar figures were obtained from French efforts at bird rehabilitation after the same disaster, and few of the 1500 diving birds cleaned after the Santa Barbara blowout survived.

It is believed that most deaths are the result of diseases, such as pneumonia, which attack the birds after they are weakened by the physical effects of the oil (feather matting, loss of buoyancy, flying difficulty, and others). However, the high death rate of cleaned birds is unexplained, so long-term toxicity of the oil cannot be ruled out.

The major studies of the effects of oil spills on species other than birds have produced a wide variety of results. Dr. Robert Holmes, the first director of a major study after the Santa Barbara blowout, has stated that plankton populations were unaffected, and, although his remark was challenged at the Massachusetts Institute of Technology symposium where it was made, it is generally agreed that visible damage to organisms other than birds has been relatively light.

On the other hand, in what is probably the best "before and after" study of a major spill, it was conclusively shown that almost the entire population of a small cove was killed by dark diesel oil from the tanker *Tampico Mara.* In March 1957, the tanker grounded at the mouth of a small, previously unpolluted cove on the Pacific coast of Baja California, Mexico, and, until destroyed by the sea, it blocked most of the cove's entrance. All signs of oil disappeared sometime between November 1957 and May 1958, but the ecology of the cove was radically changed. A few species returned within 2 months, but 2 years had elapsed before significant improvements were noted. Four years after the accident, sea urchin and abalone populations were still greatly reduced; and, at the last observations in 1967, several species present 10 years earlier had not returned.

Although toxicity studies in the ocean have been limited to a few large spills, considerable laboratory work has been done to determine the lethal concentrations of a number of chemicals on various species. Most toxic are the aromatic hydrocarbons (for example, benzene, toluene, and the xylenes), and investigators have recently shown that the low-boiling, saturated hydrocarbons are more toxic than formerly believed. The destructiveness of the *Tampico Mara* grounding was probably due to the saturated hydrocarbons, and it has been shown that aromatic hydrocarbons used to dissolve detergents in the effort to disperse oil from *Torrey Canyon* caused much of the damage. When a spill occurs at sea, a large portion of both these classes of compounds evaporates before reaching shore. This is probably the main reason that the Santa Barbara blowout was not more disastrous to shore life other than birds.

Biochemical Studies

Just enough is known about the higher-boiling, saturated hydrocarbons and the high-boiling, aromatic hydrocarbons to indicate that more study is needed. Saturated, higher-boiling compounds occur naturally in both crude oil and marine organisms, so they are probably not toxic; but work reported this year indicated that these compounds may affect the behavior of sea animals.

Blumer points out that very small amounts of certain chemicals are used by many species of sea animals as behavior signals in the vital activities of food finding, escaping from predators, homing, and reproduction. He has shown, for example, that starfish are attracted to their oyster prey by chemicals in concentrations of a few parts per billion. The responsible chemicals have not been identified, but Blumer believes that in many cases they may resemble the high-boiling, saturated hydrocarbons found in petroleum products. Because of the extreme sensitivity of the response and the similarity of the animal and petroleum chemicals, he thinks it is possible that pollution interferes with chemically stimulated behavior "by blocking the taste receptors and by mimicking natural stimuli."

Studies on chemically stimulated behavior of marine animals are in such an early stage that ideas about the role of sea oil in the process can only be considered speculative. However, the speculation indicated that the consequences—altered behavior of entire populations of commercially valuable species—are so serious that the matter deserves early attention.

Another matter still in the speculative stage, but with potentially hazardous consequences, is the significance of high-boiling, aromatic hydrocarbons. Crude oil and crude oil residues contain alkylated 4- and 5-ring aromatic hydrocarbons similar to those found in tobacco tars, but little is known about their role in the marine environment.

In 1964 Lucien Mallet, a French marine chemist, reported the presence of 3,4-benzopyrene, a known carcinogen, in sediments of the French Mediterranean. Concentrations ranged from 5.0 parts per million at a depth of 8 to 13 cm to 0.016 part per million at 200 cm. Similar concentrations have been found in other waters that had been polluted for a long time. Near the port of Villefranche, 3,4-benzopyrene in concentrations from 0.025 to 0.04 part per million have been found in plankton.

Benzopyrenes can be formed by algae, and they occur naturally in many soils in concentrations ranging from parts per million to parts per billion; thus their presence in marine sediments may not be cause for concern. However, the detection in sea cucumbers of concentrations that were slightly greater than those in the bottom sediments where these animals feed indicated that benzopyrenes in the marine environment may find their way into the food chain.

Pollutants tend to enter the food chain more easily and to pass through it with fewer changes in aquatic environments than they do in terrestrial environments. They can be introduced in solution through bottom sediments and even in dispersed droplets that are ingested by the numerous filter feeders that constitute an important part of aquatic food.

The presence of DDT in Lake Michigan's coho salmon drew public attention to the fact that some hydrocarbons pass through the aquatic food chain relatively unchanged. Work at Woods Hole has demonstrated that the ratios of olefinic hydrocarbons in zooplankton to those in livers of basking sharks and herring that feed on the plankton are so constant that they can be used to determine the feeding grounds of these species.

Obviously, studies should be conducted to see what concentrations of 3,4-benzopyrene and other potentially dangerous hydrocarbons must be in seawater or sediments before they are introduced into the food chain and whether the chemicals persist as they pass through the chain.

Priorities

Although the possible ill effects of long-term oil pollution point to the need for more studies on the complex chemical-biological relationships of oil and the environment, there is still work to be done on the immediate effects of oil spills. Dale Straugh, who now directs the large Santa Barbara study, said in a telephone interview that oil spills will undoubtedly continue and that much of the research effort should concentrate on methods of handling them.

Present alternatives are (i) to "corral" the oil and hold it at sea, (ii) to pick it up mechanically, or (iii) to treat it chemically so it will emulsify, dissolve, or sink. None of these methods is particularly successful, and research on all of them is continuing. The major requirement for further development is engineering and chemical knowledge, but biological expertise is necessary in some areas.

It is primarily biological studies, especially those after the *Torrey Canyon* incident, that precipitated the government decision not to use chemical treatment when the shore area is used as a source of fresh water or as a beach, or when it is necessary for commercially valuable species. Toxicity tests of chemicals developed to treat oil are now routinely conducted, and the Federal Water Pollution Control Administration is developing a standard procedure for such tests. This action was prompted in part by reports that a dispersal agent, Corexit, used at Santa Barbara was more toxic than earlier tests indicated.

The step beyond toxicity tests is a giant one of determining subtle and long-term effects of sunken, dissolved, or dispersed oil. Biological knowledge has advanced far enough to rule them out or to provide unquestionably safe alternatives. This task would require difficult, long-term studies on the complex interactions of oil, seawater, and marine life, and there is nothing on the horizon to indicate that these studies will progress rapidly enough to play a large role in decisions about methods of handling oil spills.

Another area in which biological knowledge could be helpful is in simply monitoring the oil that enters the oceans and determining, at least by sampling, its effects. On this horizon there seems to be some light. Several studies designed to determine the feasibility of establishing broad-based centers for enviromental study are now in progress.

The systematic monitoring of the oceans, including their oil content, is a necessary step toward development of the capability of determining the world-wide consequences of effects that at present can be measured only in the laboratory or in relatively small field studies.

20 Oil Spills—An Old Story

S. W. A. GUNN

After charting the coastline of what is now Alaska, British Columbia, and Washington, the great English seaman, Captain George Vancouver, visited California in the *Discovery* in 1793, and made this entry in his log for Sunday, 10 November (1):

The surface of the sea, which was perfectly smooth and tranquil, was covered with a thick slimy substance, which, when separated, or disturbed by any little agitation, became very luminous, whilst the light breeze that came principally from the shore, brought with it a very strong smell of burning tar, or of some such resinous substance. The next morning the sea had the appearance of dissolved tar floating upon its surface, which covered the ocean in all directions within the limits of our view; and indicated that in this neighbourhood it was not subject to much agitation.

By coincidence, this was in the very area of Santa Barbara where the undersea oil well blew up recently, and following which the Department of the Interior stated that "there is a lack of sufficient knowledge of this particular geological area"!

REFERENCE

1. J. S. Marshall, *Vancouver's Voyage* (Mitchell Press, Vancouver, 1967), p. 112.

The Oil Pollution Threat in Alaska 21

THE WILDERNESS REPORT

Oil companies already have proposed construction of immense pipelines (48 inches in diameter) that would cross Alaska. A mile length of this pipeline would contain approximately one-half million gallons of oil. A break would flood over thousands of acres of tundra and woodlands and into miles of streams and lakes to destroy nearly all life in these pristine environments. The pipe has been ordered by the oil companies for one such pipeline that would extend nearly 800 miles from Prudhoe Bay on the Arctic Coast to Valdez on Prince William Sound, and plans for construction are in their final stages. Survey work has been authorized by the Secretary of the Interior.

Thermal Pollution

Thermal pollution has been of major concern only to a minority of pollution opponents. This is a bit amazing when one considers that the 120 degree temperature range which supports life on earth is such a tiny slit in the 20 million degree galactic range from absolute zero to the unimaginable heat of the younger stars.

While some predict the return of an ice age in the wake of widespread pollution, others suggest that the ice caps will melt and flood coastal areas. Less dramatic but perhaps as important is the ecological change which could result from only an annual average two-degree-centigrade increase in the temperature of a major river.

Most power plants in the United States convert the chemical energy of fossil fuel into electrical energy. But the supply of fossil fuel is finite—and rapidly diminishing. In addition, the decrease in oxygen, increase in carbon dioxide and considerable pollution which result from the operation of conventional power plants make them unacceptable for use in the future. With this in mind, the public often turn for a remedy to advocating the use of nuclear powered generators. This solution, however, leaves us with two main problems: (1) disposal of radioactive wastes and (2) cooling of the plant. Warm water irrigation of crops may serve as a beneficial solution to the disposal of that by-product of electric power, heat. More research is urgently needed.

22   Thermal Pollution

LaMont C. Cole

Introduction

There are etymological objections to the expression "thermal pollution," but it is gaining adoption and I shall here accept it without comment as a descriptive term for unwanted heat energy accumulating in any phase of the environment.

Any isolated body drifting in space as the earth is must either increase continuously in temperature or it must dispose of all energy received from external sources or generated internally by one of two processes. The energy may either be stored in some potential form or it must be reradiated to space.

In the past the earth has stored some of the energy coming to it from outside. This was accomplished by living plants using solar energy to drive endothermic chemical reactions, thereby creating organic compounds some of which were ultimately deposited in sediments. This process had two very important effects; in protecting the organic compounds from oxidation it created a reservoir of oxygen in the atmosphere; and it also eliminated the necessity for reradiating to space the heat energy that would have been released by the oxidation of those compounds. Part of the stored organic matter gave rise to the fossil fuels, coal, oil, and natural gas, which we are so avidly burning today—and now the earth must at last radiate that heat energy back to space, or its temperature will increase.

Many of the most important problems currently facing man are ecological problems arising from the unrestrained growth of the human population and the resultant increasing strains being placed on the earth's life support system. Our seemingly insatiable demand for energy is one important source of strains on the earth's capacity to support life, and I propose here to examine it in very elementary terms.

Well over 99.999% of the earth's annual energy income is from solar radiation and this must all be returned to space in the form of radiant heat. This has gone on forever, so to speak, and conditions on earth, since before the advent of man, have reflected the necessity of maintaining this balance of incoming and outgoing radiation. A ridiculously small proportion of the sunlight reaching us is used in photosynthesis by green plants. This energy powers all of the earth's microorganisms and animals and is converted to heat by their metabolism. In addition, man can obtain useful heat energy by burning organic matter in such forms as wood, straw, cattle dung, and garbage and other refuse. This is "free" energy in the sense that the earth would have reradiated it as heat even if man had not obtained useful work from it in the meantime. Physical labor performed by man and the work done by domestic animals are also means of utilizing this solar energy.

In addition, it is solar radiation that keeps the atmosphere and hydrosphere in motion. To the extent that man can utilize the energy of the winds, of falling water and of ocean currents, or can make direct use of sunlight, he can do so without imposing increased thermal stress on the total earth environment.

The earth has some other minor sources of energy that contribute to its natural radiation balance. The tides can be used to obtain useful energy and a plant in France is now producing electricity from this source. Also, tidal friction is very gradually slowing the rotation of the earth, thereby converting kinetic energy to heat which plays a small role in maintaining the earth's surface temperature before it is radiated to space. Heat is also emerging from the interior of the earth and current concepts attribute this heat to natural radioactivity. In some local areas this heat flux is concentrated, and in a few countries man utilizes it for such purposes as heating buildings and generating electricity. Italy generates more than 400,000 kw of electricity from geothermal heat and in the United States about 85,000 kw are derived from a geyser field north of San Francisco.

This then is the inventory of energy sources available to man without affecting the surface temperature of the earth or the quantity of heat energy that it must dispose of by radiation. It is important to note this because, at least in the "developed" nations, we actually seem to be regressing from the use of these natural energy sources. Certainly windmills, animal power, and manual labor are much less in evidence today than they were during my childhood, and useful work done by sailboats seems to be a thing of the past in our culture. When we burn fossil fuels or generate electricity by nuclear or thermonuclear reactions, we must inevitably impose an increased thermal stress on the earth environment and, to the extent that this heat is undesirable, it constitutes thermal pollution.

The Earth's Radiation Balance

I assume the mean temperature of the earth's surface to be 15 C or 288 K; this may be a degree too low or too high. In order to keep the discussion sufficiently simple-minded, I shall introduce three simplifications.

First, I shall treat the earth as though its entire surface was at a uniform temperature equal to its average value, thus ignoring temperature differences due to latitude, altitude, season, and time of day. The effect of this simplification is less drastic than one might expect. It is true if one measures radiation from several bodies at different temperatures and infers the mean temperature of the surfaces from the radiation, he will obtain values that are slightly too high. For example, if we have two otherwise identical areas, one at 0 C and the other at 50 C, the average of their combined radiation will equal that which would be given off by such an area at 28 C rather than at the true mean temperature of 25 C. For the earth as a whole, the error from this source is not likely to amount to even one degree, and the other two simplifications I shall make tend to cause small errors in the opposite direction.

Second, I assume that the earth radiates as a blackbody or perfect radiator. This is probably nearly correct; and, in any case, the assumption is conservative for our purposes here. If the earth is actually a gray body rather than a black one, it will have to reach a somewhat higher temperature to dispose of the same amount of heat energy.

Finally, I assume that the earth radiates its energy to outer space which is at a temperature of O K. This is not quite correct because the portions of the sky occupied by the sun, moon, stars, and clouds of interstellar matter are at temperatures above absolute zero, and the earth's surface must therefore be very slightly warmer than it would otherwise be.

Accepting these simplifications, we can now turn to the Stefan-Boltzmann law of elementary physics which states that radiation is proportional to the fourth power of the absolute temperature, and easily calculate the amount of energy radiated from the earth to space.[1] At a temperature of 15 C (288 K) the total radiation from the earth turns out to be 2 X 10^{24} ergs/sec.

1. take the surface area of the earth as 5.1 x 10^{18} cm^2 and the value of the Stefan constant as 5.67 x 10^{-5} erg cm^{-2} deg^{-4} sec^{-1}.

Or, looked at the other way around, if we know the quantity of heat that the earth's surface must get rid of by radiation, we can calculate what its surface temperature must be for it to do so. For example, various students of the subject have concluded that the mean temperature difference between glacial and icefree periods is quite small, probably no more than 5 C (e.g., see Brooks, 1949). If we can assume that we are now about midway between these climatic types, then a rise of 3 C might be expected to melt the icecaps from Antarctica and Greenland thereby raising sea-level by some 100 m. This would drastically alter the world's coastlines as, for example, by putting all of Florida under water, and drowning most of the world's major cities. To do this would require a 4.2% increase in the earth's heat budget (an increase of 8.44 x 10^{22} ergs/sec). By the same reasoning, a 4.1% decrease in the energy budget could be expected to bring on a new ice age. As we shall see presently, however, these things are not really quite so simple and predictable.

Man's Effect on the Heat Budget

The amount of energy now being produced by man, I take to be 5 x 10^{19} ergs/sec or 25/1000 of 1% of the total radiated by the earth. Strangely enough, I am quite happy with this perhaps brash attempt to estimate a difficult quantity. Putnam (1953) estimated the fuel burned by man 16 years ago at 3.3 x 10^{19} ergs/sec. If he was correct then, and if energy demand then had been growing at the rate it is now growing, man would now be using twice what I have estimated. Kardashev (1964) estimates the energy now produced by civilization at "over 4 x 10^{19} ergs per second" which is consistent with my estimate.

There is another way of getting at the figure. The rate of combustion of fossil fuels in the United States is accurately known, as is our rate of generating electricity. Our electrical production as of 1966 corresponds to one-fifth of our fossil fuel consumption. If we assume the same ratio for the entire earth, for which we do have credible figures on electrical generation, the world energy production turns out to be 4.4 x 10^{19} ergs/sec. With this many independent estimates converging, I am happy with the figure of 5 x 10^{19} ergs/sec.

This is such a tiny part of the earth's output of energy that it is evident that the heat released by man now has an absolutely insignificant direct effect on the average temperature of the earth's surface. Will this be true if we go on increasing our demands for power? I have been hearing utility company officials assert that we must keep electrical generating capacity growing by 10% per year, but a more common projection is about 7%, at which rate the capacity would double every 10 years. I am confident that nonelectrical uses of fuel for such purposes as heating, industry, and transportation are growing at least as rapidly, and I am told that the "developing" countries are going to continue to develop. Let us examine the consequences of an energy economy that continues to grow at 7% per year.

Waggoner (1966) considers it at least possible that a warming of 1 C would cause real changes in the boundaries between plant communities. For this to occur, the earth's energy budget would have to increase by about 3×10^{22} ergs/sec. How long would it take man to cause this at an increased energy production of 7% per year? The answer is 91 years.

As already mentioned, a rise of 3 C could, in the opinion of competent authorities, melt the ice caps and produce an earth geography such as has never been seen by man, and on which there would be much less dry land for man. This would take about 108 years to achieve by present trends.

The highest mean annual temperature of any spot on earth is believed to be 29.9 C (302.9 K) at Massawa on the Red Sea in Ethiopia. I think it is safe to assume that if the average temperature of the whole earth was raised to 30 C, it would become uninhabitable. This would take 130 years under our postulated conditions—the time from the Victorian era to the present.

These calculations, rough as they are, make it clear that man is on a collision course with disaster if he tries to keep energy producti n growing by means that will impose an increased thermal stress on the earth. I have here ignored the fact that the fossil fuels, and probably uranium and thorium reserves also, would be exhausted before these drastic effects could be attained. The possibility exists, however, that a controlled fusion reaction will be achieved and bring these disastrous effects within the realm of possibility.

How can we avoid the consequences of the trends we are following? My answer would be to determine what level of human population the earth can support at a desirable standard of living without undergoing deterioration and then to move to achieve this steady state condition. I would like to see increased energy needs met by the direct utilization of solar energy. There are, however, vissionary scientists, and policy makers who will listen to them, who will grasp at any straw to keep man's exploitation of the earth forever growing. In my mind I can hear them planning to air condition part of the earth for man and for whatever then will supply his food, while the rest of the earth is allowed to radiate the excess heat by attaining a very high temperature. They will consider putting generating plants and factories on the moon and other planets and reducing the heat stress on earth by reflecting solar radiation back to space. This latter possibility brings us to consideration of some secondary effects of our expanding energy budget.

Side Effects of Energy Use

The combustion of fuel releases not only heat but also frequently smoke and various chemicals, the most important of which are water and carbon dioxide, into the environment.

Smoke and other particulate matter in the atmosphere scatters and absorbs incoming solar radiation, thus reducing the amount of energy absorbed by the surface. It has little effect on the outgoing longwave radiation, so the net effect is a tendency to cool the earth's surface. Several large volcanic eruptions within historic times have caused a year or so of abnormally low temperatures all over the earth. Perhaps the most striking case was the mighty eruption of Mt. Tomboro in the Lesser Sunda Islands in 1815. The following year, 1816, was the famous "year without a summer," during which snow fell in Boston every month. Actual measurements following the 1912 eruption of Mt. Katmai in the Aleutians showed a reduction of about 20% in the solar radiation reaching the earth.

Water vapor and carbon dioxide have an effect opposite to that of smoke; they are transparent to sunlight but absorb the longwave radiation from the earth and, by reradiating some of it back to earth, tend to raise the surface temperature. Man's combustion of fossil fuels has caused a measurable increase in the CO_2 content of the atmosphere, and now increasing numbers of jet airplanes are releasing great quantities of both water vapor and CO_2 at high altitudes. This would tend to raise the earth's temperature. However, a phenomenon of increasing frequency is the coalescence of the contrails of jet airplanes into banks of cirrus clouds which will reflect some of the incoming solar radiation back to space. Obviously, we cannot now be certain of the ultimate effects of the materials we are releasing to the atmosphere, but they certainly have the potential for changing climates.

On a more local scale, we are using prodigious quantities of water for cooling industrial plants, especially electrical generating plants, and this use is expected to increase at least as rapidly as our energy use grows[2] —perhaps more rapidly because nuclear plants waste more heat per kilowatt than plants burning fossil fuels. When heated water is discharged at a temperature above that of the air, we must expect an increase in the frequencies of mist and fog and, in winter, icing conditions.

Biological Effects of Thermal Pollution

The first and most obvious biological effect one thinks of is that bodies of water may become so hot that nothing can live in them. It is true that there are a few bacteria and blue-green algae that can grow in hot springs but even these are very unusual in water above 60 C. I know of only one case of a green alga living above 50 C—a species of *Protococcus* from Yellowstone Park. A few rotifers, nematodes, and protozoa have been found at above 50 C, and some, in a dried and encysted state, will survive much higher temperatures. In general, no higher organisms are to be expected actively living in water above about 35 C. I find it difficult to reconcile the data with the conclusion of Wurtz (1968, p. 139): "Water temperature would have to be increased to about 130 F (54.4 C) to destroy the microorganisms that are responsible for the self-purification capacity of a lake or stream." This statement is certainly incompatible with the recommendation of the National Technical Advisory Committee (1968) that: "All surface waters should be capable of supporting life forms of aesthetic value."

Another factor to be considered is the effect of temperature on the types of organisms present. Fish of any type are rare above 30 C. Diatoms, which are important members of aquatic food chains, decrease as temperature rises above 20 C, and they are gradually replaced by blue-green algae which are not important

2. Thermally more efficient electrical generating plants are considered possible: e.g., the "magnetohydrodynamic" generator (see Rosa and Hals. 1968).

as food for animals, are often toxic, and are often the source of water blooms which kill the biota and make the water unfit for domestic use. Typically at about 30 C, diatoms and blue-greens are about equally represented and green algae exceed both. At 35 C, the diatoms are nearly gone, the greens are decreasing rapidly, and the blue-greens are assuming full dominance.

So far as animals are concerned, a body of water at a temperature of 30-35 C is essentially a biological desert. The green algae, which are well above their optimum temperature, can support a few types of cladoceran, amphiphod, and isopod crustaceans; bacteria and blue-green algae may abound; and mosquito larvae may do very well; rooted plants may grow in shallow regions; and a few crayfish, carp, goldfish, and catfish may endure. Largemouth bass can survive and grow at 32 C but they do not reproduce above about 24 C. A few other forms such as aquatic insects may inhabit the water as adults but may or may not be able to complete their life cycles there. Desirable game fishes such as Atlantic salmon, lake trout, northern pike, and walleyes require water below 10 C for reproduction.

Another effect of raising the temperature of water is to reduce the solubility of gases. The amount of oxygen dissolved in water in equilibrium with the atmosphere decreases by over 17% between 20 C and 30 C. At the same time, the need of organisms for oxygen increases. As a rule of thumb, metabolic rate approximately doubles for a 10 C increase in body temperature, although the effect is sometimes greater. Krogh (1914) found that the rate of development of frog eggs is about six times as great at 20 C as at 10 C. Similar effects have been noted in the rate of development of mosquitos.

Dissolved oxygen is often in critically short supply for aquatic organisms and increased temperature aggravates the situation. This may be partially compensated by more rapid diffusion of oxygen from the air and, during daylight hours, by photosynthesis. On the other hand, decay of organic matter and other oxidative processes such as the rusting of iron are more rapid at high temperatures. In polluted water the effect of biochemical oxygen demand (BOD) is more severe at high temperatures. The addition of heat to estuaries may be more critical than in bodies of freshwater because saltwater has a slightly lower specific heat and because oxygen is less soluble in saltwater.

In contrast to the situation with gases, salts become more soluble in water as the temperature increases. Chemical reactions become more rapid and increased evaporation may further increase the concentration of dissolved salts. At the same time the rate of exchange of substances between aquatic organisms and the medium increases. Toxins are likely to have greater effects, and parasites and diseases are more likely to break out and spread. In general, water at a temperature above the optimum places a strain on metabolic processes that may make adaptation to other environmental factors more difficult. For example, the Japanese oyster can tolerate a wider range of salinity in winter than in summer (Reid, 1961, p. 267).

In addition, if the water contains plant nutrients, objectionable growths of aquatic plants may be promoted by increased temperature—extreme cases leading to heavy mortality of fishes and other animals. It has been reported that polluted water from Lake Superior which does not support algal blooms there will do so if warmed to the temperature of Lake Erie.

Still other factors come into play when a body of water is thermally stratified. In a deep cold lake such as Cayuga where we are currently threatened with a huge nuclear generating plant, the lake water mixes, usually in May, so the entire lake is well oxygenated. As the surface warms, the lake stratifies with a level of light, warm water (the epilimnion) floating with no appreciable mixing on a mass of dense cold water (the hypolimnion) in which the lake trout, their food organisms, and other things are living and consuming oxygen. This continues until the lake mixes again, usually in November, by which time the oxygen supply in the hypolimnion is seriously depleted. The power company plans to pump 750 million gallons per day from the hypolimnion at a temperature averaging perhaps 6 C and to discharge it at the surface at a temperature of about 21 C. They plan this despite a recommendation of the National Technical Advisory Committee (1968, p. 33) that: " . . . water for cooling should not be pumped from the hypolimnion to be discharged to the same body of water." The effect of this addition of heat on the average temperature of the lake will be trivially small, but the biological consequences can be out of all proportion to the amount of heating.

The heat will delay fall cooling of the epilimnion and hasten spring warming, so that the length of time the lake is stratified each year will be increased. The water from the hypolimnion is rich in available plant nutrients, and by warming it and discharging it in the lighted zone, the amount of plant growth will be increased. This means more organic matter sinking into the hypolimnion and using up oxygen when it decays. The threat to the welfare of the lake is very real.

Finally, we should comment on fluctuating temperatures. Many organisms can adapt to somewhat higher or lower temperatures if they have time. The water in reservoirs behind hydroelectric dams often becomes thermally stratified, and when it is released at the base of the dam, a stretch of cold stream is produced which can support a cold water fauna even in warm regions. But when water is only discharged during peak electrical generating hours, the stream becomes subject to severe temperature fluctuations that will exclude many sensitive organisms. Similarly, if fishes or other organisms acclimate to the warm discharge from a factory or power plant and congregate near it, they will be subjected to temperature shocks when the plant is shut down for maintenance or refueling.

Conclusion

Man cannot go on increasing his use of thermal energy without causing degradation of his environment, and if he is persistent enough, he will destroy himself. There are other energy sources that could be used, but no source can support an indefinitely growing population. As with so many other things, it is man's irresponsible proliferation in numbers that is the real heart of the problem. There is some population size that the earth could support indefinitely without undergoing deterioration, but people do not even want to consider what that number might be. I suspect that it is substantially below the present world population. One would think that any rational creature riding a space ship would take care not to damage or destroy the ship, but perhaps the word "rational" does not describe man.

REFERENCES

Brooks, C. E. P. 1949. *Climate Through the Ages.* Rev. ed. McGraw-Hill Book Co., New York.
Kardashev, N. S. 1964. Transmission of information by extraterrestrial civilizations. In: *Extraterrestrial Civilizations,* G. M. Tovmasyan (ed.). Trans. by National Aeronautics and Space Administration, Washington, D.C.
Krogh, A. 1914. On the influence of temperature on the rate of embryonic development. *Z. Allg. Physiol.,* 16: 163-177.
National Technical Advisory Committee. 1968. Water quality criteria. Report of the National Technical Advisory Committee to the Secretary of the Interior. Federal Water Pollution Control Administration, Washington, D.C.
Putnam, P. C. 1953. *Energy in the Future.* D. Van Nostrand Co., New York.
Reid, G. K. 1961. *Ecology of Inland Waters and Estuaries.* Reinhold Publishing Co., New York.
Rosa, R. J., and F. A. Hals. 1968. In defense of MHD, *Ind. Res.,* June 1968: 68-72.
Waggoner, P. E. 1966. Weather modification and the living environment. In: *Future Environments of North America,* F. F. Darling and J. F. Milton (eds.). Natural History Press, Garden City, N. Y.
Wurtz, C. B. 1968. Thermal pollution: The effect of the problem. In: *Environmental Problems,* B. R. Wilson (ed.). J. B. Lippincott Co., Philadelphia.

23   Thermal Addition: One Step From Thermal Pollution

SHARON FRIEDMAN

Many forms of aquatic and plant life are being threatened by the tons of heated water being spewed forth from electric and thermonuclear generating plants into the nation's rivers, lakes, and coastal waters.

Actually, the threat is more potential than real at present, but it could become a serious hazard as the power needs of the nation increase and more and more generating plants are built on America's waterways. As one scientist put it at a recent meeting on this problem, "Today we can still talk about thermal addition, but tomorrow we may be talking about thermal pollution."

In 1958, the electricity demand was expected to quadruple by the year 2010. In 1965, estimates for the same time period indicated that the electricity demand would increase 32 times. Now these estimates have soared to as high as 256 times the present need by 2010. This would mean that even by 1980, electricity production may amount to 2 million megawatts. If engineering designs remain the same, this production would require 200 billion gallons of cooling water per day—the equivalent of one-sixth of the total volume of fresh-water runoff per day in the United States. During dryer seasons of the year, half would be needed for cooling purposes.

The advent of thermonuclear generating plants will increase the thermal addition problem since these plants have large generating capacities ranging from 1000 to 4000 megawatts. Nuclear power plants are less efficient than traditional ones and produce about 50% more waste heat per unit of electricity. These plants may each require up to 7 billion gallons of water a day for cooling. Six months ago, the Atomic Energy Commission reported that 15 nuclear power plants were in operation in this country and that 87 more were either under construction or planned for the immediate future. Not included in these figures were the many proposed plants that are not far enough along to have applied for building permits.

Heated water is not the only problem for aquatic life brought on by the power plants. There are also metallurgical effects caused by loss of metals from power plant condenser tubes and biocidal problems caused by detergents, acids, and chlorine used to keep condenser tubes clean of fouling from biological growths and deposits. The nuclear plants may present another factor—radioactive materials.

Different environments and water temperatures mediate the effects of thermal addition. In the cooler waters of California and also those around England and Scotland, there is not much of a problem. But, he said, this does not mean we aren't concerned, since a buildup of power plants could radically change the situation.

Many species of aquatic life have different levels of temperature tolerance. For the primary producers, the grasses of the sea, a few degrees of higher temperature could make a difference, both in type and quantity, in the productivity of these organisms, which provide food and fuel for the entire ecological system.

Invertebrates, which include many economically important shellfish, also react to thermal addition. But whether the reaction is beneficial or harmful depends on the latitude of their habitats and their exposure to sun during low tides among other factors.

While all fishes face some danger from thermal addition, the migratory fishes are particularly susceptible in the mixing zones where the heated water flows into cooler natural waters. Although no large fish kills can yet be claimed on thermal addition. There is some question as to whether certain fish could carry out their life cycle in slightly elevated temperatures, and what these higher temperatures would do to their food requirements and behavioral characteristics.

Thermal addition can be avoided by the use of cooling towers where water used in cooling is cooled, in turn, by either the atmosphere alone or with the aid of giant fans. This method is commonly used in England. This is the only way it is possible to have so many generating plants located in such a small area without doing severe damage to the environment.

Cooling towers have not found favor in the United States because of their added building and maintenance expense—sometimes amounting to millions of dollars. These towers also have other drawbacks: they are huge and unsightly, and one type—an open-circuit variety—loses a significant amount of water through evaporation to the atmosphere, sometimes causing fog and ice to develop as side effects.

With more knowledge of its effects, thermal addition may be put to good use in the future. Experimenters from Scotland have reported using the heated waters from a power plant to encourage production of flounder, sole and some shellfish.

24   Executive Order on Thermal Pollution

LYNDON B. JOHNSON

If discharge of cooling water is expected to create problems by significantly increasing the temperature of the receiving waters, facilities shall be installed, or operating procedures shall be established, to maintain water temperatures within acceptable limits.

PESTICIDES

Charles F. Wurster, Jr., writing in Science[1] *in 1968, reported, "Concentrations of DDT as low as a few parts per billion in water reduced photosynthesis in laboratory cultures of four species of coastal and oceanic phytoplankton representing four major classes of algae, and in a natural phytoplankton community from Woods Hole, Massachusetts. Toxicity to diatoms increased as cell concentration decreased." This stunning report forced us to totally reconceive the role of pesticides in our environment. Not only are organisms being killed, but the very machinery for harnessing sunlight is being disrupted.*

The public must re-examine its answer to the question, "What is a pest?" Such taxonomic terms as "germ," "weed," and "bug" become, under careful scrutiny, vague categories of ignorance and misinformation. Yet the onslaught against these culturally-frowned-on organisms is carried forward with the greatest confidence that the "right thing" is being done. Arrogance combined with ignorance has hatched a serious threat to the life-process itself. American agriculture is so deeply involved in this warfare on pests that immediate "pull-out" would be economically disastrous. To de-escalate will mean a depreciation in the superficial quality of agricultural products and a downturn in the efficiency of food production.

Can we ever return to a pre-pesticide agriculture? Do we want to? How many bridges were burned as we escalated our dependence on a pesticide-employing agriculture? If there are bridges that must be rebuilt, how much time will be required to rebuild them? How many species will become extinct during the "pull-out?" Or, as the demand for food increases, will we employ even more pesticides to satisfy the urgency of immediate production?

---

[1]From "DDT Reduces Photosynthesis by Marine Phytoplankton" by Charles F. Wurster, Jr., *Science* 159:1474-1475. 29 March 1968. Copyright 1968 by the American Association for the Advancement of Science.

Effects

25   The Effects of Pesticides

WILLIAM A. NIERING

The dramatic appearance of Rachel Carson's *Silent Spring* (1962) awakened a nation to the deleterious effects of pesticides. Our technology had surged ahead of us. We had lost our perspective on just how ruthlessly man can treat his environment and still survive. He was killing pesty insects by the trillions, but he was also poisoning natural ecosystems all around him. It was Miss Carson's mission to arrest this detrimental use of our technological achievements. As one might have expected, she was criticized by special vested industrial interests and, to some degree, by certain agricultural specialists concerned with only one aspect of our total environment. However, there was no criticism, only praise, from the nation's ecosystematically oriented biologists. For those who found *Silent Spring* too dramatic an approach to the problem, the gap was filled two years later by *Pesticides and the Living Landscape* (1964) in which Rudd further documented Miss Carson's thesis but in more academic style.

The aim of this chapter is to summarize some of the effects of two pesticides —insecticides and herbicides—on our total environment, and to point up research and other educational opportunities for students of environmental science. The insecticide review will be based on representative studies from the literature, whereas the herbicide review will represent primarily the results of the author's research and experience in the Connecticut Arboretum at Connecticut College. Although some consider this subject controversial, there is really no controversy in the mind of the author—the issue merely involves the sound ecological use of pesticides only where necessary and without drastically contaminating or upsetting the dynamic equilibrium of our natural ecosystems. I shall not consider the specific physiological effects of pesticides, but rather their effects on the total environment—plants, animals, soil, climate, man—the biotic and abiotic aspects.

Environmental science or ecosystematic thinking should attempt to coordinate and integrate all aspects of the environment. Although ecosystems may be managed, they must also remain in a relative balance or dynamic equilibrium, analogous to a spider's web, where each strand is intimately interrelated and interdependent upon every other strand.

The Impact of Insecticides

Ecologists have long been aware that simplifying the environment to only a few species can precipitate a catastrophe. Our highly mechanized agricultural operations, dominated by extensive acreages of one crop, encourage large numbers of insect pests. As insurance against insect damage, vast quantities of insecticides are applied with little regard for what happens to the chemical once it is on the land. Prior to World War II, most of our insecticides were nonpersistent organics found in the natural environment. For example, the pyrethrins were derived from dried chrysanthemum flowers, nicotine sulphate from tobacco, and rotenone from the tropical derris plants. However, research during World War II and thereafter resulted in a number of potent persistent chlorinated hydrocarbons (DDT, dieldrin, endrin, lindane, chlordane, heptachor and others) to fight the ever-increasing hordes of insects, now some 3000 species plaguing man in North America.

In 1964, industries in the United States produced 783 million lb. of pesticides, half insecticides and the other half herbicides, fungicides, and rodenticides. The application of these chemicals on the nation's landscape[1] has now reached the point where one out of every ten acres is being sprayed with an average of 4 lb. per acre (Anonymous, 1966).

Positive Effects of Target Organisms

That market yields and quality are increased by agricultural spraying appears to have been well documented. Data from the National Agricultural Chemical Association show net increased yields resulting in from $5.00 to $100.00 net gains per acre on such crops as barley, tomatoes, sugar beets, pea seed, and cotton seed. However, Rudd (1964) questions the validity of these figures, since there is no explanation just how they were derived. His personal observations on the rice crop affected by the rice leaf miner outbreak in California are especially pertinent. The insect damage was reported as ruining 10% to 20% of the crop. He found this to be correct for some fields, but most of the fields were not damaged at all. In this situation, the facts were incorrect concerning the pest damage. It appears that not infrequently repeated spraying applications are merely insurance sprays and in many cases actually unnecessary. Unfortunately, the farmer is being forced to this procedure in part by those demanding from agriculture completely insect-free produce. This has now reached ridiculous proportions. Influenced by advertising, the housewife now demands perfect specimens with no thought of a regard for how much environmental contamination has resulted to attain such perfection. If we could relax our standards to a moderate degree, pesticide contamination could be greatly reduced. Although it may be difficult to question that spraying increases yields and quality of the marketable products, there are few valid data available on how much spraying is actually necessary, how much it is adding to consumer costs, what further pests are aggravated by spraying, and what degree of resistance eventually develops.

Negative Effects on Nontarget Organisms

Although yields may be increased with greater margins of profit, according to available data, one must recognize that these chemicals may adversely affect

---

1. Dr. George Woodwell estimates that there are 1 billion lbs. of DDT now circulating in the biosphere.

a whole spectrum of nontarget organisms not only where applied but possibly thousands of miles from the site of application. To the ecologist concerned with the total environment, these persistent pesticides pose some serious threats to our many natural ecosystems. Certain of these are pertinent to review.

1. *Killing of nontarget organisms.* In practically every spray operation, thousands of nontarget insects are killed, many of which may be predators on the very organisms one is attempting to control. But such losses extend far beyond the beneficial insects. In Florida, an estimated 1,117,000 fishes of at least 30 species (20 to 30 tons), were killed with dieldrin, when sand flies were really the target organism. Crustaceans were virtually exterminated—the fiddler crabs survived only in areas missed by the treatment (Harrington and Bidlingmayer, 1958).

In 1963, there was a "silent spring" in Hanover, New Hampshire. Seventy per cent of the robin population—350 to 400 robins—was eliminated in spraying for Dutch elm disease with 1.9 lb. per acre DDT (Wurster et al., 1965). Wallace (1960) and Hickey and Hunt (1960) have reported similar instances on the Michigan State University and University of Wisconsin campuses. Last summer, at Wesleyan University, my students observed dead and trembling birds following summer applications of DDT on the elms. At the University of Wisconsin campus (61 acres), the substitution of methoxychlor has resulted in a decreased bird mortality. The robin population has jumped from three to twenty-nine pairs following the change from DDT to methoxychlor. Chemical control of this disease is often overemphasized, with too little attention directed against the sources of elm bark beetle. Sanitation is really the most important measure in any sound Dutch elm disease control program (Matthysse, 1959).

One of the classic examples involving the widespread destruction of nontarget organisms was the fire ant eradication program in our southern states. In 1957, dieldrin and heptochlor were aerially spread over two and one-half million acres. Wide elimination of vertebrate populations resulted; and recovery of some populations is still uncertain (Rudd, 1964). In the interest of science, the Georgia Academy of Science appointed an ad hoc committee to evaluate this control-eradication program (Bellinger et al., 1965). It found that reported damage to crops, wildlife, fish, and humans had not been verified, and concluded, furthermore, that the ant is not really a significant economic pest but a mere nuisance. Here was an example where the facts did not justify the federal expenditure of $2.4 million in indiscriminate sprays. Fortunately, this approach has been abandoned, and local treatments are now employed with Mirex, a compound with fewer side effects. Had only a small percentage of this spray expenditure been directed toward basic research, we might be far ahead today in control of the fire ant.

2. *Accumulation in the food chain.* The persistent nature of certain of these insecticides permits the chemical to be carried from one organism to another in the food chain. As this occurs, there is a gradual increase in the biocide at each higher trophic level. Many such examples have been reported in the literature. One of the most striking comes from Clear Lake, California, where a 46,000-acre warm lake, north of San Francisco, was sprayed for pesty gnats in 1949, 1954, and 1957, with DDD, a chemical presumably less toxic than DDT. Analyses of

the plankton revealed 250 times more of the chemical than originally applied, the frogs 2000 times more, sunfish 12,000, and the grebes up to an 80,000-fold increase (Cottam, 1965; Rudd, 1964). In 1954 death among the grebes was widespread. Prior to the spraying, a thousand of these birds nested on the lake. Then for 10 years no grebes hatched. Finally, in 1962, one nestling was observed, and the following year three. Clear Lake is popular for sports fishing, and the flesh of edible fish now caught reaches 7 ppm. which is above the maximum tolerance level set by the Food and Drug Administration.

In an estuarine ecosystem, a similar trend has been reported on the Long Island tidal marshes, where mosquito control spraying with DDT has been practiced for some 20 years (Woodwell et al., 1967). Here the food chain accumulation shows plankton 0.04 ppm, shrimp 0.16 ppm, minnows 1 to 2 ppm, and ring-billed gull 75.5 ppm. In general, the DDT concentrations in carnivorous birds were 10 to 100 times those in the fish they fed upon. Birds near the top of the food chain have DDT residues about a million times greater than concentration in the water. Pesticide levels are now so high that certain populations are being subtly eliminated by food chain accumulations reaching toxic levels.

3. *Lowered reproductive potential.* Considerable evidence is available to suggest a lowered reproductive potential, especially among birds, where the pesticide occurs in the eggs in suffcient quantities either to prevent hatching or to decrease vigor among the young birds hatched. Birds of prey, such as the bald eagle, osprey, hawks, and others, are in serious danger. Along the northeast Atlantic coast, ospreys normally average about 2.5 young per year. However, in Maryland and Connecticut, reproduction is far below this level. In Maryland, ospreys produce 1.1 young per year and their eggs contain 3 ppm DDT, while in Connecticut, 0.5 young ospreys hatch and their eggs contain up to 5.1 ppm DDT. These data indicate a direct correlation between the amount of DDT and the hatchability of eggs—the more DDT present in the eggs, the fewer young hatched (Ames, 1966). In Wisconsin, Keith (1964) reports 38% hatching failure in herring gulls. Early in the incubation period, gull eggs collected contained over 200 ppm DDT and its cogeners. Pheasant eggs from DDT-treated rice fields compared to those from unsprayed lands result in fewer healthy month-old chicks from eggs taken near sprayed fields. Although more conclusive data may still be needed to prove that pesticides such as DDT are the key factor, use of such compounds should be curtailed until it is proved that they are not the causal agents responsible for lowering reproductive potential.

4. *Resistance to sprays.* Insects have a remarkable ability to develop a resistance to insecticides. The third spray at Clear Lake was the least effective on the gnats, and here increased resistance was believed to be a factor involved. As early as 1951, resistance among agricultural insects appeared. Some of these include the codling moth on apples, and certain cotton, cabbage, and potato insects. Over 100 important insect pests now show a definite resistance to chemicals (Carson, 1962).

5. *Synergistic effects.* The interaction of two compounds may result in a third much more toxic than either one alone. For example, Malathion is relatively "safe" because detoxifying enzymes in the liver greatly reduce its toxic properties.

However, if some compound destroys or interrupts this enzyme system, as certain organic phosphates may do, the toxicity of the new combination may be increased greatly. Pesticides represent one of many pollutants we are presently adding to our environment. These subtle synergistic effects have opened a whole new field of investigation. Here students of environmental science will find many challenging problems for future research.

6. *Chemical migration.* After two decades of intensive use, pesticides are now found throughout the world, even in places far from any actual spraying. Penguins and crab-eating seals in the Antarctic are contaminated, and fish far off the coasts of four continents now contain insecticides ranging from 1 to 300 ppm in their fatty tissues (Anonymous, 1966).

The major rivers of our nation are contaminated by DDT, endrin, and dieldrin, mostly in the parts per trillion range. Surveys since 1957 reveal that dieldrin has been the main pesticide present since 1958. Endrin reached its maximum, especially in the lower Mississippi River, in the fall of 1963 when an extensive fish kill occurred and has since that time decreased. DDT and its cogeners, consistently present since 1958, have been increasing slightly (Breidenbach et al., 1967).

7. *Accumulation in the ecosystem.* Since chlorinated hydrocarbons like DDT are not readily broken down by biological agents such as bacteria, they may not only be present but also accumulate within a given ecosystem. On Long Island, up to 32 lb. of DDT have been reported in the marsh mud, with an average of 13 lb. presumed to be correlated with the 20 years of mosquito control spraying (Woodwell et al., 1967). Present in these quantities, burrowing marine organisms and the detritus feeders can keep the residues in continuous circulation in the ecosystem. Many marine forms are extremely sensitive to minute amounts of insecticides. Fifty per cent of a shrimp population was killed with endrin 0.6 parts per billion (ppb). Even 1 ppb will kill blue crabs within a week. Oysters, typical filter feeders, have been reported to accumulate up to 70,000 ppb. (Loosanoff, 1965). In Green Bay along Lake Michigan, Hickey and Keith (1964) report up to 0.005 ppm wet weight of DDT, DDE, and DDD in the lake sediments. Here the accumulation has presumably been from leaching or run-off from surrounding agricultural lands in Door County, where it is reported that 70,000 pounds of DDT are used annually. Biological concentration in Green Bay is also occurring in food chain organisms, as reported at Clear Lake, California. Accumulation of biocides, especially in the food chain, and their availability for recycling pose a most serious ecological problem.

8. *Delayed response.* Because of the persistent nature and tendency of certain insecticides to accumulate at toxic levels in the food chain, there is often a delayed response in certain ecosystems subjected either directly or indirectly to pesticide treatment. This was the case at Clear Lake, where the mortality of nontarget organisms occurred several years after the last application. This is a particularly disturbing aspect, since man is often the consumer organisms accumulating pesticide residues. In the general population, human tissues contain about 12 ppm DDT-derived materials. Those with meatless diets, and the Eskimos, store less; however, agricultural applicators and formulators of pesticides

may store up to 600 ppm DDT or 1000 ppm DDT-derived components. Recent studies indicate that dieldrin and lindane are also stored in humans without occupational exposure (Durham, 1965). The possibility of synergistic effects involving DDT, dieldrin, lindane, and other pollutants to which man is being exposed may result in unpredictable hazards. In fact, it is now believed that pesticides may pose a genetic hazard. At the recent conference of the New York Academy of Science, Dr. Onsy G. Fahmy warned that certain chlorinated hydrocarbons, organophosphates and carbamates were capable of disrupting the DNA molecule. It was further noted that such mutations may not appear until as many as 40 generations later. Another scientist, Dr. M. Jacqueline Verrett, pointed out that certain fungicides (folpet and captan) thought to be nontoxic have chemical structures similar to thalidomide.

We are obviously dealing with many biological unknowns in our widespread use of presumably "safe" insecticides. We have no assurance that 12 ppm DDT in our human tissue, now above the permissible in marketable products for consumption, may not be resulting in deleterious effects in future generations. As Rudd warns (1964): " . . . it would be somewhat more than embarrassing for our 'experts' to learn that significant effects do occur in the long term. One hundred and eight million human guinea pigs would have paid a high price for their trust."

Of unpredicted delayed responses, we have an example in radiation contamination. In the Bravo tests on Bikini in 1954, the natives on Rongelap Atoll were exposed to radiation assumed to be safe. Now more than a decade later, tumors of the thyroid gland have been discovered in the children exposed to these presumably safe doses (Woodwell et al., 1966). Pesticides per se or synergisms resulting from their interaction could well plague man in now unforeseen or unpredictable ways in the future.

The Sound Use of Herbicides

In contrast to insecticides, herbicides are chemical weed-killers used to control or kill unwanted plants. Following World War II, the chlorinated herbicide 2, 4-D began to be used widely on broadleaf weeds. Later, 2, 4, 5-T was added, which proved especially effective on woody species. Today, over 40 weed-killers are available. Although used extensively in agriculture, considerable quantities are used also in aquatic weed control and in forestry, wildlife, and right-of-way vegetation management. Currently, large quantities are being used as defoliators in Vietnam.

Although herbicides in general are much safer than insecticides in regard to killing nontarget organisms and in their residual effects, considerable caution must be exercised in their proper use. One of the greatest dangers in right-of-way vegetation management is their indiscriminate use, which results in habitat destruction. Drift of spray particles and volatility may also cause adverse effects on nontarget organisms, especially following indiscriminate applications. In the Connecticut Arboretum, shade trees have been seriously affected as a result of indiscriminate roadside sprays (Niering, 1959). During the spring of 1957, the town sprayed the marginal trees and shrubs along a roadside running through the

Arboretum with 2, 4-D and 2, 4, 5-T (1 part chemical: 100 parts water). White oaks overarching the road up to 2 feet in diameter were most seriously affected. Most of the leaves turned brown. Foliage of scarlet and black oaks of similar size exhibited pronounced leaf curling. Trees were affected up to 300 feet back from the point of application within the natural area of the Arboretum. White oak twigs near the sprayed belt also developed a striking weeping habit as twig elongation occurred—a growth abnormality still conspicuous after 10 years.

The effectiveness of the spray operation in controlling undesirable woody growth indicated a high survival of unwanted tree sprouts. Black birch and certain desirable shrubs were particularly sensitive. Shrubs affected were highly ornamental forms often planted in roadside beautification programs. The resulting ineffectiveness of the spray operation was indicated by the need for cutting undesirable growth along the roadside the following year.

In the agricultural use of herbicides, drift effects have been reported over much greater distances. In California, drift from aerial sprays has been reported up to 30 miles from the point of application (Freed, 1965).

Although toxicity of herbicides to nontarget organisms is not generally a problem, it has been reported in aquatic environments. For example, the dimethylamine salt of 2, 4-D is relatively safe for bluegill at 150 ppm, but the butyl, ethly, and isopropyl esters are toxic to fish at around 1 ppm (R. E. Johnson, personal communication). Studies of 16 aquatic herbicides on *Daphnia magna,* a microcrustacean, revealed that 2, 4-D (specific derivation not given) seemed completely innocuous but that several others (Dichlone, a quinone; Molinate, a thiolcarbamate; Propanil, an anilide; sodium arsenite and Dichlopenil, a nitrile) could present a real hazard to this lower food chain organism (Crosby and Tucker, 1966).

Effects of rights-of-way. The rights-of-way across our nation comprise an estimated 70,000,000 acres of land, much of which is now subjected to herbicide treatment (Niering, 1967). During the past few decades, indiscriminate foliar applications have been widespread in the control of undesirable vegetation, erroneously referred to as brush (Goodwin and Niering, 1962). Indiscriminate applications often fail to root-kill undesirable species, therefore necessitating repeated retreatment, which results in the destruction of many desirable forms. Indiscriminate sprays are also used for the control of certain broadleaf weeds along roadsides. In New Jersey, 19 treatments were applied during a period of 6 years in an attempt to control ragweed. This, of course, was ecologically unsound, when one considers that ragweed is an annual plant typical of bare soil and that repeated sprayings also eliminate the competing broadleaved perennial species that, under natural successional conditions, could tend to occupy the site and naturally eliminate the ragweed. Broadcast or indiscriminate spraying can also result in destruction of valuable wildlife habitat in addition to the needless destruction of our native flora—wildflowers and shrubs of high landscape value.

Nonselective spraying, especially along roadsides, also tends to produce a monotonous grassy cover free of colorful wildflowers and interesting shrubs. It is economically and aesthetically unsound to remove these valuable species naturally occurring on such sites. Where they do not occur, highway beautification programs plant many of these same shrubs and low-growing trees.

Recognizing this nation-wide problem in the improper use of herbicides, the Connecticut Arboretum established, over a decade ago, several right-of-way demonstration areas to serve as models in the sound use of herbicides (Niering, 1955; 1957; 1961). Along two utility rights-of-way and a roadside crossing the Arboretum, the vegetation has been managed following sound ecological principles, (Egler, 1954; Goodwin and Niering, 1959; Niering 1958). Basic techniques include basal and stump treatments. The former involves soaking the base of the stem for 12 inches; the stump technique involves soaking the stump immediately after cutting. Effective formulations include 2, 4, 5-T in a fuel oil carrier (1 part chemical: 20 parts oil). Locally, stem-foliage sprays may be necessary, but the previous two techniques form the basic approach in the selective use of weed-killers. They result in good root-kill and simultaneously preserve valuable wildlife habitat and aesthetically attractive native species, all at a minimum of cost to the agency involved when figured on a long-range basis. In addition to these gains, the presence of good shrub cover tends to impede tree invasion and to reduce future maintenance costs (Pound and Egler, 1953; Niering and Elger, 1955).

Another intriguing use of herbicides is in naturalistic landscaping. Dr. Frank Egler conceived this concept of creating picturesque natural settings in shrubby fields by selectively eliminating the less attractive species and accentuating the ornamental forms (Kenfield, 1966). At the Connecticut Arboretum we have landscaped several such areas (Niering and Goodwin, 1963). This approach has unlimited application in arresting vegetation development and preserving landscapes that might disappear under normal successional or vegetational development processes.

Future Outlook

Innumerable critical moves have recently occurred that may alter the continued deterioration of our environment. Secretary Udall has banned the use of DDT, chlordane, dieldrin, and endrin on Department of the Interior lands. The use of DDT has been banned on state lands in New Hampshire and lake trout watersheds in New York State; in Connecticut, commercial applications are limited to dormant sprays. On Long Island, a temporary court injuction has been granted against the Suffolk Couty Mosquito Control Board's use of DDT in spraying tidal marshes. The Forest Service has terminated the use of DDT, and in the spring of 1966 the United States Department of Agriculture banned the use of endrin and dieldrin. Currently, the Forest Service has engaged a top-level research team in the Pacific Southwest to find chemicals highly selective to individual forest insect pests and that will break down quickly into harmless components. The Ribicoff hearing, which has placed Congressional focus on the problem of environmental pollution and Gaylord Nelson's bill to ban the sale of DDT in the United States are all enlightened endeavors at the national level.

The United States Forest Service has a selective program for herbicides in the National Forests. The Wisconsin Natural Resources Committee has instituted a selective roadside right-of-way maintenance program for the State. In Connecticut, a selective approach is in practice in most roadside and utility spraying.

Although we have considerable knowledge of the effects of biocides on the total environment, we must continue the emphasis on the holistic approach in studying the problem and interpreting the data. Continued observations of those occupationally exposed and of residents living near pesticide areas should reveal invaluable toxicological data. The study of migrant workers, of whom hundreds have been reported killed by pesticides, needs exacting investigation.

The development of more biological controls as well as chemical formulations that are specific to the target organism with a minimum of side effects needs continuous financial support by state and federal agencies and industry. Graduate opportunities are unlimited in this field.

As we look to the future, one of our major problems is the communication of sound ecological knowledge already available rather than pseudoscientific knowledge to increase the assets of special interest groups (Egler, 1964; 1965; 1966). The fire ant fiasco may be cited as a case in point. And as Egler (1966) has pointed out in his fourth most recent review of the pesticide problem: " . . . 95% of the problem is not in scientific knowledge of pesticides but in scientific knowledge of human behavior. . . . There are power plays . . . the eminent experts who deal with parts not ecological wholes."

One might ask, is it really good business to reduce the use of pesticides? Will biological control make as much money? Here the problem integrates political science, economics, sociology, and psychology. Anyone seriously interested in promoting the sound use of biocides must be fully cognizant of these counter forces in our society. They need serious study, analysis, and forthright reporting in the public interest. With all we know about the deleterious effects of biocides on our environments, the problem really challenging man is to get this scientific knowledge translated into action through the sociopolitical pathways available to us in a free society. If we fail to communicate a rational approach, we may find that technology has become an invisible monster as Egler has succinctly stated (1966).

Pesticides are the greatest single tool for simplifying the habitat ever conceived by the simple mind of man, who may yet prove too simple to grasp the fact that he is but a blind strand of an ecosystem web, dependent not upon himself, but upon the total web, which nevertheless he has the power to destroy.

Here environmental science can involve the social scientist in communicating sound science to society and involve the political scientist in seeing that sound scientific knowledge is translated into reality. Our survival on this planet may well depend on how well we can make this translation.

References

Ames, P. L. 1966. DDT residues in the eggs of the osprey in the northeastern United States and their relation to nesting success. *J. Applied Ecol.,* 3 (suppl.): 87-97.
Anonymous. 1966. Fish, wildlife and pesticides. U.S. Dept. of Interior, Supt. of Doc. 12 p.
Bellinger, F., R. E. Dyer, R. King, and R. B. Platt. 1965. A review of the problem of the imported fire ant. *Bull. Georgia Acad. Sci.,* Vol. 23, No. 1.
Breidenbach, A. W., C. G. Gunnerson, F. K. Kawahara, J. J. Lichtenberg, and R. S. Green. 1967. Chlorinated hydrocarbon pesticides in major basins, 1957-1965. *Public Health Rept.* 82: 139-156.
Carson, Rachel. 1962. *Silent Spring.* Houghton Mifflin, Boston, 368 p.

Cottam, C. 1965. The ecologists' role in problems of pesticide pollution. *Bio-Science,* 15: 457-463.
Crosby, D. G., and R. K. Tucker. 1966. Toxicity of aquatic herbicides to *Daphnia magna. Science,* 154: 289-290.
Dill, N. H. 1962-63. Vegetation management. *New Jersey Nature News,* 17: 123-130; 18: 151-157.
Durham, W. F. 1965. Effects of pesticides on man. *In* C. O. Chichester, ed., *Research in Pesticides.* Academic Press, Inc., New York.
Egler, F. E. 1954. Vegetation management for rights-of-way and roadsides. *Smithsonian Inst. Rept. for 1953:* 299-322.
————. 1964a. Pesticides in our ecosystem. *Am. Scientist,* 52: 110-136.
————. 1964b. Pesticides in our ecosystem: communication II: *BioScience,* 14: 29-36.
————.1965. Pesticides in our ecosystem: communication III. *Assoc. Southeastern Biologist Bull.,* 12: 9-91.
————. 1966. Pointed perspectives. Pesticides in our ecosystem. *Ecology,* 47: 1077-1084.
Freed, V. H. 1965. Chemicals and the control of plants. *In* C. O. Chichester, ed., *Research in Pesticides.* Academic Press, Inc., New York.
Goodwin, R. H., and W. A. Niering. 1959. The management of roadside vegetation by selective herbicide techniques. *Conn. Arboretum Bull.,* 11: 4-10.
————. 1962. What is happening along Connecticut's roadsides. *Conn. Arboretum Bull.,* 13: 13-24.
Harrington, R. W., Jr., and W. L. Bidlingmayer. 1958. Effects of dieldrin on fishes and invertebrates of a salt marsh. *J. Wildlife Management,* 22: 76-82.
Hickey, J. J., and L. Barrie Hunt. 1960. Initial songbird mortality following a Dutch elm disease control program. *J. Wildlife Management,* 24: 259-265.
Hickey, J. J., and J. A. Keith. 1964. Pesticides in the Lake Michigan ecosystem. *In* The Effects of Pesticides on Fish and Wildlife. U.S. Dept Interior Fish and Wildlife Service.
Keith, J. A. 1964. Reproductive success in a DDT-contaminated population of herring gulls, p. 11-12. *In* The Effects of Pesticides on Fish and Wildlife. U.S. Dept. Interior Fish and Wildlife Service.
Kenfield, W. G. 1966. *The Wild Gardner in the Wild Landscape.* Hafner, New York. 232 p.
Loosanoff, V. L. 1965. Pesticides in sea water. *In* C. O. Chichester, ed., *Research in Pesticides.* Academic Press, Inc., New York.
Matthysse, J. G. 1959. An evaluation of mist blowing and sanitation in Dutch elm disease control programs. N.Y.

Battle of Coral Sea   26

Newsweek Magazine

The starfish that is threatening to topple the Pacific islands is *Acanthaster planci* (popular name: Crown of Thorns), a creature that grows up to 2 feet in diameter, has about sixteen arms and consumes an area twice its size daily. The starfish dines on living coral, the material that protects islands from erosion by ocean waves and, indeed, is even the stuff of which many islands themselves are constructed. Already starfish have eaten away 100 square miles of Australia's 1,200-mile Great Barrier Reef and 90 per cent of the coral along a 24-mile stretch of Guam's coastline. Dr. Richard H. Chesher, associate professor of marine science at Guam University, reports that the Crown of Thorns has also invaded the coral beds off eleven other islands, including Borneo, Fiji, Palau, Saipan, Wake and Midway.

For decades the Crown of Thorns was extremely rare—only one specimen was found during a months-long survey of marine life on the Great Barrier Reef in 1928. But today Pacific waters abound with a species that scientists think may spawn twice a year, laying as many as a million eggs each time. And by destroying the living coral, the starfish are destroying the natural habitat for an entire system of marine life upon which millions of islanders rely for their protein food. "People will starve," says Dr. Porter Kier, chairman of the Paleo-Biology Department of the Smithsonian Institution in Washington, D.C. "It could affect all the marine environments of the world."

No one can explain the proliferation. The Crown of Thorns has only two known enemies: the conch-like triton snail and, strangely enough, the living coral, which consumes many of the tiny larvae. But many scientists speculate that the starfish population has been kept down by small larva-eating organisms called micro-feeders. And they contend further than man is guilty of disturbing the delicate ecological balance by killing off these micro-feeders with dredging and channel-building projects conducted constantly since World War II. Kier also maintains that the organisms are being destroyed by "too much DDT, too much dynamite, and too much residual radiation from past atomic tests."

The Australian Government conducted a study of the Crown of Thorns five years ago, but for reasons not explained the findings have been kept secret. And so late this month Kier and some 60 other scientists will join Chesher on Guam for their own survey of the life style of the starfish in order to find methods to control its population explosion. But the destruction it has already caused is irreversible. Says one scientist: "Nobody has even seen a destroyed reef come to life again."

Monitoring

27   ## Monitoring Pesticide Pollution

PHILIP A. BUTLER

The widespread use of synthetic organochloride pesticides, reports of their persistence in the environment, and the repeated demonstrations of their toxicity to nontarget fauna alerted marine biologists to their potentially disastrous effects in the estuarine environment. Soon after World War II, detailed studies of DDT applications to salt marshes for mosquito control showed increased mortality of fish and shellfish. Such acute effects were readily identified, and measures could be initiated to prevent or at least restrict such applications.

But biologists became even more concerned with the probability that continued terrestrial applications of persistent pesticides would result in their being carried in surface water, adsorbed on silt and debris, through river basins and eventually into estuaries. Here, their chronic presence at subacute levels might cause irreversible changes before their presence was apparent.

The estuary is an extraordinarily important environment to a wide array of fish, shellfish, and other elements of the biota that are important for commercial or esthetic reasons.

Permanent residents of estuaries, such as the oyster, are accustomed to widely fluctuating levels of various environmental properties and are relatively tolerant to unusual changes. Oysters can close their valves and "withdraw" from the environment, when, for example, unacceptable amounts of fresh water or silt are temporarily present. Some animals, however, including many kinds of crabs, shrimp, and fish, use the estuary only as a nursery area or as a part of their migration pathway, and are physiologically adjusted to the estuary for only a particular segment of their life span. As a consequence, they are especially susceptible to drastic environmental changes. Low levels of pollutants might interfere with olfaction, for example, and prevent salmon from finding their "home" stream; and chemicals that changed the osmoregulating ability of crustaceans could prevent shrimp and crabs from migrating to their brackish-water growing areas.

The many possibilities for subtle harmful changes resulting from the accidental or intentional transport of pesticides into estuaries prompted the Bureau of Commercial Fisheries to initiate a program in 1958 to assess the extent of the problem.

The program had two major objectives: to determine the acute and chronic toxicity of the commonly used pesticides to representative estuarine animals under controlled test conditions; and to monitor the seasonal levels of polychlorinated pesticide pollution in the nation's estuaries where production of living marine resources is commercially important. This report describes the development of the monitoring segment of the program and summarizes regional trends in pesticide pollution levels as revealed by 3 years of data collection.

Development of Program

It seemed likely that pesticide pollution in estuaries would be not only intermittent but also at such low concentrations in the water mass that automated sensing devices would be generally unsatisfactory. Consequently, the first requirement for successful monitoring was the selection of a suitable bioassay technique.

The Bureau of Commercial Fisheries Biological Laboratory at Gulf Breeze, Florida, had been engaged for more than 20 years in studies on the ecology and management of the eastern oyster, *Crassostrea virginica*. Much was known about its physiology, and it appeared to be a desirable animal for preliminary tests.

Typically, a mature oyster is feeding 90% of the time and transports about 16 liters of water an hour through its gill system to extract the planktonic food. Its ability and tendency to pick up and store metal ions, present in only trace amounts in the surrounding water, are well known. The oyster is physiologically active the entire year throughout much of its extensive geographical range. Most important, it is sedentary and easily handled.

Exploratory experiment with oysters consisted in recording on a kymograph their shell movements and rates of water transport ("pumping") before and during exposure to controlled amounts of pesticides in aquariums with flowing seawater (Butler et al., 1960). Under normal conditions, the oyster closes its valves briefly up to 10 times an hour to expel accumulated pseudofeces. These experimental oysters showed intense physiological irritation after 10 hours exposure to 1 ppm of dieldrin. The valves were almost continually opening and closing. It was obvious that the feeding process could not be normal. The oysters pumped water and fed, however, when the concentration of dieldrin was lowered to 0.1 ppm.

After 2 weeks of continuous exposure to 0.1 ppm of dieldrin, however, the experimental oysters were only half as active as controls. The oysters quickly returned to their normal level of activity when the addition of dieldrin was stopped. This inhibition of the pumping rate in oysters exposed to environmental pollutants can be measured objectively but the technique is tedious and time-consuming.

The interference with normal activity suggested that oyster growth, or rate of shell disposition, would decrease in polluted water. To test this hypothesis, shell deposition in young oysters was measured before and after exposure to known concentrations of pesticides. Linear growth of the oyster does not proceed uniformly. An initial increase in the peripheral deposition of new shell is followed by a period during which this thin shell is strengthened by internal deposits. During this second stage, there may be no measurable increase in length. To encourage the immediate deposition of new shell, the edges of the valves are ground until all new and thin shell is removed. The oyster then occupies all of the shell cavity and has no alternative, in growing, except to deposit new shell on the periphery (Butler, 1965). Linear shell deposition amounts to about 0.5 mm per day for at least 5 days under average conditions in the laboratory, when the oyster has a continuous supply of unfiltered seawater.

In the presence of a toxicant, the oyster deposits smaller and smaller amounts of new shell as the concentration of the toxicant is increased. Thus, it is possible to determine the concentrations of a particular pesticide that causes a 50% decrease in shell growth as compared to control oysters under otherwise similar conditions and to relate the toxicity of one pesticide to that of any other pesticide tested under similar conditions.

In parallel experiments, we found that oysters remove and store chlorinated hydrocarbon pesticides present in the surrounding water at concentrations as low as 0.1 part per billion. Oysters continue to build up such residues in their tissues at uniform rates as long as the toxicant is present. This biological magnification may produce DDT residues, for example, 70,000 times as high as the DDT concentration in the test water supply. An important consideration in a monitor program is the fact that the oyster flushes these residues out of its tissues at a uniform rate when the water supply is no longer contaminated. By sampling an oyster population regularly, it is possible to determine when the water supply becomes contaminated and when the contamination stops. It is possible to get some idea of the magnitude of the pollution load in the estuary by extrapolation from laboratory experiments.

Since oysters are not universally present in estuaries of interest to commercial fisheries, tests were undertaken to determine the relative efficiency of other common mollusks in storing pesticide residues. In general, the eastern oyster, the Pacific oyster (*Crassostrea gigas*), the soft clam (*Mya arenaria*), and any of several mussels are equally suitable. The hard clam (*Mercenaria mercenaria*) is the least efficient at storing pesticides of any mollusks evaluated (Butler, 1966).

With the problem of a suitable bioassay animal solved, we were able to consider the other prerequisites of a successful monitor program. The sampling had to have continuity and be done at least monthly. The assistance and cooperation of many people were required because of the length of the coastlines to be covered. To accomplish analytical uniformity, which was essential, it seemed desirable to have all analyses made by the same laboratory, although this arrangement greatly increased the difficulties in handling the samples.

The program that finally evolved was made possible by entering into formal and informal research contracts with state conservation agencies and university and federal marine laboratories in 15 coastal states. We developed a technique for homogenizing the samples with a desiccant consisting of sodium sulfate plus 10% by weight of Quso, a micro-fine, precipitated silica. This desiccant prevents spoilage of the sample and degradation of pesticide residues for at least 30 days without refrigeration. As a result, samples could be sent by ordinary mail to the Gulf Breeze laboratory for analysis. We analyze samples by gas liquid chromatography with electron capture using two different columns, so that 10 of the most commonly used organochloride pesticides can be quantified at levels above 10 ppb.

In the nearly 4 years the program has been in effect, about 170 permanent stations have been established on the Atlantic, Gulf, and Pacific coasts, and more than 5000 samples have been analyzed.

Summary of Findings

Data collected during the first 3 years of this project do not indicate any consistent upward or downward trends in estuarine pesticide pollution. Distinct seasonal and geographic differences in pollution levels are apparent, however, as well as regional differences in sources and kinds of pesticide pollution. Although each sample is screened for 10 or more pesticides, DDT (including its metabolities) is the only one commonly present. Dieldrin is next in frequency of occurrence, followed by endrin, toxaphene, and mirex.

In the estuaries of Washington, less than 3% of the samples have been contaminated and the DDT residues have always been less than 0.05 ppm. On the Atlantic Coast, oysters from Maine estuaries are the least contaminated; about 10% of the samples had residues of DDT, all at levels below 0.05 ppm. Oyster samples from the other states monitored[1] contained DDT residues more often than not. In some areas that are intensively farmed, oyster samples always

---

1. Alabama, California, Delaware, Florida, Georgia, Maryland, Mississippi, New Jersey, New York, North Carolina, South Carolina, Texas, Virginia.

contain DDT residues, but the amounts of DDT plus metabolites are usually less than 0.5 ppm. Only rarely has the residue exceeded 1.0 ppm. The highest residue of DDT observed in oysters, 5.4 ppm, was the result of a single incident of gross pollution.

It should be pointed out that these DDT residues are not of sufficient magnitude to constitute a human health problem. Their presence indicates, however, the ubiquity of DDT in the estuarine food web.

Analyses of residue data from individual river basins that drain predominantly agricultural lands show characteristic seasonal trends. Typically, there is a pronounced peak in the late spring and a lesser increase in the fall. The height of these peaks may vary tenfold from one basin to another, depending on the farming practices. In one basin on the Texas coast, three seasonal peaks in DDT residue levels reflect the intensive truck farming in an area where the mild climate permits three harvests each year.

In the river basins receiving significant amounts of municipal wastes as well as agricultural runoff, the seasonal residue pattern is similar but the magnitude of the residues is proportionately higher. By contrast, in estuaries that receive industrial wastes containing pesticides, seasonal residue patterns are erratic and occasionally indicate single, massive injections of a pollutant into the drainage system such as would happen when waste-control systems are breached. In two areas, the monitor data demonstrated the industrial discharge of pesticide wastes whose presence had been unsuspected by the state agencies responsible for clean water programs.

Several times it has been possible to identify specific sources of pesticide pollution by placing trays of oysters at intervals in the drainage system when natural beds of oysters did not occur. Near and above the river mouth, where the water becomes too fresh for oysters, we have substituted the brackish water clam (*Rangia cuneata*) and the freshwater Asiatic clam (*Corbicula fluminea*) as bioassay animals.

In one locality where a specific pollution source was suspected, trays of oysters were located at about 2-mile intervals upstream toward an industrial complex. Pesticide residues in oysters analyzed during the succeeding 10 months at the several stations, listed in order of their nearness to the pollution source, averaged as follows: 25.0, 17.0, 5.0, 3.0, 0.05, and 0.02 ppm. Analysis of the residue data at any one of these stations demonstrated the intermittency and variation in the amount of waste discharged.

Programs for control of noxious insects involving direct application of insecticides to a salt marsh, constitute still another important source of estuarine pollution. Although the use of the persistent pesticides for this purpose is declining with the increased knowledge of the harmful side effects, DDT is still popular because it is cheap and effective. The 1-pound-per-acre, or less, application rates seem disarmingly small, yet the persistence of this chemical is such that the accumulation of residues in the fauna may reach disastrous levels.

In one bay in New York, for example, DDT residues in soft clam populations are higher by an order of magnitude than at any of 15 other stations routinely sampled on Long Island. This unusually high residue is not caused by the use of more insecticide there for the control of mosquitos, but is a result of the bay being isolated from the sea for much of the year. Since bay water is not diluted by tidal action, the residues accumulate in the environment where they are adsorbed on silt and plankton that the clams ingest as they feed.

A different situation exists in an estuary of northwest Florida, where the stable fly (*Stomoxys calcitrans*) is an obnoxious pest during the summer tourist period. This fly lays its eggs it windrows of seaweed along the beaches, where the larvae then develop. Present control methods consist of spraying the windrows with a DDT formulation three or four times during the early part of the summer. The total amount of DDT used in spraying the approximately 100 miles of beach is relatively small. We calculated that if all of this DDT were evenly dispersed in the estuary at a single time the concentration would be less than 0.001 ppm. Chemical analyses of DDT residues in the plankton following the spray program, however, showed average accumulations of about 0.07 ppm. The DDT is washed into the estuary by tidal action in a relatively short time and, since there is only one tide a day in this area, the flushing rate is relatively slow. As a result, the DDT may persist adsorbed on silt or plankton for a matter of weeks. Plankton makes up the food supply of various small fish including the pinfish (*Lagodon rhomboides*). Analysis of random samples of this fish showed pesticide residues in the range of 0.1 to 0.5 ppm. The level of these residues increased the longer the fish were in the estuary, i.e., the older they were. In turn, pinfish are fed upon by various water birds, including the loon (*Gavia immen*). One analysis made of the liver of a loon shot in the vicinity showed that it contained about 180 ppm of DDT. Mullet (*Mugil cephalus*) are herbivorous fish that feed largely on plankton and consequently build up relatively large residues of DDT. In one series of analyses, for example, mullet gonads contained 3 to 10 ppm of DDT. At the top of this food chain is the bottlenose dolphin (*Tursiops truncatus*) which feeds extensively on mullet. Blubber samples from a small series of porpoise found dead in this area contained DDT residues ranging up to 800 ppm.

Evidence is substantial in the freshwater habitat that the accumulation of about 4 ppm of DDT in fish eggs may cause complete mortality of the brood. Apparently a similar situation exists in one estuary on the Texas coast. Levels of DDT residues in the ovary of the speckled seatrout (*Cynoscion nebulosus*) were as high as 8 ppm in the prespawning period in 1968, and there was no evidence of successful spawning later in the year. In a second estuary 100 miles away, ovarian DDT residues in seatrout were about 0.2 ppm and a normal number of young of the year were observed.

These data demonstrate the importance of trophic magnification of persistent pesticides in the food web and indicate that even relatively small applications of pesticides in pest control programs can be magnified astoundingly at higher trophic levels. Pesticides are, of course, not all bad. Many are essential to the production and protection of foodstuffs and other agricultural products, in the management of our natural resources, and for the amelioration of our daily existence.

Our difficulties arise from the use of broad spectrum toxicants that may contaminate the environment for months and years. These persistent pesticide chemicals, resistant to decay, may be carried by surface drainage waters to areas far from the point of application. Through the process of co-distillation, they pass into the atmosphere or are airborne on dust particles and carried by winds to every part of the globe, to contaminate even the polar regions and the mid-ocean environment. The use of such pesticides must be limited to those purposes for which there is no substitute. They must not be used on the basis of economy and expediency. Theoretically, all pesticides are used on a cost-benefit ratio. It appears, however, that even after a quarter century of use and research on DDT, we still do not know the true extent of the damage it has inflicted on the environment. It is essential that laboratory and field tests to evaluate synthetic pesticides be so thorough that we can be assured they will have no irreversible effect on the environment.

REFERENCES

Butler, Philip A. 1965. Reaction of some estuarine mollusks to environmental factors. In: Biological problems in water pollution, third seminar 1962, p. 92-104. U.S.P.H.S. Publication No. 999-WP-25.
————. 1966. Pesticides in the marine environment. *J. App. Ecol.,* 3 (Suppl): 253-259.
Butler, Philip A., Alfred J. Wilson, Jr., and Alan J. Rick. 1960. Effect of pesticides on oysters. *Proc. Nat. Shellfish Assoc.* 51: 23-32.

Control

28   Pesticide Pollution Control

H. PAGE NICHOLSON

Pesticide Pollution History

Water pollution by pesticides began to occur about 22 years ago when the organic insecticides developed just before and during World War II reached the public market. There followed an almost explosive expansion of chemical pesticides; today there are more than 650 basic kinds, of which at least 200 are of first importance. The tonnage of pesticides sold in the United States increased by 84 percent in the decade 1955-1965. Production of basic pesticides in the United States in 1965 totaled 437,500 tons (396,900 metric tons).

Fish kills associated with rainfall runoff following application of chlorinated hydrocarbon insecticides in agriculture were the first evidence that a new form of water pollution was occurring. Sporadic scattered kills were climaxed in 1950 by the almost simultaneous occurrence of kills in 15 streams tributary to the Tennessee River in Alabama. Subsequent investigation indicated that the kills were caused by insecticides washed from cotton fields with its attendant intense thunder showers.

The first recovery and identification of a water-polluting pesticide was made in 1953 by personnel at the Robert A. Taft Sanitary Engineering Center in Cincinnati, Ohio, who recovered DDT from the Detroit River and Lake St. Clair. The first quantitation was achieved in 1957, when DDT was detected in the Mississippi River at Quincy, Illinois, and at New Orleans, in the Missouri River at Kansas City, and in the Columbia River at Bonneville, Oregon, in concentrations ranging from 1 microgram to 20 micrograms per liter.

Present Status of Knowledge

The two principal sources of water pollution by pesticides today are runoff from the land and discharges of industrial waste, either from industries that manufacture or formulate pesticides or from those that use these compounds in their manufacturing processes. Less important causes of pollution are (i) activities designed to control undesirable aquatic life, (ii) careless use of pesticides, and (iii) occasional accidents in transportation. Instances of careless use have been decreasing as a result of intensive educational campaigns sponsored by agricultural, conservation, water-pollution-control and public-health agencies and by the pesticide manufacturing industry.

Aquatic animals far removed from areas where pesticides are known to have been used may have chlorinated hydrocarbon insecticide residues in their tissues. Sladen, Menzie, and Reichel demonstrated that Adélie penguins and a crabeater seal, species that seldom range beyond the limits of the Antarctic ice pack, contained residues of DDT and its metabolites. Both of these animals feed on crustacea obtained from the sea.

It is evident that contamination of the aquatic environment by pesticides, primarily by the chlorinated hydrocarbon insecticides, is widespread. This is, in part, because these insecticides possess the characteristic of persistence—they degrade slowly in the environment. As a result, control of their distribution is lost soon after they are applied for the purpose of insect control. Persistence, one of the factors that has made the chlorinated hydrocarbon insecticides so desirable from the standpoint of insect control, then becomes an undesirable attribute.

In part, widespread environmental contamination by chlorinated hydorcarbon insecticides is a result of the extensive use made of these compounds. This group constituted approximately 52 percent of all insecticides and 30 percent of all pesticides produced in the United States in 1965. DDT retained its position of some years' standing as the pesticide produced in greatest quantity, an estimated 70,000 tons (63,000 metric tons).

29   Fewer Pesticides—More Control

ROBERT VAN DEN BOSCH

Recently, as a member of a research team concerned with cotton pest control, I strongly advocated the use of DDT over alternative materials, because of its less severe impact on the agroecosystem. The advocacy of DDT earned me a somewhat heretical reputation among my colleagues, in the light of my long experience as a specialist in biological control!

Actually, I realize that nature's way does not always work, and that chemical pest control is frequently necessary for economical crop production. I believed that DDT was the ecologically safer chemical choice in cotton. But what I learned at the Rochester conference[1] came as a shock and convinced me that the use of DDT and certain other organochlorines should be curtailed and eventually stopped.

The chemical alternatives to DDT are disturbing, but until better things come along, these appear to be the safer materials. As for a moratorium on the use of DDT, it will be interesting to see how the agricultural economy of Arizona and the health and welfare of its citizenry hold up under the recently invoked year-long ban on DDT there. The ban is no assurance that all is well with chemical pest control in Arizona. Indeed, if the situation is at all comparable to that in California, it probably borders on the chaotic. But at least Arizona has stopped pouring DDT into the biosphere and is merely tearing up its own environment with alternative materials.

In general, the synthetic organic insecticides are ecologically crude and engender serious problems: resurgence of target pests, outbreaks of nontarget species, and pest resistance to pesticides. These have contributed to a steady increase in the use of insecticides in recent years. For example, in California pest control costs of its major crops, citrus and cotton, have risen sharply over the past decade. A critical analysis nationwide would reveal a similar pattern: bollworms in Texas cotton, spider mites in deciduous fruit orchards, cabbage loopers in vegetable crops, and so forth.

For the past two decades, the pest control field has been dominated by toxicologists and chemical company sales personnel—persons often either ignorant of or indifferent to ecological principles. Fortunately, entomologists are beginning to appreciate the ecological pitfalls that attend the unilateral use of synthetic insecticides. The concept of integrated control is gaining acceptance[2] This concept recognizes the ecological nature of pest control and has its objective pest population management rather than simple pest kill. Integrated control does not reject chemical insecticides but attempts, instead, to integrate them into pest management systems. Its advocates are not "anti-insecticide," but they do reject ecologically untenable materials and practices, and they plead for more sophis-

1. First Rochester Conference on Toxicity, University of Rochester, Rochester, New York, 4-6 June 1968.
2. R. F. Smith and H. T. Reynolds, *Proc. Food Agr. Organ. Symp. Integrated Control* 1, 11 (1966).

ticated materials and a voice in their development. . . . Greater pesticide efficacy and reduced environmental pollution will result. . . .

Japanese View on Defoliation 30

YOSIAKI ITÔ[1]

From the ecological point of view, we fear that such wide-scale application of herbicides will deal a deadly blow to tropical forest ecosystems and cause serious damage to human beings and property. Even the report by the Mid-west Research Institute admits the danger that the large-scale destruction of the vegetation in the high temperature and humidity of tropical forests may cause rapid erosion of organic matter in the soil and may turn the forest areas with the richest biological productivity into semipermanent lateritic barrens. The report also expressed fear that precious wild animals including the douc langur will be exterminated by the spraying. Moreover, it is possible that these herbicides will either kill small animals and fish, which are the important protein source for the natives, or contaminate them with poisonous residues. We recognize that such methods which cause these dangers are also the means of conducting war.

As ecologists, we share a world responsibility to prevent the destruction of nature by the thoughtless action of humans. At the 15th general meeting of the Ecological Society of Japan held at Ueda City, 2 June 1968, we resolved to demand that the United States immediately stop the large-scale military use of herbicides and forest burning in Vietnam. We also hope that ecologists everywhere will support our stand and take action on it. (The above resolution was also signed by 121 members of the Ecological Society.)

REFERENCE

1. *Assessment of Ecological Effects of Extensive or Repeated Use of Herbicides* (Midwest Research Institute, Kansas City, Mo., 1 Dec. 1967).

31   Gardening Without DDT

TIME MAGAZINE

Dibrom is morbid spelled backward. Happily, it is also one of many pest controls that can keep gardens green without the dangers of DDT and similar chlorinated hydrocarbon insecticides. Others are helpfully summarized in the current issue of *Cry California,* an ecologically astute magazine that deserves to be better known outside its state.

The best defense against common pests, says *Cry California,* is simply to keep the garden well watered, fed and weeded. A strong blast of water from the garden hose is often effective against leafhoppers and spittlebugs. Such natural predators as birds, ladybugs and lacewings wreak havoc with aphids, caterpillars and oak moths. When poisons must be used, the problem is how to avoid overkill. The preferred pesticides are "botanicals," or natural poisons extracted from plants—for example, nicotine sulphate, rotenone and pyrethrum. Their effectiveness, though, is limited to certain chewing pests and sucking insects, such as Diabrotica and thrips. Some synthetic poisons, for example diazinon, kill more kinds of bugs than botanicals but are also more persistent. The newest synthetic poisons are the highly toxic "systemics" (Di-syston and Meta-systox-R), which kill sucking pests after being adsorbed by plants. On the market for only two years, systemics may eventually prove undesirable for garden use.

Thoughtful gardeners should choose the least toxic control available; if it is a poison, they should buy the smallest quantity necessary. Above all, says *Cry California,* swear off DDT and other chlorinated hydrocarbons. The ecosystem you save will be your own.

Fertilizers

The application of fertilizer to upland areas will seriously affect life in a pond or lake which receives the drain-off. Eutrophication in a confined body of water often follows as readily from the run-off following fertilization of nearby fields as it would from the direct introduction of sewage into the water.

Lake Tahoe and Soil Pollution 32

DAVID E. ELRICK

Fertilizers are applied to the soil and it is the behavior of these chemicals both on or in the soil that will determine any subsequent transport which could lead to water pollution. Under normal conditions small amounts of some nutrients are transported. For example, fall applications of nitrogen fertilizers in the temperate climates will probably lead to an increased leaching of nitrogen as both nitrate (and nitrite) nitrogen are mobile and will move in some manner associated with the percolating water. Under normal growth conditions, microbial mineralization and nitrification will convert some of the organic and ammonium forms of nitrogen in the upper layers of the soil to the nitrate form. Phosphorus compounds are relatively immobile within the soil (movement is generally of the order of centimeters).

All of North America is involved because nitrate nitrogen is mobile within the soil and the real problem involves the long range effects of slowly increasing the nitrogen content of our groundwater supplies throughout the continent.

33   Lake Tahoe: Measured for Pollution

EDWARD S. DEEVEY, JR.

One can only have arrived at the conclusion that mineral fertilizers pose no threat to Lake Tahoe by supposing the volume of Lake Tahoe to be infinite, like God's bounty to undeserving man. This kind of notion has survived the collapse of the whaling industry and now promises to outlive Lake Erie and Lake Baikal. It has been claimed that the annual increment of fertilizer to the entire state of Nevada, 2000 tons (2×10^{15} μg) of nitrogen, could not be detected by any means, "including a biological one," if mixed all at once into Lake Tahoe. This may be true in plant food circles, but limnologists use methods appropriate to the concentrations they encounter. Although no analyses of Tahoe waters are readily available to me, (and I have not studied the lake myself), the total nitrogen in so pure a lake is unlikely to exceed 100 μg/liter and is probably closer to 20; soluble nitrogen may be presumed to vary seasonally between 1 and 20 μg/liter. Tahoe is one of the deepest lakes in the world. Its boundaries are circumscribed in a map on p. 17 of G. E. Hutchinson's *Treatise on Limnology,* vol. 1 (Wiley, New York, 1957), and its volume is 124 km^3, or 1.24×10^{14} liters. Thus the hypothetical addition of 20×10^{14} μg of soluble nitrogen (16 μg/liter) might easily double the concentration; the difference would be easily detectable by standard micromethods, and ultramicromethods are available if needed.

Commercial fertilizers usually contain as much phosphorus as nitrogen, whereas the two elements are ordinarily present in natural waters in the proportion of N:P = 7:1 by weight. Doubling the nitrogen concentration might therefore entail a sevenfold increase of phosphorus. Ignoring sewage as a source of algal nutrients, we may use the 2×10^{15} μg of nitrogen, taken as the annual increment of fertilizer to Nevada, to estimate the current input of phosphorus to the lake. The lake itself occupies 0.18 percent of the state's area, and I will suppose that the drainage basin occupies 0.3 percent. The predevelopment concentration of total phosphorus would be of the order of 5 μg/liter. If the basin received its proportionate share of Nevada's fertilizer, with phosphorus equal to nitrogen, the current rate of application of phosphorus would yield an increment of 0.05 μg/liter per year to the lake. If only half the phosphorus, or 0.025 μg/liter per year, reaches the lake, its waters would be enriched by 1 μg/liter, or 20 percent, in the course of 40 years, or a little more than one generation. The amount of the increase is probably small, compared with sewage pollution, but algae know what to do with a scarce element when it suddenly becomes available.

The present mode of harvesting Lake Tahoe's productivity—angling for salmonid fishes—is admittedly obsolete, even atavistic; technological progress could easily find more efficient ways of utilizing an enriched lake. Most citizens, however, would find the price of such progress rather high, for Lake Tahoe, apart from its quite exceptional beauty, is poorly sited, and much too deep, for an experiment in growing algae.

Solid Wastes and Sewage

"Recycle" may well become the key word of the seventies. New industries will likely spring up to assume the task of returning materials to the system. As things now stand, an observer from another planet might reasonably conclude, given the way products are blithely junked, that reservoirs of raw products are bottomless; or that our science is so very clever that we create materials out of nothing. In truth, however, resources are in a finite supply and we must learn to recycle them. When we do this we will immediately solve much of our disposal problem. For example, it has been estimated recently that if all the paper used in this country were recycled, sixty percent of the country's trash disposal problems would be solved. In addition, the hodgepodge of materials that usually goes into the dump makes "mining" of these materials at a future date difficult. The electric toaster, purchased at a discount store, is now thrown into the "sanitary land fill" because it is "cheaper to buy a new one than to fix the old." Reprocessing the materials in the toaster will be more difficult than was the initial process of claiming them from the system.

Part of the present Administration's monetary package for cleaning up the environment provides for the construction of sewage treatment plants. Such plants are designed to "detoxify" the effluent before it is discharged into waterways. Research and development is underway to find efficient methods for returning the effluent to the system free of odor and disease. The valuable nutrients contained in sewage would then be available for recycling rather than being unproductively relegated to septic tanks, river beds or the ocean.

AEC Scientists Push Project to Eliminate All Wastes

34

NEAL STANFORD

If you think splitting the atom and harnessing its power was incredible, if you think putting men on the moon is fantastic, let me tell you about something two Atomic Energy Commission scientists are working on that can only be called apocalyptic. They are working on a project to eliminate all waste! Yes, make this a wasteless world! It sounds like the millennium.

Did you know that each person in the United States produces 4.8 pounds per day of solid waste? That by the year 2000 each person will produce 6.8 pounds per day? That over the 35-year period from 1965 to 2000 almost 10 billion tons of solid refuse will have been accumulated in the United States?

If this were all compacted and disposed of in sanitary landfill, it would cover the state of Delaware 10 feet deep! It would cover the state of Rhode Island 20 feet deep! At the cost of $1 a foot (the cost of sanitary landfill in Los Angeles), this layer of solid waste would represent a total investment of about half a trillion dollars!

Industrial Wastes Added

To the solid wastes of municipal refuse has to be added the solid wastes of industrial origin—junked cars, waste material resulting from mining of solid fuels, metals. The management of waste materials, or, better, its elimination, would quite obviously be an unparalleled boon to mankind. It would be the material equivalent of perpetual motion.

At the moment, the ability to create something from basic elements, use it as a product or service, and then economically reduce it back to its basic elements for future use (with no adverse effect on nature) sounds like fantasy. It smacks of alchemy. What it would mean to mankind staggers the imagination: a pollution-free world; a wasteless society; a control over matter such as man has never had.

The process involved in this concept is called "the fusion torch." It rests upon the prospect of man being able to tame the hydrogen—or fusion—bomb, just as he tamed the nuclear—or fission—bomb. Controlled atomic fission made possible nuclear reactors.

Controlled atomic fusion would not only allow man on a large scale and economic basis to desalt water, process urban sewage, perform plasma chemistry, produce electricity through fuel cells, but also to recycle essentially all solid waste.

Return to Raw Form

That last operation constitutes the fusion-torch concept, or closing the cycle from use to reuse. What this means in layman's language is that waste products would be converted back to elemental form. There would be no waste products to dispose of. There would rather be a supply of basic raw materials for reuse.

When fusion reactors become available, a volume of materials equal to thousands of tons per day could be handled in a single plant. That would take care of urban wastes even in the volume produced today. It is said that if just 10,000 megawatts were used for processing via the fusion torch, the entire wastes of a city with a population in the millions could be converted into raw materials each day.

Who are these modern Merlins—the men working to make possible a wasteless world? Drs. Bernard J. Eastlund and William C. Gough, of the AEC's division of research, as well as the many scientists, physicists, and engineers working on the problem of controlled thermonuclear fusion.

It can be reported that at present new progress has been made both in the United States and in the Soviet Union in this field. The Soviets, it is understood, have made particularly great strides recently.

Ultimate Solution?

In this matter of waste management, two possibilities exist today. Now the fusion-torch concept provides the third—or ultimate—solution. Waste disposal produces no economic return. Partial recycle involves some economic penalty. But this prospect of closing the cycle of use of a resource back to resource makes waste itself a resource.

The fusion-torch concept is a bit complicated for the layman, so it may be better to let the nuclear scientists working on it explain it in their own words.

This is how Drs. Eastlund and Gough describe their fusion-torch concept: "This closing the basic link from used back to resource would be accomplished by vaporizing and ionizing solids (for example, ores or waste products) in the plasma and then separating the elements from the mixture of ionized species.

A fusion plasma is able to vaporize solids easily by the propagation of shock waves. This is because of the plasma's tremendously large flux of random kinetic energy and its high thermal conductivity."

To control fusion energy, say Drs. Eastlund and Gough, "we must heat a dilute gas of fusion fuel to temperatures of hundreds of millions of degrees, then contain it long enough (and at sufficient purity) for an appreciable fraction of the fuel to react." That first goal, they say, was achieved five years ago when plasmas above the ideal ignition temperature were obtained for a self-sustaining fusion reactor. So the problem now is to confine the hot plasmas.

These two scientists say that progress to this end "has been accelerating as the result of increased correlation between theory and experiment, also the use of advanced computers for plasma simulation."

They become quite enthusiastic in explaining their fusion-torch concept: "The fusion torch would close the basic link from user back to resource. Waste products would be converted back to elemental form.

"When a solid is injected into the fusion torch, the interaction results in the transformation of an ultrahigh temperature hydrogen plasma into a low-temperature plasma composed of ionic species characteristic of the solid, irrespective of a solid's chemical composition or mechanical properties.

Attainment Held-Possible

"The number of processes needed for complete recovery of elements from waste products would equal the number of types of waste products present. The fusion torch probably would handle all species in one central recovery plan."

Drs. Eastlund and Gough, while immersed in their research on fusion and on fusion-torch physics, certainly have a vision, a vision, as they put it, "of the future—large cities, operated electrically by clean, safe fusion reactors that eliminate the city's waste products and generate the city's raw materials."

They conclude: "The vision is there. Its attainment does not appear to be blocked by nature. Its achievement depends on the will and the desire of men to see that it is brought about."

35   Shock at Sea

TIME MAGAZINE

When the Norwegian author-explorer Thor Heyerdahl sailed across half the Pacific on a balsawood raft 22 years ago, he recalls, "We on *Kon Tiki* were thrilled by the beauty and purity of the ocean." During his recent attempt to sail from Africa to Central America in a boat made of papyrus reeds, which he was forced to abandon last month 600 miles from his goal, Heyerdahl's old thrill was replaced by shock. In Manhattan he reported to the Norwegian Mission at the United Nations: "Large surface areas in mid-ocean as well as nearer the continental shores on both sides were visibly polluted by human activity."

Heyerdahl and his six-man crew were astonished and depressed by the quantity of jetsam bobbing hundreds of miles from land. Almost every day, plastic bottles, squeeze tubes and other signs of industrial civilization floated by the expedition's leaky boat. What most appalled Heyerdahl were sheets of "pelagic particles." At first he assumed that his craft was in the wake of an oil tanker that had just cleaned its tanks. But on five occasions he ran into the same substances covering the water so thickly, he told *Time* Researcher Nancy Williams, that "it was unpleasant to dip our toothbrushes into the sea. Once the water was too dirty to wash our dishes in."

The particles, some of which Heyerdahl collected for later analysis, are roughly the size of a pea. Oily and sometimes encrusted with tiny barnacles, they smell like a combination of putrefying fish and raw sewage. Heyerdahl hopes that his experience will stir the U.N. to propose new international regulations to keep the oceans clean. "Modern man seems to believe that he can get everything he needs from the corner drugstore," says the explorer. "He doesn't understand that everything has a source in the land or sea, and that he must respect those sources. If the indiscriminate pollution continues, we will be sawing off the branch we are sitting on."

Radioactive and Chemical and Biological Warfare Materials

Radioiodine Fallout over the Midwest in May   36

LESTER MACHTA

Abstract. High concentration of radioiodine in milk, found preferentially over the midwestern United States after atmospheric nuclear tests in May 1962, 1965, and 1966, can best be explained by high-reaching intense thunderstorms that scavenge passing radioactivity from the upper troposphere and lower stratosphere.

Fallout after nuclear tests, including 8-day radioiodine, I^{131}, has been documented. Radioiodine enters man by passage from the nuclear cloud and through atmosphere, pasture, cow, and milk. I now illustrate the manner in which one atmospheric phenomenon increases the likelihood of contamination of milk in the Midwest in May or therebouts, in contrast to other parts of the country and other months.

Nuclear clouds passed over the United States during May of 3 years between 1961 and 1967. The highest concentrations of radioiodine in milk occurred in the Midwest during each episode. The air concentrations are the highest readings, preceding the peak milk concentrations, from the closest station to each milkshed. All the highest concentrations in milk, apart from Charleston, South Carolina, occurred in the Midwest. The highest values during episodes in January and in September through December 1961-67 were not preferentially in the Midwest.

Crops may be contaminated by deposition of radioiodine with precipitation or directly by ground-level radioiodine, or by both. It is argued that during the three May episodes almost all radioiodine was deposited with rainwater.

Three other episodes with little or no rain but with much I^{131} in milk were examined for their ratios of I^{131} in milk to gross beta activity in ground-level air; such ratios roughly indicate the contributions of dry fallout to contamination of milk. During dry weather the ratios are less than 3 on all but three of 17 sites; the highest is only 15, while equivalent ratios run to scores. These higher ratios suggest that a mechanism other than dry fallout enhanced the contamination of milk in May.

Nor is there correlation between milk contamination and gross beta radioactivity during the three May episodes. For example, in May 1966 the highest

Midwest concentrations were 9 pc/m³ in air and more tha 100 pc/liter in milk, while Denver, Colorado, and Phoenix, Arizona, reported 14 pc/m³ and only 20 and 30 pc/liter, respectively. Since the latter stations had little rain, the air:milk ratios agree with the previous dry-weather ratios.

Unfortunately a direct link between concentrations of radioiodine in the upper atmosphere, in rainwater falling on a milkshed, and subsequently in milk is unavailable because of the lack of appropriate measurements. The ability of rain to scavenge fission products from the atmosphere and of contaminated rainwater to enhance concentrations in milk is universally acknowledged. There are a few reports of radioiodine in rainwater in the Midwest in May 1962, and many observations of gross beta radioactivity in rainwater during all three episodes. But, because of the isolated nature of thundershowers and other difficulties, it has not always been possible to document adequately even gross beta contaminations in rainwater in all milksheds. In some instances the evidence of significant gross beta concentration in rainwater over the Midwest is clear: on 17 May 1966 Jefferson City, Missouri, reported a concentration about 30 times greater than did any non-Midwest station after the nuclear test of 9 May 1966.

The Midwest suffers severe weather in the spring. It is the severe thunderstorms from which some tornadoes spawn that concern us rather that the high incidence of tornadoes. Florida and the Southwest have the most thunderstorms in summer. Two characteristics set the Midwest in May apart from the rest of the United States: there is high incidence of nocturnal storms, and the cloud tops reach to great heights. While the nocturnal frequency is of unknown significance, one may argue that high-reaching rainclouds by day and by night account for the greater fallout of I^{131} in the Midwest during May.

Clouds from atmospheric nuclear detonations equivalent to more than about 10 kilotons rise initially into the upper troposphere or lower stratosphere or the upper atmosphere—above about 10 km. These higher altitudes contain a larger fraction of the radioactivity and stronger winds than does the lower troposphere. The stronger winds normally effect faster transit to the United States, with less decay and dilution.

37   Nerve Gas: Dugway Accident Linked to Utah Sheep Kill

PHILIP M. BOFFEY

[In March, 1968,] some 6000 sheep grazing in Skull Valley, Utah, were killed or sickened by a mysterious ailment that attacked the central nervous system. The sheep were located near the Dugway Proving Ground, the Army's chief site for field testing chemical and biological weapons, so suspicions were immediately aroused that the sheep had been felled by a lethal substance originating at Dugway. These suspicions were heightened when it was subsequently revealed that Dugway had tested highly toxic nerve agents the day before the sheep became ill. Circumstantial evidence publicly available indicated that the primary cause of the sheep deaths was VX, a persistent nerve agent that was used in an aircraft spray test at Dugway the day before the sheep started dying.

Scientists have found traces of the nerve agent in the dead sheep and in nearby vegetation and snow water; they have established that the sheep were poisoned by an organic phosphate compound, of which the nerve agent is one; and they have shown that low doses of the nerve agent fed to healthy sheep will produce the same symptoms as those found in the sick Skull Valley sheep. There is evidence that the sheep ingested the nerve agent primarily by eating contaminated vegetation, and that the toxic material persisted in the area for at least three weeks after the incident. As a result of the unfortunate incident, a high-level advisory committee, headed by Surgeon General William H. Stewart, has recommended stringent new safety procedures for Dugway, and the Army last week adopted them *in toto*.

How the agent escaped from Dugway may never be known beyond doubt, but investigators suggest that a combination of circumstances conspired to bring about the sheep slaughter. There was an accident during the spray test at Dugway; shortly thereafter a change in weather conditions apparently carried the agent toward the sheep and then precipitated it around them; and sheep turned out to be unusually susceptible to the agent. Had any of these factors been absent, it is conceivable—though unprovable—that there would have been no "Dugway incident."

Academy Changes Army Gas Dump Plan   38

PHILIP M. BOFFEY

The Army intended to ship some 27,000 tons of chemical weapons from as far away as Denver, Colo., to the Naval Ammunition Depot at Earle, N.J., where they were to be loaded on four old Liberty ships, towed at least 145 miles out to sea, and then sunk with the ships in at least 7200 feet of water. But critics in Congress charged that a railroad accident might spew lethal chemicals over the countryside and that the chemicals might cause serious ecological damage to the ocean.

The Academy panel, which was headed by George B. Kistiakowsky, Harvard chemist and science adviser to the late President Eisenhower, generally agreed with the critics. It recommended that two of the five chemical materials involved be deactivated and that the other three be dumped in the ocean only as a last resort. Although the Army had previously argued that deactivation was time-consuming, costly, and dangerous, the panel said the government should minimize risks to humans and the environment "even though this may complicate and make more costly its own operations."

The panel said that clusters of bomblets loaded with GB, a liquid nerve gas, should be disassembled and neutralized chemically by acid or alkaline hydrolysis. It said that under the Army's original plans there was a "remote possibility" that a "catastrophic explosion" could be caused by a sniper's bullet or a railroad or ship collision. The Pentagon indicated it would carry out this recommendation.

The panel also said that liquid mustard agent, which is currently stored in bulk containers, should be burned in government establishments where local air pollution would not be a serious problem. The panel said that while there was virtually no danger of a catastrophic accident with mustard, it was concerned about possible adverse effects on the oceanic ecosphere when the mustard eventually leaked out of its containers. The Pentagon also agreed to comply with this recommendation.

The panel said the other three materials involved—namely, GB nerve gas rockets imbedded in concrete and steel "coffins," steel containers contaminated by toxic chemicals, and canisters of CS riot control agent imbedded in drums filled with concrete—could be dumped at sea without serious harm if no other suitable means of disposal can be found. However, the panel urged the Army to convene a group of technical and demolition experts to determine if it is feasible to demilitarize the nerve gas rockets, and the Army agreed to form such a group.

The Academy study, by implication, pointed to two glaring oversights on the part of the Army. It noted that while "various chemical warfare agents have been repeatedly disposed of in the oceans by the United States and other nations . . . we have no information regarding possible deleterious effects of these operations on the ecosphere of the seas." The panel also suggested that the Army should assume that all chemical weapons will require eventual disposal and should consequently build disposal facilities that will not require dumping at sea.

Conservation

Something will have gone out of us as a people if we ever let the remaining wilderness be destroyed; if we ever permit the last virgin forests to be turned into comic books and plastic cigarette cases; if we drive the few remaining wild species into zoos or extinction; if we pollute the last clear air and dirty the last clean streams and push out paved roads through the last of the silences.

Wallace Stegner
The Living Wilderness
Winter 68-69

The sentiments expressed in the above quotation, valid and important as they are, refer only to the "soul of a people." Most conservationists of less than a decade ago were "blue sky boys." The public has recently started to become aware that conservation of our resources must be argued on more than aesthetic grounds. The selections that follow demonstrate the complexity involved in the conservation issue.

Encroachment

Frontierism will likely be long in dying since man has always been able to go "just over the hill" or "around the bend" when his nest was fouled or his resources dwindled. But now, for the first time in history, our species has been permanently turned back. Man may make occasional excursions to planets in his own solar system, but the other stars are too far away.

The greatest experiment of mankind may just be getting under way. That is, how to live on a finite spaceship with finite resources and be obliged to repair the life support system. But a mature ecosystem is self-sustaining and requires none of man's time to repair it. We call this the wilderness. Thoreau's words, "In wilderness is the preservation of the world," take on new meaning in a period of accelerated encroachment.

39   # The Wail of Kashmir

LEE MERRIMAN TALBOT

A striking example of man's growing impact on the land is the Great Thar Desert in western India. At the time of Christ, Indian rhinoceros roamed in grass jungles in the middle of what is now desert. And for the past 80 years the desert has been advancing into the rest of India at the rate of one-half mile a year along its whole long perimeter. That means that in 80 years, an estimated 56,000 square miles, or an area equal to that of Wisconsin, has been turned into shifting sand.

The mechanics of this land degradation seem clear. The starting point is the mature forest with its wildlife, fertile soil, and abundant water. The lumber is cut, often clear-cut with young growth destroyed. The land is then cultivated for a time, then grazed and overgrazed. There can be no replacement of trees or grass, for everything green is eaten by ravenous livestock. When there is nothing left for cattle, goats take over, and when the goats have left, nothing remains but sand or blowing dust. This story holds true, with the same plot and characters, but with different stage scenery and costumes, throughout much of the world.

To illustrate the effect of this land-use pattern on wilderness, let us consider Kashmir, the ancient Moguls' "paradise on earth." This is a lovely mountain land in northernmost India, lying at about the same latitude as San Francisco, and bordered by Tibet, China, and Pakistan. The British with the local maharajah set aside magnificent wild areas here. But when independence came, here as in most former colonies, the tendency during the first burst of nationalism was to reject all that smacked of the previous "imperialism" or "colonialism." Parks and wilderness areas were thought of as something kept away from the people by the former rulers rather than as a resource maintained for them, so the first reaction was to destroy them, to take "what was rightfully ours." On top of this came political and military unrest with a side effect of a large population suddenly armed but with little discipline. Among the results have been large-scale poaching leading to the virtual extermination of the Kashmir stag, heavy forest cutting, and overgrazing.

Through much of Kashmir up to and above timberline one runs into herders and livestock. In less than ten years much of this land changed from dense conifer forest or park lands like the best of our Sierra or Rockies, to what are approaching high-altitude deserts, with the vegetation pulled apart, cut, overgrazed, and burned out—and the soil, too.

Economic need, destructive land use, and destructive nationalism form a constantly recurring pattern deadly to wilderness. Until all three of these factors are somewhat ameliorated it is hard to be optimistic about the future of wilderness lands throughout the world.

As my last example I would like to mention an area not usually thought of as living wilderness—the Middle East. Much of it is arid desert, but when Moses led the children of Israel through the Sinai wilderness, it was a live wilderness with wildlife and trees. Today one can go for days through that country and never see a living thing. The mountains above the Promised Land were cloaked with dense forest, with pine, oak, and cedar; and in the more open areas, Asiatic lions stalked abundant wildlife. Today these mountains are largely dead stone skeletons, and the last small remnant of the Asiatic lions is to be found 3,000 miles to the east. There are still two more or less living wilderness areas left—in northern Lebanon and western Syria. Until recently, protected by inaccessibility and unsettled conditions, the forest here remained intact; but within the last few years, lumbering and cultivation have begun to move into these last forests. When the land's fertility has been cropped out and the trees have been cut off, the crops will give way to grazing. Once overgrazing has gone far enough, the starving animals preventing grass, brush, and tree reproduction, the area will assume the desert aspect of most of the Middle East.

This remnant biblical wilderness illustrates one of the very real economic values of wilderness that, perhaps, is not often thought of in our country. It would be easy to say, looking at most of the desert Middle Eastern lands, that this area never did support much life, or that the old records of forests and crops are wrong, or that if there were trees here once there has since been a climactic change. But in these remaining wild forest areas we have the living proof that this was not the case. North Lebanon and western Syria provide a point of reference by which one may judge the condition of the land as it was, see what man has done to the rest of the land, and therefore see what can be done with what land is left.

Deserts On The March 40

PAUL B. SEARS

By the time of Charlemagne, who was an enlightened ruler, the onslaught against the forests of western Europe was under way, to continue through the thirteenth century. By the end of the Middle Ages the land was largely divested of its trees, as the Mediterranean region had been before the Christian era, and stringent laws against cutting came into being. Whatever advanced ideas had been inherited from Rome were soon lost to sight. Fields were used, then abandoned. Feudal lords shifted their headquarters from one castle to another, to get away, it has been said, from the accumulated filth. But the coefficient of toleration of filth was so high in those days that the moving was more likely to have been for the purpose of tapping new sources of food as the old sections of the fief played out. Eventually, after a period of rest, the abandoned fields had to be used again. Such a system is unsound. Recuperation takes too long, and too much of the land at a time remains idle. Paintings and sculptured figures of the period portray human beings who are wan and rickety, and since these portrayals were commonest in sacred art, most of us still have the feeling that anaemia and sainthood are inseparable. Actually the trouble was due to inadequate diet and malnutrition on a huge scale, such as we find in backward rural communities.

41   Encroachment Of The Present

KENNETH S. NORRIS

A casual observer might suggest that there would be no problem in carrying out a population study of desert animals by driving 5 miles or so beyond Palm Springs into the completely barren dunes, and as an added protection walking about a thousand feet off the road before beginning work. I did this and had a motel built right in the middle of my study plot. Thus, ended one half-finished doctoral thesis problem, and thus arose much concern regarding the undisturbed character of the barren dunes.

Surely one could expect to maintain a trapline of drop-can lizard traps along the margins of uninhabited austere Pisgah Crater, 35 miles out of Barstow, which is itself far out in the desert. These traps are buried flush with the ground and unobtrusively covered by a plywood sheet on top of which is sprinkled local dirt for camouflage. I did this too, and over a 2-year period about 20% of my traps were pulled from the ground, shot full of bullet holes, or carried completely away. I cannot know how many times undisturbed traps were raided of the animals I sought. An entire aspect of my work, thus, became insecure, and this project also had to be abandoned.

On my own campus, as a student and later as a staff member, I watched a magnificent natural canyon disappear under buildings and the pavement of parking lots. Deer once visited UCLA every year or so to have their fawns. A fox family used to live where the present University elementary school is now located. A colony of bats and chaparral plants and animals once lived where the music, social science, and art buildings now stand. Furthermore, near our campus urbanization has all but eliminated opportunities for teaching in nature.

The Los Angeles basin, not so many years ago, had extensive marshes, the nesting grounds for avocets and least terns, and great populations of spade-foot toads, but now it is covered with a vast slum-in-the-making of housing tracts, which is uniformly repellant to naturalists. We felt we were being excluded by social change from our lands, like the American Indians, and like them, we needed reservations to protect ourselves.

A Letter From The Arctic   42

SAM WRIGHT

Samuel Wright "A Letter From The Arctic" was written February 15, 1969, reproduced in a limited number of copies on a flat tin of gelatin, and flown out by bush pilot in a small plane. It was written on the author's second trip to the Brooks Range, where he and his wife are spending their second winter in a 12 x 12 foot log cabin at Big Lake, 200 miles from Fairbanks, north of the Arctic Circle. On a previous trip "north of timberline," in the summer of 1967, he went for two reasons: one reason was that he "had never been there"; another was to look for white spruce which Robert Marshall had planted as seeds twenty-seven years before, north of present timber.

As I write this, a great caravan of heavily laden trucks is growling over a new winter road which yesterday reached the Eskimo village in Anaktuvuk Pass at the central top of the range. Yesterday wrote the end of Anaktuvuk Pass as it was, a small village of inland Eskimos still dependent upon migrating herds of caribou. It may have written the beginning of the end of the great caribou herds, majestic mountain sheep and the wolf. It was certainly the end of thousands of years of solitude, as the great diesel trucks thundered up the John River valley on their way to the "North Slope" and the great oil strike near Prudhoe Bay on the Arctic Ocean.

For many millenia this great range of mountains north of the Yukon in Alaska not only sheltered caribou herds and bands of mountain sheep, but provided breeding grounds for myriad birds. Athabascan Indians and inland Eskimos shared this great wilderness, living out their lives as an integral part of a balanced ecology. To the Indian and caribou hunting Eskimo, this was more than home. It was ten thousand years of Eden, where the bear and wolf gave their pelts, and the fish flashing in lakes and streams after break-up were fat and abundant.

This is the way it was in what is now called the Brooks Range, that great escarpment which stretches over 500 miles from Canada to the western coast, north of the Arctic Circle in Alaska. Because of its inaccessability and because the winters are long and cold, this last great wilderness on the American continent is still relatively pristine, a resource from which man can yet gain sustenance for his spirit, know his roots, and perhaps save his soul.

At this moment in history this great wilderness is doomed. Domestication has already begun. Until yesterday, Anaktuvuk Pass was accessible only by airplane, and just twenty years ago there was no village in this mountain sheltered valley on the route of the caribou. For hundreds of years it had been a camping place of the Nunamiut (inland people) until a school, church and airstrip drew the nomadic Eskimos into a permanent settlement. With the projection of a railroad, and a forty-eight inch crude oil pipeline over the range in the immediate future, the arrival of the road at Anaktuvuk Pass signals not only the end of a way of life for the Nunamiut but for the wilderness itself.

Who speaks for wilderness? Nearly everyone says it is a value we must not lose, and expresses regret at what seems to be the inevitable ambition of civilization to bring every niche on earth under domestication. But when a choice for wilderness or domestication is to be made, progress, money, exploitation, if not encouraged are condoned. With the North Slope oil strike already producing millionaires, and an estimate of enough reserves to make the United States virtually independent of foreign sources, few question that the fields will be brought into full production. But need we destroy a wilderness in the process?

We are fortunate in Alaska that such potential wealth lies beneath the northern tundra. The State is blessed at a time in history when such income can materially enrich the lives of all. Will we use it to create a balanced ecology for our time, and live in harmony with the land as its native population did for centuries, or will we destroy the very resource of serenity and beauty we hope to buy with our newly found wealth?

It is a question of balancing values. Today, oil may be high in our hierarchy of values, but there may come a day, closer than we realize, when the values of the wilderness will be worth more to us than all the oil on earth—as important as the issue of war and peace.

We must not think only of ourselves, but of our children and all to come. We need to reserve this last great wilderness, from the Yukon River to the North Slope, with the exception of settled areas around the Seward Peninsula. Through her aids of cold and inaccessibility, nature reserved the oil on the North Slope for our day. We can no longer count on nature to reserve for the future. It is up to us to preserve the wilderness. The issue could be life or death.

What are the values of wilderness which can be spoken of so strongly that I use terms of life and death? They are those qualities which have made us what we are as a people, a nation—qualities of self-reliance, spontaneity, and affirmation. These have been shared by others throughout the history of man, but they have been nurtured by the wilderness, which in our past history has so amply blessed us. . . .

Any reasonable person whose values are not these is beholden to nurture and protect that quality of life which comes from and is symbolized in wilderness, *wherever* he lives. There are many who do not know the wilderness first hand, but because it exists their lives are enhanced. This quality is not confined to the wilderness, but without the wilderness resource, there is a question as to how long this quality will survive. Where so much of contemporary life is dribbled second hand through many fingers, the only place where life remains unequivocally first hand is in the wilderness.

What is this quality of life which came from the wilderness and still is nurtured there? It is aliveness. Aliveness is given to those who live wild, not bred to domesticity. That the wild has taken on negative, unwarranted connotations over the years beyond the aliveness it represents is unfortunate. It is this quality of aliveness which is affirmation. In wildness is not only the preservation of the world, as Thoreau says, but it is that quality which makes of life more than existence.

It is this "more than existence," a sense of adventure, a risk-taking, which has projected man into the frontiers of both inner and outer space. The answer is not domestication, but a recognition that wildness is not predatory but a relationship. Without a quality of wildness, man ceases to be human.

There is no time left. If there is any natural resource which deserves our full attention, it is wilderness. We must preserve any wilderness area left on this planet we have now seen from the moon to be our home or the opportunity is lost forever. Fortunately, the Brooks Range is in the State of Alaska in the United States of America, and we can save it now. Next month, tomorrow, will be too late.

In our technological age, the domestication of the Eskimo village in Anaktuvuk Pass is inevitable. But what is not inevitable is the domestication of this last great arctic wilderness, the Brooks Range. The choice is ours. Whether by action or indifference, the choice will be made.

The Public And The Wilderness

In 1968, a long-standing proposal for the creation of a nationwide system of trails was signed into law. The Appalachian trail will extend from Maine to Georgia, a distance of about 2000 miles. The Pacific Crest will run about 2350 miles, from Canada to Mexico. Additional side and connecting trails will likely be added. How much "togetherness" is possible in the wilderness before it ceases to be wilderness?

It is possible to lower the vehicle density in some established National Parks while actually increasing the Parks' accessibility to more people (reading 43). However, some naturalists strongly maintain that only the able-bodied and self-sufficient should be permitted access to the most rugged areas of the wilderness (reading 44).

43 National Parks: Traffic Jams Turn Attention To Roads

LUTHER J. CARTER

Many of our (national) parks are no longer a place of escape and repose, but a massive traffic jam as nerve-racking as a 5 o'clock urban rush. Senator Frank E. Moss of Utah, in a speech on 1 August in the United States Senate.

The Park Service is investigating the capabilities, costs, and possible effects on terrain and natural communities of monorails, tramways, minirails, helicopters, hydrofoils, and other systems.

Consider how this hypothetical system would operate on a tour of Yellowstone. Assume that a Chicago family of four stops off for a quick tour of a few of the park's most famous spectacles. After arriving at Gardner, at Yellowstone's north entrance, they leave their car and take one of the monorail trains which make frequent stops at park entrance points. They are now on Yellowstone's "mainline" system, designed to move people about quickly between those principal park attractions and visitor centers which earlier were linked by road. This elevated system allows them sweeping scenic views, while itself intruding far less conspicuously upon the landscape than the road it has replaced.

The Chicagoans begin their tour with stops at Old Faithful geyser and Canyon Village. At the latter, the family (which includes small children for whom rugged hikes and back-country trips are out of the question) leaves the monorail and boards a minirail train for a 6-mile round trip to Yellowstone Canyon. Some parts of the canyon may be seen from the train itself, though it passes well back from the north rim of the canyon and is not visible from the south rim. The visitors make frequent stops, however, walking to various overlooks, then boarding other trains to make their way around the circuit. Later, the family gets back on the monorail but then leaves it again briefly for an excursion by aerial tramway to the summit of Mount Washburn. The family's visit to Yellowstone ends back at Gardner—after a tour of about 150 miles in which no one had to fight traffic.

We Must Earn Again For Ourselves What We Have Inherited   44
(A Lesson in Wilderness Economics)

GARRETT HARDIN

To some it may seem anathema to mention wilderness and economics in the same breath. Certainly, in the past, some of the most dangerous enemies of wilderness have been men who spoke the economic lingo. Despite this historic tar I think the brush of economics is a proper one for painting a picture of wilderness as a problem in human choice.

Economics may be defined as the study of choice necessitated by scarcity. There is something improper in speaking of the "economics of abundance" as Stuart Chase once did. With true abundance all economics ceases, except for the ultimately inescapable economics of time. Of the economics of time there is no general theory, and perhaps cannot be. But for the *things* of the world there is an economics, something that can be said.

Although there really is no such thing as an economics of abundance, the belief that there is is one of the suppurating myths of our time. This belief had its origin partly in a genuine economic phenomenon, "the economy of scale." For complex artifacts in general the unit cost goes down as the scale of manufacture increases. In general, the more complex the artifact, the more striking the economy of scale: the cost per unit to build a million automobiles per year is far, far less than the cost per unit when only one is manufactured. Because artifacts are so pervasive in modern life, most of us unconsciously assume "the bigger the better," and "the more the cheaper." It takes a positive effort of imagination to realize that there are things the supply of which cannot be multiplied indefinitely. Natural resources in general, and wilderness in particular, fall in this group.

This is obvious enough to Sierra Club members. It should be obvious to everyone, but it is not. Discussing some proposed improvements in a national park the *Toronto Financial Post* recently said: "During 1968 and early 1969, campsites will be expanded and roads paved to enable the visitor to enjoy the wilderness atmosphere that was nearly inaccessible only a few years ago." This is an astonishing sentence, but I will bet you would have to argue with the writer for quite a while before he could be made to see the paradox in proposing to "build a road into the wilderness."

Wilderness cannot be multiplied; and it can be subdivided only a little. It is not increasing; we have to struggle to keep it from decreasing. But population increases steadily. The ratio of the wilderness available to each living person becomes steadily less—and bear in mind that this is only a statistical abstraction: were we to divide up the wilderness among even a small fraction of the total population there would be no wilderness available to anyone. So what should we do?

The first thing to do is to see where we stand, to see what the possibilities are, to make a calendar of possibilities without (initially) making any judgment of their desirability. On the first level of analysis there are just three possibilities.

1. The wilderness can be opened to everyone. The end result of this is completely predictable: absolute destruction. Only a nation with a small population, perhaps no greater than one percent of our present population, a nation that does not have at its disposal our rapid means of transportation could maintain a wilderness that was open to all.

2. We can close the wilderness to everyone. In a limited sense, this action would preserve the wilderness. But it would be a wilderness like Bishop Berkeley's "tree in the quad" when no one is there: does wilderness really exist if no one experiences it? Such an action would save wilderness for the future but it would do no one any good now.

3. We can allow only limited access to the wilderness. This is the only course of action that can be rationally defended. Only a small percent of a large population can ever enjoy the wilderness. With suitable standards and a detailed study of the variables, we can (in principle) work out a theory for maximizing the enjoyment of wilderness under a system of limited access.

Whatever theory we adopt we shall have to wrestle with the problem of choice, the problem of determining what small number from among a vast population shall have the opportunity to enjoy this scarce good, wilderness. It is this problem of choice that I wish to explore here.

What I have to say applies not only to wilderness in the sense in which that term is understood by all good outdoorsmen, but also to all other kinds of outdoor recreational areas—to national parks, to ski areas and the like. All of these can be destroyed by localized overpopulation. They differ in their "carrying capacity," to use a term taken from game management. The carrying capacity of a Coney Island (for those who like it, and there are such people) is very high; the carrying capacity of wilderness, in the sense defined by Howard Zahniser, is very low. In the Wilderness Bill of 1964 Zahniser's felicitous definition stands for all to admire:

A wilderness, in contrast with those areas where man and his own works dominate the landscape is hereby recognized as an area where the earth and its community of life are untrammeled by man, where man himself is a visitor who does not remain.

The carrying capacity of Coney Island is, I suppose, something like 200 people per acre; the carrying capacity of a wilderness may be less than one person per square mile. Whatever the capacity, as population inexorably increases, each type of recreational area sooner or later comes up against the problem of allocation of a scarce resource among a more than sufficient number of claimants. The problem of limited access must be faced.

How shall we limit access? How shall we choose from among the too-abundant petitioners those few who shall be allowed to come in? Let's run over the various possibilities.

First: By the market place. We can auction off the natural resource, letting the richest purchase it, or purchase tickets for admission. In our part of the world and in our time most of us unhesitatingly label this method "unfair." Perhaps it is. But don't forget that many an area of natural beauty that we enjoy today was passed down to us unspoiled in an estate of the wealthy of past times. This method of allotment has at least the virtue that it preserves natural treasures until a better, or perhaps we should merely say a more acceptable, method of distribution can be devised. The privilege of wealth has in the past carried many of the beauties of nature through the first, destructive eras of nascent democracy to the more mature stages when people are capable of appreciating beauty. A somewhat different privilege in China, the privilege of religion, preserved the "dawn redwood" in temple gardens while all the rest of the species was being cut for timber and fuel by the impoverished people outside.

Second: By queues. Wilderness could be made available on a first come, first served basis, up to the extent of the carrying capacity. People would simply line up each day in a long queue and a few would be allowed in. It would be a fatiguing and wasteful system, but it would be "fair." But it might not be stable.

Third: By lottery. This would be eminently "fair," and it would not be terribly fatiguing or wasteful. In earlier days, the decision of a lottery was regarded as the choice of God. We cannot recapture this consoling belief (now that "God is dead"), but we still are willing to abide by the results of a lottery. Hunting rights in several states where big game abounds are allocated by lottery.

Fourth: By merit. Whether one regards this as "unfair" or "fair" depends on the complexion of one's political beliefs. Whether it is fair or not, I will argue that it is the best system of allocation.

Anyone who argues for a merit system of determining rights immediately raises an *argumentum ad hominem.* He immediately raises the suspicion that he is about to define "merit" in such a way as to include himself in the meritorious group. The suspicion is justified, and because it is justified it must be met.

To carry conviction, he who proposes standards must show that his argument is not self-serving. What I hereby propose as a criterion for admission to the wilderness is great physical vigor. I explicitly call your attention to this significant fact: *I myself cannot pass the test I propose.* I had polio at the age of four, and got around moderately well for more than 40 years, but now I require crutches. Until today, I have not traded on my infirmity. But today I must, for it is an essential part of my argument.

I am not fit for the wilderness I praise. I cannot pass the test I propose. I cannot enter the area I would restrict. Therefore I claim that I speak with objectivity. The standard I propose is not an example of special pleading in my own interest. I can speak loudly where abler men would have to hesitate. I hope that what I have the right to say can be accepted by all.

To restrict the wilderness to physically vigorous people is inherently sensible. What is the *experience* of wilderness? Surely it has two major components. The first is *the experience of being there,* the experience (to use Thoreau's words) of being refreshed "by the sight of inexhaustible vigor," of being emotionally overwhelmed by the vast and titanic forces of nature.

The experience of being there is part of the experience of wilderness, but only a part. Dropped down from a line by helicopter into the middle of a wilderness we would miss an important part of the total experience, namely *the experience of getting there.* The exquisite sight, sound and smell of wilderness is many times more powerful if it is earned through physical achievement, if it comes at the end of a long and fatiguing journey for which vigorous good health is a necessity.

Practically speaking, this means that no one should be able to enter a wilderness by mechanical means. He should have to walk many miles on his own two feet, carrying all his provisions with him. In some cases, entrance might be on horse or mule back, or in a canoe, or by snowshoes; but there should be no automobiles, no campers, no motorcycles, no tote-goats, no outboard motors, no airplanes. Just unmechanized man and nature—this is a necessary part of the prescription of the wilderness experience.

That mechanical aids threaten wilderness is already recognized by the managers of our wildernesses. Emergency roads, it is said, should be used sparingly. I submit that this cautious policy is not cautious enough. I submit that there should be *no* emergency roads, that the people who go into the wilderness should go in without radio transmitters, that they should know for certain that if an emergency arises they can get no help from the outside. If injured, they must either somehow struggle to the outside under their own power, or (if lucky) catch the attention of another rare wanderer in the wilderness and get him to help. For people who are physically prepared for it, the wilderness is not terribly dangerous—but such danger as there is, is a precious part of the total experience. The knowledge that one is *really* on one's own is a powerful tonic. It would be a sentimental cruelty to deprive the wilderness adventurer of the tonic knowledge that death is possible.

There is not even a public interest in making the wilderness safe. Making great and spectacular efforts to save the life of an individual makes sense only when there is a shortage of people. I have not lately heard that there is a shortage of people.

There is, however, a public interest in making the wilderness as difficult and dangerous as it legitimately can be. There is, I think, a well-founded suspicion that our life has become, if anything, too safe for the best psychological health, particularly among the young. The ever-greater extension of the boundaries of legal liability has produced a controlled and fenced-in environment in which it is almost impossible to hurt oneself—unless one tries. The behavior of the young clearly indicates that they really try. Drag races, road races, "rumbles," student sit-ins, marches, and tauntings of the police—all these activities look like the behavior of people looking for danger. I do not wish to deny that these activities spring from other motivations as well, e.g., idealistic political beliefs. I am only saying that it looks like a deliberate seeking of danger is part of the motivation of our obstreperous young. I think they are right to seek danger. I think we should tear down some of the fences that now deprive people of the possibility of danger. I think that a wilderness without rescue services would, in a small way, contribute to the stability of society.

There is another respect in which the interests of society could be furthered by a rigorous wilderness. From time to time a president of the United States tries to improve the physical condition of the average citizen by pummeling him with rhetoric. The verbal assault consists principally of the words "responsibility," "duty," and "patriotism." I'm afraid these rhetorical duds no longer move the young. The negative motivation of shame is, in general, not as effective as the positive motivation of prestige. A wilderness that can be entered only by a few of the most physically fit of the population will act as an incentive to myriads more to improve their physical condition. The motivation will be more effective if we have (as I think we should) a graded series of wilderness and park areas. Areas in which the carrying capacity is reckoned at one person per thousand acres should be the most difficult to enter; those with a capacity of one per hundred acres should be easier; those with one per ten, still easier, and so on. Yosemite Valley should, I suggest, be assigned a carrying capacity of about one per acre, which might mean that it could be opened to anyone who could walk ten miles. All automobile roads should come to a dead end ten miles short of the Valley. At first, of course, the ten-mile walkers would be a very small class, but once the prestige factor took effect more and more people would be willing to walk such a distance. Then the standard should be made more rigorous.

I am sure other details of such a system would eventually have to be faced and worked out. It might be necessary to combine it with a lottery. Or some independent, easily administered test of physical fitness might be instituted. These are details, and in principle can be solved, so I will not spend time on them. But whatever the details, it is clear that many of our present parks, forests, and other recreation areas should be forever closed to people on crutches, to small children, to fat people, to people with heart conditions, and to old people in their usual state of physical disrepair. On the basis of their lack of merit, such people (and remember, I am a member of this deprived group) should give up all claim of right to the wilderness experience.

The poet Goethe once said, "We must earn again for ourselves what we have inherited," recognizing that only those things that are earned can be precious. To be precious the heritage of wilderness must be open only to those who can earn it again for themselves. The rest, since they cannot gain the genuine treasure by their own efforts, must relinquish the shadow of it.

We need not be so righteous as to deny the excluded ones all experience of the out-of-doors. There is no reason in the world why we cannot expand our present practice of setting up small outdoor areas where we permit a high density of people to get a tiny whiff of the outdoors. Camping cheek by jowl with thousands of others in an outdoor slum does not appeal to me personally (I have not visited Yosemite Valley in thirty years) but there *are* people who simply love this slummy togetherness—a fact that Sierra Clubbers sometimes forget or find hard to believe. By all means, let us create some *al fresco* slums for the people —but not in the likes of Yosemite Valley, which is too good for this purpose. But there will be little loss if some of the less attractive forest areas are turned into outdoor slums to relieve the pressure on the really good areas. We must have lakes that fairly pollute with water skiers, in order that we may be able to set aside other lakes for quiet canoeing. At the terminus of six-lane highways we must have beaches that fairly writhe with oily bodies and vibrate to a steady cacaphony of transistor radios—in order to maintain other beaches, difficult of access, on which we forbid all noise makers.

The qualities we seek in wilderness can be achieved only by adopting a policy of variety in management, and selling the concept of merit as the ticket for entrance to the most restricted areas.

The idea of wilderness is a difficult one, but it is precisely because it is difficult that clarifying it is valuable. In discovering how to justify a restricted good to a growing nation of 200 million people we find a formula that extends beyond wilderness to a whole spectrum of recreational activities in the national commons. The solution of this difficult case erects a framework into which other cases can be easily fitted.

The Fate Of Wildlife

Extinction is the rule. Species die out naturally through change over time or by failure to adapt. Or they are killed off by men, who hunt, change habitats and introduce predators, competitors and diseases. The readings in this group are concerned exclusively with extinction through the agency of man. Fisher, Simpson and Vincent[1] have estimated that from 70 to 80 percent of extinctions and significant population declines are due to man. What is especially alarming is that the great majority of these extinctions or declines have occurred since 1600, the beginning of the age of colonization. As men more densely crowd the globe, the figures for many species' life spans will undoubtedly continue to plunge.

Fisher et al. have estimated (from fossil records) the average life of a bird species to be two million years. The average duration of a mammal species is something over 6,000,000 years. Island populations evolve faster and become extinct faster than mainland populations. In a shocking island example from the West Indies, before colonization by man, a bird species lasted about 180,000 years. After aboriginal man appeared, this number plummeted to 30,000 years. The figure dropped to 12,000 when the European colonizers came on the scene.

Animals from the Amazon Basin   45

PAUL GREGORY HELTNE

History shows that precisely the resources and species thought to be inexhaustible are those in greatest danger of misuse and extinction. Laymen and scientists alike generally consider the flow of products from the "green sea" of the Amazon Basin to be limitless. It is not.

From 19 Sept.—12 Oct. 1966, I explored the forests near the Peruvian towns of Pebas, Santa Clara, Iquitos, and Pucallpa in order to survey the area for the study of primates. I flew over or boated through the intervening miles. Wherever I inquired, army officers, missionaries, and natives insisted that animals and good forest could be found *"en el centro"* (meaning directly away from the major waterway in the area). However, after half-day treks into forests of a type in which experience led me to expect many animals, I found none, even though I had been previously assured that I was in a "good" area. The sounds of the forests where I walked were chiefly those of insects. Visible were small birds, small lizards, and colorful tree frogs, joined only occasionally by a bird of medium size. Not once

---

1. *Wildlife in Danger.* James Fisher, Noel Simpson, Jack Vincent, and members and correspondents of the Survival Service Commission of the International Union for Conservation of Nature and Natural Resources. New York: Viking, 1969.

did I see any mammals or any large birds or reptiles. The usually common armadillo trails were extremely rare; feces or signs of feeding or resting were extremely scattered, and no nests were spotted. A colleague who has worked the Amazon from the Colombian border into Brazil and another who has worked the headwaters of the Pachitea River confirm these observations.

Wherever land is high enough to permit farming, slash-and-burn agriculture degrades the soil, completing the depredation of the forests which was begun by lumbering. In places the destructive trend has progressed to an "anticlimax" of pastureland. The second-growth forests, soon to be recut in their turn, are of poor quality and produce mainly wind—dispersed seeds. These are probably poor or inefficient food sources and can support little animal life in comparison with the original forests, though it is true that in slashed areas the collapse of the vertical stratification contributes to the abundance of a few species. Losses of forests to lumbering and farming, and animals to hunting practices are inevitable corollaries of the burgeoning populations along the river. (Not only dried monkeys but also fresh rat-sized rodents are for sale in the open meat market in Iquitos.) Road building will soon send colonizers into frontier areas which are now inaccessible.

However, the fur and live animal export markets threaten wildlife over a wider range. Demand always exceeds the fur traders' supply, though tens of thousands of skins are shipped from Iquitos every year. Select species such as tapir, peccary, ocelot, and jaguar are being severely depleted over truly vast regions because of the desirability of their hides. All animals must be sought further and further into the forests each year. The trends set in motion by agriculture and the fur trade are compounded by exportation. Many animal exporters are unable to fill their huge orders—mostly from the U.S.—and mainly for experimental animals. The methods of hunting and capture are those most devastating to the breeding populations. My experiences lead me to conclude that through human intervention many species' ranges are being truncated, perhaps irreversibly, over large areas.

Editor's Footnote To Letter

In August, 1968, a bill was passed (HR-11618) to prohibit any species threatened with extinction from being imported unless it is to be used for educational and scientific purposes. Many pet shop owners objected to the law as it would hurt business.

46   Whales: Decline Continues Despite Limitations On Catch

JOHN WALSH

Whaling as an industry has gone past the point of diminishing returns. As for the whales themselves, conservationists say their very survival is threatened. In the case of the largest whale of all, the great blue whale, some observers feel it may be too late now for that leviathan no matter what is done.

Since World War II, whalers have gone about their work with a growing effidience that is putting them out of business. So grim are the statistics of the industry that only three nations—Japan, Norway, and the Soviet Union—still engage in pelagic whaling, that is, whaling from ocean-going ships.

Hope for the whales lies mainly in the efforts of the International Whaling Commission, which was established in 1946. Fifteen nations now belong to the commission, including the principal whaling nations, but the organization is an entirely voluntary one, and resistance to putting into effect an international inspection system on whale catches has contributed as much as anything to pessimism about the future of the whales.

Signs of the situation can be read in the decline of the "yield" and reduction in Antartic whaling fleets in recent years. In the 1964-65 whaling season (December to April) there were 15 whaling expeditions to the Antarctic. In 1966-67 there were nine expeditions (four Japanese, three Russian, and two Norwegian). The catch last season was four blue whales, 2893 fin whales, and 12,893 of the smaller sei whales, or the equivalent by IWC reckoning of 3511 blue whale units (a blue whale unit equals two and a half humpback whales, two fin whales, or six sei whales). Some 4960 sperm whales were also reported caught in the Antarctic. The year before, when there were ten expeditions to the Antarctic whaling grounds, an equivalent of 4089 whale units were caught, 578 more than last season.

The best-known work of the IWC has been the setting of catch limits for the Antarctic. A recommendation on safe catch limits is given each year to the commission by its scientific committee made up mainly of scientists drawn from the fisheries' ministries of the commission's member countries. This year the committee recommended a catch limit of between 3100 and 3600 blue whale units. At its annual meeting held late in June in London, a limit of 3100 was put forward but was rejected as too low. Norway, which is faced with competition from the powerful Japanese and Russian whaling fleets and was unable to catch its full quota last year, asked for a limit of 3500. After hard bargaining, the limit for the coming season was put at 3500. (This, in effect, means fin and sei whales. Because the blue whale population has declined from an estimated 100,000 thirty years ago to about 1000 today, the blue whale is now completely protected.) In 1965-66 the catch limit was 4500 blue whale units; last season it was 3500.

The commission at its meeting also decided to extend the ban on killing humpback whales in the North Pacific area for a further three years and to extend to the whole of the Southern Hemisphere the ban on the taking of blue whales, thus making the ban complete.

Saving the whales would seem to require that catch limits be extended to all regions and to the activities of land stations. Outside Antarctica last season, 24 land stations and seven factory ships accounted for 29,536 whales and a total of 929,194 barrels of oil compared to 600,130 barrels from the 1966-67 catch in Antarctic waters. There is a fear, apparently well-grounded, that the reduction of quotas in the Antarctic will drive whalers to heighten the attack on sperm whales outside Antarctic waters where female breeding stocks are found.

The obvious weakness of the IWC is that it depends on voluntary cooperation without sanction of international law. In recent years, the commission has been able to speak with greater certainty about whale stocks because of advances made in the study of whale population dynamics and because of the help of its own scientific committee and of a whale stock assessment group formed by the United Nations Food and Agricultural Organization. Concerning noncooperation from some nations that conduct whaling from shore stations and do not belong to the commission and concerning infractions by its members, the commission must speak softly since it carries no stick.

A perennial disappointment for the commission has been its failure to achieve a workable inspection system. In 1963, an agreement was reached on an international observer scheme which would have placed inspectors from other nations on whale-catching ships. The agreement was never implemented and ran out last year. Supervision of catches now depends on government inspectors who sail on their own country's vessels. This year a working group of the commission recommended that a system of regional inspection schemes should be initiated to provide for stationing of inspectors of one nation on factory ships or land stations of another. Work on the scheme, however, seems to be in abeyance.

The great difficulty for the commission is that the pelagic whaling nations are reluctant to see restrictions tightened further. The Japanese depend on the whale catch as an important source of food protein, and Japanese owners have a big unamortized investment in their commercial whaling fleet. The Soviet Union, with its formidable state-owned whaling fleet, might be more amenable to mothballing part of the fleet during a period of low-catch limitation, set to allow whale stocks to recover. But the Soviets, who have worked on a lower national quota than the Japanese, have been pushing for a bigger share for themselves of whatever total is being taken.

The IWC is explicitly barred from setting national quotas. These are set by the pelagic whaling nations on the basis of the IWC total catch limit, and each year it seems to get harder. The three interested parties met in London after the recent IWC meeting to try to work out shares, but failed to agree.

What almost everyone, from the pelagic whaling nations and elsewhere, does agree on is that the writing is on the wall for the whales. Conservation principles and long-run economic interests both dictate that lower kill quotas be set to raise substainable yields in the long run. But logic and sentiment seem to need the support of workable law.

47   The End Of Whale Oil Soap

RALPH TAYLOR

For over a century, Caswell-Massey has been making superb soaps from a specially prepared extract of whale oil—soaps unrivaled for richness, unmatched for the sheer luxury of their lather. Today, the demand for Caswell-Massey Whale Oil Soaps has never been greater. And it is precisely when these leviathans of lather are at their peak of popularity that we have decided to make no more. With this public notice, we are ceasing production of Caswell-Massey Whale Oil Extract Soaps. What prompts this unprecedented action on our part? The real fear that the whale, if unprotected, stands in mortal danger of extinction. And far be it from us, America's oldest chemists and perfumers, in any way to encourage the hunting down of these noble giants of the deep, not to precipitate their demise! Hopefully, by stopping the manufacture of Whale Oil Soaps, we may encourage others in commerce to follow our example and thus Save The Whale.

The Tortoise And The Jet   48

DAEL WOLFLE

The tortoise beat the hare. Can it also beat the jet? The racetrack is Aldabra, an uplifted coral atoll in the Indian Ocean, 260 miles north-west of Madagascar and 400 miles east of Africa. The tortoise is the giant land tortoise, and Aldabra is its only remaining home in the Indian Ocean. The jets are of the United States and British air forces, which want to develop Aldabra for military use.

Obscure and almost uninhabited, Aldabra has a rich and unique ecosystem. It is the breeding place of the frigate bird for the entire Indian Ocean, and home of the last colony of flightless birds in the Indian Ocean. Of its 22 species of land birds, 12 species or subspecies are found nowhere else. About a quarter of its species of invertebrates are believed to be found only on the island. Aldabra is a major breeding place of the increasingly rare edible green turtle and the hawksbill turtle. Of some 175 species of higher plants known on the island, 18 or more are unique. When still undisturbed, such islands provide ideal opportunities to study evolutionary processes. Aldabra is the ecologically richer of the last two nearly undisturbed uplifted coral atolls in the world. Raymond Fosberg, of the National Academy of Sciences staff, calls the island "scientifically, the most important area of its size remaining in that part of the world." The Royal Society is sending an expedition there in August [1967] and would like to establish a small, permanent research station.

The air forces, however, need an airfield in that region and consider other islands much less satisfactory. The Secretary said that, if the decision is made to go ahead with military development, "our object . . . would be to make sure that changes in the ecosystem of the island are kept to a minimum."

But it is doubtful that there can be dual use. The atoll is too small. Road, harbor, causeway, and other construction would bring major physical alterations and connect the now separated islands of the atoll. The larger birds would be a hazard to aircraft, and some species would probably have to be exterminated. The home of the giant land tortoise is precisely the best part of the island for airfield construction. The suggestion that the airfield be surrounded by a wall seems unsatisfactory. A wall could exclude the tortoise, the flightless birds, and some other animals, but could not contain their imported enemies. Nor is temporary development and use a satisfactory compromise; once a species is destroyed, or an environment drastically invaded, there is no return to the original state. The current program to study what little remains of native Hawaiian plant and animal life is evidence of the need to study island ecologies before invasion brings ecological chaos.

Will the jet replace the tortoise on Aldabra? Perhaps. Military needs rightfully have high priority, and man has powerful weapons. He can win over tortoises, passenger pigeons, the blue whale, the Great Auk, the Moa, and other animals, and he can win most easily in the fragile ecology of a small island. The decision between the tortoise and the jet will be a governmental and a political one. The jet can win, but the more virgin areas we destroy, the more we impoverish our natural heritage. British and American government councils must weigh this fact in deciding whether to build on Aldabra or elsewhere.

49   Loss Of Wild Genetic Stocks

KENNETH S. NORRIS

Naturalists are growing increasingly aware that to let any species become extinct is a deeply serious error. The mere presumption of humans obliterating other species is reason enough to avoid this error, but a practical reason also exists for saving species. Each organism contains within it a genetic code that has been buffeted, altered, and molded through long geologic time, fitting that organism to the subtle and varied complex of environmental stresses imposed by nature. Each organism is thus a magnificently intricate response system whose subsystems and structures mesh together for survival. Each is a marvel of adaptation.

Modern genetics has revealed so much of the living blueprint in recent years that one may predict with some confidence that our means for altering the genetic constitutions of our domestic animals and plants may increase manyfold in the coming years. The raw materials will most likely be these natural systems, tested and approved by nature. Already we often return to wild plants or animals for genetic materials to diversify and strengthen our in-bred food stocks. Genetic modification will probably become a much more sophisticated applied science, placing great power in human hands, and we will need nature as its basis. The use of such a "gene bank" will likely extend far beyond application to our present domestic animals and plants, to subtle use in bringing many organisms, now useless from the human standpoint, under our control. Crops may one day thrive on salt flats or on barren desert slopes as a result.

An Example of Conservation Controversy

The two letters that follow appeared after Stone and Vasey (authors of second letter) outlined in an article in Science *why fire and flood were necessary to maintain alluvial forest redwoods. The first letter was written by a conservationist with the best of intentions.*

The conservationist will likely meet less resistance from vested interest groups in the seventies than he did in the fifties. Nevertheless, controversy will occur even when informed citizens with the same major objectives get together. Reading 50 illustrates a typical example of a controversy between two groups wearing white hats. Just because the nation appears to be rapidly mobilized to save the environment does not mean the problems will be easily solved. In some respects, ecologists would again welcome the days of black and white hats. What does one do when all hats are white?

Alluvial-Flat Redwoods: Impact of Flood Control **50**

BESTOR ROBINSON

In the article "Preservation of coast redwood on alluvial flats" Stone and Vasey have done a splendid job of summarizing the growth characteristics of the coast redwood and describing the effect of fire and silt deposition in eliminating competing forest species. They conclude that the survival of the giant redwood groves is threatened by the proposal construction of flood control dams unless man employs such tools as herbicides, fire, and chainsaws as a substitute for floods and resultant siltation.

Whether any of these tools should be used for park or forest improvement is beside the point. The facts do not support the conclusion that floods and siltation are necessary for the survival of these magnificent redwood groves in the Eel River basin.

Since minor differences in soil, exposure, and precipitation often result in major variations in the species composition of a forest, I will confine my comments to the redwood forests of the Eel River basin.

First, it should be noted that large or "giant" redwoods, that is, over 150 cm in diameter at breast height, are not confined to the alluvial flats that are subject to flood and silt deposit. They are found in almost solid strands in this basin wherever the following conditions coexist:

1. Adequate soil depth for nutrition and prevention of windthrow.

2. Benches, flats, and slopes sufficiently moderate to prevent soil creep or excessive erosion.

3. Adequate summer moisture to substitute for this region's deficient rainfall. This substitute moisture is provided by either moderate depth of water table (alluvial flats), underground seepage from higher slopes, or condensation of ocean summer fogs. Most of these groves and forests are above maximum flood level and many of them show no evidence of fire scar or fire-blackened bark.

The survival vigor of the solid stands of redwood is based on the fact that although fire and siltation may help, neither of these agents is necessary.

The redwood, given proper growing conditions as previously outlined, has weapons and competitive advantages that enable it to become a climax species as against its competitors in this region—Douglas fir, tan oak, and bay. (Grand fir will not be discussed since it is not a major competitive species in the Eel River basin.)

The bay tree is slow of growth and only partially shade-tolerant. Even when given an equal start on cleared land, it is, in a few decades, shaded out by the redwood and reduced to the status of a scattered understory of weak growth.

The tan oak, like the bay tree, cannot compete with the redwood in height. Although it sprouts from the stump after a fire and is vigorous in reproduction, it has a short life on sites suitable for redwood, and usually succumbs to heart rot. It does, however, compete vigorously with the redwood for a longer period than the bay tree.

The Douglas fir, if sprouted on cleared land at the same time as the redwood, will live to maturity as a large competing tree, finally yielding to the redwood because of its shorter lifespan. But in an established redwood forest, Douglas fir, because of low shade-tolerance plus vigorous root competition by the redwood, seldom succeeds in reaching the region of sunlight.

It should also be noted that, in a dense climax forest of redwood, the mat of redwood roots in the top 15 cm of soil deprives all seedlings of moisture sufficient to survive the first summer. Floods and resulting silt deposits on alluvial flats do eliminate most of the tan oak and Douglas fir. This favorable factor in the continued survival of mature redwoods is more than outweighed by the three undesirable effects of flooding:

1. The silt deposit produces a new seed bed without a surface mat of redwood roots. For several years, depending on the depth of silt, this deposit is free of competition from redwood roots and permits competing trees to survive beyond the critical initial years.

2. The physical undermining and toppling of several thousand large trees such as occurred during the 1955 and 1964 floods are an intolerable loss.

3. The power of streams to move boulders and large cobbles increases exponentially with the volume of the flow. The Eel River bed in many places was raised

a meter or more as a result of these recent floods; the raised bed was normally confined to gravel beds adjacent to the alluvial-redwood flats. This resulted in the raising of the water table and the death of many mature redwoods from what is locally known as "sour root."

If the facts and conclusions stated above are sound, there is only one answer to the basic question. The construction of flood control dams on the Eel River and its tributaries would aid in the preservation of the giant redwood groves on the adjacent alluvial flats.

EDWARD C. STONE
RICHARD B. VASEY

The greatest threat to the alluvial-flat redwoods may, in the long run, turn out to be the lay conservationists. This is ironical because they were largely responsible for getting these redwoods placed under park protection in the first place. Unfortunately, however, they have failed to fully appreciate the dynamic character of the ecosystem involved. They have focused their attention on preserving the trees now standing, ignoring the rest of the ecosystem which was responsible for these redwoods being present and upon which their replacements must depend. Protection from man, fires, and floods has been their goal. They have attached little importance to the fact that fires and floods were critical elements in the system under which the alluvial-flat redwoods developed and have actively opposed any man-generated substitutes.

It is essentially from this position that Bestor Robinson writes today. For 31 years as a director of the Sierra Club and an active conservationist, he is protection-oriented and is a strong advocate of flood control because he wants to keep the alluvial-flat redwoods from being washed away. He has dismissed as insignificant the impact such action might have on the functioning of the alluvial-flat ecosystem of which these redwoods are only part. The crux of his argument is that, because there are big trees on the slopes and benches where flooding does not occur, siltation per se is not necessary in order for the redwood to maintain its competitive position on the alluvial flats; he even goes so far as to suggest that siltation, by creating a competition-free seedbed, aids the survival of competing species and is therefore undesirable. Apparently, he is unaware that he cannot readily extrapolate from one ecosystem to another.

We are fully aware that nearly pure stands of large redwoods exist off the alluvial flats. But the ecology that has contributed to their development is not the same as that which has contributed to the development of the alluvial-flat redwoods. It was the ecology of the alluvial-flat redwood that we considered in the paper to which Robinson takes exception.

Robinson argues that because the potential competitors of redwood are short-lived they could not possibly replace redwood. Obviously he is not familiar with the facts. In the absence of floods and fires, seedlings and saplings of bay, tan oak, and grand fir will actively maintain a suppressed understory on the alluvial flats. Only an opening in the canopy is needed for these species to develop into full-fledged competitors. Thus when a redwood falls—as some do each year —these waiting competitors are on hand ready to take its place. Not always will there be a redwood seedling in the right place at the right time to compete for space when an opening occurs. It is in this way that the alluvial-flat redwoods will eventually be replaced with a mixture of bay, tan oak, and grand fir if flooding and fire are removed from the ecosystem and man fails to actively intervene. It is unimportant how big or for how long redwood can grow when once established on the alluvial flats. The important fact is that periodically a redwood tree falls and there are competing species ready to take its place.

All the evidence we have been able to collect to date suggests that time is running out for the alluvial-flat redwoods and that flood control could be the final blow unless man actively intervenes with herbicides, the ax, or the chainsaw. Strong support behind a program of active intervention is urgently needed. Our hope is that it will not be too late in coming.

How Simple Answers Backfire

To know what is ecologically correct behavior often depends on a complex weighting of an ensemble of factors. We are now discovering that many time-honored ecological dicta are inadequate, if not downright erroneous. This is illustrated in the next selection. Smokey the Bear has taught us that fire in the wilderness is bad. Is it always?

Forest Fires: Suppression Policy Has Its Ecological Drawbacks

51

MARK OBERLE

In California and the Southwest, tree-ring studies of ponderosa pine forests have indicated that ground fires—small blazes that spread through the turf and underbrush but not the treetops—swept through these areas at least once in a decade during prehistoric times. By preventing even these moderate ground fires from periodically clearing accumulations of litter from the forest floor, the policy of total fire suppression has made some woods easy targets for disastrous fires. In primitive times, periodic fires also prevented an understory of competing shade-resistant trees from developing, and thus gave the ponderosa forests an open, park-like appearance. But, in the absence of fire, understory trees have crowded the forest and weakened the taller pines through competition, Harold H. Biswell, professor of forestry at the University of California, Berkeley, told *Science*. Crown fires—the huge conflagrations that spread through the forest canopy—rarely occurred in primitive California forests, Biswell added, but this understory of trees has formed a new intermediate level of fuel between the canopy and the forest floor that encourages crown fires.

One biologist has advanced the theory that fire-exclusion policies may be a factor in the near-extinction of the California condor. Raymond B. Cowles of the University of California at Santa Barbara has suggested that the condor needs relatively long runways for takeoffs, and clearings on ridgetops for feeding. With the prevention of fires, Cowles said, dense plant growth has reclaimed these clearings and thus has narrowed the condor's ecological niche.

In Alaska, the permafrost layer complicates the relationship of fire to wildlife populations. "Fire has been an important part of the ecology of interior Alaska," said David R. Klein, leader of the Cooperative Wildlife Research Unit at the University of Alaska. When fire is excluded from many lowland sites, an insulating carpet of moss tends to accumulate and raise the permafrost level, he said, and permafrost close to the surface encourages the growth of black spruce, a low-growing species with little timber or food value. "These areas are veritable deserts," Klein said. Bear, deer, moose, and other animals depend on lightning fires to maintain a constant cycle of vegetation types for food and cover.

Harold Biswell of the University of California, Berkeley, argues that underbrush and leaf litter in ponderosa pine and some mixed conifer forests should be removed much as they were before white man came—by means of small ground fires every few years. When Biswell advanced this forest-management proposal, in the early 1950's, the idea received so much flak from government foresters that he claims he was forced to do his research on private land. His burning technique involves setting a fire on a hilltop at a time of year when only the upper layer of pine needles is dry enough to burn, and letting the fire creep down the slope under close supervision. The technique involves extensive initial cutting of underbrush in forests with thick undergrowth, and heavy investments of manpower to control the low-intensity blaze, but Biswell claims that the investment pays off in fire hazard reduction.

In 1962, a crown fire whipped through a forest adjacent to his prescribed burning plot at Hobergs, California, but as soon as the fire reached his land it dropped out of the tree-tops and crept through the forest floor, where it was easily controlled. His prescribed burning causes minimal soil erosion and has no adverse effects on long-term soil fertility or water-holding ability, Biswell says. He estimates that his technique may be applicable to 4 million acres in California alone.

"The public," said one administrator, "can't see why we allow a fire we set in November to burn when we'll jump in with a thousand men to put out a wildfire that starts in June."

All the Way to the End

Compare the position argued for in Peugnet's letter (reading 52) with the attitude expressed in Garrett Hardin's "We Must Earn Again for Ourselves What We Have Inherited," (reading 44). How valid is it to maintain virgin wilderness if "restoration" to its original state can occur? This raises the heated issue of how important it is to be able to say, "This has not been altered by technological man." Is it just as satisfactory to be able to say, "This has been altered by technological man, but the restoration has likely made it the way it was before man"?

Will the oceans perish from good intentions? Paul Ehrlich's article "Eco-catastrophe!" (reading 53) suggests how the oceans may die. A valuable exercise would be to determine how many readings in this book contain information alluded to in Ehrlich's article.

Flyspeck on Glacier Peak   52

AMÉDEÉ A. PEUGNET

The 450-acre site of the Kennecott mine is a mere flyspeck in the 458,000-acre Glacier Peak area. The region "which is largely inaccessible except by helicopter or by foot" would be made relatively accessible to the public, with a minimum expenditure of public funds, by the road which Kennecott would have to build. Also, without cost to the public, a reasonably large and potentially beautiful lake would result from the operation. A foregone conclusion cannot be made that the tailings would either pollute streams or destroy fish. It should be obvious that the excavation from which both ore and waste are derived could eventually contain the tailings. Any deleterious effect that the proposed pit might have on the wilderness area would be of short duration, especially if the rather common practice of "restoration" were put into effect, and would be more that offset by the lake created. One has only to visit the numerous abandoned mining areas in the Americas to be impressed by the rapidity with which Nature reclaims her own, even without human efforts. This, true even in arid areas, is much more rapid in areas of reasonable amounts of rainfall. On completion of mining and restoration, there would exist in this huge wilderness an ideal, ready-made, site on which appropriate authority could erect facilities for public enjoyment, and from which to exercise safety, fire protection, and other functions required in large public recreation areas. Roads, piped water, and sanitary facilities would already exist, together with a lake sufficiently large to provide recreation to many, but not so large that it could not be adequately policed for safety.

Since real "national wealth" consists of the industry of its people and its natural resources, it would be a serious error to deprive a nation of possibly a not inconsiderable portion of its natural wealth. It should not be forgotten that mining claims of the kind in question are, to a large extent, won by aching feet, backs, and heads; not infrequently at the cost of life. The fact that our country is largely self-sufficient in many of its mineral requirements is, to no small extent, a result of the lowly, unsung, prospector. The very existence of 91,000 mining claims, of any nature or worth, is mute testimony to the existence of a large highly mineralized area. The closing off of huge potential areas of mineral wealth augurs ill with respect to our deficiencies in gold, silver, and other minerals. Let us not hastily write off large portions of our national inheritance.

53   Eco-catastrophe!

PAUL R. EHRLICH

The end of the ocean came late in the summer of 1979, and it came even more rapidly than the biologists had expected. There had been signs for more than a decade, commencing with the discovery in 1968 that DDT slows down photosynthesis in marine plant life. It was announced in a short paper in the technical journal, *Science,* but to ecologists it smacked of doomsday. They knew that all life in the sea depends on photosynthesis, the chemical process by which green plants bind the sun's energy and make it available to living things. And they knew that DDT and similar chlorinated hydrocarbons had polluted the entire surface of the earth, including the sea.

But that was only the first of many signs. There had been the final gasp of the whaling industry in 1973, and the end of the Peruvian anchovy fishery in 1975. Indeed, a score of other fisheries had disappeared quietly from over—exploitation and various eco-catastrophes by 1977. The term "eco-catastrophe" was coined by a California ecologist in 1969 to describe the most spectacular of man's attacks on the systems which sustain his life. He drew his inspiration from the Santa Barbara offshore oil disaster of that year, and from the news which spread among naturalists that virtually all of the Golden State's seashore bird life was doomed because of chlorinated hydrocarbon interference with its reproduction. Eco-catastrophes in the sea became increasingly common in the early 1970's. Mysterious "blooms" of previously rare microorganisms began to appear in offshore waters.

Red tides—killer outbreaks of a minute single-celled plate—returned to the Florida Gulf coast and were sometimes accompanied by tides of other exotic hues. It was clear by 1975 that the entire ecology of the ocean was changing. A few types of phytoplankton were becoming resistant to chlorinated hydrocarbons and were gaining the upper hand. Changes in the phytoplankton community led inevitably to changes in the community of zooplankton, the tiny animals which eat the phytoplankton. These changes were passed on up the chains of life in the ocean to the herring, plaice, cod and tuna. As the diversity of life in the ocean diminished, its stability also decreased.

Other changes had taken place by 1975. Most ocean fishes that returned to fresh water to breed, like the salmon, had become extinct, their breeding streams so dammed up and polluted that their powerful homing instinct only resulted in suicide. Many fishes and shellfishes that bred in restricted areas along the coasts followed them as onshore pollution escalated.

By 1977 the annual yield of fish from the sea was down to 30 million metric tons, less than one-half the per capita catch of a decade earlier. This helped malnutrition to escalate sharply in a world where an estimated 50 million people per year were already dying of starvation. The United Nations attempted to get all chlorinated hydrocarbon insecticides banned on a worldwide basis, but the move was defeated by the United States. This opposition was generated primarily by the American petrochemical industry, operating hand in glove with its subsidiary, the United States Department of Agriculture. Together they persuaded the government to oppose the U.N. move—which was not difficult since most Americans believed that Russia and China were more in need of fish products than was the United States. The United Nations also attempted to get fishing nations to adopt strict and enforced catch limits to preserve dwindling stocks. This move was blocked by Russia, who, with the most modern electronic equipment, was in the best position to glean what was left in the sea. It was, curiously, on the very day in 1977 when the Soviet Union announced its refusal that another ominous article appeared in *Science*. It announced that incident solar radiation had been so reduced by a worldwide air pollution that serious effects on the world's vegetation could be expected.

Apparently it was a combination of ecosystem destabilization, sunlight reduction, and a rapid escalation in chlorinated hydrocarbon pollution from massive Thanodrin applications which triggered the ultimate castastrophe. Seventeen huge Soviet-financed Thanodrin plants were operating in underdeveloped countries by 1978. They had been part of a massive Russian "aid offensive" designed to fill the gap caused by the collapse of America's ballyhooed "Green Revolution".

It became apparent in the early '70s that the "Green Revolution" was more talk than substance. Distribution of high yield "miracle" grain seeds had caused temporary local spurts in agricultural production. Simultaneously, excellent weather had produced record harvests. The combination permitted bureaucrats, especially in the United States Department of Agriculture and the Agency for International Development (AID), to reverse their previous pessimism and indulge in an outburst of optimistic propaganda about staving off famine. They raved about the approaching transformation of agriculture in the underdeveloped countries (UDCs). The reason for the propaganda reversal was never made clear. Most historians agree that a combination of utter ignorance of ecology, a desire to justify past errors, and pressure from agroindustry (which was eager to sell pesticides, fertilizers, and farm machinery to the UDCs and agencies helping the UDCs) was behind the campaign. Whatever the motivation, the results were clear. Many concerned people, lacking the expertise to see through the Green Revolution drivel, relaxed. The population-food crisis was "solved."

But reality was not long in showing itself. Local famine persisted in northern India even after good weather brought an end to the ghastly Bihar famine of the mid-'60s. East Pakistan was next, followed by a resurgence of general famine in northern India. Other foci of famine rapidly developed in Indonesia, the Philippines, Malawi, the Congo, Egypt, Columbia, Ecuador, Honduras, the Dominican Republic, and Mexico.

Everywhere hard realities destroyed the illusion of the Green Revolution. Yields dropped as the progressive farmers who had first accepted the new seeds found that their higher yields brought lower prices—effective demand (hunger plus cash) was not sufficient in poor countries to keep prices up. Less progressive farmers, observing this, refused to make the extra effort required to cultivate the "miracle" grains. Transport systems proved inadequate to bring the necessary fertilizer to the fields where the new and extremely fertilizer-sensitive grains were being grown. The same systems were also inadequate to move produce to markets. Fertilizer plants were not built fast enough, and most of the underdeveloped countries could not scrape together funds to purchase supplies, even on concessional terms. Finally, the inevitable happened, and pests began to reduce yields in even the most carefully cultivated fields. Among the first were the famous "miracle rats" which invaded Philippine "miracle rice" fields early in 1969. They were quickly followed by many insects and viruses, thriving on the relatively pest-susceptible new grains, encouraged by the vast and dense plantings, and rapidly acquiring resistance to the chemicals used against them. As chaos spread until even the most obtuse agriculturists and economists realized that the Green Revolution had turned brown, the Russians stepped in.

In retrospect it seems incredible that the Russians, with the American mistakes known to them, could launch an even more incompetent program of aid to the underdeveloped world. Indeed, in the early 1970's there were cynics in the United States who claimed that outdoing the stupidity of American foreign aid would be physically impossible. Those critics were, however, obviously unaware that the Russians had been busily destroying their own environment for many years. The virtual disappearance of sturgeon from Russian rivers caused a great shortage of caviar by 1970. A standard joke among Russian scientists at that time was that they had created an artificial caviar which was indistinguishable from the real thing—except by taste. At any rate the Soviet Union, observing with interest the progressive deterioration of relations between the UDCs and the United States, came up with a solution. It had recently developed what it claimed was the ideal insecticide, a highly lethal chlorinated hydrocarbon complexed with a special agent for penetrating the external skeletal armor of insects. Announcing that the new pesticide, called Thanodrin, would truly produce a Green Revolution, the Soviets entered into negotiations with various UDCs for the construction of massive Thanodrin factories. The USSR would bear all the costs; all it wanted in return were certain trade and military concessions.

It is interesting now, with the perspective of years, to examine in some detail the reasons why the UCDs welcomed the Thanodrin plan with such open arms. Government officials in these countries ignored the protests of their own scientists that Thanodrin would not solve the problems which plagued them. The governments now knew that the basic cause of their problems was overpopulation, and that these problems had been exacerbated by the dullness, daydreaming, and cupidity endemic to all governments. They knew that only population control and limited development aimed primarily at agriculture could have spared them the horrors they now faced. They knew it, but they were not about to admit it. How much easier it was simply to accuse the Americans of failing to give them proper aid; how much simpler to accept the Russian panacea.

And then there was the general worsening of relations between the United States and the UDCs. Many things had contributed to this. The situation in America in the first half of the 1970's deserves our close scrutiny. Being more dependent on imports for raw materials than the Soviet Union, the United States had, in the early 1970's, adopted more and more heavy-handed policies in order to insure continuing supplies. Military adventures in Asia and Latin America had further lessened the international credibility of the United States as a great defender of freedom—an image which had begun to deteriorate rapidly during the pointless and fruitless Viet-Nam conflict. At home, acceptance of the carefully manufactured image lessened dramatically, as even the more romantic and chauvinistic citizens began to understand the role of the military and the industrial system in what John Kenneth Galbraith had aptly named "The New Industrial State."

At home in the USA the early '70s were traumatic times. Racial violence grew and the habitability of the cities diminished, as nothing substantial was done to ameliorate either racial inequities or urban blight. Welfare rolls grew as automation and general technological progress forced more and more people into the category of "unemployable." Simultaneously a taxpayers' revolt occurred. Although there was not enough money to build the schools, roads, water systems, sewage systems, jails, hospitals, urban transit lines, and all the other amenities needed to support a burgeoning population, Americans refused to tax themselves more heavily. Starting in Youngstown, Ohio in 1969 and followed closely by Richmond, California, community after community was forced to close its schools or curtail educational operations for lack of funds. Water supplies, already marginal in quality and quantity in many places by 1970, deteriorated quickly. Water rationing occurred in 1723 municipalities in the summer of 1974, and hepatitis and epidemic dysentery rates climbed about 500 percent between 1970-1974.

Air pollution continued to be the most obvious manifestation of environmental deterioration. It was, by 1972, quite literally in the eyes of all Americans. The year 1973 saw not only the New York and Los Angeles smog disasters, but also the publication of the Surgeon General's massive report on air pollution and health. The public had been partially prepared for the worst by the publicity given to the U.N. pollution conference held in 1972. Deaths in the late '60s caused by smog were well known to scientists, but the public had ignored them because they mostly involved the early demise of the old and sick rather than people dropping dead on the freeways. But suddenly our citizens were faced with nearly 200,000 corpses and massive documentation that they could be the next to die from respiratory disease. They were not ready for that scale of disaster. After all, the U.N. conference had not predicted that accumulated air pollution would make the planet uninhabitable until almost 1990. The population was terrorized as TV screens became filled with scenes of horror from the disaster areas. Especially vivid was NBC's coverage of hundreds of unattended people choking out their lives outside of New York's hospitals. Terms like nitrogen oxide, acute bronchitis and cardiac arrest began to have real meaning for most Americans.

The ultimate horror was the announcement that chlorinated hydrocarbons were now a major constituent of air pollution in all American cities. Autopsies of smog disaster victims revealed an average chlorinated hydrocarbon load in fatty tissue equivalent to 26 parts per million of DDT. In October, 1973, the Department of Health, Education and Welfare announced studies which showed unequivocally that increasing death rates from hypertension, cirrhosis of the liver, liver cancer and a series of other diseases had resulted from the chlorinated hydrocarbon load. They estimated that Americans born since 1946 (when DDT usage began) now had a life expectancy of only 49 years, and predicted that if current patterns continued, this expectancy would reach 42 years by 1980, when it might level out. Plunging insurance stocks triggered a stock market panic. The president of Velsicol, Inc., a major pesticide producer, went on television to "publicly eat a teaspoonful of DDT" (it was really powdered milk) and announce that HEW had been infiltrated by Communists. Other giants of the petrochemical industry, attempting to dispute the indisputable evidence, launched a massive pressure campaign on Congress to force HEW to "get out of agriculture's business." They were aided by the agro-chemical journals, which had decades of experience in misleading the public about the benefits and dangers of pesticides. But by now the public realized that is had been duped. The Nobel Prize for medicine and physiology was given to Drs. J.L. Radomski and W.B. Deichmann, who in the late 1960's had pioneered in the documentation of the long-term lethal effects of chlorinated hydrocarbons. A Presidential Commission with unimpeachable credentials directly accused the agrochemical complex of "condemning many millions of Americans to an early death." The year 1973 was the year in which Americans finally came to understand the direct threat to their existence posed by environmental deterioration.

And 1973 was also the year in which most people finally comprehended the indirect threat. Even the president of Union Oil Company and several other industrialists publicly stated their concern over the reduction of bird populations which had resulted from pollution by DDT and other chlorinated hydrocarbons. Insect populations boomed because they were resistant to most pesticides and had been freed, by the incompetent use of those pesticides, from most of their natural enemies. Rodents swarmed over crops, multiplying rapidly in the absence of predatory birds. The effect of pests on the wheat crop was especially disastrous in the summer of 1973, since that was also the year of the great drought. Most of us can remember the shock which greeted the announcement by atmospheric physicists that the shift of the jet stream which had caused the drought was probably permanent. It signalled the birth of the Midwestern desert. Man's air-polluting activities had by then caused gross changes in climatic patterns. The news, of course, played hell with commodity and stock markets. Food prices skyrocketed, as savings were poured into hoarded canned goods. Official assurances that food supplies would remain ample fell on deaf ears, and even the government showed signs of nervousness when California migrant field workers went out on strike again in protest against the continued use of pesticides by growers. The strike burgeoned into farm burning and riots. The workers, calling themselves "The Walking Dead," demanded immediate compensation for their shortened lives, and crash research programs to attempt to lengthen them.

It was in the same speech in which President Edward Kennedy, after much delay, finally declared a national emergency and called out the National Guard to harvest California's crops, that the first mention of population control was made. Kennedy pointed out that the United States would no longer be able to offer any food aid to other nations and was likely to suffer food shortages herself. He suggested that, in view of the manifest failure of the Green Revolution, the only hope of the UDCs lay in population control. His statement, you will recall, created an uproar in the underveloped countries. Newspaper editorials accused the United States of wishing to prevent small countries from becoming large countries and thus threatening American hegemony. Politicians asserted that President Kennedy was a "creature of the giant drug combine" that wished to shove its pills down every woman's throat.

Among Americans, religious opposition to population control was very slight. Industry in general also backed the idea. Increasing poverty in the UDCs was both destroying markets and threatening supplies of raw materials. The seriousness of the raw material situation had been brought home during the Congressional Hard Resources hearings in 1971. The exposure of the ignorance of the cornucopian economists had been quite a spectacle—a spectacle brought into virtually every American's home in living color. Few would forget the distinguished geologist from the University of California who suggested that economists be legally required to learn at least the most elementary facts of geology. Fewer still would forget that an equally distinguished Harvard economist added that they might be required to learn some economics, too. The overall message was clear: America's resource situation was bad and bound to get worse. The hearings had led to a bill requiring the Departments of State, Interior, and Commerce to set up a joint resource procurement council with the express purpose of "insuring that proper consideration of American resource needs be an integral part of American foreign policy."

Suddenly the United States discovered that it had a national consensus: population control was the only possible salvation of the underdeveloped world.

But that same consensus led to heated debate. How could the UDCs be persuaded to limit their populations, and should not the United States lead the way by limiting its own? Members of the intellectual community wanted America to set an example. They pointed out that the United States was in the midst of a new baby boom: her birth rate, well over 20 per thousand per year, and her growth rate of one percent per annum were among the very highest of the developed countries. They detailed the deterioration of the American physical and psychic environments, the growing health threats, the impending food shortages, and the insufficiency of funds for desperately needed public works. They contended that the nation was clearly unable or unwilling to properly care for the people it already had. What possible reason could there be, they queried, for adding any more? Besides, who would listen to requests by the United States for population control when that nation did not control her own profligate reproduction?

Those who opposed population controls for the U.S. were equally vociferous. The military-industrial complex, with its all-too-human mixture of ignorance and avarice, still saw strength and prosperity in numbers. Baby food magnates, already worried by the growing nitrate pollution of their products, saw their market disappearing. Steel manufacturers saw a decrease in aggregate demand and slippage for that holy of holies, the Gross National Product. And military men saw, in the growing population-food-environment crisis, a serious threat to their carefully nurtured Cold War. In the end, of course, economic arguments held sway, and the "inalienable right of every American couple to determine the size of its family," a freedom invented for the occasion in the early '70s, was not compromised.

The population control bill, which was passed by Congress early in 1974, was quite a document, nevertheless. On the domestic front, it authorized an increase from 100 to 150 million dollars in funds for "family planning" activities. This was made possible by a general feeling in the country that the growing army on welfare needed family planning. But the gist of the bill was a series of measures designed to impress the need for population control on the UDCs. All American aid to countries with overpopulation problems was required by law to consist in part of population control assistance. In order to receive any assistance each nation was required not only to accept the population control aid, but also to match it according to a complex formula. "Overpopulation" itself was defined by a formula based on U.N. statistics, and the UDCs were required not only to accept aid, but also to show progress in reducing birth rates. Every five years the status of the aid program for each nation was to be re-evaluated.

The reaction to the announcement of this program dwarfed the response to President Kennedy's speech. A coalition of UDCs attempted to get the U.N. General Assembly to condemn the United States as a "genetic aggressor." Most damaging of all to the American cause was the famous "25 Indians and a dog" speech by Mr. Shankarnarayan, Indian Ambassador to the U.N. Shankarnarayan pointed out that for several decades the United States, with less than six percent of the people of the world had consumed roughly 50 percent of the raw materials used every year. He described vividly America's contribution to worldwide environmental deterioration, and he scathingly denounced the miserly record of

United States foreign aid as "unworthy of a fourth-rate power, let alone the most powerful nation on earth."

It was the climax of his speech, however, which most historians claim once and for all destroyed the image of the United States. Shankarnarayan informed the assembly that the average American family dog was fed more animal protein per week than the average Indian got in a month. "How do you justify taking fish from protein-starved Peruvians and feeding them to your animals?" he asked. "I contend," he concluded, "that the birth of an American baby is a greater disaster for the world than that of 25 Indian babies." When the applause had died away, Mr. Sorensen, the American representative, made a speech which said essentially that "other countries look after their own self-interest, too." When the vote came, the United States was condemned.

This condemnation set the tone of U.S.-UDC relations at the time the Russian Thanodrin proposal was made. The proposal seemed to offer the masses in the UDCs an opportunity to save themselves and humiliate the United States at the same time; and in human affairs, as we all know, biological realities could never interfere with such an opportunity. The scientists were silenced, the politicans said yes, the Thanodrin plants were built, and the results were what any beginning ecology student could have predicted. At first Thanodrin seemed to offer excellent control of many pests. True, there was a rash of human fatalities from improper use of the lethal chemical, but, as Russian technical advisors were prone to note, these were more than compensated for by increased yields. Thanodrin use skyrocketed throughout the underdeveloped world. The Mikoyan design group developed a dependable , cheap agricultural aircraft which the Soviets donated to the effort in large numbers. MIG sprayers became even more common in UDCs than MIG interceptors.

Then the troubles began. Insect strains with cuticles resistant to Thanodrin penetration began to appear. And as streams, rivers, fish culture ponds and onshore waters became rich in Thanodrin, more fisheries began to disappear. Bird populations were decimated. The sequence of events was standard for broadcast use of synthetic pesticide: Great success at first, followed by removal of natural enemies and development of resistance by the pest. Populations of crop-eating insects in areas treated with Thanodrin made steady comebacks and soon became more abundant than ever. Yields plunged, while farmers in their desperation increased the Thanodrin dose and shortened the time between treatments. Death from Thanodrin poisoning became common. The first violent incident occurred in the Canete Valley of Peru, where farmers had suffered a similar chlorinated hydrocarbon disaster in the mid—'50s. A Russian advisor serving as an agricultural pilot was assaulted and killed by a mob of enraged farmers in January, 1978. Trouble spread rapidly during 1978, especially after the word got out that two years earlier Russia herself had banned the use of Thanodrin at home because of its serious effects on ecological systems. Suddenly Russia, and not the United States, was the *bete noir* in the UDCs. "Thanodrin parties" became epidemic, with farmers, in their ignorance, dumping carloads of Thanodrin concentrate into the sea. Russian advisors fled, and four of the Thanodrin plants were leveled to the ground. Destruction of the plants in Rio and Calcutta led to hundreds of thousands of gallons of Thanodrin concentrate being dumped directly into the sea.

Mr. Shankarnarayan again rose to address the U.N., but this time it was Mr. Potemkin, representative of the Soviet Union, who was on the hot seat. Mr. Potemkin heard his nation described as the greatest mass killer of all time as Shankarnarayan predicted at least 30 million deaths from crop failures due to overdependence on Thanodrin. Russia was accused of "chemical aggression," and the General Assembly, after a weak reply by Potemkin, passed a vote of censure.

It was January, 1979, that huge blooms of a previously unknown variety of diatom were reported off the coast of Peru. The blooms were accompanied by a massive die-off of sea life and of the pathetic remainder of the birds which had once feasted on the anchovies of the area. Almost immediately another huge bloom was reported in the Indian ocean, centering around the Seychelles, and then a third in the South Atlantic off the African coast. Both of these were accompanied by spectacular die-offs of marine animals. Even more ominous were growing reports of fish and bird kills at ocean points where there were no spectacular blooms. Biologists were soon able to explain the phenomena: the diatom had evolved an enzyme which broke down Thanodrin; that enzyme also produced a breakdown product which interfered with the transmission of nerve impulses, and was therefore lethal to animals. Unfortunately, the biologists could suggest no way of repressing the poisonous diatom bloom in time. By September, 1979, all important animal life in the sea was extinct. Large areas of coastline had to be evacuated, as windrows of dead fish created a monumental stench.

But stench was the least of man's problems. Japan and China were faced with almost instant starvation from a total loss of the seafood on which they were so dependent. Both blamed Russia for their situation and demanded immediate mass shipments of food. Russia had none to send. On October 13, Chinese armies attacked Russia on a broad front. . . .

A pretty grim scenario. Unfortunately, we're a long way into it already. Everything mentioned as happening before 1970 has actually occurred; much of the rest is based on projections of trends already appearing. Evidence that pesticides' harmful long-term lethal effects on human beings has started to accumulate, and recently Robert Finch, Secretary of the Department of Health, Education and Welfare expressed his extreme apprehension about the pesticide situation. Simultaneously the petrochemical industry continues its unconscionable poison-peddling. For instance, Shell Chemical has been carrying on a high-pressure campaign to sell the insecticide Azodrin to farmers as a killer of cotton pests. They continue their program even though they know that Azodrin is not only ineffective, but often *increases* the pest density. They've covered themselves nicely in an advertisement which states, "Even if an overpowering migration (sic) develops, the flexibility of Azodrin lets you gain control fast. Just increase the dosage according to label recommendations." It's a great game—get people to apply the poison and kill the natural enemies of the pests. Then blame the increased pests on "migration" and sell even more pesticides!

Right now fisheries are being wiped out by over-exploitation, made easy by modern electronic equipment. The companies producing the equipment know this. They even boast in advertising that only their equipment will keep fishermen in business until the final kill. Profits must obviously be maximized in the short run. Indeed, Western society is in the process of completing the rape and murder of the planet for economic gain. And, sadly, most of the rest of the world is eager for the opportunity to emulate our behavior. But the underdeveloped peoples will be denied that opportunity—the days of plunder are drawing inexorably to a close.

Most of the people who are going to die in the greatest cataclysm in the history of man have already been born. More than three and a half billion people already populate our moribund globe, and about half of them are hungry. Some 10 to 20 million will starve to death *this year.* In spite of this, the population of the earth will increase by 70 million souls in 1969. For mankind has artificially lowered the death rate of the human population, while in general birth rates have remained high. With the input side of the population system in high gear and the output side slowed down, our fragile planet has filled with people at an incredible rate. It took several million years for the population to reach a total of two billion people in 1930, while a *second two billion will have been added by 1975!* By that time some experts feel that food shortages will have escalated the present level of world hunger and starvation into famines of unbelievable proportions. Other experts, more optimistic, think the ultimate food-population collision will not occur until the decade of the 1980's. Of course a more massive famine may be avoided if other events cause a prior rise in the human death rate.

Both worldwide plague and thermonuclear war are made more probable as population growth continues. These, along with famine, make up the trio of potential "death rate solutions" to the population problem—solutions in which the birth rate-death rate imbalance is redressed by a rise in the death rate rather than by a lowering of the birth rate. Make no mistake about it, *the imbalance will be redressed.* The shape of the population growth curve is one familiar to the biologist. It is the outbreak part of an outbreak-crash sequence. A population grows rapidly in the presence of abundant resources, finally runs out of food or some other necessity, and crashes to a low level or extinction. Man is not only running out of food, he is also destroying the life support systems of the Spaceship Earth. The situation was recently summarized very succinctly: "It is the top of the ninth inning. Man, always a threat at the plate, has been hitting Nature hard. It is important to remember, however, that NATURE BATS LAST."

Conflicts and Guidelines

Fundamental changes in the way of looking at the environment must occur before the public can develop an eco-conscience. An "attitude toward" the environment is necessary (reading 54), perhaps even an eco-religion. Legislation alone does not change people's minds, though it may provide a necessary impetus (especially if the legislation is enforced). Once an individual is convinced of a need for action and desires to convince others, some guidelines may be helpful (reading 55).

54   Four Conflicts in Conservation

CHARLES A. DAMBACH

Because the conflicts in conservation are many, of varying degrees of complexity and importance, and derive from diverse origins, it is necessary to sort them into some kinds of sets or groups so they can be better examined. There are a variety of ways in which to do this. I suggest dividing them into *four groups.* One concerns conflicts arising out of such cultural sources as historical antecedents, concepts of ownership and rights, religious and philosophical beliefs, the way in which emotions are affected, and the conservation related legends and myths which prevail. There are many examples. Historically, we have always been on the frontier of new lands, of new discoveries, which made available new resources. Even now there is the frontier of outer space. We are thus conditioned to an infinite and expanding resource base.

I. Deep in our religious beliefs is the prevailing concept that man was created to have dominion over the earth, that he can and should master nature. The first view runs counter to the idea of a finite limit to resources; the matter runs counter to the concept of man as a part of nature.

Edward Teller stated this view cogently when he observed: "It is true that conditions are wretched in many countries, but even where life is hard people are objecting not because they look back to a happier past but rather because they demand a better future which they know can be realized. Human fertility is undoubtedly great, but so far human ingenuity has proved greater. I suspect that ultimately the population of the earth will be limited not by any scarcity but rather by our ability to put up with each other."

In a similar vein, Thomas B. Nolan (1958) during a symposium conducted by the Resources for the Future organization said, "I believe that the prospect of impending shortages or unsuitable supplies will continue to inspire research and technical advances that will make it possible to resolve such problems well in advance of the doom we often are prone to foresee. We probably need to fear not the exhuastion of physical resources but the dangers of inadequate or belated utilization of our intellectual resources. . . ." It is beliefs such as these which support confidence in planned obsolescence and the defense of waste which are the antithesis of the advocation of prudent use of resources.

There is the basic and vigorously defended concept that each individual has a right to do what he wishes with resources reduced to possession, for instance, cutting into lumber the great oak that may have been a community landmark for a century or logging the redwoods that may otherwise be enjoyed indirectly by nonowners or vicariously by an apartment dweller thousands of miles away.

Elements of such basic beliefs are evident in many of the conservation controversies which exist. Unfortunately, they are not readily resolvable by adult education. An editor of a large city daily once set me straight on this subject after I had confronted him with what I believed was overwhelming evidence concerning a local conservation controversy. The editor's answer in the press and on the air to that evidence was to quote an old but unfortunately valid cliche that "a man convinced against his will is of the same opinion still." This could be amended to say a man convinced against his basic beliefs is really not convinced at all.

II. Another broad set of conservation conflicts are those based on different economic, social, and other self-interests of individuals and groups. These are more readily identified. Sometimes they are amenable to settlement by bargaining. They also represent, however, some of the more complex and difficult problems to resolve because of the great range of interests involved. Their resolution is often elusive due to inadequate means with which to assess related public values and the lack of mechanisms whereby the interests of indirect users can be properly evaluated. The cross currents of conflicts in this category are often strong if not violent. The conflicts which fit into this category are many, and need no elaboration. Senator Gaylord Nelson stated the situation well in speaking at the annual meeting of the National Wildlife Federation in 1965, when he said, "What we have done in this country is to develop a vast network of special-interests conservation. We have lost our broad vision of the public interests, and we have fallen to quarrelling over little pieces of it."

III. There is another group of conservation conflicts which emanates from a source more difficult to describe. These are conflicts generated by dissidents who exist in virtually every community. Often they are well-meaning individuals and groups. Unfortunately, however, there are many who seek personal recognition through exploiting otherwise readily resolvable conservation conflicts. I can perhaps best illustrate the nature of this source of conflict with a personal experience. I served for 5 years as the administrative head of the Division of Wildlife of the newly organized State of Ohio Department of Natural Resources, in the period 1950 to 1955. During that tour of duty, I arrived at the office one day to find on my desk a stack of petitions sent over from the Governor's office with 3156 signatures. The petitions implored the Governor to direct the chief of the Division of Wildlife to stock nearby thirty-seven hundred acre Buckeye Lake with fish. In 1951 when this episode occurred, the scientists in the Division had records of fish populations for this body of water which indicated that stocking would be superfluous.

It is one thing for an administrator to listen to a confident group of scientists backed by filing cabinets full of data declaring the inadvisability of stocking a body of water and another to convey that message effectively to more than three thousand signers of a petition and a general public inclined to agree with them.

As a scientist trained in the management of wildlife resources, my first inclination was to stand firm on the scientific evidence and deny the petitioners. As an educator, however, it occurred to me that here was an opportunity to demonstrate the wisdom of the scientist and to gain support not only for our position in this matter but to gain respect upon which to base future actions. The decision was to choose the latter course. The method chosen involved a gamble. We proposed to stock the lake if we were unable through demonstration to convince the petitioners and their backers that the lake was adequately stocked. A public demonstration was arranged. For their part, the petitioners invited key political figures, members of their organizations, the press, the radio, and anyone interested to the demonstration. For our part, we agreed to place test nets in the water at points where fishing was reputedly at its worst and lift them publicly for all to see. To assure that the demonstration was conducted in a scientific manner, we used two standard test nets and placed them in the water just 24 hours before the appointed time for them to be lifted and witnessed. Also to assure scientific validity and for other reasons, a rotation of guards was employed for the full 24 hours.

At the appointed time for the demonstration, hundreds of people crowded on the pier to watch the lifting of the nets. Note now the following quote from an editorial which appeared in the *Newark Advocate* (1951), the local daily newspaper, a few days later:

A whispering campaign said there was no fish in Buckeye Lake. That libel has now been erased officially. . . . A test was made under the most unfavorable conditions near the lake's shore at the park where much boat activity and other conditions prevailed which fish don't like. In one trap 967 were taken. . . . In another trap some 400 fish of a similar variety were taken. . . . The fish management boys were pleased.. . . . And now the wise boys are changing their tune. Instead of singing a doleful song of no fish, they are asking why the conservation authorities don't seine a third of the fish out of the lake. Their point is Buckeye Lake is overpopulated. As Ralph Edwards would say, 'People are indeed funny.'

Although there is much humor in the incident, one can become easily discouraged from efforts to resolve conflicts by educational methods when agitation, not conservation, is the objective.

But there is a sequel to the story which illustrates that while not many conservation conflicts can be resolved totally through adult education, much can be done to contribute to their resolution. The residents of the State of Ohio, and more recently residents of many other states, now enjoy millions of hours of virtually restriction-free recreational fishing not formerly available. This came about despite many deep-seated beliefs about over-fishing and putting little fish back and protecting fish on their spawning beds. It came about because of repeated demonstrations of this kind and educational programs which afforded interested parties an opportunity to have their questions answered. Confidence in the judgment of scientists was achieved, and a willingness to resolve conflict by experimentation, by trial, and by test was permitted.

There remain, of course, enough unanswered questions that groups still looking for a cause by which to gain recognition have plenty of room in which to operate.

IV. Let me draw your attention now to the fourth category of sources of conservation conflicts: those arising out of ignorance. There are many conservation problems for which we do not have good answers or, at best, but partial answers. Who knows, for example, the necessary physical dimensions of a unit of coastal redwoods essential to their perpetuation as man found them? Who knows with full assurance the specific cause of the degradation of the waters of Lake Erie? Who knows with certainty the cause of the great increase in red wing blackbirds which have become a scourge to crops in the Midwest? Who knows when man will, if he can, discover a substitute for silver which can be used satisfactorily in the photographic process or which will find acceptance as a medium of exchange for goods and services?

There will continue to be controversy over conservation problems which we do not understand. And understanding becomes more difficult as the problems become more complex and as individuals become more specialized. A scientist may be an expert in one resource area but no better informed than the average lay person in others. Under these circumstances, it is easy for an aggressive proponent with little knowledge to win support for a cause out of all proportion to the evidence substantiating it. Paul B. Sears had a favorite way of expressing this situation by noting that some people he knew knew a great deal about things which just aren't so.

Guidelines for Action in Saving the Environment   **55**

CHARLES H. W. FOSTER

In evaluating the validity of a position or the desirability of a project, the following guidelines might usefully be employed by an organization.

Be prepared. Always have the necessary facts at hand and your homework done prior to facing the issue.

Be right. Nothing is more transparent than the distortion of facts to a predetermined conclusion. Knowing when you are wrong—and being big enough to admit it—will enhance rather than hurt an organization's image.

Be practical. Natural area protectionists are frequently accused of being blue-sky advocates, and many are. Being practical, however, is *not* the same as compromising on principle.

Be wise in time. Knowing when to espouse an issue, or undertake a project, is perhaps the real key to success. A prophet achieves much personal satisfaction but rarely lives long enough to see his cause realized.

From these few remarks you should be able to sense my personal conviction that the natural area movement is important and promising—but one whose essence must be action. This will require close teamwork between governmental and private agencies, and within the private sector itself. In my judgment, private leadership must carry the main burden if the movement is to be ultimately successful. I am encouraged by the evidence of interest and cooperation expressed at this symposium and know that my fellow state administrators will join with me in offering their support.

POPULATION

and FOOD

The growth curve so familiar to the biologist describes the pattern of development of living units from the relatively simple cellular level of organization on through the complexly structured individuals, populations, and the ecosystem. Growth experiences a series of stages. At the population level, the initial stage is characterized by both a high birth and a high death rate. Growth progresses slowly. The next stage finds the death rate falling with the birth rate remaining high. Now the mass of individuals expands explosively. As the food energy supply becomes more difficult for the population to obtain, the third stage is ushered in. This final stage witnesses an acceleration in the death rate, a decrease in the birth rate, or both. At any rate, the growth rate will eventually become stable unless an energy input in the form of food occurs.

The Population Crisis

The current world-wide population of 3.6 billion will swell to 5.03 billion in 1985 if present population increase trends continue. Even with effective family planning, the earth will know 4.65 billion that year. The difference between effective planning and no planning, then, is a mere 385 million.

In the year 2000, effective family planning may allow us to hold the population down to 6 billion; but if current trends persist, the population will nearly double and stand at 7.15 billion.

Clearly, "too many people" is the most crucial problem facing us during the remaining three decades of this century. This somber prospect demands a fundamental—not trifling—modification of our child-bearing attitudes and behavior. Yet, as Henry David Thoreau said, "There are a thousand hacking at the branches of evil to one who is striking at the root."

The Population Crisis Is Here Now 56

WALTER E. HOWARD

Preface

At the present world rate of population growth of 2% per year, a mere dozen people a thousand years ago could have produced the present world population, and in another thousand years each one of us could have 300 million living descendants. Obviously, that cannot be—something must be done. Either the birth rate must be significantly curtailed or the death rate drastically increased.

The world's overpopulation crisis is of a magnitude beyond human comprehension, yet the government and the public remain seemingly indifferent. Better awareness and a more forthright leadership are obviously needed, from biologists and politicians alike. Will you help? A vastly increased rate of involuntary premature deaths can be prevented only by an informed public, here and abroad, following dynamic leadership. No population can continue to increase indefinitely, no matter how much food there is. If civilization is to be viable, we must end the arrogant assumption that there are unlimited resources and infinite air and water. People must develop much greater voluntary restraint in reproduction —or conception itself will have to come under government control.

This earth does not have the resources necessary to provide even the present world population with the degree of affluence that the middle-class citizen enjoys. Even though the average birth rate in the United States has declined during the past decade from about seven children per family to fewer than three, the population density has been growing much more rapidly than before. The reason is the high population base level; there are now so many more women that their "small" families add a greater number of new people to the population each year than did their grandmothers, even with much larger families.

No population can continue to grow beyond certain limits; eventually, involuntary self-limitation—in the form of premature deaths from starvation, pestilence, and wars—will prevent any further increase in density. Since all finite space is limited, it is an indisputable fact that birth rates and death rates must someday be balanced. Already the rich are devouring the poor—the survival of the fittest.

Introduction

The intent of this article is not to alarm the reader unnecessarily. But how is that possible? Alarm is called for; man should be alarmed. Man must be aware of his dilemma, for if he attempts to feed the world without effective control of the birth rate, he actually is only deferring the starvation of an even greater number of people to a later date.

The world is facing this acute overpopulation situation specifically because of advances in agriculture and health, through science and technology, and a lack of similar progress in the field of sensible birth control. Families are not having more babies, it is just that more now survive.

Passion between the sexes must, of course, remain a basic human right, but it cannot include the having of children at will. While intercourse remains an individual and private matter, procreation must become of public concern. Conception should not be a euphemism for sexual relations. The obvious goal for all societies wishing an abundant life and freedom from want should be a low-birth-rate, low-death-rate culture. Man's responsibility to the next generation includes a primary duty of limiting the size of that generation.

Our problem is uncontrolled human fertility—not underproduction and maldistribution—and corrective action is being dangerously delayed by wishful thinking that some miracle will solve the problem. There is a prodigious need for immediate public awareness of the current critical situation, since overpopulation is intimately involved with political, economic, and sociological problems—in fact, with everyone's peace, security, and general well-being. All of the world's desperate needs—ample food, permanent peace, good health, and high-quality living—are unattainable for all human beings both now and in the foreseeable future for one obvious reason: there are too many people. A soaring population means a shrinking of man's space on this earth.

Not only is population growth the most basic conservation problem of today, but its dominating influence will affect the ultimate survival of mankind. Man can no longer be indifferent to this basic population problem. Its severity behooves all to act now. Hunger and overpopulation will not go away if we do not discuss them, and the bringing of too many babies into this world is not just someone else's problem; it is everyone's concern. The destiny of overpopulation is erosion of civilized life.

The World's Population

To appreciate the recent rapidity with which the world's population has grown—it took from the beginning of man until 1850 to reach a population of one billion people, only 80 years more (1930) to reach two billion, then only 30 years (1960) to reach the three billion mark, and in less than 15 years after 1960 we expect four billion. In the next 25 years after that, the population is expected to increase by another three and one-half billion people. If there have been about 77 billion births since the Stone Age, then about 1 out of every 22 persons born since then is alive today. But in only 30 or 40 years from now, if current rates of increase continue, 1 out of every 10 people ever born will be living at that time. The youth of today might see the United States with a population equal to what India has now.

Only a small proportion of the world's population has made the demographic transition of attaining both a lower fertility and a lower mortality; most have decreased only the premature death rate. The population has continued to increase rapidly because reductions in fertility have not been sufficient to offset the effects of current reductions in mortality produced by technological sanitation, disease control, and pesticide use.

The reproductive potential of the world is grim, for 40 to 45% of the people alive today are under 15 years old. How can this tremendous number of babies soon be fed solid foods? And look how soon those who survive will be breeding.

Even though technology exists that could manufacture enough intrauterine devices for every woman, the problems of distribution and the shortage of doctors make it impossible for the devices to be inserted fast enough to control the world's population growth. Within a few years the number of people dying each year from causes related to poor nutrition will equal what is now the entire population of the United States.

In the United States if the fertility and mortality trends of 1950-60 should be reestablished, replacing the 1968 low birth rate, in only 150 years our country alone could exceed the current world population of over 3.3 billion, and in 650 years there would be about one person per square foot. This will not happen, of course, because either the birth rate will decline, or more likely, the death rate will increase.

Rate of Population Increase

The basic factor is the difference between birth and death rates, not what the levels of births and deaths happen to be. Continued doubling of a population soon leads to astronomical numbers. If the world population increase continued at the low rate of only 2%, the weight of human bodies would equal the weight of the earth in about 1500 years.

The world population is reported to be currently growing by 180,000 a day, more than a million a week, or about 65 million a year, and each year it increases in greater amounts. If current trends continue, the population will reach about 25 billion in only 100 years.

Prior to Christ, it took about 40,000 years to double the population, but the current growth rate of about 2% would require only 35 years to double the present population. Populations that grow by 3% per year double within a generation and increase eighteen-fold in 100 years.

Population Dynamics

If 90% of a population survives long enough to reproduce, an average of 2.3 children per family will keep the population stable. Only a very slight increase to 2.5 children would produce an increase of 10% per generation, and 3.0 children per family would cause an increase of 31% per generation. If child-bearing families averaged 3.0 children, about one woman in four would need to be childless for the population to remain stable.

A sustained geometric increase in human beings is, of course, impossible; once the population's base level of density is high, as it now is, birth rates cannot continue much above the death rates for long without a truly impossible density being produced. As the base population density rises, even a lower birth rate can still mean that there will be a greater absolute increase in total numbers than was occuring before, when population was less and birth rates were higher.

Obviously, if input (natality) continues to exceed outgo (mortality), any finite space must eventually fill up and overflow. Populations increase geometrically, whereas food and subsistence increase arithmetically. The geometric ratio of population growth is also known as the ever-accelerating growth rate, the logistic curve, the well-known S-shaped or sigmoid growth curve, and compound interest.

When populations of people are exposed to stressing pressures, including those due to overpopulation, they may respond in a strange way of breeding earlier and more prolifically, further aggravating the situation. The principal way in which man differs from other animals is in his intellect, his ability to read and communicate, to learn, to use tools, and his society; and he also differs from other species in that he attempts to protect the unfit and all "surplus" births.

Predisposition to Overpopulate

Nature has seen to it that all organisms are obsessed with a breeding urge and provided with the biological capacity to overproduce, thereby ensuring survival of the species. Since man now exercises considerable control over so many of the natural factors which once controlled his population, he must also learn to control his innate trait to reproduce excessively.

It is not a question of whether this earth has the resources for feeding a much greater population than is now present—of course, it has. The point is that the human population is now growing too fast for food production ever to catch up without stringent birth control.

Carrying Capacity and Self-Limitation

No matter how far science and technology raise the carrying capacity of the earth for people, involuntary self-limiting forces will continue to determine man's upper population density. Surplus populations do not just quietly fade away—quite the contrary. Before surplus individuals die, they consume resources and contribute in general to other population stresses, all of which make the environment less suitable, thus lowering its carrying capacity. Man needs space to live as much as do plants and animals.

The balance of nature is governed primarily by the suitability of the habitat and species-specific self-limitation, where members of each species involuntarily prevent any further increase in their kind. This self-limitation consists of undesirable stresses which cause individual births in a family to be unwanted or cause a compensating increase in death rates. Members of the population become their own worst enemy in the sense that they are responsible for the increased rates of mortality and, perhaps, also some reduction in natality.

Nearly all organisms that are well-adapted to their environment have built-in mechanisms for checking population growth before the necessary food and cover are permanently destroyed. But nature's population control processes are unemotional, impartial, and truly ruthless, a set of conditions that educated men will surely wish to avoid.

Instead of man learning how to conquer nature, he may annihilate it, destroying himself in the process. In current times at least, there is no hope that man as a species will voluntarily limit his birth rate to the low level (zero or even minus replacement) that the overall population must have. Also, unfortunately, when a population level is below carrying capacity the innate desire to have larger families then becomes very strong, making human husbandry difficult to practice.

Nature does not practice good husbandry—all its components are predisposed to overpopulate and, in fact, attempt to do so, thus causing a high rate of premature deaths. If food supply alone were the principal factor limiting the number of people, man would long ago have increased to a density where all of the food would have been consumed and he would have become an extinct species.

When other organisms follow a population growth curve similar to what man is currently experiencing—and they do this only in disturbed (usually man-modified) environments—they can then become so destructive to their habitat that the subsequent carrying capacity may be dramatically reduced if not completely destroyed, thus causing not only mass individual suffering and a high rate of premature deaths but also a permanent destruction of the ecosystem.

Whenever man's population density has been markedly reduced through some catastrophe, or his technology has appreciably increased the carrying capacity of his habitat (environment), the growth rate of his population increases. The population then tends to overcompensate, temporarily growing beyond the upper limits of the carrying capacity of the environment. The excess growth is eventually checked, however, by the interaction of a number of different kinds of self-limiting population stress factors. These include such forces as inadequate food and shelter, social stress factors, competition for space, wars, an increase in pestilence, or any of many other subtle vicissitudes of life that either increase the death rate, reduce successful births, or cause individuals to move elsewhere. Unfortunately, in the developed countries, science and technology are developing at an exponential rate, so the population growth may not again be sufficiently halted by self-limitation until the earth's resources are largely exploited or a world famine or other drastic mortality factor appears.

Although nature practices survival of the fittest, man believes that all who are born should be given every opportunity to live to an old age. If this is to be our objective, and I am sure it will, then we have only one other alternative, i.e., to restrict the number of births. And to accomplish this, it seems better to reduce conception rather than to rely on abortions. Abortions are a solution, however, when other means of preventing conceptions have broken down. Surprising to most people, abortions induced by a doctor are safer than childbearing.

There is a need too for man to establish a stable relationship with the environment. Man must recognize that he also responds to many, in fact, most of the laws of nature. And his population checks are largely famine, pestilence, and war. Man has transferred himself from being just a member of the ecosystem to a dominant position, where he now mistakenly assumes that the ecosystem is his to control at will. He forgets that he is part of nature. To see his true place in the world he must not attempt to transcend too much over nature, but to discover and assimilate all he can about the truth of nature and his own role in nature.

Only self-limitation can stem the population tide, and the only voice man has in the matter is whether it will be done involuntarily by nature's undesirable stresses, as witnessed by the history of civilization, or will be done consciously by not allowing his kind to exceed an optimum carrying capacity.

Socio-Economic Situations

It is incongruous that student unrest is so great and race problems so much in the front, yet almost everyone seems unaware that the basic cause of most of these socio-economic stresses is overpopulation, about which almost nothing is said by all of these energetic and sometimes vociferous groups. The daily economic pressures of individuals attempting to provide a decent civilization, especially for themselves, may lead to the ultimate destruction of all ecosystems. Surplus individuals do not quietly fade away.

In spite of man's power of conscious thought, the only species so endowed, he seldom thinks beyond his lifetime or his own family's particular needs. The great desire of most people to provide their children and themselves with all of today's advantages is an important factor in reducing family size. That is not enough, however, for these families are still raising the population level.

At the same time that the world's population is increasing, both the number and the percentage of the "have-nots" increase and, in addition, the gap widens between the "haves" and "have-nots." As tragic as it may sound, when an underdeveloped country's population density is growing rapidly, both health and agricultural aid from the United States may not only be wasted but may severly aggravate the already deplorable social and economic situation in that country.

In industrially developed countries, middle-class couples often have fewer children than they would like (if they only had more money, domestic help, etc.), whereas in underdeveloped countries and ghettos the reverse is too frequently true. High birth rates tend to nullify national efforts to raise average per capita income since there is less money for savings and developmental investments. Neither families nor a nation can escape when life is held close to the margin of subsistence.

Overpopulation inevitably commits too many people to poverty and despair. With perpetual pregnancies the bonds of welfare become inescapable, for unskilled parents cannot feed a large family from the wages they can earn. No matter how you look at it, families of more than two or three children intensify the problem of national development, and this happens whether the parents are poor, middle class, or wealthy.

A complete reorientation of social values and attitudes regarding births is urgently needed now. We need new baby ethics, an awareness of the tragedies associated with too many babies. Bringing births and deaths into balance will demand great social, economic, and political changes.

With reference to our affluence, we cannot turn back—if for no other reason than the fact that there are now too many people to permit going back—to a less materialistic existence without cars, pesticides, diesel exhaust, sewage and garbage disposal, etc. The stork has passed the plow. Food prices in developing nations are rising faster than the purchasing power.

Economic Interests

Man seems to be governed by economic self-interest. Societies become conditioned to the tenets of the economists—that money can buy anything. Without the basic resources there can be no wealth and affluence; but, unfortunately, the exploitation of resources seems to be considered the very foundation of all "progress."

"Progress" is the magic word. It means to increase property values and returns on one's investment; it is the deity of modern civilization. Yet, do any of us really know what we are progressing toward? Too often, the chamber-of-commerce form of "progress" is the next man's destruction.

Man seems to be more concerned with the quality of his goals than with the quantity of his goods. The more slowly a population increases the more rapid is the growth of both its gross and per capita income.

The harmful consequences of overpopulation are blindly overlooked by those who favor an expanding population for reasons of military strength, economic progress, scientific and agricultural development, and eugenics.

Man's economic dreams, his selfishness, and his materialism interfere with his awareness of the fate of the unborn. He is too busy in the United States in covering two acres per minute with houses, factories, and stores. His highways are now equivalent to paving the entire state of Indiana. Every day, California loses 300 acres of agricultural land.

Unfortunately, little planning has been done on how the socio-economic problems can be handled once the population growth is stopped. If the rush of today's living and industrial development or defense spending just slows down, a painful recession is upon us. We have no government study on how the nation could exist without a growing population.

Resource Management

Insidious economic pressures seem to prevent any effective management of resources in a manner that would provide for their utilization in perpetuity. Concrete and pavement surely are not the epitome of the human species' fulfillment. An ecological appreciation of resource management is needed, and ecological ethics must replace ecological atrocities.

Man is rapidly depleting the nonreplenishable resources. Half of the energy used by man during the past 2000 years was used in the last century. Man is reported to have mined more in the past 100 years than during all previous time. But, every barrel has a bottom; unbridled technology promises to speed us faster toward that bottom. Our planet's resources diminish faster as society's affluence is increased. Our qualitative sense of appreciation of our environment seems to be replaced by mere quantitative values. Why cannot civilization fulfill its obligation of being a competent steward of all resources?

It is inevitable that the limited legacy of natural resources must steadily yield in the face of the current explosion in the world population. As the population swells, open spaces are inundated by a flood of housing, and resources shrink faster. The United States and other developed nations are consuming a disproportionately large share of the world's nonrenewable and other resources at an ever-accelerating rate, perhaps 20 to 30 times as much on a per capita basis as are individuals in undeveloped countries. In 1954, the United States was reported to be using about 50% of the raw-material resources consumed in the world each year, and by 1980 it might be 80%. But we do not have an endless earth of boundless bounty. Any finite resource is subject to eventual exhaustion.

Effect of Science and Technology

The world may have sufficient resources, but it has never provided enough food and other necessities of life for all people at any one time. As technology improved, enabling better utilization of resources, the population similarly increased, so that there have always been many who died prematurely, as Malthus predicted.

No one anticipated the scope and rapidity of the technological changes that have occurred in Western society. About one-third of the people now consume about two-thirds of the world's food production, while the other two-thirds go undernourished. But, unfortunately, these starving people reproduce at a high rate. As individual aspirations rise and per capita resources fall, the widening gap between the haves and the have-nots could well generate some serious social and political pressures.

In recent times spectacular gains have been made in controlling mass killers such as typhus, malaria, yellow fever, small pox, cholera, plague, and influenza; but no corresponding checks have been made on birth rates. It is ironic that the root of our overpopulation problem is technical advances brought about by our increasing intellect (the knowledge explosion of the last hundred years).

Technology can produce almost anything, but only at the usually recognized high price of resource consumption and waste accumulation. As our technology advances, the amount of resources utilized per person also increases, and the supply is not endless.

Technology and science can and do progress at an ever-increasing rate, but can social, political, and religious views change rapidly enough to cope with this "progress"? The fruits of all our scientific and technological advances will be ephemeral if the world's population continues to explode. Our intelligence is so powerful that it may destroy us because we lack the wisdom and insight to recognize and correct what we are doing to ourselves and, especially, to future generations. We are passing on an enormous population problem to the next generation.

Pollution and Waste Disposal

Affluent societies have also been labeled "effluent" societies. That man is a highly adaptable species that can live in polluted environments, in extremely crowded conditions, in situations of acute malnutrition, and in some of the most depressing of environments is well exemplified today. But why should he? And how much lower can he sink and still survive as a "successful" species?

Mushrooming with the population are pollution and litter. We produce 70% of the world's solid wastes but have only 10% of the world's population. There is a need to make the reuse and disposal of rubbish more economical.

Popular Solutions and Misconceptions

Hopeful but inadequate panaceas include synthetic foods (proteins and vitamins), hydroponics, desalinization of seawater, food from the ocean, more agricultural research, fertilizers, irrigation, the vast unused lands, land reforms, government regulation, price support, migrations, redistribution of food and wealth, and private enterprise.

Science and technology may find a way to produce more food and to accommodate more people, but in the end this, of course, will only make matters that much worse if birth control is not effective. It should be obvious that the only solution is a drastically reduced birth rate or a greatly increased death rate. The one inescapable fact about a country's population—about the world's population —is that the death rate must someday equal the birth rate, regardless of how plentiful food may be.

Unfortunately, a basic American philosophy is the belief that our free-enterprise system can produce anything that is necessary, a false cornucopian faith that our population growth is not a real threat. Our overpopulation-under-development dilemma is not a matter of increasing production to meet the demand for more food; rather, the only solution is to limit demand for food so that production may someday catch up to the population's needs.

Role of Family Planning

There is no question that family planning has made great progress. But today's society and religious groups must recognize the urgency for adopting the pill, IUD, other chemical and mechanical devices (both undependable), sterilization, abortion—in fact, any means of limiting childbirth. The promotion of some form of effective means of artificial birth control is the only moral, human, and political approach available to prevent the misery and suffering which will result if people are permitted to have as many "planned" children as they want.

Despite the great benefits of family planning programs, especially the benefits to the families concerned, family planning is not a euphemism for birth control. We need to develop a social and cultural philosophy that even a family of three children is too large and to overcome the fear of some ethic and religious sects that other groups may multiply faster, becoming more dominant. Family planning per se has little relevance to the underdeveloped countries of the world or to poverty groups in the more advanced countries. Therefore anything other than government control of conception may be self-defeating.

Sexual Desire and Love of Children

The basic conflict with the overpopulation problem is that of desires—actually drives—and the fact that most young women are fecund; without either the strong drives or the ability of women to conceive, there would be no problem. As with all organisms, man's potential fecundity and predisposition to overproduce are the basic causes for his excess fertility over deaths. Most babies are the consequence of passion, not love. But children are loved.

Motherhood must become a less significant role for women. We must forego some of our love for children and learn to be content with fewer numbers. What is needed in the way of governmental control of births is not control of an individual's behavior but control of the consequence of such behavior, the prevention of intemperate breeding.

There is no question that children make family ties more intimate, but man has already done too well toward "fathering" the country. Compassionate relations between spouses, not the having of children, must become the primary goal of marriages in the future. There is no need to find drugs that destroy sexual desire; the objective is to control the conception rate, not frequency of intercourse.

Is Having Children a Basic Right?

One price that society must be willing to pay for sustained world peace is a stringent universal birth-control program, which will require revolutionary revisions of modes of thought about our basic human rights with regard to family planning.

The increasing disparity between population density and food supply, by itself, justifies effective birth control regardless of the "morality" associated with depriving parents of the right to have as many planned children as they choose.

Having too many children can no longer be dismissed as an act of God, for it is now truly the consequence of a complacent society that is unwilling to take any of many steps available for preventing surplus births. Our primitive reproductive instincts cannot be condoned in the face of modern survival rates. The two are no longer in balance.

To say that the opportunity to decide the number and spacing of children is a basic human right is to say that man may do whatever he wants with nature without thought of its inevitable consequence to future generations. Our legal and ethical right should be to have only enough children to replace ourselves.

No longer can we consider procreation an individual and private matter. Intercourse, yes, but not unregulated numbers of conceptions since they affect the welfare of all other individuals living at that time plus those to be born in the future.

Religious Complications

It needs to be said over and over again that the bringing of surplus children into this world, whether from personal desire or from religious edicts, destines not only some of these children but many others to a premature death. Overproduction actually lowers the maximum density that can be sustained for normal life spans, thereby increasing the number of souls in need of salvation.

The "morality" of birth control in today's burgeoning human population has taken on an entirely new aspect. God clearly never meant for man to overpopulate this earth to the point where he would destroy many other forms of life and perhaps even himself. The religious doctrines we lean on today were established before science and technology had dramatically raised the carrying capacity for man.

The question of complete abstinence as the only acceptable means of family regulation is as ludicrous as compulsory euthanasia. The mortal sin, if there is one, in God's eyes surely would be associated with those who do *not* practice birth control, for to let babies come "as they naturally do" will prove to be a form of murder—through starvation, pestilence, and wars resulting from excess babies. It must be recognized that the number of children can no longer be left to "the will of God" or to our own desires and family plans, and if population controls are to be successful, they may have to be determined by government regulations.

Religious views that do not condone rigorous birth control must realize that every surplus birth their philosophy promotes will guarantee, on the average, a horrible death some day to more than one individual.

Although the Christian attitude implies that everything on this earth was created for man's use, in reality man is inescapably also part of nature.

Some form of compulsory control of birth rates is essential, although I see no reason why various religious groups cannot be permitted to achieve birth limitations in whatever manner they choose. If a woman or a couple exceeds the limit set by society, however, then they must be dealt with by law compelling them to be sterilized, to have an abortion, or by some other repayment to society.

Birth control is not murder, as some claim, but lack of it in today's over-populated world most surely will be. For those who strongly oppose the setting of any limit on the number of children a family can have, I ask them to tell the rest of us just how they think the premature death rate should be increased to offset their extra births.

Wealth vs. Number of Children

Civilization can no longer endure a way of life in which people believe they have the right to have as many children as they can afford. This is hypocritical, for those who can "afford" luxurious living are already utilizing many times their share of the limited food and other resources, and also they are contributing much more pollution to the environment than are the have-nots. The affluent population needs to be made aware of the overpopulation problems, for they often desire to have more children per family than those who are in poverty.

Too much of today's religious climate makes birth control a politically sensitive area, thus constraining public officials. But, as citizens, are we not justified in asking why our governmental officials have not done more to make us aware of the urgency of population control—political sensitivities notwith-standing?

Governments should be guiding the development of a better life and world to live in, but if it does not recognize the need for human husbandry, then it will be fostering the ultimate destruction of the earth rather than the goals it seeks.

Man, in spite of his intellect, is so concerned with the present that he too often turns a deaf ear to alarming sounds of the future. Another difficulty in stabilizing the population is that our standard of living and our economy cannot survive in a static state.

Limiting Size of Families

We can no longer be prophets and philosophers; we must act. The biomag-nification of births must be brought to an abrupt halt. Procreation must come under governmental control if no other way can be found. Perhaps what is needed is a system of permits for the privilege of conceiving, or compulsory vasectomies of all man and sterilization of all women who have been responsible for two births.

Since the taboo against birth control is inviolable to some, regardless of the dire consequences of overpopulation, laws must be passed to regulate conceptions and births. Each individual needs to have the right to produce or adopt only a replacement for himself or herself.

The general public must be made to realize that from now on, for a married couple to have more than two children or three at most, is a very socially irresponsible act. We must advocate small families. When business is good and living has quality, marriages will naturally tend to be earlier and births more numerous; therefore, only through the development of new nonfamilial rewards can later marriages be made to appear attractive to people. Taxes now subsidize children, whereas we should be taxed for the privilege of having children.

A rising age at marriage is an effective way of reducing births, and, sociologically and economically, it gives women more time to become better educated, acquire nonfamily sorts of interests, and develop greater cautions toward pregnancy.

Up to now, only death has been of public concern; procreation has remained an individual and highly cherished private matter. But this privilege cannot continue, and regulation of the number of conceptions, or at least births, must also become a government function.

Population Control or Premature Deaths

Man must decide whether the future growth of populations will be governed by famine, pestilence, and war, or whether he will use his intellect to control birth rates artificially. If the population growth is not controlled by lower birth rates, hundreds of millions of people must soon die prematurely each year.

Man must use his intellect to counteract his excessive fertility, for all species have been endowed by nature to be overfecund. If he does not, the extra individuals will be eliminated by the natural process of "struggle for existence—survival of the fittest," which causes all surplus individuals to die prematurely as a result of nature's ruthless laws of involuntary "self-limitation" whenever the carrying capacity has been exceeded. That territoriality and aggression are life-preserving functions of the social order of animals is frightening when man applies these same principles to his own species.

There have always been hungry people in the world, but both the total number of individuals and the percentage of the total population that are destined to go hungry in the future will be dramatically increased if birth rates are not drastically checked. Many like to think that nature will somehow take care of things. They fail to remember how nature has taken care of many species that were no longer adaptable to existence on this earth—they are now preserved as fossils.

Modern public-health methods and medical technology have lessened the chronic hunger, general economic misery, and other vicissitudes that once caused high mortality rates. But, sooner or later, any increase in births over deaths will be balanced by an increase in the rate of premature deaths.

Human Husbandry and Quality Living

Human husbandry implies that we regulate the population density before the natural self-limiting demographic and societal stress factors do it for us. But human motivation will always work against good human husbandry, because to each individual who has quality living, a large family will seem desirable.

The population of the world is so great that what used to be a ripple when it doubled now means catastrophic effects because of the great numbers involved and the lack of this earth's ability to support them. Man is not practicing good husbandry when he lets his population density expand beyond the carrying capacity.

The most important thesis regarding the need for human husbandry is that human beings will not voluntarily restrict their number of children to just two when economic, social, and political conditions appear to be personally favorable. A quality society with quality existence is now unattainable in many parts of the world, and may soon be unattainable any place in the world. The "economic" struggle of overpopulation is the world's greatest threat to quality living, enriched leisure, and even man's ultimate existence.

Conclusion

The ultimate goal must be a zero population growth. To achieve "quality living" instead of nature's "survival of the fittest," as has persisted throughout the history of mankind, the birth rate must not continue to exceed the death rate. If the birth rate of nations and the world are not greatly reduced, an ever-increasing amount of starvation and other types of premature deaths are inevitable. There is a prodigious need for mankind to practice human husbandry (Human Husbandry, a guest editorial in *BioScience*. 18: 372-373, 1968, by Walter E. Howard).

A conscientious regulation of fertility is needed, or a calamitous rise in premature mortality rates is inevitable. Without this tremendous voluntary restraint or the development of a strong social stigma against bearing more than two or three children, the rate of conceptions must come under some form of governmental control. It can no longer be a basic human right to have as many children as one wants, especially if such action dooms others to a premature death.

Even though the above picture is bleak, the world is not going to come to an end. In fact, none of the people who read this article are going to starve, but their very existencē is going to cause others who are less well off to perish. As overpopulation becomes worse, the percentage of the people who will fall into this nonsurviving unfit category must obviously increase. If babies of the future are to live, there must be fewer of them now.

How To Save The Ship 57

PAUL R. EHRLICH

A ship has hit the rocks and is sinking. The passengers scream for help. Some jump overboard and are devoured by the circling sharks. A group of distinguished scientists is on board. One of their number suggests that they can help man the pumps. "Oh, no!" shout the others. "That might hurt the captain's feelings. Besides, pumping is not our business. It's outside our field of competence." You can guess what they do. They appoint a committee to study the problem, with subcommittees on marine engineering and navigation. They announce to the passengers that in two or three years the committee will produce a wonderful report which will be acceptable to the passengers, the captain, and the steamship line. Not so passive are the politicians. Some jump up to say that the passengers don't understand the political realities of the situation. Other more progressive politicians grab thimbles and start bailing, stopping every few seconds to accept praise for their valiant efforts.

That about sums up the situation on the population control front in the United States and in much of the rest of the world.

Some Consequences of Population Growth

The Social Consequences Of Population Growth 58

BENJAMIN VIEL

It has been demonstrated that families lacking access to contraceptive means of birth control, particularly in Latin America, often turn in desperation to the harsh alternative of abortion. Some evidence for this fact is presented in the following provocative essay by a distinguished Chilean physician. According to Dr. Viel, the rate of induced abortion in Latin America is highest among the middle classes, which do not practice contraception on a wide scale. Extremely poor families, he asserts, seldom resort to abortion or contraception because "ignorance and demoralization probably destroy the capacity of poor women to combat family growth." Under such circumstances, birth rates are very high.

The most disturbing part of Dr. Viel's essay is his hypothesis that women in large, poor families may unconsciously wish for the death of their newest-born children. While the evidence for this hypothesis is still inconclusive, it merits further attention. The degree to which unconscious infanticide exists in Latin

America—and the degree to which it may occur among large families in the United States and elsewhere—can only be ascertained through research. Such research is urgently needed.

When we refer to population growth and its effects, we should differentiate clearly between normal growth, which parallels the increase in the means of subsistence, and accelerated growth, which takes place more rapidly than the increase in resources available to support life. Far from stimulating progress and giving rise to evolutionary processes, accelerated growth has been the cradle of wars and revolutions. It has slowed down production and vastly increased human misery and hunger.

Starting somewhat arbitrarily with the year 1930, we have had normal growth in the developed regions of the world and accelerated growth in all the regions we call underdeveloped or developing. In the latter areas, mortality rates have dropped swiftly as a result of techniques imported from the industrialized world. Populations have consequently grown fast, but there has been no parallel growth in productivity or in the sources of employment.

Latin America today is a typical victim of this speedup in population growth. Its predicament has been caused largely by the reduction of infectious diseases through new drugs and more effective methods of administering and distributing medical resources. Both the new drugs and the improved methods are imports from abroad. Instead of creating a biological balance between the South American and his environment, they have helped to destroy the equilibrium already in existence. Death rates have dropped much faster than they would have fallen through improvements in nutrition brought about by an increase in the means of subsistence.

Between 1930 and 1968, the population of Latin America more than doubled, and at the present rate of growth, it will have tripled between 1960 and the end of this century.

What are the social implications of this enormously rapid growth? In offering an analysis, I will, as a doctor, start with those effects which lie closest to the field of medicine.

Unconscious Infanticide

It comes as a shock to realize that infanticide has grown more widespread during the twentieth century. This phenomenon exists at a frequency and in a form that is unknown to the great majority of people in Latin America.

I do not speak of deliberate infanticide such as the outright killing of the newborn, which is very rare, or the abandonment of infants, which is tragically on the increase, at least in Chile. Rather, I refer to infanticide of the unconscious type, in which the mother allows her child to die without even admitting to herself that she desires the child's death.

In a careful study in Santiago, Dr. Aníbal Faúndes found that for first-born infants, 60 of every 1,000 died during their first year. Among the third- or fourth-born, however, infant deaths rose to about 100. After 10 or more children were born to the same couples, the number of deaths during the first year of life reached 300 for every 1,000 infants. Since there is no biological phenomenon that entirely explains this increase in mortality, we must consider the possibility that a major cause is the growing lack of concern on the part of the mother towards additional children who burden her with more work than she can endure.

This hypothesis is supported by the experience of almost any pediatrician. Mothers come to him when they detect the least symptoms of illness in their first-born children. After they have had five or six children, however, these same mothers bring in their infants only when they are seriously ill.

In developing countries such as those of Latin America, the multiplicity of births per family may provoke unconscious infanticide and thereby serve as an important cause of high infant mortality rates. High mortality, moreover, continues through the preschool years. We must face the shameful fact that out of every 100 deaths in Latin America, 44 are of persons less than five years old. In Argentina and Uruguay, where birth rates are lower than elsewhere in the continent, mortality rates in the younger ages are also lower. Only 18 out of every 100 deaths in these two countries occur among children under five.

Induced Abortion

When the mother's life is not imperiled by pregnancy or childbirth, induced abortion is considered illegal throughout Latin America. Both the mother who submits to such an abortion and the person who performs it are liable to punishment. Yet we have had an extremely high rate of induced abortion. The result has been widespread non-enforcement of the law. If the law *were* enforced, we would soon face a grave shortage of police, judges and jails.

How common are induced abortions in Latin America? Their illegal status has led to vast underreporting, and we must therefore resort to indirect means of evaluating their frequency.

Assuming that in 1960 the use of reliable contraceptives was very rare among Latin American women and that the age distribution was "young" in all Latin American countries except Argentina and Uruguay, we may then state that the theoretical birth rate (without abortion) in these countries could not have been lower than 50*. From the differences between this theoretical rate and the actual birth rates in 1960, as shown in Table 1, we can obtain a rough idea of the frequency of induced abortion.

This table indicates that induced abortion is more frequent in Brazil, Chile and Peru than in other countries. Although the relationship is not very close, the table also suggests that the actual birth rate tends to be higher where the percentage of urban population is smaller. In other words, the incidence of provoked abortion rises with urbanization.

In 1964, the U.N. Regional Center for Demographic Training and Research (CELADE) conducted a random-sample survey of abortion and contraception among women of reproductive age in several Latin American cities. Table 2 gives the results. San José, the capital of Costa Rica, had an abortion rate of 33 per

*Birth and death rates are given per 1,000 people per year.

TABLE 1: Difference Between Theoretical and Actual Birth Rates, 1960.

Country	Actual Birth Rate	Difference from Theoretical Birth Rate of 50	Percentage of Population Urban
Brazil	33.0	−17.0	40.4
Chile	33.0	−17.0	66.2
Perú	38.2	−11.8	47.1
Venezuela	42.8	− 7.2	63.7
Colombia	44.6	− 5.4	50.6
México	44.7	− 5.3	50.7
Honduras	47.2	− 2.8	22.5
Salvador	48.5	− 1.5	38.5
Costa Rica	49.2	− 0.8	34.5

1,000 woman-years; Caracas and Mexico City also had very high rates. Comparing these results with those of Table 1, we may state that where the frequency of abortion is low at the national level, it is very often high in urban areas. The varying rates of abortion in different countries therefore tend to reflect the varying degrees of urbanization.

Table 2 also reveals an inverse relationship between the abortion rate and the percentage of women in each sample using contraceptives.

TABLE 2: Abortion, Contraception and Family Size
in Seven Latin American Countries, 1964.

City	Abortions per 1,000 Woman-Years	Percentage of Women Using Contraceptives	Average Number of Children
Mexico City	37	13.7	3.3
Caracas	34	24.4	3.0
San José of Costa Rica	33	27.2	3.0
Bogotá	26	21.8	3.2
Panama City	24	na	2.7
Rio de Janeiro	21	na	2.3
Buenos Aires	21	41.8	1.5

Other investigations bear out the urban-rural differential in provoked abortion. Surveys by the population department of the Colombian Association of Medical Schools reveal that the rate of induced abortions reached 16 per 100 pregnant women in Bagotá and 20 or more in other cities, while in rural communities it averaged only about 8. Likewise, in Santiago, Chile, the induced abortion rate as determined by surveys reached 35, while in the rural community of Calera it was less than 7.

What are some of the reasons for this urban-rural differential? In the rural areas, particularly where the climate is favorable as it is in most of Latin America, children do not constitute a great housing problem; they use the home mainly for sleeping. Even before they reach the age of 15, moreover, they help with the farm work. But in the cities, conditions are much different. Children remain in the home for a much longer time, creating a serious housing problem. Far from contributing substantially to the family's income, they constitute a financial burden even after the age of 15. Moreover, they are increasingly born into families where the mother works outside the home. It is under such circumstances that women turn to abortion when they lack effective contraceptive devices. In the cities, too, it is much easier to find the facilities for abortion.

Considering the fact that in Latin America there is a growing trend towards urbanization, it is easy to conclude that, unless an attempt is made to prevent them, induced abortions will become tragically more prevalent in the next decade.

The trend towards a gradual increase in illegal abortions in Chile can be traced as far back as 1937. In that year, records first became available of the number of women hospitalized for complications which arose from illegal abortions performed outside the hospital. Certainly such cases represent only a fraction of all illegal abortions, since illegal abortions without complications are not recorded. It should also be noted that these hospital cases do not represent all the socioeconomic classes. They are heavily weighted towards the low-income groups. When complications of abortion arise in women who are economically well off, the patients are usually hospitalized in private clinics where it is easy to falsify the diagnosis.

The Chilean record reveals a gradual increase in hospital abortion rates, nationwide, and in Santiago, between 1937 and 1967. It also reveals that abortion is more frequent in Santiago than in the rest of the country. Outside Santiago, the problem appears to have been minimized by the low rate of abortion in the rural areas, even though the rate in other Chilean cities is as high as in Santiago —sometimes even higher. Since 1966, the level of hospital abortions has stabilized, particularly in Santiago. This stabilization appears to have been caused by a birth control program which has been in effect since 1965 and which has been applied more extensively in Santiago than elsewhere.

In conjunction with studies of hospital abortions in Chile between 1937 and 1967, a decrease has also been observed in infant mortality rates. It is thus clear that there is an inverse relationship between abortion and infant mortality. While infant mortality rates have dropped, the frequency of illegal abortion has risen. There is a logical explanation to this relationship. Years ago, high infant mortality severely limited the size of families. In recent decades, however, medical advances and the availability of powdered milk have decreased infant mortality without stimulating any significant change in the economic conditions of the home. Women, the most responsible members of Latin American society, are attacking the problem of excessive family size by resorting more and more to illegal abortions.

It is interesting to note that the greatest frequency of induced abortion exists among married women. From studies recently conducted in Santiago and San José, we can see that the yearly rate of induced abortions for married women was 49 per 1,000 women in Santiago and 26.5 in Costa Rica, while for single girls it was only 19 in Santiago and 11.5 in Costa Rica. The old belief that illegal abortion is resorted to mainly by single women who wish to hide premarital relationships is erroneous. This practice undoubtedly exists, but its extent is very small compared with the number of married women with children who seek abortion to prevent a further increase in family size.

Abortion and Socioeconomic Class

It has been shown that a definite relationship exists between socioeconomic class and the frequency of abortions. If we assume that fertility is roughly equal in all classes, then abortion must be considered a rare phenomenon in the extreme classes and a very common one in the middle-income classes. Wealthy women resort less often to abortion for the simple reason that they use contraceptive methods to a much greater extent than other women. Middle-income women submit to illegal abortion much more frequently because they seldom use contraceptives to prevent unwanted births. In the very low-income classes, however, abortion is rare and the birth rate is extremely high. The ignorance and demoralization caused by destitution probably destroy the capacity of the poor woman to combat family growth.

In studying the frequency of abortion, researchers use the degree of education as a measure of socioeconomic status. Table 3 shows the percentage of women in three educational groups who have resorted to abortion in three Latin American cities.

TABLE 3: Abortion and Educational Status

Level of Education	Percentage of women having resorted to one or more abortions		
	Santiago	Bogotá	Mexico City
None	27.3	26.0	29.6
Primary School	39.3	28.8	34.2
Secondary School and above	24.3	19.1	24.8

If we assume that educational levels roughly coincide with economic classes, then Table 3 bears out the statement that abortions are sought primarily by women in the middle socioeconomic classes.

Throughout Latin America, women in these classes generally hire domestics who, in addition to receiving a salary, live in the homes of their employers. Practically every middle-class family has one or more domestic workers. For this type of hired help, abortion can be called a professional disease. Faced with pregnancy, domestics must choose between losing their jobs and resorting to induced abortion. Most well-off families will not hire domestics who are mothers.

In the methods as well as the frequency of abortion, we can discern distinct differences according to socioeconomic class. When a woman from the high-income group decides to have an abortion, she seeks out a professionally trained doctor and she generally pays an expensive fee. At a somewhat lower economic level, however, the woman resorts to a non-professional whose competance is as low as the fee he charges. This woman may suffer complications from the methods used by the unskilled practitioner.

In the poorest classes, a woman is likely to perform a crude abortion on herself by inserting a stiff implement or sewing needle through the neck of the uterus. She seeks help only when hemorrhaging begins.

While complications requiring hospitalization may result from abortions performed by unskilled "specialists," they almost always follow from abortions performed by the pregnant woman herself.

The foregoing conclusions, based on research in Chile, reflect practices throughout Latin America. Illegally induced abortions result in the deaths of many young women. They are the cause of an incalculable number of gynecological infections that lead to a serious interruption of medical practice, because proper attention for women during childbirth and for newborn children is made difficult by the need to care for so many complications of abortion. Medical care for these complications drains a large fraction of the funds allocated to health programs by the Latin American countries.

We may conclude that unless something is done to reduce the problem, abortion will continue to increase in direct proportion both to the rate of urbanization in our countries and to the expected drop in infant mortality.

Control of Illegal Abortion

The punishment of abortion by law in Chile has failed miserably, even though authorities have long had access to the names and addresses of women who are hospitalized each year because of complications of illegal abortion. Since no attempt has even been made to initiate court proceedings, many people ask: "Why not adopt the policy of Japan and make all abortions legal?" This proposal reflects a very superficial analysis of the problem. First of all, there are strong moral objections to making abortions legal. Secondly, such a policy would be completely impractical. It is true that the Soviet Union and Japan, among many other countries, have legalized abortions, but in the Soviet Union there is a doctor for every 460 people, and in Japan the ratio of doctors to the total population is only slightly smaller. In Chile, one of the medically more advanced countries in Latin America, there is only one doctor for every 1,600 persons. If doctors were authorized to practice abortion, and even more importantly, if they had the legal *obligation* to practice abortion on request, Chile would not have enough doctors to handle the demand. Nor would there be enough hospital beds—even for one day of hospitalization—unless Chile accepted a significant reduction in the present insufficient number of beds used for normal obstetric care.

There is, finally, a strong medical objection to legalizing abortion. Giving a woman the means to exercise very high fertility is incompatible with her good health and with the normalcy of her last-born children. Therefore, an indiscriminate policy of legalizing abortion is not an acceptable solution.

What about other proposed remedies? There is no doubt that reducing abortion by abstinence would require a return to the harsh times of Malthus. No one could seriously consider such an approach. It is equally wrong to maintain that abortion can be prevented by improving the living standards of the family and guaranteeing the education of children. Housing space is becoming continuously smaller because every day there are more people to be housed. Education is expensive, and government programs are seldom on par with the educational requirements of countries having high birth rates.

The truth is that a humane, effective solution to the very serious problem of illegal abortion cannot be other than the use of contraceptives. This brings together the two demographic goals which must be sought in today's world—first, the reduction of the rate of population increase to the point where it parallels the rise in production, and second, the reduction of the population explosion within the family which forces women to expose themselves to a cruel operation.

Those persons who are against birth control join forces with those seeking legalized abortion to maintain that the contraceptive methods known today are incapable of replacing abortion and reducing the birth rate to any significant extent. It is even argued that illegal abortion tends to increase when a birth control plan based on contraception is started. The evidence, however, is to the contrary.

In our own experience with a birth control program in the western district of Santiago between 1964 and 1968, we observed a considerable drop in the number of induced abortions that resulted in complications requiring hospital care. Table 4 shows the estimated population of fertile women (aged 15-44) in the area studied, the cumulative number and percentage of women using intrauterine devices, the number of hospitalized abortions, and the percentage of women in the 15-44 age group who resorted to abortion.

TABLE 4: Abortion and Contraception in West Santiago, 1964-1968.

Year	Females Aged 15-44	Women Using IUD's (Cumulative Number)	Per-cent	Hospi-talized Abortions	Percent of 15-44 Age Group
1964	81,642	4,073	5.0	5,282	6.5
1965	84,747	8,222	9.9	6,237	7.4
1966	87,994	14,579	17.1	4,731	5.4
1967	101,909	26,147	28.5	4,265	4.2
1968	104,283	36,377	38.3	3,727	3.6

The number of hospitalized abortions in 1968 amounted to only about 70 percent of those in 1964. This drop can only be attributed to the free distribution and use of the intrauterine device and other effective contraceptives.

In maintaining that a contraceptive program can reduce the number of illegally induced abortions to the extent shown in Table 4, we do not claim that abortion can be eliminated. The contraceptives available today, even the most effective ones, involve a certain percentage of failure and are not suitable for all women.

Abortion will therefore continue to be a serious problem. Nevertheless, a reduction in abortions to the point where they do not require the use of over 10 percent of the beds in gyneco-obstetric wards would be a real triumph.

Population Growth and Employment

Despite high infant mortality and the increasing use of illegal abortions, Latin American countries are experiencing very rapid population growth at rates which, with the exception of Argentina and Uruguay, range between 2 and 3.5 percent annually.

Sustained high fertility has raised the percentage of young people in Latin America, and the majority of the Latin American nations find that over half their people are under 20. Every year the number of new job candidates is so great that the labor market cannot absorb all of them. The consequence of this phenomenon is increasing unemployment.

When Europe experienced a decline in its mortality rates as a result of better hygiene and improved nutrition, she also enjoyed the benefits of an extraordinary economic expansion arising from a successful industrial revolution. Furthermore, Europe had a safety-valve—emigration—which enabled her to colonize other continents when her own labor market failed to absorb all the new candidates for employment. Conditions in Latin America today are much different.

Latin America's labor market is growing too slowly to absorb all the workers which modern medicine and public health measures have saved from premature death. Furthermore, the continent lacks almost completely the migratory outlet which Europe long enjoyed.

There is another point of comparison which is unfavorable to Latin America. When the population growth rates of the European nations increased—and they were never as high as those occurring today in Latin America—the industrial machinery of that time required a large number of human laborers. But the slow economic expansion of Latin America today is being achieved through more automated industrial machines which are continuously replacing muscle power. Every day we see how factories which once employed 1,000 workers are modernizing their machinery and producing more and better products with only half as many workers.

The mechanization of agriculture has increased productivity and reduced the number of farm laborers. Those who do not find new jobs in the rural environment must migrate to the cities, where they face very serious problems created by a type of industrial production which requires fewer and fewer workers and which selects only the most qualified persons. Skills are demanded which cannot be acquired in the rural environment.

The continent's cities are growing, partly as a result of their own natural increase, but largely because of rural migration caused by the mechanization of agriculture. The growing mass of urban unemployed is seriously inflating the service expenditures of the Latin American countries, and it is disturbing the social peace.

This trend affects not only the city laborer and the farm worker. Intellectuals are also victims of technological progress. Without a doubt, if Latin America had the capital to purchase many more electronic computers, the middle classes would be as seriously riddled with unemployment as the classes of blue-collar workers and farm workers are now.

What are the political consequences of population growth which is too rapid for the economy to absorb? If a young man cannot find work, his natural reaction is to blame the socioeconomic system. It is not strange that energy is spent in resisting the economic and social structures prevalent today.

The intense and growing political activity of the youth of Latin America, which has assumed more and more violent forms in recent times, is the natural reaction to the uncertain future which is faced by young people who cannot find employment in the labor market.

For young intellectuals, the circumstances of the unemployed man give further incentive to protest and rebellion. Universities join in the violence. Strike after strike interrupts the periods of study. Students who should leave our universities technically trained are handicapped by an inadequate preparation, and thus they help widen the gap between the high-technology developed world and the low-technology underdeveloped world.

The Loss of Values

Youth has always been rebellious, but perhaps in no period of history has its rebellion been more vehement than now. In former times, fathers spoke to their sons with absolute faith in the moral and intellectual values which had guided their own lives. Today, men who are approaching 50—the generation holding power—sense that their faith is wavering. They can no longer hand down a given set of values to their sons with complete sincerity.

The multicellular family which constituted the basis of Latin American life in the past has been swept away by the population increase. The ancestral home of the grandparents, parents and grandchildren has been replaced by the apartment in the cooperative which the new generation views less as a home than as a bedroom.

We were taught in the cradle that work was a virtue, and that every person should cultivate his talents to the maximum. But we are living in a world in which overzealous work, far from being virtuous, is anti-social. One man's excessive work leaves another man unemployed.

We were taught that savings would guarantee the education of our children, that they would be an insurance against our old age. But we are living at a time when inflation has so throughly destroyed savings that anyone who saves what he earns is destined to be poor.

Having lost faith in the moral values which were absolute pillars of our upbringing, we do not understand the upcoming generation. We have lost the confidence to promote an evolutionary movement which will deliver us from a revolutionary force of dire consequences. If the Latin American population continues to grow ever more rapidly, a revolution led by illiterate and impoverished masses will be the logical result.

Given this dangerous prospect, it is very difficult to understand those traditional elements of Latin American society which so vehemently resist the effort to reduce the rate of population growth. Yet this rate must come down if we are to relieve the family tensions that lead mothers to unconscious infanticide and abortion. And it must come down if we are to relieve the social tensions which lead men to rebellion and violence, seeking changes which are possible only in a climate of peaceful dialogue.

Birth Control and Economic Development 59

STEPHEN ENKE

Most less-developed countries have population increases approaching 3 percent a year. Death rates have fallen dramatically in the past several decades, but annual birthrates remain at around 4 percent of population. Income per head is rising slowly.

Enough is known about the main parameters that a demographic-economic computer model can be used to assess the effects of declining fertility rates on various indices of economic welfare in a typical less-developed country. Thus halving in 30 years a 3.025 gross rate of reproduction results in income per head increasing 3.0 percent a year instead of 1.7 percent a year with no fertility change. Halving fertility also results in a third more capital per worker after 30 years.

A large birth-control program might directly cost about $5 a year per "acceptor." About 25 percent of the population aged 15 through 49 would have to practice contraception on an average to halve the gross reproduction rate in 30 years. During this period the total cost might be roughly $200 million for a less-developed country that started with a population of 10 million. Accumulated benefits could be $16 billion. The benefit to cost ratio is roughly 80 to 1.

Population Policy

Two myths have been too long in dying regarding the population question in the United States. The myth that the poor want no more children than the non-poor has become the basis for government policy. Birth control programs have been "poverty oriented" with the assumption generally made that lack of education and family planning services are at the root of the large family. However, Judith Blake Davis, Department of Demography, University of California at Berkeley, writing in Science in 1969, has presented data supporting the position that poor families do indeed want more children than non-poor ones. Apparently when there is little else to live for, children serve as a means of obtaining fulfillment.

The following paper by Kingsley Davis (reading 60) deals with the second myth. Professor Davis makes a distinction between population planning and population control. This now classic document emphasizes that "planning" may be successful while "control" fails.

60 Population Policy: Will Current Programs Succeed?

KINGSLEY DAVIS

Throughout history the growth of population has been identified with prosperity and strength. If today an increasing number of nations are seeking to curb rapid population growth by reducing their birth rates, they must be driven to do so by an urgent crisis. My purpose here is not to discuss the crisis itself but rather to assess the present and prospective measures used to meet it. Most observers are suprised by the swiftness with which concern over the population problem has turned from intellectual analysis and debate to policy and action. Such action is welcome relief from the long opposition, or timidity, which seemed to block forever any governmental attempt to restrain population growth, but relief that "at last something is being done" is no guarantee that what is being done is adequate. On the face of it, one could hardly expect such a fundamental reorientation to be quickly and successfully implemented. I therefore propose to review the nature and (as I see them) limitations of the present policies and to suggest lines of possible improvement.

The Nature of Current Policies

With more than 30 nations now trying or planning to reduce population growth and with numerous private and international organizations helping, the degree of unanimity as to the kind of measures needed is impressive. The consensus can be summed up in the phrase "family planning." President Johnson declared in 1965 that the United States will "assist family planning programs in nations which request such help." The Prime Minister of India said a year later, "We must press forward with family planning. This is a programme of the highest importance." The Republic of Singapore created in 1966 the Singapore Family Planning and Population Board "to initiate and undertake population control programmes" (1).

As is well known, "family planning" is a euphemism for contraception. The family-planning approach to population limitation, therefore, concentrates on providing new and efficient contraceptives on a national basis through mass programs under public health auspices. The nature of these programs is shown by the following enthusiastic report from the Population Council (2):

No single year has seen so many forward steps in population control as 1965. Effective national programs have at last emerged, international organizations have decided to become engaged, a new contraceptive has proved its value in mass application, . . . and surveys have confirmed a popular desire for family limitation . . .

An accounting of notable events must begin with Korea and Taiwan . . . Taiwan's program is not yet two years old, and already it has inserted one IUD (intrauterine device) for every 4-6 target women (those who are not pregnant, lactating, already sterile, already using

contraceptives effectively, or desirous of more children). Korea has done almost as well
. . . has put 2,200 full-time workers into the field, . . . has reached operational levels for
a network of IUD quotas, supply lines, local manufacture of contraceptives, training of
hundreds of M.D.'s and nurses, and mass propaganda . . .

Here one can see the implication that "population control" is being achieved
through the dissemination of new contraceptives, and the fact that the "target
women" exclude those who want more children. One can also note the technological emphasis and the medical orientation.

What is wrong with such programs? The answer is, "Nothing at all, if they
work." Whether or not they work depends on what they are expected to do as
well as on how they try to do it. Let us discuss the goal first, then the means.

Goals

Curiously, it is hard to find in the population-policy movement any explicit
discussion of long-range goals. By implication the policies seem to promise a great
deal. This is shown by the use of expressions like *population control* and *population planning* (as in the passages quoted above). It is also shown by the characteristic style of reasoning. Expositions of current policy usually start off by lamenting
the speed and the consequences of runaway population growth. This growth, it
is then stated, must be curbed—by pursuing a vigorous family-planning program.
That family planning can solve the problem of population growth seems to be
taken as self-evident.

For instance, the much-heralded statement by 12 heads of state, issued by
Secretary-General U Thant on 10 December 1966 (a statement initiated by John
D. Rockefeller III, Chairman of the Board of the Population Council), devotes
half its space to discussing the harmfulness of population growth and the other
half to recommending family planning (3). A more succinct example of the typical
reasoning is given in the Provisional Scheme for a Nationwide Family Planning
Programme in Ceylon (4):

The population of Ceylon is fast increasing. . . . (The) figures reveal that a serious situation
will be created within a few years. In order to cope with it a Family Planning programme
on a nationwide scale should be launched by the Government.

The promised goal—to limit population growth so as to solve population
problems—is a large order. One would expect it to be carefully analyzed, but it
is left imprecise and taken for granted, as is the way in which family planning
will achieve it.

When the terms *population control* and *population planning* are used, as
they frequently are, as synonyms for current family-planning programs, they are
misleading. Technically, they would mean deliberate influence over all attributes
of a population, including its age-sex structure, geographical distribution, racial
composition, genetic quality, and total size. No government attempts such full
control. By tacit understanding, current population policies are concerned with
only the *growth* and *size* of populations. These attributes, however, result from

the death rate and migration as well as from the birth rate; their control would require deliberate influence over the factors giving rise to all three determinants. Actually, current policies labeled population control do not deal with mortality and migration, but deal only with the birth input. This is why another term, *fertility control,* is frequently used to describe current policies. But, as I show below, family planning (and hence current policy) does not undertake to influence most of the determinants of human reproduction. Thus the programs should not be referred to as population control or planning, because they do not attempt to influence the factors responsible for the attributes of human populations, taken generally; nor should they be called fertility control, because they do not try to affect most of the determinants of reproductive performance.

The ambiguity does not stop here, however. When one speaks of controlling population size, any inquiring person naturally asks, What is "control"? Who is to control whom? Precisely what population size, or what rate of population growth, is to be achieved? Do the policies aim to produce a growth rate that is nil, one that is very slight, or one that is like that of the industrial nations? Unless such questions are dealt with and clarified, it is impossible to evaluate current population policies.

The actual programs seem to be aiming simply to achieve a reduction in the birth rate. Success is therefore interpreted as the accomplishment of such a reduction, on the assumption that the reduction will lessen population growth. In those rare cases where a specific demographic aim is stated, the goal is said to be a short-run decline within a given period. The Pakistan plan adopted in 1966 (5, p. 889) aims to reduce the birth rate from 50 to 40 per thousand by 1970; the Indian plan (6) aims to reduce the rate from 40 to 25 "as soon as possible"; and the Korean aim (7) is to cut population growth from 2.9 to 1.2 percent by 1980. A significant feature of such stated aims is the rapid population growth they would permit. Under conditions of modern mortality, a crude birth rate of 25 to 30 per thousand will represent such a multiplication of people as to make use of the term *population control* ironic. A rate of increase of 1.2 percent per year would allow South Korea's already dense population to double in less than 60 years.

One can of course defend the programs by saying that the present goals and measures are merely interim ones. A start must be made somewhere. But we do not find this answer in the population-policy literature. Such a defense, if convincing, would require a presentation of the *next* steps, and these are not considered. One suspects that the entire question of goals is instinctively left vague because thorough limitation of population growth would run counter to national and group aspirations. A consideration of hypothetical goals throws further light on the matter.

Industrialized nations as the model. Since current policies are confined to family planning, their maximum demographic effect would be to give the underdeveloped countries the same level of reproductive performance that the industrial nations now have. The latter, long oriented toward family planning, provide a good yardstick for determining what the availability of contraceptives can do to population growth. Indeed, they provide more than a yardstick; they are actually the model which inspired the present population policies.

What does this goal mean in practice? Among the advanced nations there is considerable diversity in the level of fertility (8). At one extreme are countries such as New Zealand, with an average gross reproduction rate (GRR) of 1.91 during the period 1960-64; at the other extreme are countries such as Hungary, with a rate of 0.91 during the same period. To a considerable extent, however, such divergencies are matters of timing. The birth rates of most industrial nations have shown, since about 1940, a wave-like movement, with no secular trend.

The average level of reproduction during this long period has been high enough to give these countries, with their low mortality, an extremely rapid population growth. If this level is maintained, their population will double in just over 50 years—a rate higher than that of world population growth at any time prior to 1950, at which time the growth in numbers of human beings was already considered fantastic. The advanced nations are suffering acutely from the effects of rapid population growth in combination with the production of ever more goods per person (9). A rising share of their supposedly high per capita income, which itself draws increasingly upon the resources of the underdeveloped countries (who fall farther behind in relative economic position), is spent simply to meet the costs, and alleviate the nuisances, of the unrelenting production of more and more goods by more people. Such facts indicate that the industrial nations provide neither a suitable demographic model for the nonindustrial peoples to follow nor the leadership to plan and organize effective population-control for them.

Zero population growth as a goal. Most discussions of the population crisis lead logically to zero population growth as the ultimate goal, because *any* growth rate, if continued, will eventually use up the earth. Yet hardly ever do arguments for population policy consider such a goal, and current policies do not dream of it. Why not? The answer is evidently that zero population growth is unacceptable to most nations and to most religious and ethnic communities. To argue for this goal would be to alienate possible support for action programs.

Goal peculiarities inherent in family planning. Turning to the actual measures taken, we see that the very use of family planning as the means for implementing population policy poses serious but unacknowledged limits on the intended reduction in fertility. The family-planning movement, clearly devoted to the improvement and dissemination of contraceptive devices, states again and again that its purpose is that of enabling couples to have the number of children they want. "The opportunity to decide the number and spacing of children is a basic human right," say the 12 heads of state in the United Nations declaration. The 1965 Turkish Law Concerning Population Planning declares (10):

Article 1. Population Planning means that individuals can have as many children as they wish, whenever they want to. This can be ensured through preventive measures taken against pregnancy. . . .

Logically, it does not make sense to use *family* planning to provide *national* population control or planning. The "planning" in family planning is that of each separate couple. The only control they exercise is control over the size of *their* family. Obviously, couples do not plan the size of the nation's population, any more than they plan the growth of the national income or the form of the highway network. There is no reason to expect that the millions of decisions about family size made by couples in their own interest will automatically control population for the benefit of society. On the contrary, there are good reasons to think they will not do so. At most, family planning can reduce reproduction to the extent that unwanted births exceed wanted births. In industrial countries the balance is often negative—that is, people have fewer children as a rule than they would like to have. In underdeveloped countries the reverse is normally true, but the elimination of unwanted births would still leave an extremely high rate of multiplication.

Actually, the family-planning movement does not pursue even the limited goals it professes. It does not fully empower couples to have only the number of offspring they want because it either condemns or disregards certain tabooed but nevertheless effective means to this goal. One of its tenets is that "there shall be freedom of choice of method so that individuals can choose in accordance with the dictates of their consciences" (11), but in practice this amounts to limiting the individual's choice, because the "conscience" dictating the method is usually not his but that of religious and government officials. Moreover, not every individual may choose: even the so-called recommended methods are ordinarily not offered to single women, or not all offered to women professing a given religious faith.

Thus, despite its emphasis on technology, current policy does not utilize all available means of contraception, much less all birth-control measures. The Indian government wasted valuable years in the early stages of its population-control program by experimenting exclusively with the "rhythm" method, long after this technique had been demonstrated to be one of the least effective. A greater limitation on means is the exclusive emphasis on contraception itself. Induced abortion, for example, is one of the surest means of controlling reproduction, and one that has been proved capable of reducing birth rates rapidly. It seems peculiarly suited to the threshold stage of a population-control program —the stage when new conditions of life first make large families disadvantageous. It was the principal factor in the halving of the Japanese birth rate, a major factor in the declines in birth rate of East-European satellite countries after legalization of abortions in the early 1950s, and an important factor in the reduction of fertility in industrializing nations from 1870 to the 1930s (12). Today, according to *Studies in Family Planning* (13), "abortion is probably the foremost method of birth control throughout Latin America." Yet this method is rejected in nearly all national and international population-control programs. American foreign aid is used to help *stop* abortion (14). The United Nations excludes abortion from family planning, and in fact justifies the latter by presenting it as a means of combating abortion (15). Studies of abortion are being made in Latin America under the presumed auspices of population-control groups, not with the intention of legalizing it and thus making it safe, cheap, available, and hence more effective for population control, but with the avowed purpose of reducing it (16).

Although few would prefer abortion to efficient contraception (other things being equal), the fact is that both permit a woman to control the size of her family. The main drawbacks to abortion arise from its illegality. When performed, as a legal procedure, by a skilled physician, it is safer than childbirth. It does not compete with contraception but serves as a backstop when the latter fails or when contraceptive devices or information are not available. As contraception becomes customary, the incidence of abortion recedes even without its being banned. If, therefore, abortions enable women to have only the number of children they want, and if family planners do not advocate—in fact decry—legalization of abortion, they are to that extent denying the central tenet of their own movement. The irony of anti-abortionism in family-planning circles is seen particularly in hair-splitting arguments over whether or not some contraceptive agent (for example, the IUD) is in reality an abortifacient. A Mexican leader in family planning writes (17):

One of the chief objectives of our program in Mexico is to prevent abortions. If we could be sure that the mode of action (of the IUD) was not interference with nidification, we could easily use the method in Mexico.

The questions of sterilization and unnatural forms of sexual intercourse usually meet with similar silent treatment or disapproval, although nobody doubts the effectiveness of these measures in avoiding conception. Sterilization has proved popular in Puerto Rico and has had some vogue in India (where the new health minister hopes to make it compulsory for those with a certain number of children), but in both these areas it has been for the most part ignored or condemned by the family-planning movement.

On the side of goals, then, we see that a family-planning orientation limits the aims of current population policy. Despite reference to "population control" and "fertility control," which presumably means determination of demographic results by and for the nation as a whole, the movement gives control only to couples, and does this only if they use "respectable" contraceptives.

The Neglect of Motivation

By sanctifying the doctrine that each woman should have the number of children she wants, and by assuming that if she has only that number this will automatically curb population growth to the necessary degree, the leaders of current policies escape the necessity of asking why women desire so many children and how this desire can be influenced (18, p. 41; 19). Instead, they claim that satisfactory motivation is shown by the popular desire (shown by opinion surveys in all countries) to have the means of family limitation, and that therefore the problem is one of inventing and distributing the best possible contraceptive devices. Overlooked is the fact that a desire for availability of contraceptives is compatible with *high* fertility.

Given the best of means, there remain the questions of how many children couples want and of whether this is the requisite number from the standpoint of population size. That it is not is indicated by continued rapid population growth in industrial countries, and by the very surveys showing that people want contraception—for these show, too, that people also want numerous children.

The family planners do not ignore motivation. They are forever talking about "attitudes" and "needs." But they pose the issue in terms of the "acceptance" of birth control devices. At the most naive level, they assume that lack of acceptance is a function of the contraceptive device itself. This reduces the motive problem to a technological question. The task of population control then becomes simply the invention of a device that *will* be acceptable (20). The plastic IUD is acclaimed because, once in place, it does not depend on repeated *acceptance* by the woman, and thus it "solves" the problem of motivation (21).

But suppose a woman does not want to use *any* contraceptive until after she has had four children. This is the type of question that is seldom raised in the family-planning literature. In that literature, wanting a specific number of children is taken as complete motivation, for it implies a wish to control the size of one's family. The problem woman, from the standpoint of family planners, is the one who wants "as many as come," or "as many as God sends." Her attitude is construed as due to ignorance and "cultural values," and the policy deemed necessary to change it is "education." No compulsion can be used, because the movement is committed to free choice, but movie strips, posters, comic books, public lectures, interviews, and discussions are in order. These supply information and supposedly change values by discounting superstitions and showing that unrestrained procreation is harmful to both mother and children. The effort is considered successful when the woman decides she wants only a certain number of children and uses an effective contraceptive.

In viewing negative attitudes toward birth control as due to ignorance, apathy, and outworn tradition, and "mass-communication" as the solution to the motivation problem (22), family planners tend to ignore the power and complexity of social life. If it were admitted that the creation and care of new human beings is socially motivated, like other forms of behavior, by being a part of the system of rewards and punishments that is built into human relationships, and thus is bound up with the individual's economic and personal interests, it would be apparent that the social structure and economy must be changed before a deliberate reduction in the birth rate can be achieved. As it is, reliance on family planning allows people to feel that "something is being done about the population problem" without the need for painful social changes.

Designation of population control as a medical or public health task leads to a similar evasion. This categorization assures popular support because it puts population policy in the hands of respected medical personnel, but, by the same token, it gives responsibility for leadership to people who think in terms of clinics and patients, of pills and IUD's, and who bring to the handling of economic and social phenomena a self-confident naiveté. The study of social organization is a technical field; an action program based on intuition is no more apt to succeed in the control of human beings than it is in the area of bacterial or viral control. Moreover, to alter a social system, by deliberate policy, so as to regulate births in accord with the demands of the collective welfare would require political power, and this is not likely to inhere in public health officials, nurses, midwives, and social workers. To entrust population policy to them is "to take action," but not dangerous "effective action."

Similarly, the Janus-faced position on birth-control technology represents an escape from the necessity, and onus, of grappling with the social and economic determinants of reproductive behavior. On the one side, the rejection or avoidance of religiously tabooed but otherwise effective means of birth prevention enables the family-planning movement to avoid official condemnation. On the other side, an intense preoccupation with contraceptive technology (apart from the tabooed means) also helps the family planners to avoid censure. By implying that the only need is the invention and distribution of effective devices, they allay fears, on the part of religious and governmental officials, that fundamental changes in social organization are contemplated. Changes basic enough to affect motivation for having children would be changes in the structure of the family, in the position of women, and in the sexual mores. Far from proposing such radicalism, spokesmen for family planning frequently state their pupose as "protection" of the family—that is, closer observance of family norms. In addition, by concentrating on *new* and *scientific* contraceptives, the movement escapes taboos attached to old ones (the Pope will hardly authorize the condom, but may sanction the pill) and allows family planning to be regarded as a branch of medicine: over-population becomes a disease, to be treated by a pill or a coil.

We thus see that the inadequacy of current population policies with respect to motivation is inherent in their overwhelmingly family-planning character. Since family planning is by definition private planning, it eschews any societal control over motivation. It merely furnishes the means, and, among possible means, only the most respectable. Its leaders, in avoiding social complexities and seeking official favor, are obviously activated not solely by expediency but also by their own sentiments as members of society and by their background as persons attracted to the family-planning movement. Unacquainted for the most part with technical economics, sociology, and demography, they tend honestly and instinctively to believe that something they vaguely call population control can be achieved by making better contraceptives available.

The Evidence of Ineffectiveness

If this characterization is accurate, we can conclude that current programs will not enable a government to control population size. In countries where couples have numerous offspring that they do not want, such programs may possibly accelerate a birth-rate decline that would occur anyway, but the conditions that cause births to be wanted or unwanted are beyond the control of family planning, hence beyond the control of any nation which relies on family planning alone as its population policy.

This conclusion is confirmed by demographic facts. As I have noted above, the widespread use of family planning in industrial countries has not given their governments control over the birth rate. In backward countries today, taken as a whole, birth rates are rising, not falling; in those with population policies, there is no indication that the government is controlling the rate of reproduction. The main "successes" cited in the well-publicized policy literature are cases where a large number of contraceptives have been distributed or where the program has been accompanied by some decline in the birth rate. Popular enthusiasm for family planning is found mainly in the cities, or in advanced countries such as Japan and Taiwan, where the people would adopt contraception in any case, program or no program. It is difficult to prove that present population policies have even speeded up a lowering of the birth rate (the least that could have been expected), much less that they have provided national "fertility control."

Let us next briefly review the facts concerning the level and trend of population in underdeveloped nations generally, in order to understand the magnitude of the task of genuine control.

Rising Birth Rates in Underdeveloped Countries

In ten Latin-American countries, between 1940 and 1959 (23), the average birth rates (age-standardized), as estimated by our research office at the University of California, rose as follows: 1940-44, 43.4 annual births per 1000 population; 1945-49, 44.6; 1950-54, 46.4; 1955-59, 47.7.

In another study made in our office, in which estimating methods derived from the theory of quasi-stable populations were used, the recent trend was found to be upward in 27 underdeveloped countries, downward in six, and unchanged in one (24). Some of the rises have been substantial, and most have occurred where the birth rate was already extremely high. For instance, the gross reproduction rate rose in Jamaica from 1.8 per thousand in 1947 to 2.7 in 1960; among the natives of Fiji, from 2.0 in 1951 to 2.4 in 1964; and in Albania, from 3.0 in the period 1950-54 to 3.4 in 1960.

The general rise in fertility in backward regions is evidently not due to failure of population-control efforts, because most of the countries either have no such effort or have programs too new to show much effect. Instead, the rise is due, ironically, to the very circumstance that brought on the population crisis in the first place—to improved health and lowered mortality. Better health increases the probability that a woman will conceive and retain the fetus to term; lowered mortality raises the proportion of babies who survive to the age of reproduction and reduces the probability of widowhood during that age (25). The significance of the general rise in fertility, in the context of this discussion, is that it is giving would-be population planners a harder task than many of them realize. Some of the upward pressure on birth rates is independent of what couples do about family planning, for it arises from the fact that, with lowered mortality, there are simply more couples.

Underdeveloped Countries with Population Policies

In discussions of population policy there is often confusion as to which cases are relevant. Japan, for instance, has been widely praised for the effectiveness of its measures, but it is a very advanced industrial nation and, besides, its government policy had little or nothing to do with the decline in the birth rate, except unintentionally. It therefore offers no test of population policy under peasant-agrarian conditions. Another case of questionable relevance is that of Taiwan, because Taiwan is sufficiently developed to be placed in the urban-industrial class of nations. However, since Taiwan is offered as the main showpiece by the sponsors of current policies in under-developed areas, and since the data are excellent, it merits examination.

TABLE 1: Decline in Taiwan's Fertility
Rate, 1951 Through 1966.

Year	Registered births per 1000 women aged 15-49	Change in rate (percent)*
1951	211	
1952	198	−5.6
1953	194	−2.2
1954	193	−0.5
1955	197	+2.1
1956	196	−0.4
1957	182	−7.1
1958	185	+1.3
1959	184	−0.1
1960	180	−2.5
1961	177	−1.5
1962	174	−1.5
1963	170	−2.6
1964	162	−4.9
1965	152	−6.0
1966	149	−2.1

*The percentages were calculated on un-
rounded figures. Source of data through
1965, *Taiwan* Demographic Fact Book
(1964, 1965); for 1966, *Monthly Bulletin of
Population Registration Statistics of Taiwan*
(1966, 1967).

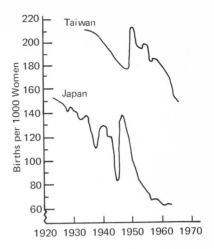

FIGURE 1. Birth rates per 1000 women
aged 15 through 49 in Japan and Taiwan.

Taiwan is acclaimed as a showpiece because it has responded favorably to
a highly organized program for distributing up-to-date contraceptives and has
also had a rapidly dropping birth rate. Some observers have carelessly attributed
the decline in birth rate—from 50.0 in 1951 to 32.7 in 1965—to the family-
planning campaign (26), but the campaign began only in 1963 and could have
affected only the end of the trend. Rather, the decline represents a response to
modernization similar to that made by all countries that have become industrialized (27). By 1950 over half of Taiwan's population was urban, and by 1964 nearly
two-thirds were urban, with 29 percent of the population living in cities of 100,000
or more. The pace of economic development has been extremely rapid. Between
1951 and 1963, per capita income increased by 4.05 percent per year. Yet the
island is closely packed, having 870 persons per square mile (a population density
higher than that of Belgium). The combination of fast economic growth and rapid
population increase in limited space has put parents of large families at a relative
disadvantage and has created a brisk demand for abortions and contraceptives.
Thus the favorable response to the current campaign to encourage use of the IUD
is not a good example of what birth-control technology can do for a genuinely
backward country. In fact, when the program was started, one reason for expect-
ing receptivity was that the island was already on its way to modernization and
family planning (28).

At most, the recent family-planning campaign—which reached significant
proportions only in 1964, when some 46,000 IUD's were inserted (in 1965 the
number was 99,253, and in 1966, 111,242) (29; 30, p. 45)—could have caused the

increase observable after 1963 in the rate of decline. Between 1951 and 1963 the average drop in the birth rate per 1000 women (see Table 1) was 1.73 percent per year; in the period 1964-66 it was 4.35 percent. But one hesitates to assign all of the acceleration in decline since 1963 to the family-planning campaign. The rapid economic development has been precisely of a type likely to accelerate a drop in reproduction. The rise in manufacturing has been much greater than the rise in either agriculture or construction. The agricultural labor force has thus been squeezed, and migration to the cities has skyrocketed (31). Since housing has not kept pace, urban families have had to restrict reproduction in order to take advantage of career opportunities and avoid domestic inconvenience. Such conditions have historically tended to accelerate a decline in birth rate. The most rapid decline came late in the United States (1921-33) and in Japan (1947-55). A plot of the Japanese and Taiwanese birth rates (Fig. 1) shows marked similarity of the two curves, despite a difference in level. All told, one should not attribute all of the post-1963 acceleration in the decline of Taiwan's birth rate to the family-planning campaign.

The main evidence that *some* of this acceleration is due to the campaign comes from the fact that Taichung, the city in which the family-planning effort was first concentrated, showed subsequently a much faster drop in fertility than other cities (30, p. 69; 32). But the campaign has not reached throughout the island. By the end of 1966, only 260,745 women had been fitted with an IUD under auspices of the campaign, whereas the women of reproductive age on the island numbered 2.86 million. Most of the reduction in fertility has therefore been a matter of individual initiative. To some extent the campaign may be simply substituting sponsored (and cheaper) services for those that would otherwise come through private and commercial channels. An island-wide survey in 1964 showed that over 150,000 women were already using the traditional Ota ring (a metallic intrauterine device popular in Japan); almost as many had been sterilized; about 40,000 were using foam tablets; some 50,000 admitted to having had at least one abortion; and many were using other methods of birth control (30, pp. 18, 31).

The important question, however, is not whether the present campaign is somewhat hastening the downward trend in the birth rate but whether, even if it is, it will provide population control for the nation. Actually, the campaign is not designed to provide such control and shows no sign of doing so. It takes for granted existing reproductive goals. Its aim is "to integrate, through education and information, the idea of family limitation *within the existing attitudes, values, and goals* of the people" [30, p. 8 (italics mine)]. Its target is *married* women who do not want any more children; it ignores girls not yet married, and women married and wanting more children.

With such an approach, what is the maximum impact possible? It is the difference between the number of children women have been having and the number they want to have. A study in 1957 found a median figure of 3.75 for the number of children wanted by women aged 15 to 29 in Taipei, Taiwan's largest city; the corresponding figure for women from a satellite town was 3.93; for women from a fishing village, 4.90; and for women from a farming village, 5.03. Over 60 percent of the women in Taipei and over 90 percent of those in farming villages wanted 4 or more children (33). In a sample of wives aged 25 to 29 in Taichung, a city of over 300,000, Freedman and his co-workers found the average number of children wanted was 4; only 9 percent wanted less than 3, 20 percent wanted 5 or more (34). If, therefore, Taiwanese women used contraceptives that were 100 percent effective and had the number of children they desire, they would have about 4.5 each. The goal of the family-planning effort would be achieved. In the past the Taiwanese woman who married and lived through the reproductive period had, on the average, approximately 6.5 children; thus, a figure of 4.5 would represent a substantial decline in fertility. Since mortality would continue to decline, the population growth rate would decline somewhat less than individual reproduction would. With 4.5 births per woman and a life expectancy of 70 years, the rate of natural increase would be close to 3 percent per year (35).

In the future, Taiwanese views concerning reproduction will doubtless change, in response to social change and economic modernization. But how far will they change? A good indication is the number of children desired by couples in an already modernized country long oriented toward family planning. In the United States in 1966, an average of 3.4 children was considered ideal by white women aged 21 or over (36). This average number of births would give Taiwan, with only a slight decrease in mortality, a long-run rate of natural increase of 1.7 percent per year and a doubling of population in 41 years.

Detailed data confirm the interpretation that Taiwanese women are in the process of shifting from a "peasant-agrarian" to an "industrial" level of reproduction. They are, in typical fashion, cutting off higher-order births at age 30 and beyond (37). Among young wives, fertility has risen, not fallen. In sum, the widely acclaimed family-planning program in Taiwan may, at most, have somewhat speeded the later phase of fertility decline which would have occurred anyway because of modernization.

Moving down the scale of modernization, to countries most in need of population control, one finds the family-planning approach even more inadequate. In South Korea, second only to Taiwan in the frequency with which it is cited as a model of current policy, a recent birth-rate decline of unknown extent is assumed by leaders to be due overwhelmingly to the government's family-planning program. However, it is just as plausible to say that the net effect of government involvement in population control has been, so far, to delay rather than hasten a decline in reproduction made inevitable by social and economic changes. Although the government is advocating vasectomies and providing IUD's and pills, it refuses to legalize abortions, despite the rapid rise in the rate of illegal abortions and despite the fact that, in a recent survey, 72 percent of the people who stated an opinion favored legalization. Also, the program is presented in the context of maternal and child health; it thus emphasizes motherhood and the family rather than alternative roles for women. Much is made of the fact that opinion surveys show an overwhelming majority of Koreans (89 percent in 1965) favoring contraception (38, p. 27), but this means only that Koreans are like other people in wishing to have the means to get what they want. Unfortunately, they want sizable families: "The records indicate that the program appeals mainly to women in the 30-39 year age bracket who have four or more children, including at least two sons . . ." (38, p. 25).

In areas less developed than Korea the degree of acceptance of contraception tends to be disappointing, especially among the rural majority. Faced with this discouragement, the leaders of current policy, instead of reexamining their assumptions, tend to redouble their effort to find a contraceptive that will appeal to the most illiterate peasant, forgetting that he wants a good-sized family. In the rural Punjab, for example, "a disturbing feature . . . is that the females start to seek advice and adopt family planning techniques at the fag end of their reproductive period" (39). Among 5196 women coming to rural Punjabi family-planning centers, 38 percent were over 35 years old, 67 percent over 30. These women had married early, nearly a third of them before the age of 15 (40); some 14 percent had eight or more *living* children when they reached the clinic, 51 percent six or more.

A survey in Tunisia showed that 68 percent of the married couples were willing to use birth-control measures, but the average number of children they considered ideal was 4.3 (41). The corresponding averages for a village in eastern Java, a village near New Delhi, and a village in Mysore were 4.3, 4.0, and 4.2, respectively (42, 43). In the cities of the regions women are more ready to accept birth control and they want fewer children than village women do, but the number they consider desirable is still wholly unsatisfactory from the standpoint of population control. In an urban family-planning center in Tunisia, more than 600 of 900 women accepting contraceptives had four living children already (44). In Bangalore, a city of nearly a million at the time (1952), the number of offspring desired by married women was 3.7 on the average; by married men, 4.1 (43). In the metropolitan area of San Salvador (350,000 inhabitants) a 1964 survey (45) showed the number desired by women of reproductive age to be 3.9, and in seven other capital cities of Latin America the number ranged from 2.7 to 4.2. If women in the cities of underdeveloped countries used birth-control measures with 100 percent efficiency, they will would have enough babies to expand the city populations senselessly, quite apart from the added contribution of rural-urban migration. In many of the cities the difference between actual and ideal number of children is not great; for instance, in the seven Latin-American capitals mentioned above, the ideal was 3.4 whereas the actual births per women in the age range 35 to 39 was 3.7 (46). Bombay City has had birth-control clinics for many years, yet its birth rate (standardized for age, sex, and marital distribution) is still 34 per 1000 inhabitants and is tending to rise rather than fall. Although this rate is about 13 percent lower than that for India generally, it has been about that much lower since at least 1951 (47).

Is Family Planning the "First Step" in Population Control?

To acknowledge that family planning does not achieve population control is not to impugn its value for other purposes. Freeing women from the need to have more children than they want is of great benefit to them and their children and to society at large. My argument is therefore directed not against family-planning programs as such but against the assumption that they are an effective means of controlling population growth.

But what difference does it make? Why not go along for awhile with family planning as an initial approach to the problem of population control? The answer is that any policy on which millions of dollars are being spent should be designed to achieve the goal it purports to achieve. If it is only a first step, it should be so labeled, and its connection with the next step (and the nature of that next step) should be carefully explained. In the present case, since no "next step" seems ever to be mentioned, the question arises, Is reliance of family planning in fact a basis for dangerous postponement of effective steps? To continue to offer a remedy as a cure long after it has been shown merely to ameliorate the disease is either quackery or wishful thinking, and it thrives most where the need is greatest. Today the desire to solve the population problem is so intense that we are all ready to embrace any "action program" that promises relief. But postponement of effective measures allows the situation to worsen.

Unfortunately, the issue is confused by a matter of semantics. "Family planning" and "fertility control" suggest that reproduction is being regulated according to some rational plan. And so it is, but only from the standpoint of the individual couple, not from that of the community. What is rational in the light of a couple's situation may be totally irrational from the standpoint of society's welfare.

The need for societal regulation of individual behavior is readily recognized in other spheres—those of explosives, dangerous drugs, public property, natural resources. But in the sphere of reproduction, complete individual initiative is generally favored even by those liberal intellectuals who, in other spheres, most favor economic and social planning. Social reformers who would not hesitate to force all owners of rental property to rent to anyone who can pay, or to force all workers in an industry to join a union, balk at any suggestion that couples be permitted to have only a certain number of offspring. Invariably they interpret societal control of reproduction as meaning direct police supervision of individual behavior. Put the word *compulsory* in front of any term describing a means of limiting births—*compulsory sterilization, compulsory abortion, compulsory contraception*—and you guarantee violent opposition. Fortunately, such direct controls need not be invoked, but conservatives and radicals alike overlook this in their blind opposition to the idea of collective determination of a society's birth rate.

That the exclusive emphasis on family planning in current population policies is not a "first step" but an escape from the real issues is suggested by two facts. (i) No country has taken the "next step." The industrialized countries have had family planning for half a century without acquiring control over either the birth rate or population increase. (ii) Support and encouragement of research on population policy other than family planning is negligible. It is precisely this blocking of alternative thinking and experimentation that makes the emphasis on family planning a major obstacle to population control. The need is not to abandon family-planning programs but to put equal or greater resources into other approaches.

New Directions in Population Policy

In thinking about other approaches, one can start with known facts. In the past, all surviving societies had institutional incentives for marriage, procreation, and child care which were powerful enough to keep the birth rate equal to or in excess of a high death rate. Despite the drop in death rates during the last century and a half, the incentives tended to remain intact because the social structure (especially in regard to the family) changed little. At most, particularly in industrial societies, children became less productive and more expensive (48). In present-day agrarian societies, where the drop in death rate has been more recent, precipitate, and independent of social change (49), motivation for having children has changed little. Here, even more than in industrialized nations, the family has kept on producing abundant offspring, even though only a fraction of these children are now needed.

If excessive population growth is to be prevented, the obvious requirement is somehow to impose restraints on the family. However, because family roles are reinforced by society's system of rewards, punishments, sentiments, and norms, any proposal to demote the family is viewed as a threat by conservatives and liberals alike, and certainly by people with enough social responsibility to work for population control. One is charged with trying to "abolish" the family, but what is required is selective restructuring of the family in relation to the rest of society.

The lines of such restructuring are suggested by two existing limitations on fertility. (i) Nearly all societies succeed in drastically discouraging reproduction among unmarried women. (ii) Advanced societies unintentionally reduce reproduction among married women when conditions worsen in such a way as to penalize childbearing more severely than it was penalized before. In both cases the causes are motivational and economic rather than technological.

It follows that population-control policy can de-emphasize the family in two ways: (i) by keeping present controls over illegitimate childbirth yet making the most of factors that lead people to postpone or avoid marriage, and (ii) by instituting conditions that motivate those who do marry to keep their families small.

Postponement of Marriage

Since the female reproductive span is short and generally more fecund in its first than in its second half, postponement of marriage to ages beyond 20 tends biologically to reduce births. Sociologically, it gives women time to get a better eduction, acquire interests unrelated to the family, and develop a cautious attitude toward pregnancy (50). Individuals who have not married by the time they are in their late twenties often do not marry at all. For these reasons, for the world as a whole, the average age of marriage for women is negatively associated with the birth rate: a rising age at marriage is a frequent cause of declining fertility during the middle phase of the demographic transition; and, in the late phase, the "baby boom" is usually associated with a return to younger marriages.

Any suggestion that age at marriage be raised as a part of population policy is usually met with the argument that "even if a law were passed, it would not be obeyed." Interestingly, this objection implies that the only way to control the age at marriage is by direct legislation, but other factors govern the actual age.

Roman Catholic countries generally follow canon law in stipulating 12 years as the minimum *legal* age at which girls may marry, but the actual average age at marriage in these countries (at least in Europe) is characteristically more like 25 to 28 years. The actual age is determined, not by law, but by social and economic conditions. In agrarian societies, postponement of marriage (when postponement occurs) is apparently caused by difficulties in meeting the economic prerequisite for matrimony, as stipulated by custom and opinion. In industrial societies it is caused by housing shortages, unemployment, the requirement for overseas military service, high costs of education, and inadequacy of consumer services. Since almost no research has been devoted to the subject, it is difficult to assess the relative weight of the factors that govern the age at marriage.

Encouraging Limitation of Births Within Marriage

As a means of encouraging the limitation of reproduction within marriage, as well as postponement of marriage, a greater rewarding of nonfamilial than of familial roles would probably help. A simple way of accomplishing this would be to allow economic advantages to accrue to the single as opposed to the married individual, and to the small as opposed to the large family. For instance, the government could pay people to permit themselves to be sterilized (51); all costs of abortion could be paid by the government; a substantial fee could be charged for a marriage license; a "child-tax" (52) could be levied; and there could be a requirement that illegitimate pregnancies be aborted. Less sensationally, governments could simply reverse some existing policies that encourage childbearing. They could, for example, cease taxing single persons more than married ones; stop giving parents special tax exemptions; abandon income-tax policy that discriminates against couples when the wife works; reduce paid maternity leaves; reduce family allowances (53); stop awarding public housing on the basis of family size; stop granting fellowships and other educational aids (including special allowances for wives and children) to married students; cease outlawing abortions and sterilizations; and relax rules that allow use of harmless contraceptives only with medical permission. Some of these policy reversals would be beneficial in other than demographic respects and some would be harmful unless special precautions were taken. The aim would be to reduce the number, not the quality, of the next generation.

A closely related method of de-emphasizing the family would be modification of the complementarity of the roles of men and women. Men are now able to participate in the wider world yet enjoy the satisfaction of having several children because the housework and childcare fall mainly on their wives. Women are impelled to seek this role by their idealized view of marriage and motherhood and by either the scarcity of alternative roles or the difficulty of combining them with family roles. To change this situation women could be required to work outside the home, or compelled by circumstances to do so. If, at the same time, women were paid as well as men and given equal educational and occupational opportunities, and if social life were organized around the place of work rather than around the home or neighborhood, many women would develop interests that would compete with family interests. Approximately this policy is now followed in several Communist countries, and even the less developed of these currently have extremely low birth rates (54).

That inclusion of women in the labor force has a negative effect on reproduction is indicated by regional comparisons (18, p. 1195; 55). But in most countries the wife's employment is subordinate, economically and emotionally, to her family role, and is readily sacrificed for the latter. No society has restructured both the occupational system and the domestic establishment to the point of permanently modifying the old division of labor by sex.

In any deliberate effort to control the birth rate along these lines, a government has two powerful instruments—its command over economic planning and its authority (real or potential) over education. The first determines (as far as policy can) the economic conditions and circumstances affecting the lives of all citizens; the second provides the knowledge and attitudes necessary to implement the plans. The economic system largely determines who shall work, what can be bought, what rearing children will cost, how much individuals can spend. The schools define family roles and develop vocational and recreational interests; they could, if it were desired, redefine the sex roles, develop interests that transcend the home, and transmit realistic (as opposed to moralistic) knowledge concerning marriage, sexual behavior, and population problems. When the problem is viewed in this light, it is clear that the ministries of economics and education, not the ministry of health, should be the source of population policy.

The Dilemma of Population Policy

It should now be apparent why, despite strong anxiety over runaway population growth, the actual programs purporting to control it are limited to family planning and are therefore ineffective. (i) The goal of zero, or even slight, population growth is one that nations and groups find difficult to accept. (ii) The measures that would be required to implement such a goal, though not so revolutionary as a Brave New World or a Communist Utopia, nevertheless tend to offend most people reared in existing societies. As a consequence, the goal of so-called population control is implicit and vague; the method is only family planning. This method, far from de-emphasizing the family, is familistic. One of its stated goals is that of helping sterile couples to *have* children. It stresses parental aspirations and responsibilities. It goes along with most aspects of conventional morality, such as condemnation of abortion, disapproval of premarital intercourse, respect for religious teachings and cultural taboos, and obeisance to medical and clerical authority. It deflects hostility by refusing to recommend any change other than the one it stands for: availability of contraceptives.

The things that make family planning acceptable are the very things that make it ineffective for population control. By stressing the right of parents to have the number of children they want, it evades the basic question of population policy, which is how to give societies the number of children they need. By offering only the means for *couples* to control fertility, it neglects the means for societies to do so.

Because of the predominantly pro-family character of existing societies, individual interest ordinarily leads to the production of enough offspring to constitute rapid population growth under conditions of low mortality. Childless or single-child homes are considered indicative of personal failure, whereas having three to five living children gives a family a sense of continuity and substantiality (56).

Given the existing desire to have moderate-sized rather than small families, the only countries in which fertility has been reduced to match reduction in mortality are advanced ones temporarily experiencing worsened economic conditions. In Sweden, for instance, the net reproduction rate (NRR) has been below replacement for 34 years (1930-63), if the period is taken as a whole, but this is because of the economic depression. The average replacement rate was below unity (NRR $= 0.81$) for the period 1930-42, but from 1942 through 1963 it was above unity (NRR $= 1.08$). Hardships that seem particularly conducive to deliberate lowering of the birth rate are (in managed economies) scarcity of housing and other consumer goods despite full employment, and required high participation of women in the labor force, or (in freer economies) a great deal of unemployment and economic insecurity. When conditions are good, any nation tends to have a growing population.

It follows that, in countries where contraception is used, a realistic proposal for a government policy of lowering the birth rate reads like a catalogue of horrors: squeeze consumers through taxation and inflation; make housing very scarce by limiting construction; force wives and mothers to work outside the home to offset the inadequacy of male wages, yet provide few childcare facilities; encourage migration to the city by paying low wages in the country and providing few rural jobs; increase congestion in cities by starving the transit system; increase personal insecurity by encouraging conditions that produce unemployment and by haphazard political arrests. No government will institute such hardships simply for the purpose of controlling population growth. Clearly, therefore, the task of contemporary population policy is to develop attractive substitutes for family interests, so as to avoid having to turn to hardship as a corrective. The specific measures required for developing such substitutes are not easy to determine in the absence of research on the question.

In short, the world's population problem cannot be solved by pretense and wishful thinking. The unthinking identification of family planning with population control is an ostrich-like approach in that it permits people to hide from themselves the enormity and unconventionality of the task. There is no reason to abandon family-planning programs; contraception is a valuable technological instrument. But such programs must be supplemented with equal or greater investments in research and experimentation to determine the required socioeconomic measures.

REFERENCES AND NOTES

1. *Studies in Family Planning, No. 16* (1967).
2. *Ibid., No. 9* (1966), p. 1.

3. The statement is given in *Studies in Family Planning (I*, p. 1), and in *Population Bull.* 23, 6 (1967).
4. The statement is quoted in *Studies in Family Planning* (*I*, p. 2).
5. *Hearings on S. 1676, U.S. Senate, Subcommittee on Foreign Aid Expenditures, 89th Congress, Second Session, April 7, 8, 11* (1966), pt. 4.
6. B. L. Raina, in *Family Planning and Population Programs*. B. Berelson, R. K. Anderson, O. Harkavy, G. Maier, W. P. Mauldin, S. G. Segal, Eds. (Univ. of Chicago Press, Chicago, 1966).
7. D. Kirk, *Ann. Amer. Acad. Polit. Soc. Sci.* 369, 53 (1967).
8. As used by English-speaking demographers, the world *fertility* designates actual reproductive performance, not a theoretical capacity.
9. K. Davis, *Rotarian* 94, 10 (1959); *Health Educ. Monographs* 9, 2 (1960); L. Day and A. Day, *Too Many Americans* (Houghton Mifflin, Boston, 1964); R. A. Piddington, *Limits of Mankind* (Wright, Bristol, England, 1956).
10. *Official Gazette* (15 Apr. 1965); quoted in *Studies in Family Planning* (*I*, p. 7).
11. J. W. Gardner, Secretary of Health, Education, and Welfare, "Memorandum to Heads of Operating Agencies" (Jan. 1966), reproduced in *Hearings on S. 1676 (5)*, p. 783.
12. C. Tietze, *Demography* 1, 119 (1964); *J. Chronic Diseases* 18, 1161 (1964); M. Muramatsu, *Milbank Mem. Fund Quart.* 38, 153 (1960); K. Davis, *Population Index* 29, 345 (1963); R. Armijo and T. Monreal, *J. Sex Res.* 1964, 143 (1964); Proceedings World Population Conference, Belgrade, 1965; Proceedings International Planned Parenthood Federation.
13. *Studies in Family Planning, No. 4* (1964), p. 3.
14. D. Bell (then administrator for Agency for International Development), in *Hearings on S. 1676 (5)*, p. 862.
15. *Asian Population Conference* (United Nations, New York, 1964), p. 30.
16. R. Armijo and T. Monreal, in *Components of Population Change in Latin America* (Milbank Fund, New York, 1965), p. 272; E. Rice-Wray, *Amer. J. Public Health* 54, 313 (1964).
17. E. Rice-Wray, in "Intra-Uterine Contraceptive Devices," *Excerpta Med. Intern. Congr. Ser. No. 54* (1962), p. 135.
18. J. Blake, in *Public Health and Population Change*, M. C. Sheps and J. C. Ridley, Eds. (Univ. of Pittsburgh Press, Pittsburgh, 1965).
19. J. Blake and K. Davis, *Amer. Behavioral Scientist*, 5, 24 (1963).
20. See "Panel discussion on comparative acceptability of different methods of contraception," in *Research in Family Planning*, C. V. Kiser, Ed. (Princeton Univ. Press, Princeton, 1962), pp. 373-86.
21. "From the point of view of the woman concerned, the whole problem of continuing motivation disappears, . . ." [D. Kirk, in *Population Dynamics*, M. Muramatsu and P. A. Harper, Eds. (Johns Hopkins Press, Baltimore, 1965)].
22. "For influencing family size norms, certainly the examples and statements of public figures are of great significance . . . also . . . use of mass-communication methods which help to legitimize the small-family style, to provoke conversation, and to establish a vocabulary for discussion of family planning." [M. W. Freymann, in *Population Dynamics*, M. Muramatsu and P. A. Harper, Eds. (Johns Hopkins Press, Baltimore, 1965)].
23. O. A. Collver, *Birth Rates in Latin America* (International Population and Urban Research, Berkeley, Calif., 1965), pp. 27-28; the ten countries were Colombia, Costa Rica, El Salvador, Ecuador, Guatemala, Honduras, Mexico, Panamá, Peru, and Venezuela.
24. J. R. Rele, *Fertility Analysis through Extension of Stable Population Concepts.* (International Population and Urban Research, Berkeley, Calif., 1967).
25. J. C. Ridley, M. C. Sheps, J. W. Lingner, J. A. Menken, *Milbank Mem. Fund Quart.* 45, 77 (1967); E. Arriaga, unpublished paper.
26. "South Korea and Taiwan appear successfully to have checked population growth by the use of intrauterine contraceptive devices" [U. Borell, *Hearings on S. 1676* (5), p. 556].
27. K. Davis, *Population Index* 29, 345 (1963).
28. R. Freedman, *ibid.* 31, 421 (1965).
29. Before 1964 the Family Planning Association had given advice to fewer than 60,000 wives in 10 years and a Pre-Pregnancy Health Program had reached some 10,000; and, in the current campaign, 3650 IUD's were inserted in 1965, in a total population of 2 1/2 million women of reproductive age. See *Studies in Family Planning No. 19* (1967), p. 4, and R. Freedman *et al., Population Studies* 16, 231 (1963).
30. R. W. Gillespie, *Family Planning on Taiwan* (Population Council, Taichung, 1965).
31. During the period 1950-60 the ratio of growth in the city to growth of the noncity population was 5:3; during the period 1960-64 the ratio was 5:2; these ratios are based on data of Shaohsing Chen, *J. Sociol. Taiwan* 1, 74 (1963) and data in the United Nations *Demographic Yearbooks*.
32. R. Freedman, *Population Index* 31, 434 (1965). Taichung's rate of decline in 1963-64 was roughly double the average in four other cities, whereas just prior to the campaign its rate of decline had been much less than theirs.

33. S. H. Chen, *J. Soc. Sci. Taipei* 13, 72 (1963).
34. R. Freedman *et al., Population Studies* 16, 227 (1963); *ibid.,* p. 232.
35. In 1964 the life expectancy at birth was already 66 years in Taiwan, as compared to 70 for the United States.
36. J. Blake, *Eugenics Quart.* 14, 68 (1967).
37. Women accepting IUD's in the family-planning program are typically 30 to 34 years old and have already had four children. [*Studies in Family Planning No. 19* (1967), p. 5].
38. Y. K. Cha, in *Family Planning and Population Programs,* B. Berelson *et al.,* Eds. (Univ. of Chicago Press, Chicago, 1966).
39. H. S. Ayalvi and S. S. Johl, *J. Family Welfare* 12, 60 (1965).
40. Sixty percent of the women had borne their first child before age 19. Early marriage is strongly supported by public opinion. Of couples polled in the Punjab, 48 percent said that girls *should* marry before age 16, and 94 percent said they should marry before age 20 (H. S. Ayalvi and S. Johl, *ibid.,* p. 57). A study of 2380 couples in 60 villages of Uttar Pradesh found that the women had consummated their marriage at an average age of 14.6 years [J. R. Rele, *Population Studies* 15, 268 (1962)].
41. J. Morsa, in *Family Planning and Population Programs,* B. Berelson *et al.,* Eds. (Univ. of Chicago Press, Chicago, 1966).
42. H. Gille and R. J. Pardoko, *ibid.,* p. 515; S. N. Agarwala, *Med. Dig. Bombay* 4, 653 (1961).
43. *Mysore Population Study* (United Nations, New York, 1961), p. 140.
44. A. Daly, in *Family Planning and Population Programs,* B. Berelson *et al.,* Eds. (Univ. of Chicago Press, Chicago, 1966).
45. C. J. Goméz, paper presented at the World Population Conference, Belgrade, 1965.
46. C. Miro, in *Family Planning and Population Programs,* B. Berelson *et al.,* Eds. (Univ. of Chicago Press, Chicago, 1966).
47. *Demographic Training and Research Centre (India) Newsletter* 20, 4 (Aug. 1966).
48. K. Davis, *Population Index* 29, 345 (1963). For economic and sociological theory of motivation for having children, see J. Blake [Univ. of California (Berkeley)], in preparation.
49. K. Davis, *Amer. Economic Rev.* 46, 305 (1956); *Sci. Amer.* 209, 68 (1963).
50. J. Blake, *World Population Conference [Belgrade, 1965]* (United Nations, New York, 1967), vol. 2, pp. 132-36.
51. S. Enke, *Rev. Economics Statistics* 42, 175 (1960);———, *Econ. Develop. Cult. Change* 8, 339 (1960);———, *ibid.* 10, 427 (1962); A. O. Krueger and L. A. Sjaastad, *ibid.,* p. 423.
52. T. J. Samuel, *J. Family Welfare India* 13, 12 (1966).
53. Sixty-two countries, including 27 in Europe, give cash payments to people for having children [U.S. Social Security Administration, *Social Security Programs Throughout the World, 1967* (Government Printing Office, Washington, D.C., 1967), pp. xxvii-xxviii].
54. Average gross reproduction rates in the early 1960's were as follows: Hungary, 0.91; Bulgaria, 1.09; Romania, 1.15; Yugoslavia, 1.32.
55. O. A. Collver and E. Langlois, *Econ. Develop. Cult. Change* 10, 367 (1962); J. Weeks, [Univ. of California (Berkeley)], unpublished paper.
56. Roman Catholic textbooks condemn the "small" family (one with fewer than four children as being abnormal [J. Blake, *Population Studies* 20, 27 (1966)].
57. Judith Blake's critical readings and discussions have greatly helped in the preparation of this article.

Ideology and Faith

61   Soviet Population Theory

DAEL WOLFLE

A genuine difference of opinion seems to have opened among Russian economists and demographers over the Marxist doctrine that overpopulation can exist only under capitalism and that in a Communist world of constantly expanding production, economic and cultural advances automatically bring population into balance with resources. Primary emphasis on economic and social progress and planning has not been abandoned, but that there is need for concurrent population planning is the message of a number of recent articles in *Literaturnaya Gazeta* and other Russian publications that Robert Cook analyzes in the October issue of the *Population Bulletin,* published by the Population Reference Bureau.*

Some of these articles defend the traditional Marxist position, but others, by a number of authors, recognize inadequacies of the traditional position. Some authors ridicule projections of a possible world population of 3, 4, or even 13 million people that have been advanced as possibilities if we use solar energy more effectively for photosynthesis, cultivate the land more intensively, and grow plants in the ocean on the scale possible on land. They criticize these estimates as exercises in arithmetic that make no economic or social sense, and contend that we should plan for "a comfortable way of life" for the world's population, that we must "create conditions worthy of humanity," and that the goal should be the "maximum per capita happiness of the people" rather than the maximum number of people.

Several authors deny that Russia has a population problem but recognize that many other countries do. And, indeed, population has been growing more slowly in Russia than in most of the less developed nations. Nevertheless, the comparison with other countries makes it probable that Russia will be accused, as the United States has been, of advocating population control measures for the less developed parts of the world but of failing to practice at home what it preaches to others. Russia has, however, already cut some of the ground from under such accusations by several actions that will reduce the Russian birth rate: relegalizing abortion, substantially reducing family allowances, and announcing that the government will no longer support illegitimate children.

The United Nations Population Commission met in Geneva from 30 October through 10 November. Although observers noted no further change in Soviet attitudes, it is nevertheless noteworthy that three times in 1966 the U.S.S.R. joined with the U.S. and other countries in voting affirmatively on the United Nations actions in the population field.

*Population Reference Bureau, 1755 Massachusetts Avenue, N.W., Washington, D.C.

Agreement within the U.N. not only strengthens current U.N. population programs but also increases a bit the likelihood that we may be able to move on to a problem that most of us have been dodging. Kingsley Davis has pointed out that the increasingly widespread endorsement of contraception throughout the world, with justification on the grounds that married couples should be free to decide for themselves how many children they will have, is completely insufficient for reducing the rate of population growth and constitutes only the barest beginning of a social policy on population. The current Russian debate will be most constructive if it helps the U.N., and individual countries, advance to the stage of meaningful analysis of population planning and adoption of measures to curb the runaway growth of the world's population.

Do Roman Catholic Countries Have the Highest Birth Rates?   **62**

POPULATION REFERENCE BUREAU, INC.

Recently the Population Reference Bureau released a 1968 "World Population Data Sheet" containing up-to-date demographic information for 136 countries. This information was widely reported by the press. Amid the commentary, however, an old misconception reappeared—namely, that Roman Catholic countries have the world's highest birth rates. Typical was one editorial which said: "The birth rate in the 'havenot' and Catholic nations soars while the literacy rate and per capita income level remain stagnant."

Several errors cloud this brief statement. Not only do United Nations figures show that birth rates are not soaring anywhere in the world, but many Roman Catholic nations have achieved some of the lowest such rates on record. Furthermore, per capita incomes in European Catholic nations range from $350 to $1,500; their weighted average is higher than per capita income in all but a very few countries of non-Catholic Asia or Africa. And if the literacy rate remains stagnant in most of Europe's Catholic countries, it is mainly because they conquered illiteracy long ago.

The big difference between high and low birth-rate nations, according to demographers, is not whether they are Catholic or non-Catholic but whether they are economically underdeveloped or advanced. In the advanced countries of the West, the industrial revolution spurred a gradual reduction of mortality and a gradual spread of literacy—two trends followed by a slow, spontaneous decline in birth rates. As a rule this downtrend in natality proceeded only a generation or so after the drop in mortality, and the excess of births over deaths was therefore not great enough to cause a "population explosion" in the sense of that term today. The annual rate of population growth in Europe in the nineteenth century

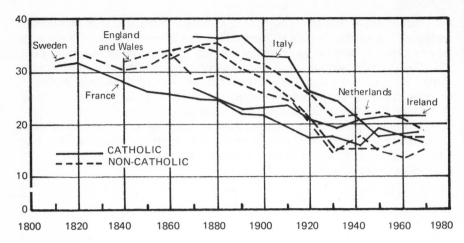

FIGURE 1. Birth rate trends in selected Catholic and non-Catholic countries of Europe.

never reached 1 percent a year. In some developing countries today, growth exceeds 3 percent. This contrast is strikingly shown in Figure 2, which compares trends in births and deaths in highly developed Sweden and still developing Mexico.

Despite such discrepancies, some observers have speculated that a European-style demographic transition will occur in the underdeveloped countries. The facts, however, run contrary to such an assumption.

In the economically depressed regions of Asia, Africa and Latin America, two demographic realities stand out as distinctly different from their counterparts in the West. First, illiteracy remains very high, and in many countries the number of illiterates is actually growing. No widespread or marked decline in birth rates has ever been recorded under such conditions. Secondly, the death rate in these regions has been drastically reduced within just a few decades through a highly effective infusion of modern public health techniques. People there have not had time to adjust to the fact that many more children and adults are surviving than before, and they continue to produce babies at a very high rate. This widening gap between births and deaths is the direct cause of the world's accelerating population growth. It can be seen in both Catholic and non-Catholic nations. But so can the modern pattern of low death rates and *low* birth rates be seen in both Catholic and non-Catholic nations.

The European Example

Europe offers a clear example of modern demographic trends. What is the impact of Roman Catholicism on the birth rates there?

Based on population, the Roman Catholic countries of Europe are Ireland, Austria, Belgium, France, Luxembourg, Czechoslovakia, Hungary, Poland, Italy, Portugal and Spain. (West Germany, with a population evenly divided between Catholics and Protestants, is not counted in this tabulation.) Experts within the

Catholic Church, the World Council of Churches and the United Nations differ markedly in their definitions of a Catholic country. Some rule out any nation with a communist government, others accept certain communist governments but not all, and still others accept any nation in which over half the people are Roman Catholics. We have used this last definition because it leads to the fewest contradictions and because in Europe, at least, birth rates have run counter to government policy as often as they have reflected it.

Taken together, the 11 Roman Catholic countries of Europe have an average annual birth rate of only 18.1 babies per 1,000 people. The birth rate for the 15 non-Roman Catholic countries averages out to virtually the same: 18.0. In short, there is no evidence in Europe

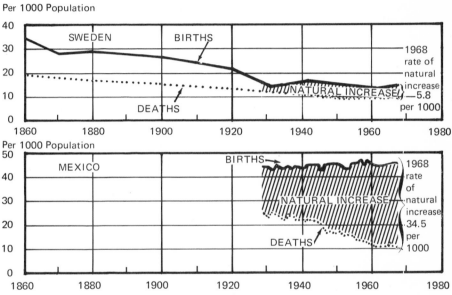

FIGURE 2. Natural increase trends, Sweden vs. Mexico.

for the widely-held belief that Roman Catholicism exerts a buoyant force on overall birth rates. Even when compared by a more sensitive gauge of natality—birth rates specifically for women in the child-bearing ages of 15-44—Catholic and non-Catholic nations are very much alike (Figure 3).

Looking at the statistics in more detail, one finds that considerably lower-than-average natality rates occur in the three European countries where branches of the Greek Orthodox Catholic religion claim a majority following. For these countries—Romania, Bulgaria and Greece—the average birth rate is only 15.4. Three nations with heavily Roman Catholic populations—Ireland, Portugal and Spain—are among the least industrialized in Europe, but even they have birth rates just barely above the low European average of 18.0. And they are low indeed when compared with the figures of 35 to 50 that prevail in Asia, Africa and Latin America.

Particularly interesting are two countries at the extremes of Europe's birth-rate spectrum, both under communist control. Roman Catholic Hungary, where abortions are easily and legally obtained, has the world's lowest birth rate at 13.6, while non-Catholic Albania's rate is a lofty 34.0. Abortions, incidentally, are legal merely on the grounds of a woman's wishes in Hungary and Bulgaria; they are legal for a liberal variety of medical, eugenic and social reasons in Czechoslo-vakia, Poland, Yugoslavia, Norway, Sweden, Iceland, Denmark and Finland; they are harder to get but still permissible in Switzerland, Romania, East Germany and the United Kingdom; they are severely limited to urgent medical reasons in West Germany, Italy, Greece, the Netherlands, Portugal, Austria, France and Belgium; and they are legally forbidden in Ireland and Spain. Despite the varying strictures against them, however, abortions do take place in great numbers throughout Europe. The International Planned Parenthood Federation estimates that at least a one-to-one ratio exists between illegal abortions and live births in Austria, Belgium, France, West Germany and Italy.

Significantly, the historic transition from large to small families in the West began in two Roman Catholic nations—France and Ireland. In the former country, birth rates began falling nearly 200 years ago, long before the trend was observed elsewhere. (France's head start is shown in Figure 1, which clearly reveals the similarity in birth trends for both the Catholic and non-Catholic nations of Europe). The decline in France was caused by "the prevention of births within marriage by contraceptive means," according to Alfred Sauvy, former Director of the French National Institute for Demographic Studies. It occurred despite a strongly pro-natalist government policy and it quickly spread across all class lines, with much less discrepancy between city and rural fertility than is common in most countries today. The French experience of the late 18th and early 19th centuries was a classic example of population restraint that is spontane-ously exercised by the people in the face of governmental and ecclesiastical opposition.

Crisis Area: Latin America

One region where Roman Catholicism coincides with high birth rates is, of course, Latin America. Here birth rates range from the low 20's for two temperate countries to above 45 for several nations in Central America, the Caribbean and tropical South America. The continental average is 40. Responding to modern medicine and public health measures, moreover, Latin America's death rate has dropped from over 20 to 10 in just a few decades—and is now only a fraction higher than that of the United States. These death rates are not directly compara-ble because of the higher proportion of young people in the developing world. When widely differing age distributions are taken into account, mortality rates in Latin America turn out to be somewhat higher than those of the developed countries. Still, no other large area of the world so dramatically combines a modern low death rate with a traditional high birth rate. Tropical Latin Ameri-ca's population is growing explosively by over three percent a year, and if present trends continue the number of people throughout the continent will double to some 536 million by 1992.

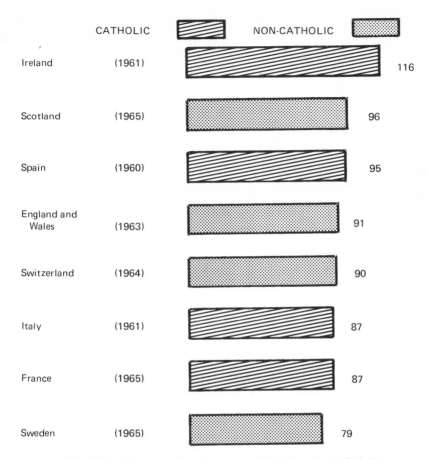

FIGURE 3. Birth rates per 1000 women aged 15-44 in selected Catholic and non-Catholic countries of Europe.

Even in heavily Roman Catholic Latin America, however, there are valid reasons for attributing high birth rates less to religious doctrine than to economic levels of living. Church influence against formal birth control programs is quite strong, but its control over sexual behavior within families is usually overrated. Surveys conducted by the United Nations Latin American Demographic Center (CELADE) and Cornell University, for example, have demonstrated a striking lack of religious influence on the number of children born to women in six Latin American cities. Using the frequency of attendance at Mass as a gauge of religiosity, the studies show that "devout" Catholic women have slightly *fewer* children, on the average, than women who are only "nominally" Catholic. There is, on the other hand, a strong link between education and fertility. In some of the cities surveyed by CELADE, women with less than a primary school education have at least one more child than their better educated counterparts—regardless of the degree of their religious conviction.

Thus it is Latin America's economic and educational levels, rather than its formal religious beliefs, that put it on common ground with the high-fertility regions of Africa and Asia. National per capita incomes on the continent range from $80 to $960 but still average only $350 a year, and illiteracy still holds a third of the population in its grasp. Thus, it is significant to note that the only major Latin American nations with birth rates under 30—Argentina (21.5) and Uruguay (23-25)—are also the two with the highest literacy levels. Furthermore they have the continent's highest per capita incomes ($740 and $540) outside of heavily subsidized Puerto Rico and oil-rich Venezuela, where the distribution of wealth is extremely uneven. As with many of their Latin neighbors, Argentines and Uruguayans frequently resort to birth control in its most extreme form— abortion. The ratio of aborted to live births in Uruguay, according to some sources, may be as high as three to one. In Chile, where statistics are more reliable, studies show that of every 100 pregnancies 25 end in artificially induced abortions.

The Policy of the Church

Italy, home of the Vatican, did not experience the transition to modern low birth rates until quite recently. At the insistence of the dictator Mussolini, a series of laws was passed in the 1920's which encouraged, through strong incentives and severe penalties, an *increase* in the national birth rate. Italians promptly responded to this suasion by *reducing* their output of bambinos. Under Il Duce the birth rate fell from about 26 in 1922 to 21 in 1940. Today it hovers just slightly above the European average at 18.9, and large areas of northern Italy record some of the lowest regional birth rates in the world. Since the Italian limitation of natural increase is being practiced around the very headquarters of the Roman Catholic Church, it raises a central question: What *is* the attitude of the Church toward population growth?

Today the Vatican finds itself in the rather paradoxical position of recognizing the dangers of the population explosion while barring the use of reliable contraceptives. Even this delicate balancing act, however, is a major advance over the traditional doctrines espoused in Pope Pius XI's famous 1930 Encyclical, "Casti Connubii."

This Encyclical warned that "since the conjugal act is destined primarily for the begetting of children, those who in exercising it deliberately frustrate its natural power and purpose sin against nature and commit a deed which is shameful and intrinsically vicious."

The harsh tone of "Casti Connubii" sounds medieval compared with that of Papal Representative the Reverend Father Stanislas de Lestapis, who addressed a United Nations meeting in Rome only 24 years later. "The choice of the number of children in the bosom of the family," he said in 1954, "is the sole personal responsibility of the spouses ... who not only take into consideration their personal welfare but also the welfare of their children ... and finally the general welfare of the human community, present and future."

It was this public statement, more than any other, which recognized the moral obligation of married couples to assure that hyperfertility does not endanger the family or the wider society. Subsequent announcements from the Holy See, notably the 1967 Encyclical, "On the Development of Peoples," have enlarged the theme adumbrated by Father Lestapis. This recent Encyclical from Pope Paul displays a truly broad and penetrating concern for demographic trends.

"It is true," the Pope announced, "that too frequently an accelerated demographic increase adds its own difficulties to the problems of development: the size of the population increases more rapidly than the available resources, and things are found to have reached apparently an impasse. . . . It is certain that public authorities can intervene, within the limit of their competence, by favoring the availability of appropriate information and by adopting suitable measures, provided that these be in conformity with the moral law."

Pope Paul also stressed the obligation of Catholic couples not to have more children than they can adequately provide for. "It is for the parents to decide on the number of their children," he said, "taking into account their responsibilities towards God, themselves, the children they have already brought into the world, and the community to which they belong."

The spirit of this message is one with which reasonable people around the world can feel at home. As it reveals quite clearly, the Roman Catholic Church is now directing the concern of its followers to the population problem. The Church is unrealistic only in that it offers conscientious Catholics just two means of birth control—complete or periodic abstinence. No chemical, physiological or mechanical methods have yet been approved. But while these limitations are profound, it is unfair to indict Roman Catholicism for encouraging oversized families or for promoting high birth rates. Even with respect to the means of birth control, the Church is not monolithically consistent. Richard Cardinal Cushing of Boston has several times declared that U.S. Catholics "do not seek to impose by law their moral views on other members" of a pluralistic society. The Reverend Father Dexter Hanley, S. J., a prominent Jesuit scholar who directs the Institute of Law, Human Rights and Social Values at Georgetown University, likewise affirms that "the government must allow each individual to choose the most adequate method of family planning in accord with his moral standards." These liberal views echo the expressed thought of many other Roman Catholic priests around the world.

The demographic evidence, finally, will not support a broad indictment of Church influence against population restraint. In Europe, where birth rates are low, there is virtually no differential between Catholic and non-Catholic countries. In Latin America, where birth rates are still high, religion is demonstrably less of a factor than levels of literacy and income. The figures speak for themselves.

Population Control

63 Population Control, Sterilization, and Ignorance

THOMAS EISNER
ARI VAN TIENHOVEN
FRANK ROSENBLATT

We recently submitted a questionnaire to students and faculty at Cornell University designed to test attitudes and preferences concerning family size and contraceptive technique. The 1059 respondents (74 percent males) were a mixed lot who represented the physical and biological sciences, humanities, and social sciences and who included faculty (294), graduate students (174), upperclassmen (264), and freshmen (327). Given the level of education of the sample, the results were unexpected in several respects.

First, although there was general agreement (84 percent) on the desirability of limiting family size, a substantial majority (65 percent) said it wanted three children (39 percent) or more (26 percent). Only 30 percent favored two children, and a mere 5 percent expressed preference for one or none. Choice was in no major way affected by age, sex, marital status, parenthood, or professional specialty. Even the respondents whom we expected to be most concerned about the population crisis (for example, graduate students and young faculty in biology) included a minimum of 50 percent with a desire for three children or more.

As regards contraception, about one-half favored "the pill" over all other available means as a way both to space children (53 percent) and to maintain family size at its desired limit (50 percent). Other contraceptive appliances such as condoms, diaphragms, and intrauterine devices were each given top preference by no more than 13 percent of the sample. Voluntary sterilization, either of man or woman, was judged as decidedly undesirable. Only 6 percent opted in favor of vasectomy as the preferred form of contraception once full family size had been achieved; the corresponding number favoring ligation of the oviducts was 2 percent. A majority (52 percent of males and 61 percent of females) said they would *never* undergo sterilization, even after having had the desired number of children. The operation was judged to be as undesirable as abortion and abstinence for prevention of family growth beyond the set limit. It is of interest in this connection that the consequences of sterilization are not generally understood. For example, asked whether vasectomy would abolish the ability to ejaculate, nearly half the respondents (49 percent) confessed to ignorance or expressed either certainty or probability that emission would no longer accompany orgasm. Biology students scored no better than nonbiologists, and graduate students, even after marriage and parenthood, seemed to be no better informed than freshmen. The only exceptional group was the biology faculty, but, even there, 30 percent were either misinformed or uninformed on this point. Comparable ignorance prevails with respect to oviduct ligation: 37 percent of respondents were certain, or thought it probable, that the operation would interfere with the menstrual cycle.

We are bothered by these results. Perhaps of least general concern is the probability that proponents of voluntary sterilization are backing a hopeless or nearly hopeless cause. But what are we to make of the educated youth growing up among us that is either unconcerned about population growth or, at the very least, unable or unwilling to apply to itself the simple arithmetic of compound interest? And what, if any, are the prospects for improved sex education when ignorance about the reproductive system is widespread even among those who should know best?

Abortion

History of Abortion 64

James R. Newman

Abortion is an ancient practice, but even in antiquity it provoked sharp differences of opinion. Plato, in the *Republic,* approved abortion to prevent the birth of incestuous offspring; Aristotle, always a practical fellow, looked upon it as a useful Malthusian governor. The Hippocratic oath, on the other hand, contains the words "I will not give to a woman a pessary to produce abortion"; Seneca and Cicero condemned abortion on ethical grounds; and the Justinian Code prohibited it. There seems little doubt, however, that in the Roman Empire and the Hellenistic world abortion was, as one authority has stated, "very common among the upper classes." The Christian Church took a stern stand against this "pagan attitude," and pronounced abortion a sin. In many states the law followed church doctrine and made the sin a crime. But in Anglo-Saxon law abortion was considered "an ecclesiastical offense only."

65   Those Smelly Roman Lamps

ASHLEY MONTAGU

Since the discovery in recent years that certain airborne odors, "phero-
mones," are capable of producing a number of reproductive changes, including
abortion, in a variety of different animals, it is of great interest to note that the
phenomenon had been noted for the human female as early as the first century
A.D. Pliny the Elder (about A.D. 23-79) wrote, "One feels pity and even shame
in realizing how trivial is the origin of the proudest of animals, when the smell
of lamps being put out usually causes abortion."[1]

Pliny's "usually" (plerisque) undoubtedly represents a gross exaggeration. I
wonder how true this observation was? It would be of interest to know what was
burned by Romans in the lamps they customarily used. What would have been
released by Roman lamps that might have had the effect stated by Pliny?

KIFFIN A. ROCKWELL

Four hundred years before Pliny, Aristotle wrote: "Mares miscarry at the
scent of an extinguished lamp; this happens also to some women." This is the
probable source of Pliny and others who make the same remark . . . Montagu will
find out about lamps if he plows on through the *Natural History*. The ancients
preferred clear olive oil for lighting, but burned anything they could, including
castor oil and tallow. The wicks were of any capillary material — papyrus waste,
rope, and wool were used, and the wick might contain sulfur to help it catch.
There were many nauseous possibilities. . . .

66   Abortion—or Compulsory Pregnancy?

GARRETT HARDIN

The problem of abortion is usually seen as one of justifying a particular surgical
operation on the assumption that great social loss is incurred by it. This approach leads to intractable administrative problems: rape is in principle impossible to prove, the paternity of a child is always in doubt, the probability of
defective embryos is generally low, and the socioeconomic predicament of the
supplicant has little power to move the men who sit in judgment. These difficulties vanish when one substitutes for the problem of permissive abortion the

1. Pliny, *Natural History*, H. Rackham, Transl. (Harvard Univ. Press, Cambridge, Mass., 1952), p.
   534.

inverse problem of compulsory pregnancy. The latter is a special case of compulsory servitude, which the Western world has agreed, in principle, has no valid justification. Unfortunately, state legislatures are now in a process of setting up systems for the management of compulsory pregnancy. The experience of Scandinavia indicates that women do not accept bureaucratic management of their unwanted pregnancies; therefore we can confidently predict that the reform bills now going through our legislatures will have little effect on the practice of illegal abortion. Only the abolition of compulsory pregnancy will solve the erroneously conceived "abortion problem."

The year 1967 produced the first fissures in the dam that had prevented all change in the abortion-prohibition laws of the United States for three-quarters of a century. Two states adopted laws that allowed abortion in the "hardship cases" of rape, incest, and probability of a deformed child. A third approved the first two "indications," but not the last. All three took some note of the mental health of the pregnant woman, in varying language; how this language will be translated into practice remains to be seen. In almost two dozen other states, attempts to modify the laws were made but foundered at various stages in the legislative process. It is quite evident that the issue will continue to be a live one for many years to come.

The legislative turmoil was preceded and accompanied by a fast-growing popular literature. The word "abortion" has ceased to be a dirty word—which is a cultural advance. However, the *word* was so long under taboo that the ability to think about the *fact* seems to have suffered a sort of logical atrophy from disuse. Popular articles, regardless of their conclusions, tend to be over-emotional and to take a moralistic rather than an operational view of the matter. Nits are picked, hairs split. It is quite clear that many of the authors are not at all clear what question they are attacking.

It is axiomatic in science that progress hinges on asking the right question. Surprisingly, once the right question is asked the answer seems almost to tumble forth. That is a retrospective view; in prospect, it takes genuine (and mysterious) insight to see correctly into the brambles created by previous, ill-chosen verbalizations.

The abortion problem is, I think, a particularly neat example of a problem in which most of the difficulties are actually created by asking the wrong question. I submit further that once the right question is asked the whole untidy mess miraculously dissolves, leaving in its place a very simple public policy recommendation.

Rape as a Justification

The wrong question, the one almost invariably asked, is this: "How can we justify an abortion?" This assumes that there are weighty public reasons for encouraging pregnancies, or that abortions, per se, somehow threaten public peace. A direct examination of the legitimacy of these assumptions will be made later. For the present, let us pursue the question as asked and see what a morass it leads to.

Almost all the present legislative attempts take as their model a bill proposed by the American Law Institute which emphasizes three justifications for legal abortion: rape, incest, and the probability of a defective child. Whatever else may be said about this bill, it is clear that it affects only the periphery of the social problem. The Arden House Conference Committee[1] estimated the number of illegal abortions in the United States to be between 200,000 and 1,200,000 per year. A California legislator, Anthony C. Beilenson,[2] has estimated that the American Law Institute bill (which he favors) would legalize not more than four percent of the presently illegal abortions. Obviously, the "problem" of illegal abortion will be scarcely affected by the passage of the laws so far proposed in the United States.

I have calculated[3] that the number of rape-induced pregnancies in the United States is about 800 per year. The number is not large, but for the woman raped the total number is irrelevant. What matters to her is that she be relieved of her unwanted burden. But a law which puts the burden of proof on her compels her to risk a second harrowing experience. How can she *prove* to the district attorney that she was raped? He could really know whether or not she gave consent only if he could get inside her mind; this he cannot do. Here is the philosopher's "egocentric predicament" that none of us can escape. In an effort to help the district attorney sustain the illusion that he can escape this predicament, a talented woman may put on a dramatic performance, with copious tears and other signs of anguish. But what if the raped woman is not an actress? What if her temperament is stoic? In its operation, the law will act against the interests of calm, undramatic women. Is that what we want? It is safe to say also that district attorneys will hear less favorably the pleas of poor women, the general assumption of middle-class agents being that the poor are less responsible in sex anyway.[4] Is it to the interest of society that the poor bear more children, whether rape-engendered or not?

A wryly amusing difficulty has been raised with respect to rape. Suppose the woman is married and having regular intercourse with her husband. Suppose that following a rape by an unknown intruder she finds herself pregnant. Is she legally entitled to an abortion? How does she know whose child she is carrying anyway? If it is her husband's child, abortion is illegal. If she carries it to term, and if blood tests then exclude the husband as the father, as they would in a fraction of the cases, is the woman then entitled to a *delayed* abortion? But this is ridiculous: this is infanticide, which no one is proposing. Such is the bramble bush into which we are led by a *reluctant* consent for abortion in cases of rape.

How Probable Must Deformity Be?

The majority of the public support abortion in cases of a suspected deformity

1. Mary Steichen Calderone (ed.), *Abortion in the United States,* New York: Hoeber-Harper, 1958, p. 178.
2. Anthony C. Beilenson, "Abortion and Common Sense," *Per/Se,* 1 (1966), p. 24.
3. Garrett Hardin, "Semantic Aspects of Abortion," *ETC.,* 24 (1967), p. 263.
4. Lee Rainwater, *And the Poor Get Children,* Chicago: Quadrangle Books, 1960, p. *IX* and chap. 1.

of the child[5] just as they do in cases of rape. Again, however, if the burden of proof rests on the one who requests the operation, we encounter difficulties in administration. Between 80,000 and 160,000 defective children are born every year in the United States. The number stated depends on two important issues: (a) how severe a defect must be before it is counted as such and (b) whether or not one counts as birth defects those defects that are not *detected* until later. (Deafness and various other defects produced by fetal rubella may not be detected until a year or so after birth.) However many defective infants there may be, what is the prospect of detecting them before birth?

The sad answer is: the prospects are poor. A small percentage can be picked up by microscopic examination of tissues of the fetus. But "amniocentesis"—the form of biopsy required to procure such tissues—is itself somewhat dangerous to both mother and fetus; most abnormalities will not be detectable by a microscopic examination of the fetal cells; and 96 to 98 percent of all fetuses are normal anyway. All these considerations are a contraindication of routine amniocentesis.

When experience indicates that the probability of a deformed fetus is above the "background level" of 2 to 4 percent, is abortion justified? At what level? 10 percent? 50? 80? Or only at 100 percent? Suppose a particular medical history indicates a probability of 20 percent that the baby will be defective. If we routinely abort such cases, it is undeniable that four normal fetuses will be destroyed for every one abnormal. Those who assume that a fetus is an object of high value are appalled at this "wastage." Not uncommonly they ask, "Why not wait until the baby is born and then suffocate those that are deformed?" Such a question is unquestionably rhetoric and sardonic; if serious, it implies that infanticide has no more emotional meaning to a woman than abortion, an assumption that is surely contrary to fact.

Should The Father Have Rights?

Men who are willing to see abortion-prohibition laws relaxed somewhat, but not completely, frequently raise a question about the "rights" of the father. Should we allow a woman to make a unilateral decision for an abortion? Should not her husband have a say in the matter? (After all, he contributed just as many chromosomes to the fetus as she.)

I do not know what weight to give this objection. I have encountered it repeatedly in the discussion section following a public meeting. It is clear that some men are disturbed at finding themselves powerless in such a situation and want the law to give them some power of decision.

Yet powerless men are—and it is nature that has made them so. If we give the father a right of veto in abortion decisions, the wife has a very simple reply to her husband: "I'm sorry, dear, I wasn't going to tell you this, but you've forced my hand. This is not your child." With such a statement she could always deny her husband's right to decide.

Why husbands should demand power in such matters is a fit subject for depth

---

5. Alice S. Rossi, "Abortion Laws and Their Victims," *Trans-action,* 3 (September-October, 1966), p. 7.

analysis. In the absence of such, perhaps the best thing we can say to men who are "hung up" on this issue is this: "Do you really want to live for another eight months with a woman whom you are compelling to be pregnant against her will?"

Or, in terms of public policy, do we want to pass laws which give men the right to compel their wives to be pregnant? Psychologically, such compulsion is akin to rape. Is it in the public interest to encourage rape?

"Socio-Economic"—An Anemic Phrase

The question "How can we justify an abortion?" proves least efficient in solving the real problems of this world when we try to evaluate what are usually called "socio-economic indications." The hardship cases—rape, incest, probability of a deformed child—have been amply publicized, and as a result the majority of the public accepts them as valid indicators; but hardship cases constitute only a few percent of the need. By contrast, if a woman has more children than she feels she can handle, or if her children are coming too close together, there is little public sympathy for her plight. A poll[5] conducted by the National Opinion Research Center in December, 1965, showed that only 15 percent of the respondents replied "Yes" to this question: "Please tell me whether or not you think it should be possible for a pregnant woman to obtain a legal abortion if she is married and does not want any more children." Yet this indication, which received the lowest rate of approval, accounts for the vast majority of instances in which women want—and illegally get—relief from unwanted pregnancy.

There is a marked discrepancy between the magnitude of the need and the degree of public sympathy. Part of the reason for this descrepancy is attributable to the emotional impact of the words used to describe the need. "Rape," "incest," "deformed child"—these words are rich in emotional connotations. "Socio-economic indications" is a pale bit of jargon, suggesting at best that the abortion is wanted because the woman lives by culpably materialistic standards. "Socio-economic indications" tugs at no one's heartstrings; the hyphenated abomination hides the human reality to which it obliquely refers. To show the sort of human problem to which this label may be attached, let me quote a letter I received from one woman. (The story is unique, but it is one of a large class of similar true stories.)

I had an illegal abortion 2-1/2 years ago. I left my church because of the guilt I felt. I had six children when my husband left me to live with another woman. We weren't divorced and I went to work to help support them. When he would come to visit the children he would sometimes stay after they were asleep. I became pregnant. When I told my husband, and asked him to please come back, he informed me that the woman he was living with was five months pregnant and ill, and that he couldn't leave her—not at that time anyway.

I got the name of a doctor in San Francisco from a Dr. friend who was visiting here from there. This Dr. (Ob. and Gyn.) had a good legitimate practice in the main part of the city and was a kindly, compassionate man who believes as you do, that it is better for everyone not to bring an unwanted child into the world.

It was over before I knew it. I thought I was just having an examination at the time. He

even tried to make me not feel guilty by telling me that the long automobile trip had already started a spontaneous abortion. He charged me $25. That was on Fri. and on Mon. I was back at work. I never suffered any ill from it.
The other woman's child died shortly after birth and six months later my husband asked if he could come back. We don't have a perfect marriage but my children have a father. My being able to work has helped us out of a deep financial debt. I shall always remember the sympathy I received from that Dr. and wish there were more like him with the courage to do what they believe is right.

Her operation was illegal, and would be illegal under most of the "reform" legislation now being proposed, if interpreted strictly. Fortunately some physicians are willing to indulge in more liberal interpretations, but they make these interpretations not on medical grounds, in the strict sense, but on social and economic grounds. Understandably, many physicians are unwilling to venture so far from the secure base of pure physical medicine. As one Catholic physician put it:

Can the patient afford to have another child? Will the older children have sufficient educational opportunities if their parents have another child? Aren't two, three or four children enough? I am afraid such statements are frequently made in the discussion of a proposed therapeutic abortion. (But) we should be doctors of medicine, not socio-economic prophets.[6]

To this a non-Catholic physician added: "I sometimes wish I were an obstetrician in a Catholic hospital so that I would not have to make any of these decisions. The only position to take in which I would have no misgivings is to do no interruptions at all."[7]

Who Wants Compulsory Pregnancy?

The question "How can we justify an abortion?" plainly leads to great difficulties. It is operationally unmanageable: it leads to inconsistencies in practice and inequities by any moral standard. All these can be completely avoided if we ask the right question, namely: *"How can we justify compulsory pregnancy?"*

By casting the problem in this form, we call attention to its relationship to the slavery issue. Somewhat more than a century ago men in the Western world asked the question: "How can we justify compulsory servitude?" and came up with the answer: *"By no means whatever."* Is the answer any different to the related question: "How can we justify compulsory pregnancy?" Certainly pregnancy is a form of servitude; if continued to term it results in parenthood, which is also a kind of servitude, to be continued for the best years of a woman's life. It is difficult to see how it can be argued that this kind of servitude will be more productive of social good if it is compulsory rather than voluntary. A study[8] made of Swedish children born when their mothers were refused the abortions they had requested showed that unwanted children, as compared with their

6. Calderone (ed.), *op. cit.,* p. 103.
7. *Ibid.,* p. 123.
8. Hans Forssman and Inga Thuwe, "One Hundred and Twenty Children Born after Application for Therapeutic Abortion Refused," *Acta Psychiatrica Scandinavica,* 42 (1966), p. 71.

controls, as they grew up were more often picked up for drunkenness, or antisocial or criminal behavior; they received less education; they received more psychiatric care; and they were more often exempted from military service by reason of defect. Moreover, the females in the group married earlier and had children earlier, thus no doubt tending to create a vicious circle of poorly tended children who in their turn would produce more poorly tended children. How then does society gain by increasing the number of unwanted children? No one has volunteered an answer to this question.

Of course if there were a shortage of children, then society might say that it needs all the children it can get—unwanted or not. But I am unaware of any recent rumors of a shortage of children.

Alternatives: True and False

The end result of an abortion—the elimination of an unwanted fetus— is surely good. But is the act itself somehow damaging? For several generations it was widely believed that abortion was intrinsically dangerous, either physically or psychologically. It is now very clear that the widespread belief is quite unjustified. The evidence for this statement is found in a bulky literature which has been summarized in Lawrence Lader's *Abortion*[9] and the collection of essays brought together by Alan Guttmacher.[10]

In tackling questions of this sort, it is imperative that we identify correctly the alternatives facing us. (All moral and practical problems involve a comparison of alternative actions.) Many of the arguments of the prohibitionists implicitly assume that the alternatives facing the woman are these:

abortion————no abortion

This is false. A person can never do nothing. The pregnant woman is going to do something, whether she wishes to or not. (She cannot roll time backward and live her life over.)

People often ask: "Isn't contraception better than abortion?" Implied by this question are these alternatives:

abortion————contraception

But these are not the alternatives that face the woman who asks to be aborted. She *is* pregnant. She cannot roll time backward and use contraception more successfully than she did before. Contraceptives are never foolproof anyway. It is commonly accepted that the failure rate of our best contraceptive, the "pill," is around one percent, i.e., one failure per hundred woman-years of use. I have earlier shown[11] that this failure rate produces about a quarter of a million unwanted pregnancies a year in the United States. Abortion is not so much an alternative to contraception as it is a subsidiary method of birth control, to be used when the primary method fails—as it often does.

The woman *is* pregnant: this is the base level at which the moral decision

9. Lawrence Lader, *Abortion,* Indianapolis: Bobbs-Merrill, 1966.
10. Alan F. Guttmacher (ed.), *The Case for Legalized Abortion,* Berkeley, California: Diablo Press, 1967.
11. Garrett Hardin, "A Scientist's Case for Abortion," *Redbook* (May 1967), p. 62.

begins. If she is pregnant against her will, does it matter to society whether or not she was careless or unskillful in her use of contraception? In any case, she is threatening society with an unwanted child, for which society will pay dearly. The real alternatives facing the woman (and society) are clearly these:

abortion————*compulsory pregnancy*

When we recognize that these are the real, operational alternatives, the false problems created by pseudo-alternatives vanish.

Is Potential Value Valuable?

Only one weighty objection to abortion remains to be discussed, and this is the question of "loss." When a fetus is destroyed, has something valuable been destroyed? The fetus has the potentiality of becoming a human being. A human being is valuable. Therefore is not the fetus of equal value? This question must be answered.

It can be answered, but not briefly. What does the embryo receive from its parents that might be of value? There are only three possibilities: substance, energy, and information. As for the substance in the fertilized egg, it is not remarkable: merely the sort of thing one might find in any piece of meat, human or animal, and there is very little of it—only one and a half micrograms, which is about a half of a billionth of an ounce. The energy content of this tiny amount of material is likewise negligible. As the zygote develops into an embryo, both its substance and its energy content increase (at the expense of the mother); but this is not a very important matter—even an adult, viewed from this standpoint, is only a hundred and fifty pounds of meat!

Clearly, the humanly significant thing that is contributed to the zygote by the parents is the information that "tells" the fertilized egg how to develop into a human being. This information is in the form of a chemical tape called "DNA," a double set of two chemical supermolecules each of which has about three billion "spots" that can be coded with any one of four different possibilities, symbolized by *A, T, G,* and *C.* (For comparison, the Morse code offers three possibilities in coding: dot, dash, and space.) It is the particular sequence of these four chemical possibilities in the DNA that directs the zygote in its development into a human being. The DNA constitutes the information needed to produce a valuable human being. The question is: is this information precious? I have argued elsewhere[12] that it is not:

Consider the case of a man who is about to begin to build a $50,000 house. As he stands on the site looking at the blueprints a practical joker comes along and sets fire to the blueprints. The question is: can the owner go to the law and collect $50,000 for his lost blueprints? The answer is obvious: since another set of blueprints can be produced for the cost of only a few dollars, that is all they are worth. (A court might award a bit more for the loss of the owner's time, but that is a minor matter.) The moral: *a nonunique copy of information that specifies a valuable structure is itself almost valueless.*

12. Garrett Hardin, "Blueprints, DNA, and Abortion: A Scientific and Ethical Analysis," *Medical Opinion and Review,* 3:2 (1967), p. 74.

This principle is precisely applicable to the moral problem of abortion. The zygote, which contains the complete specification of a valuable human being, is not a human being, and is almost valueless. . . . The early stages of an individual fetus have had very little human effort invested in them; they are of very little worth. The loss occasioned by an abortion is independent of whether the abortion is spontaneous or induced. (Just as the loss incurred by the burning of a set of blueprints is independent of whether the causal agent was lightning or an arsonist.)

A set of blueprints is not a house; the DNA of a zygote is not a human being. The analogy is singularly exact, though there are two respects in which it is deficient. These respects are interesting rather than important. First, we have the remarkable fact that the blueprints of the zygote are constantly replicated and incorporated in every cell of the human body. This is interesting, but it has no moral significance. There is no moral obligation to conserve DNA—if there were, no man would be allowed to brush his teeth and gums, for in this brutal operation hundreds of sets of DNA are destroyed daily.

The other anomaly of the human information problem is connected with the fact that the information that is destroyed in an aborted embryo *is* unique (unlike the house blueprints). But it is unique in a way that is without moral significance. A favorite argument of abortion-prohibitionists is this: "What if Beethoven's mother had had an abortion?" The question moves us; but when we think it over we realize we can just as relevantly ask: "What if Hitler's mother had had an abortion?" Each conceptus is unique, but not in any way that has a moral consequence. The *expected* potential value of each aborted child is exactly that of the average child born. It is meaningless to say that humanity loses when a *particular* child is not born, or is not conceived. A human female, at birth, has about 30,000 eggs in her ovaries. If she bears only 3 children in her lifetime, is there any meaningful sense in which we can say that mankind has suffered a loss in those other 29,997 fruitless eggs? (Yet one of them might have been a super-Beethoven!)

People who worry about the moral danger of abortion do so because they think of the fetus as a human being, hence equate feticide with murder. Whether the fetus is or is not a human being is a matter of definition, not fact; and we can define any way we wish. In terms of the human problem involved, it would be unwise to define the fetus as human (hence tactically unwise ever to refer to the fetus as an "unborn child"). Analysis based on the deepest insights of molecular biology indicates the wisdom of sharply distinguishing the information for a valuable structure from the completed structure itself. It is interesting, and gratifying, to note that this modern insight is completely congruent with common law governing the disposal of dead fetuses. Abortion-prohibitionists generally insist that abortion is murder, and that an embryo is a person; but no state or nation, so far as I know, requires the dead fetus to be treated like a dead person. Although all of the states in the United States severely limit what can be done with a dead human body, no cognizance is taken of dead fetuses up to about five months' prenatal life. The early fetus may, with impunity, be flushed down the toilet or thrown out with the garbage—which shows that we never have regarded it as a human being. Scientific analysis confirms what we have always known.

The Management of Compulsory Pregnancy

What is the future of compulsory pregnancy? The immediate future is not hopeful. Far too many medical people misconceive the real problem. One physician has written:

Might not a practical, workable solution to this most difficult problem be found by setting up, in every hospital, an abortion committee comprising a specialist in obstetrics and gynecology, a psychiatrist, and a clergyman or priest? The patient and her husband—if any—would meet with these men who would do all in their power to persuade the woman not to undergo the abortion. (I have found that the promise of a postpartum sterilization will frequently enable even married women with all the children they can care for to accept this one more, final pregnancy.) If, however, the committee members fail to change the woman's mind, they can make it very clear that they disapprove of the abortion, but prefer that it be safely done in a hospital rather than bungled in a basement somewhere.[13]

What this author has in mind is plainly not a system of legalizing abortion but a system of managing compulsory pregnancy. It is this philosophy which governs pregnancies in the Scandinavian countries,[14] where the experience of a full generation of women has shown that women do not want their pregnancies to be managed by the state. Illegal abortions have remained at a high level in these countries, and recent years have seen the development of a considerable female tourist trade to Poland, where abortions are easy to obtain. Unfortunately, American legislatures are now proposing to follow the provably unworkable system of Scandinavia.

The drift down this erroneous path is not wholly innocent. Abortion-prohibitionists are showing signs of recognizing "legalization" along Scandinavian lines as one more roadblock that can be thrown in the way of the abolition of compulsory pregnancy. To cite an example: on February 9, 1966, the *Courier,* a publication of the Winona, Minnesota Diocese, urged that Catholics support a reform law based on the American Law Institute model, because the passage of such a law would "take a lot of steam out of the abortion advocate's argument" and would "defeat a creeping abortionism of disastrous importance."[15]

Wherever a Scandinavian or American Law Institute type of bill is passed, it is probable that cautious legislators will then urge a moratorium for several years while the results of the new law are being assessed (though they are easily predictable from the Scandinavian experience). As Lord Morley once said: "Small reforms are the worst enemies of great reforms." Because of the backwardness of education in these matters, caused by the long taboo under which the subject of abortion labored, it seems highly likely that our present system of compulsory pregnancy will continue substantially without change until the true nature of the alternatives facing us is more widely recognized.

13. H. Curtis Wood, Jr., "Letter to the Editor," *Medical Opinion and Review,* 3:11 (1967), p. 19.
14. David T. Smith (ed.), *Abortion and the Law,* Cleveland: Western Reserve University, 1967, p. 179.
15. Anonymous, *Association for the Study of Abortion Newsletter,* 2:3 (1967), p. 6.

Contraceptive Failure

67   ## Coping with Contraceptive Failure

GARRETT HARDIN

Every unintended pregnancy represents a failure of birth control. It is important to state this truism explicitly so that we can get on with the business of studying the system of birth control. Every system has its failures; what do we do about them? In general, we react in two ways: (1) we study the system and seek to improve it; and (2) we employ remedial actions for the failures we cannot avoid.

Let us take up the second aspect first. Of remedial measures for the unwanted child, there are only two important ones: infanticide and adoption. Infanticide has been practiced openly in many societies, though not in ours:—not openly, that is. The historical studies of William Langer have shown that infanticide was institutionalized in a cryptic way in the Western world, being particularly important in the nineteenth century. The institution was that of the "baby farmer," the obliging person of flexible conscience who took care of your unwanted child for a fee, with the implicit understanding that it would not be for long. It is this understanding that gives new meaning to the scene in Gilbert and Sullivan's *H.M.S. Pinafore* in which Little Buttercup reveals the dread secret she had hinted at earlier:

> A many years ago
> When I was young and charming,
> As some of you may know
> I practised baby-farming.

To which the chorus replies:

> Now this is most alarming!
> When she was young and charming,
> She practised baby-farming,
> A many years ago.

Why did they say "this is most alarming"? Because "alarming" rhymes with "charming," of course; and to create the mood for the coming revelation that Buttercup had mixed two babies up. But Langer's study suggests that the "alarm" had another source: Baby-farming in the Victorian world was no more respectable than bootlegging was in Prohibition days. It was an institutionalized way of dealing with failures in birth control. Many of the "best people" knew this; but they didn't speak of it. It was under taboo. In writing this scene, Gilbert was drawing on an ambiguous feeling of dread that no longer exists. He was not *merely* being funny.

Does baby-farming, in this sense, still exist? I have been informed by some who lived in Germany in the pre-Hitler days that they still had their "angel-makers," as they were called. I suspect the profession has declined since. It used to be easy to make angels: All you had to do was crowd the babies together, underfeed them somewhat, expose them a bit, and let "nature" (that is, crowd diseases) take over. With the coming of antibiotics and government inspection of nurseries, baby-farming on the old scale is hardly possible.

What used to be done professionally is now done by amateurs, less efficiently and more brutally. Parents have now taken over the executioner's role—not many parents, but *too* many. Child-ridden, impoverished, and desperate parents are responsible for thousands of "battered babies" every year and perhaps some hundreds of dead ones. Statistics are hard to come by because it is difficult to distinguish between accidents and homicides in this population.

Desire for Children

The Explosive Desire for Children 68

TIME MAGAZINE

According to Peter J. Smith, a lecturer in geophysics at the University of Liverpool, the problem—at least in the U.S.—is not lack of birth control but excess desire for children.

Citing Gallup polls going back to 1943, Smith says that the median number of children considered ideal by non-Catholic American women has always been more than two. Well-educated, middle- and upper-class women usually want fewer children than poor women. But "on the average, all parents desire more children than the number required to maintain the population equilibrium." Birth control devices are already widely available to all but a tiny fraction of U.S. citizens, Smith declares, but really effective population control cannot be achieved until there is a change in society's attitude toward procreation. As things now stand, social and institutional pressures tend to stigmatize the childless couple—not to mention the single person—as "abnormal." Smith concedes that such an attitude had its use in the past; it "evolved over millennia to ensure high enough fertility to overcome high mortality." Now, however, medical progress has made that notion obsolete. Smith proposes that the reform start with the elimination of tax advantages for big families.

Solving The Problem

69   ## The Tragedy Of The Commons

GARRET HARDIN

At the end of a thoughtful article on the future of nuclear war, Wiesner and York (1) concluded that: "Both sides in the arms race are . . . confronted by the dilemma of steadily increasing military power and steadily decreasing national security. *It is our considered professional judgment that this dilemma has no technical solution.* If the great powers continue to look for solutions in the area of science and technology only, the result will be to worsen the situation."

I would like to focus your attention not on the subject of the article (national security in a nuclear world) but on the kind of conclusion they reached, namely that there is no technical solution to the problem. An implicit and almost universal assumption of discussions published in professional and semipopular scientific journals is that the problem under discussion has a technical solution. A technical solution may be defined as one that requires a change only in the techniques of the natural sciences, demanding little or nothing in the way of change in human values or ideas of morality.

In our day (though not in earlier times) technical solutions are always welcome. Because of previous failures in prophecy, it takes courage to assert that a desired technical solution is not possible. Wiesner and York exhibited this courage; publishing in a science journal, they insisted that the solution to the problem was not to be found in the natural sciences. They cautiously qualified their statement with the phrase, "It is our considered professional judgment . . . " Whether they were right or not is not the concern of the present article. Rather, the concern here is with the important concept of a class of human problems which can be called "no technical solution problems," and, more specifically, with the identification and discussion of one of these.

It is easy to show that the class is not a null class. Recall the game of tick-tack-toe. Consider the problem, "How can I win the game of tick-tack-toe?" It is well known that I cannot, if I assume (in keeping with the conventions of game theory) that my opponent understands the game perfectly. Put another way, there is no "technical solution" to the problem. I can win only by giving a radical meaning to the word "win." I can hit my opponent over the head; or I can drug him; or I can falsify the records. Every way in which I "win" involves, in some sense, an abandonment of the game, as we intuitively understand it. (I can also, of course, openly abandon the game—refuse to play it. This is what most adults do.)

The class of "No technical solution problems" has members. My thesis is that the "population problem," as conventionally conceived, is a member of this class. How it is conventionally conceived needs some comment. It is fair to say that most people who anguish over the population problem are trying to find a way to avoid the evils of overpopulation without relinquishing any of the privileges they now enjoy. They think that farming the seas or developing new strains of wheat will solve the problem—technologically. I try to show here that the solution they seek cannot be found. The population problem cannot be solved in a technical way, any more than can the problem of winning the game of tick-tack-toe.

What Shall We Maximize?

Population, as Malthus said, naturally tends to grow "geometrically," or, as we would now say, exponentially. In a finite world this means that the per capita share of the world's goods must steadily decrease. Is ours a finite world?

A fair defense can be put forward for the view that the world is infinite; or that we do not know that it is not. But, in terms of the practical problems that we must face in the next few generations with the foreseeable technology, it is clear that we will greatly increase human misery if we do not, during the immediate future, assume that the world available to the terrestrial human population is finite. "Space" is no escape (2).

A finite world can support only a finite population; therefore, population growth must eventually equal zero. (The case of perpetual wide fluctuations above and below zero is a trivial variant that need not be discussed.) When this condition is met, what will be the situation of mankind? Specifically, can Bentham's goal of "the greatest good for the greatest number" be realized?

No—for two reasons, each sufficient by itself. The first is a theoretical one. It is not mathematically possible to maximize for two (or more) variables at the same time. This was clearly stated by von Neumann and Morgenstern (3), but the principle is implicit in the theory of partial differential equations, dating back at least to D'Alembert (1717-1783).

The second reason springs directly from biological facts. To live, any organism must have a source of energy (for example, food). This energy is utilized for two purposes: mere maintenance and work. For man, maintenance of life requires about 1600 kilocalories a day ("maintenance calories"). Anything that he does over and above merely staying alive will be defined as work, and is supported by "work calories" which he takes in. Work calories are used not only for what we call work in common speech; they are also required for all forms of enjoyment, from swimming and automobile racing to playing music and writing poetry. If our goal is to maximize population it is obvious what we must do: We must make the work calories per person approach as close to zero as possible. No gourmet meals, no vacations, no sports, no music, no literature, no art ... I think that everyone will grant, without argument or proof, that maximizing population does not maximize goods. Bentham's goal is impossible.

In reaching this conclusion I have made the usual assumption that it is the acquisition of energy that is the problem. The appearance of atomic energy has led some to question this assumption. However, given an infinite source of energy, population growth still produces an inescapable problem. The problem of the acquisition of energy is replaced by the problem of its dissipation, as J. H. Fremlin has so wittily shown (4). The arithmetic signs in the analysis are, as it were, reversed; but Bentham's goal is still unobtainable.

The optimum population is, then, less than the maximum. The difficulty of defining the optimum is enormous; so far as I know, no one has seriously tackled this problem. Reaching an acceptable and stable solution will surely require more than one generation of hard analytical work—and much persuasion.

We want the maximum good per person; but what is good? To one person it is wilderness, to another it is ski lodges for thousands. To one it is estuaries to nourish ducks for hunters to shoot; to another it is factory land. Comparing one good with another is, we usually say, impossible because goods are incommensurable. Incommensurables cannot be compared.

Theoretically this may be true; but in real life incommensurables are commensurable. Only a criterion of judgment and a system of weighting are needed. In nature the criterion is survival. Is it better for a species to be small and hideable, or large and powerful? Natural selection commensurates the incommensurables. The compromise achieved depends on a natural weighting of the values of the variables.

Man must imitate this process. There is no doubt that in fact he already does, but unconsciously. It is when the hidden decisions are made explicit that the arguments begin. The problem for the years ahead is to work out an acceptable theory of weighting. Synergistic effects, nonlinear variation, and difficulties in discounting the future make the intellectual problem difficult, but not (in principle) insoluble.

Has any cultural group solved this practical problem at the present time, even on an intuitive level? One simple fact proves that none has: there is no prosperous population in the world today that has, and has had for sometime, a growth rate of zero. Any people that has intuitively identified its optimum point will soon reach it, after which its growth rate becomes and remains zero.

Of course, a positive growth rate might be taken as evidence that a population is below its optimum. However, by any reasonable standards, the most rapidly growing populations on earth today are (in general) the most miserable. This association (which need not be invariable) casts doubt on the optimistic assumption that the positive growth rate of a population is evidence that it has yet to reach its optimum.

We can make little progress in working toward optimum population size until we explicitly exorcize the spirit of Adam Smith in the field of practical demography. In economic affairs, *The Wealth of Nations* (1776) popularized the "invisible hand," the idea that an individual who "intends only his own gain," is, as it were, "led by an invisible hand to promote . . . the public interest" (5). Adam Smith did not assert that this was invariably true, and perhaps neither did any of his followers. But he contributed to a dominant tendency of thought that has ever since interfered with positive action based on rational analysis, namely, the tendency to assume that decisions reached individually will, in fact, be the best decisions for an entire society. If this assumption is correct it justifies the continuance of our present policy of laissez-faire in reproduction. If it is correct we can assume that men will control their individual fecundity so as to produce the optimum population. If the assumption is not correct, we need to reexamine our individual freedoms to see which ones are defensible.

Tragedy of Freedom in a Commons

The rebuttal to the invisible hand in population control is to be found in a scenario first sketched in a little-known pamphlet (6) in 1833 by a mathematical amateur named William Forster Lloyd (1794-1852). We may well call it "the tragedy of the commons," using the word "tragedy" as the philosopher Whitehead used it (7): "The essence of dramatic tragedy is not unhappiness. It resides in the solemnity of the remorseless working of things." He then goes on to say, "This inevitableness of destiny can only be illustrated in terms of human life by incidents which in fact involve unhappiness. For it is only by them that the futility of escape can be made evident in the drama."

The tragedy of the commons develops in this way. Picture a pasture open to all. It is to be expected that each herdsman will try to keep as many cattle as possible on the commons. Such an arrangement may work reasonably satisfactorily for centuries because tribal wars, poaching, and disease keep the numbers of both man and beast well below the carrying capacity of the land. Finally, however, comes the day of reckoning, that is, the day when the long-desired goal of social stability becomes a reality. At this point, the inherent logic of the commons remorselessly generates tragedy.

As a rational being, each herdsman seeks to maximize his gain. Explicitly or implicitly, more or less consciously, he asks, "What is the utility *to me* of adding one more animal to my herd?" This utility has one negative and one positive component.

1) The positive component is a function of the increment of one animal. Since the herdsman receives all the proceeds from the sale of the additional animal, the positive utility is nearly $+1$.

2) The negative component is a function of the additional overgrazing created by one more animal. Since, however, the effects of overgrazing are shared by all the herdsmen, the negative utility for any particular decision-making herdsman is only a fraction of -1.

Adding together the component partial utilities, the rational herdsman concludes that the only sensible course for him to pursue is to add another animal to his herd. And another; and another . . . But this is the conclusion reached by each and every rational hersman sharing a commons. Therein is the tragedy. Each man is locked into a system that compels him to increase his herd without limit —in a world that is limited. Ruin is the destination toward which all men rush, each pursuing his own best interest in a society that believes in the freedom of the commons. Freedom in a commons brings ruin to all.

Some would say that this is a platitude. Would that it were! In a sense, it was learned thousands of years ago, but natural selection favors the forces of psychological denial (8). The individual benefits as an individual from his ability to deny the truth even though society as a whole, of which he is a part, suffers. Education can counteract the natural tendency to do the wrong thing, but the inexorable succession of generations requires that the basis for this knowledge be constantly refreshed.

A simple incident that occurred a few years ago in Leominster, Massachusetts, shows how perishable the knowledge is. During the Christmas shopping season the parking meters downtown were covered with plastic bags that bore tags reading: "Do not open until after Christmas. Free parking courtesy of the mayor and city council." In other words, facing the prospect of an increased demand for already scarce space, the city fathers reinstituted the system of the commons. (Cynically, we suspect that they gained more votes than they lost by this retrogressive act.)

In an approximate way, the logic of the commons has been understood for a long time, perhaps since the discovery of agriculture or the invention of private property in real estate. But it is understood mostly only in special cases which are not sufficiently generalized. Even at this late date, cattlemen leasing national land on the western ranges demonstrate no more than an ambivalent understanding, in constantly pressuring federal authorities to increase the head count to the point where overgrazing produces erosion and weed-dominance. Likewise, the oceans of the world continue to suffer from the survival of the philosophy of the commons. Maritime nations still respond automatically to the shibboleth of the "freedom of the seas." Professing to believe in the "inexhaustible resources of the oceans," they bring species after species of fish and whales closer to extinction (9).

The National Parks present another instance of the working out of the tragedy of the commons. At present, they are open to all, without limit. The parks themselves are limited in extent—there is only one Yosemite Valley—whereas population seems to grow without limit. The values that visitors seek in the parks are steadily eroded. Plainly, we must soon cease to treat the parks as commons or they will be of no value to anyone.

What shall we do? We have several options. We might sell them off as private property. We might keep them as public property, but allocate the right to enter them. The allocation might be on the basis of wealth, by the use of an auction system. It might be on the basis of merit, as defined by some agreed-upon standards. It might be by lottery. Or it might be on a first-come, first-served basis, administered to long queues. These, I think, are all the reasonable possibilities. They are all objectionable. But we must choose—or acquiesce in the destruction of the commons that we call our National Parks.

Pollution

In a reverse way, the tragedy of the commons reappears in problems of pollution. Here it is not a question of taking something out of the commons, but of putting something in—sewage, or chemical, radioactive, and heat wastes into water; noxious and dangerous fumes into the air; and distracting and unpleasant advertising signs into the line of sight. The calculations of utility are much the same as before. The rational man finds that his share of the cost of the wastes he discharges into the commons is less than the cost of purifying his wastes before releasing them. Since this is true for everyone, we are locked into a system of "fouling our own nest," so long as we behave only as independent, rational, free-enterprisers.

The tragedy of the commons as a food basket is averted by private property, or something formally like it. But the air and waters surrounding us cannot readily be fenced, and so the tragedy of the commons as a cesspool must be prevented by different means, by coercive laws or taxing devices that make it cheaper for the polluter to treat his pollutants than to discharge them untreated. We have not progressed as far with the solution of this problem as we have with the first. Indeed, our particular concept of private property, which deters us from exhausting the positive resources of the earth, favors pollution. The owner of a factory on the bank of a stream—whose property extends to the middle of the stream—often has difficulty seeing why it is not his natural right to muddy the waters flowing past his door. The law, always behind the times, requires elaborate stitching and fitting to adapt it to this newly perceived aspect of the commons.

The pollution problem is a consequence of population. It did not much matter how a lonely American frontiersman disposed of his waste. "Flowing water purifies itself every 10 miles," my grandfather used to say, and the myth was near enough to the truth when he was a boy, for there were not too many people. But as population became denser, the natural chemical and biological recycling processes became overloaded, calling for a redefinition of property rights.

How To Legislate Temperance?

Analysis of the pollution problem as a function of population density uncovers a not generally recognized principle of morality, namely: *the morality of an act is a function of the state of the system at the time it is performed* (10). Using the commons as a cesspool does not harm the general public under frontier conditions, because there is no public; the same behavior in a metropolis is unbearable. A hundred and fifty years ago a plainsman could kill an American bison, cut out only the tongue for his dinner, and discard the rest of the animal. He was not in any important sense being wasteful. Today, with only a few thousand bison left, we would be appalled at such behavior.

In passing, it is worth noting that the morality of an act cannot be determined from a photograph. One does not know whether a man killing an elephant or setting fire to the grassland is harming others until one knows the total system in which his act appears. "One picture is worth a thousand words," said an ancient Chinese; but it may take 10,000 words to validate it. It is as tempting to ecologists as it is to reformers in general to try to persuade others by way of the photographic shortcut. But the essense of an argument cannot be photographed: it must be presented rationally—in words.

That morality is system-sensitive escaped the attention of most codifiers of ethics in the past. "Thou shalt not . . . " is the form of traditional ethical directives which make no allowance for particular circumstances. The laws of our society follow the pattern of ancient ethics, and therefore are poorly suited to governing a complex, crowded, changeable world. Our epicyclic solution is to augment statutory law with administrative law. Since it is practically impossible to spell out all the conditions under which it is safe to burn trash in the back yard or to run an automobile without smog-control, by law we delegate the details to bureaus. The result is administrative law, which is rightly feared for an ancient reason—*Quis custodiet ipsos custodes?* —"Who shall watch the watchers themselves?" John Adams said that we must have "a government of laws and not men." Bureau administrators, trying to evaluate the morality of acts in the total system, are singularly liable to corruption, producing a government by men, not laws.

Prohibition is easy to legislate (though not necessarily to enforce); but how do we legislate temperance? Experience indicates that it can be accomplished best through the mediation of administrative law. We limit possibilities unnecessarily if we suppose that the sentiment of *Quis custodiet* denies us the use of administrative law. We should rather retain the phrase as a perpetual reminder of fearful dangers we cannot avoid. The great challenge facing us now is to invent the corrective feedbacks that are needed to keep custodians honest. We must find ways to legitimate the needed authority of both the custodians and the corrective feedbacks.

Freedom To Breed Is Intolerable

The tragedy of the commons is involved in population problems in another way. In a world governed solely by the principle of "dog eat dog"—if indeed there ever was such a world—how many children a family had would not be a matter of public concern. Parents who bred too exuberantly would leave fewer descendants, not more, because they would be unable to care adequately for their children. David Lack and others have found that such a negative feedback demonstrably controls the fecundity of birds (11). But men are not birds, and have not acted like them for millenniums, at least.

If each human family were dependent only on its own resources; *if* the children of improvident parents starved to death; *if*, thus, overbreeding brought its own "punishment" to the germ line—*then* there would be no public interest in controlling the breeding of families. But our society is deeply committed to the welfare state (12), and hence is confronted with another aspect of the tragedy of the commons.

In a welfare state, how shall we deal with the family, the religion, the race, or the class (or indeed any distinguishable and cohesive group) that adopts overbreeding as a policy to secure its own aggrandizement (13)? To couple the concept of freedom to breed with the belief that everyone born has an equal right to the commons is to lock the world into a tragic course of action.

Unfortunately this is just the course of action that is being pursued by the United Nations. In late 1967, some 30 nations agreed to the following (14):

The Universal Declaration of Human Rights describes the family as the natural and fundamental unit of society. It follows that any choice and decision with regard to the size of the family must irrevocably rest with the family itself, and cannot be made by anyone else.

It is painful to have to deny categorically the validity of this right; denying it, one feels as uncomfortable as a resident of Salem, Massachusetts, who denied the reality of witches in the 17th century. At the present time, in liberal quarters, something like a taboo acts to inhibit criticism of the United Nations. There is a feeling that the United Nations is "our last and best hope," that we shouldn't find fault with it; we shouldn't play into the hands of the archconservatives. However, let us not forget what Robert Louis Stevenson said: "The truth that is suppressed by friends is the readiest weapon of the enemy." If we love the truth we must openly deny the validity of the Universal Declaration of Human Rights, even though it is promoted by the United Nations. We should also join with Kingsley Davis (15) in attempting to get Planned Parenthood-World Population to see the error of its ways in embracing the same tragic ideal.

Conscience Is Self-Eliminating

It is a mistake to think that we can control the breeding of mankind in the long run by an appeal to conscience. Charles Galton Darwin made this point when he spoke on the centennial of the publication of his grandfather's great book. The argument is straightforward and Darwinian.

People vary. Confronted with appeals to limit breeding, some people will undoubtedly respond to the plea more than others. Those who have more children will produce a larger fraction of the next generation than those with more susceptible consciences. The difference will be accentuated, generation by generation.

In C. G. Darwin's words: "It may well be that it would take hundreds of generations for the progenitive instinct to develop in this way, but if it should do so, nature would have taken her revenge, and the variety *Homo contracipiens* would become extinct and would be replaced by the variety *Homo progenitivus*" (16).

The argument assumes that conscience or the desire for children (no matter which) is hereditary—but hereditary only in the most general formal sense. The result will be the same whether the attitude is transmitted through germ cells, or exosomatically, to use A. J. Lotka's term. (If one denies the latter possibility as well as the former, then what's the point of education?) The argument has here been stated in the context of the population problem, but it applies equally well to any instance in which society appeals to an individual exploiting a commons to restrain himself for the general good—by means of his conscience. To make such an appeal is to set up a selective system that works toward the elimination of conscience from the race.

Pathogenic Effects of Conscience

The long-term disadvantage of an appeal to conscience should be enough to condemn it; but has serious short-term disadvantages as well. If we ask a man who is exploiting a commons to desist "in the name of conscience," what are we saying to him? What does he hear?—not only at the moment but also in the wee small hours of the night when, half asleep, he remembers not merely the words we used but also the nonverbal communication cues we gave him unawares? Sooner or later, consciously or subconsciously, he senses that he has received two communications, and that they are contradictory: (i) (intended communication) "If you don't do as we ask, we will openly condemn you for not acting like a responsible citizen"; (ii) (the unintended communication) "If you *do* behave as we ask, we will secretly condemn you for a simpleton who can be shamed into standing aside while the rest of us exploit the commons."

Everyman then is caught in what Bateson has called a "double bind." Bateson and his co-workers have made a plausible case for viewing the double bind as an important causative factor in the genesis of schizophrenia (17). The double bind may not always be so damaging, but it always endangers the mental health of anyone to whom it is applied. "A bad conscience," said Nietzsche, "is a kind of illness."

To conjure up a conscience in others is tempting to anyone who wishes to extend his control beyond the legal limits. Leaders at the highest level succumb to this temptation. Has any President during the past generation failed to call on labor unions to moderate voluntarily their demands for higher wages, or to steel companies to honor voluntary guidelines on prices? I can recall none. The rhetoric used on such occasions is designed to produce feelings of guilt in noncooperators.

For centuries it was assumed without proof that guilt was a valuable, perhaps even an indispensable, ingredient of the civilized life. Now, in this post-Freudian world, we doubt it.

Paul Goodman speaks from the modern point of view when he says: "No good has ever come from feeling guilty, neither intelligence, policy, nor compassion. The guilty do not pay attention to the object but only to themselves, and not even to their own interests, which might make sense, but to their anxieties" (18).

One does not have to be a professional psychiatrist to see the consequences of anxiety. We in the Western world are just emerging from a dreadful two-centuries-long Dark Ages of Eros that was sustained partly by prohibition laws, but perhaps more effectively by the anxiety-generating mechanisms of education. Alex Comfort has told the story well in *The Anxiety Makers* (19); it is not a pretty one.

Since proof is difficult, we may even concede that the results of anxiety may sometimes, from certain points of view, be desirable. The larger question we should ask is whether, as a matter of policy, we should ever encourage the use of a technique the tendency (if not the intention) of which is psychologically pathogenic. We hear much talk these days of responsible parenthood; the coupled words are incorporated into the titles of some organizations devoted to birth control. Some people have proposed massive propaganda campaigns to instill responsibility into the nation's (or the world's) breeders. But what is the meaning of the word responsibility in this context? Is it not merely a synonym for the word conscience? When we use the word responsibility in the absence of substantial functions are we not trying to browbeat a free man in a commons into acting against his own interest? Responsibility is a verbal counterfeit for a substantial *quid pro quo*. It is an attempt to get something for nothing.

If the word responsibility is to be used at all, I suggest that it be in the sense Charles Frankel uses it (20). "Responsibility," says this philosopher, "is the product of definite social arrangements." Notice that Frankel calls for social arrangements—not propaganda.

Mutual Coercion Mutually Agreed Upon

The social arrangements that produce responsibility are arrangements that create coercion, of some sort. Consider bank-robbing. The man who takes money from a bank acts as if the bank were a commons. How do we prevent such action? Certainly not by trying to control his behavior solely by a verbal appeal to his sense of responsibility. Rather than rely on propaganda we follow Frankel's lead and insist that a bank is not a commons; we seek the definite social arrangements that will keep it from becoming a commons. That we thereby infringe on the freedom of would-be robbers we neither deny nor regret.

The morality of bank-robbing is particularly easy to understand because we accept complete prohibition of this activity. We are willing to say "Thou shalt not rob banks," without providing for exceptions. But temperance also can be created by coercion. Taxing is a good coercive device. To keep downtown shoppers temperate in their use of parking space we introduce parking meters for short periods, and traffic fines for longer ones. We need not actually forbid a citizen to park as long as he wants to; we need merely make it increasingly expensive for him to do so. Not prohibition, but carefully biased options are what we offer him. A Madison Avenue man might call this persuasion; I prefer the greater candor of the word coercion.

Coercion is a dirty word to most liberals now, but it need not forever be so. As with the four-letter words, its dirtiness can be cleansed away by exposure to the light, by saying it over and over without apology or embarrassment. To many, the word coercion implies arbitrary decisions of distant and irresponsible bureaucrats; but this is not a necessary part of its meaning. The only kind of coercion I recommend is mutual coercion, mutually agreed upon by the majority of the people affected.

To say that we mutually agree to coercion is not to say that we are required to enjoy it, or even to pretend we enjoy it. Who enjoys taxes? We all grumble about them. But we accept compulsory taxes because we recognize that voluntary taxes would favor the conscienceless. We institute and (grumblingly) support taxes and other coercive devices to escape the horror of the commons.

An alternative to the commons need not be perfectly just to be preferable. With real estate and other material goods, the alternative we have chosen is the institution of private property coupled with legal inheritance. Is this system perfectly just? As a genetically trained biologist I deny that it is. It seems to me that, if there are to be differences in individual inheritance, legal possession should be perfectly correlated with biological inheritance—that those who are biologically more fit to be the custodians of property and power should legally inherit more. But genetic recombination continually makes a mockery of the doctrine of "like father, like son" implicit in our laws of legal inheritance. An idiot can inherit millions, and a trust fund can keep his estate intact. We must admit that our legal system of private property plus inheritance is unjust—but we put up with it because we are not convinced, at the moment, that anyone has invented a better system. The alternative of the commons is too horrifying to contemplate. Injustice is preferable to total ruin.

It is one of the peculiarities of the warfare between reform and the status quo that it is thoughtlessly governed by a double standard. Whenever a reform measure is proposed it is often defeated when its opponents triumphantly discover a flaw in it. As Kingsley Davis has pointed out (21), worshippers of the status quo sometimes imply that no reform is possible without unanimous agreement, an implication contrary to historical fact. As nearly as I can make out, automatic rejection of proposed reforms is based on one of two unconscious assumptions: (i) that the status quo is perfect; or (ii) that the choice we face is between reform and no action; if the proposed reform is imperfect, we presumably should take no action at all, while we wait for a perfect proposal.

But we can never do nothing. That which we have done for thousands of years is also action. It also produces evils. Once we are aware that the status quo is action, we can then compare its discoverable advantages and disadvantages with the predicted advantages and disadvantages of the proposed reform, discounting as best we can for our lack of experience. On the basis of such a comparison, we can make a rational decision which will not involve the unworkable assumption that only perfect systems are tolerable.

Recognition of Necessity

Perhaps the simplest summary of this analysis of man's population problems is this: the commons, if justifiable at all, is justifiable only under conditions of low-population density. As the human population has increased, the commons has had to be abandoned in one aspect after another.

First we abandoned the commons in food gathering, enclosing farm land and restricting pastures and hunting and fishing areas. These restrictions are still not complete throughout the world.

Somewhat later we saw that the commons as a place for waste disposal would also have to be abandoned. Restrictions on the disposal of domestic sewage are widely accepted in the Western world; we are still struggling to close the commons to pollution by automobiles, factories, insecticide sprayers, fertilizing operations, and atomic energy installations.

In a still more embryonic state is our recognition of the evils of the commons in matters of pleasure. There is almost no restriction on the propagation of sound waves in the public medium. The shopping public is assaulted with mindless music, without its consent. Our government is paying out billions of dollars to create supersonic transport which will disturb 50,000 people for every one person who is whisked from coast to coast 3 hours faster. Advertisers muddy the air-waves of radio and television and pollute the view of travelers. We are a long way from outlawing the commons in matters of pleasure. Is this because our Puritan inheritance makes us view pleasure as something of a sin, and pain (that is, the pollution of advertising) as the sign of virtue?

Every new enclosure of the commons involves the infringement of some-body's personal liberty. Infringements made in the distant past are accepted because no contemporary complains of a loss. It is the newly proposed infringe-ments that we vigorously oppose; cries of "rights" and "freedom" fill the air. But what does "freedom" mean? When men mutually agreed to pass laws against robbing, mankind became more free, not less so. Individuals locked into the logic of the commons are free only to bring on universal ruin; once they see the necessity of mutual coercion, they become free to pursue other goals. I believe it was Hegel who said, "Freedom is the recognition of necessity."

The most important aspect of necessity that we must now recognize, is the necessity of abandoning the commons in breeding. No technical solution can rescue us from the misery of overpopulation. Freedom to breed will bring ruin to all. At the moment, to avoid hard decisions many of us are tempted to propagandize for conscience and responsible parenthood. The temptation must be resisted, because an appeal to independently acting consciences selects for the disappearance of all conscience in the long run, and an increase in anxiety in the short.

The only way we can preserve and nurture other and more precious freedoms is by relinquishing the freedom to breed, and that very soon. "Freedom is the recognition of necessity"—and it is the role of education to reveal to all the necessity of abandoning the freedom to breed. Only so, can we put an end to this aspect of the tragedy of the commons.

REFERENCES

1. J. B. Wiesner and H. F. York, *Sci. Amer.* 211 (No. 4), 27 (1964).
2. G. Hardin, *J. Hered.* 50, 68 (1959); S. von Hoernor, *Science* 137, 18 (1962).
3. J. von Neumann and O. Morgenstern. *Theory of Games and Economic Behavior* (Princeton Univ. Press, Princeton, N.J., 1947), p. 11.
4. J. H. Fremlin, *New Sci.*, No. 415 (1964), p. 285.
5. A. Smith, *The Wealth of Nations* (Modern Library, New York, 1937), p. 423.
6. W. F. Lloyd, *Two Lectures on the Checks to Population* (Oxford Univ. Press, Oxford, England, 1833), reprinted (in part) in *Population, Evolution, and Birth Control,* G. Hardin, Ed. (Freeman, San Francisco, 1964), p. 37.
7. A. N. Whitehead, *Science and the Modern World* (Mentor, New York, 1948), p. 17.
8. G. Hardin, Ed. *Population, Evolution, and Birth Control* (Freeman, San Francisco, 1964), p. 56.
9. S. McVay, *Sci. Amer.* 216 (No. 8), 13 (1966).
10. J. Fletcher, *Situation Ethics* (Westminster, Philadelphia, 1966).
11. D. Lack, *The Natural Regulation of Animal Numbers* (Clarendon Press, Oxford, 1954).
12. H. Girvetz, *From Wealth to Welfare* (Stanford Univ. Press, Stanford, Calif., 1950).
13. G. Hardin, *Perspec. Biol. Med.* 6, 366 (1963).
14. U. Thant, *Int. Planned Parenthood News,* No. 168 (February 1968), p. 3.
15. K. Davis, *Science* 158, 730 (1967).
16. S. Tax, Ed., *Evolution after Darwin* (Univ. of Chicago Press, Chicago, 1960), vol. 2, p. 469.
17. G. Bateson, D. D. Jackson, J. Haley, J. Weakland, *Behav. Sci.* 1, 251 (1956).
18. P. Goodman, *New York Rev. Books* 10 (8), 22 (23 May 1968).

19. A. Comfort, *The Anxiety Makers* (Nelson, London, 1967).
20. C. Frankel, *The Case for Modern Man* (Harper, New York, 1955), p. 203.
21. J. D. Roslansky, *Genetics and the Future of Man* (Appleton-Century-Crofts, New York, 1966), p. 177.

70   The Tragedy of the Commons Revisited

BERYL L. CROWE

There has developed in the contemporary natural sciences a recognition that there is a subset of problems, such as population, atomic war, and environmental corruption, for which there are no technical solutions (1, 2). There is also an increasing recognition among contemporary social scientists that there is a subset of problems, such as population, atomic war, environmental corruption, and the recovery of a livable urban environment, for which there are no current political solutions (3). The thesis of this article is that the common area shared by these two subsets contains most of the critical problems that threaten the very existence of contemporary man.

The importance of this area has not been raised previously because of the very structure of modern society. This society, with its emphasis on differentiation and specialization, has led to the development of two insular scientific communities—the natural and the social—between which there is very little communication and a great deal of envy, suspicion, disdain, and competition for scarce resources. Indeed, these two communities more closely resemble tribes living in close geographic proximity on university campuses than they resemble the "scientific culture" that C. P. Snow placed in contrast to and opposition to the "humanistic culture" (4).

Perhaps the major problems of modern society have, in large part, been allowed to develop and intensify through this structure of insularity and specialization because it serves both psychological and professional functions for both scientific communities. Under such conditions, the natural sciences can recognize that some problems are not technically soluble and relegate them to the nether land of politics, while the social sciences recognize that some problems have no current political solutions and then postpone a search for solutions while they wait for new technologies with which to attack the problem. Both sciences can thus avoid responsibility and protect their respective myths of competence and relevance, while they avoid having to face the awesome and awful possibility that each has independently isolated the same subset of problems and given them different names. Thus, both never have to face the consequences of their respective findings. Meanwhile, due to the specialization and insularity of modern society, man's most critical problems lie in limbo, while the specialists in problem-solving go on to less critical problems for which they can find technical or political solutions.

In this circumstance, one psychologically brave, but professionally fool-hardy soul, Garrett Hardin, has dared to cross the tribal boundaries in his article "The Tragedy of the Commons" (1). In it, he gives vivid proof of the insularity of the two scientific tribes in at least two respects: first, his "rediscovery" of the tragedy was in part wasted effort, for the knowledge of this tragedy is so common in the social sciences that it has generated some fairly sophisticated mathematical models (5); second, the recognition of the existence of a subset of problems for which science neither offers nor aspires to offer technical solutions is not likely, under the contemporary conditions of insularity, to gain wide currency in the social sciences. Like Hardin, I will attempt to avoid the psychological and professional benefits of this insularity by tracing some of the political and social implications of his proposed solution to the tragedy of the commons.

The commons is a fundamental social institution that has a history going back through our own colonial experience to a body of English common law which antidates the Roman conquest. That law recognized that in societies there are some environmental objects which have never been, and should never be, exclusively appropriated to any individual or group of individuals. In England the classic example of the commons is the pasturage set aside for public use, and the "tragedy of the commons" to which Hardin refers was a tragedy of overgrazing and lack of care and fertilization which resulted in erosion and underproduction so destructive that there developed in the late 19th century an enclosure movement. Hardin applies this social institution to other environmental objects such as water, atmosphere, and living space.

The cause of this tragedy is exposed by a very simple mathematical model, utilizing the concept of utility drawn from economics. Allowing the utilities to range between a positive value of 1 and a negative value of 1, we may ask, as did the individual English herdsman, what is the utility to me of adding one more animal to my herd that grazes on the commons? His answer is that the positive utility is near 1 and the negative utility is only a fraction of minus 1. Adding together the component partial utilities, the herdsman concludes that it is rational for him to add another animal to his herd; then another, and so on. The tragedy to which Hardin refers develops because the same rational conclusion is reached by each and every herdsman sharing the commons.

Assumptions Necessary To Avoid the Tragedy

In passing the technically insoluble problems over to the political and social realm for solution, Hardin has made three critical assumptions: (i) that there exists, or can be developed, a "criterion of judgment and a system of weighting . . . " that will "render the incommensurables . . . commensurable . . . " in real life; (ii) that, possessing this criterion of judgment, "coercion can be mutually agreed upon," and that the application of coercion to effect a solution to problems will be effective in modern society; and (iii) that the administrative system, supported by the criterion of judgment and access to coercion, can and will protect the commons from further desecration.

If all three of these assumptions were correct, the tragedy which Hardin has recognized would dissolve into a rather facile melodrama of setting up administrative agencies. I believe these three assumptions are so questionable in contemporary society that a tragedy remains in the full sense in which Hardin used the term. Under contemporary conditions, the subset of technically insoluble problems is also politically insoluble, and thus we witness a full-blown tragedy wherein "the essence of dramatic tragedy is not unhappiness. It resides in the remorseless working of things."

The remorseless working of things in modern society is the erosion of three social myths which form the basis for Hardin's assumptions, and this erosion is proceeding at such a swift rate that perhaps the myths can neither revitalize nor reformulate in time to prevent the "population bomb" from going off, or before an accelerating "pollution immersion," or perhaps even an "atomic fallout."

Eroding Myth of the Common Value System

Hardin is theoretically correct, from the point of view of the behavioral sciences, in his argument that "in real life incommensurables *are* commensurable." He is, moreover, on firm ground in his assertion that to fulfill this condition in real life one needs only "a criterion of judgment and a system of weighting." In real life, however, values are the criteria of judgment, and the system of weighting is dependent upon the ranging of a number of conflicting values in a hierarchy. That such a system of values exists beyond the confines of the nation-state is hardly tenable. At this point in time one is more likely to find such a system of values within the boundaries of the nation-state. Moreover, the nation-state is the only political unit of sufficient dimension to find and enforce political solutions to Hardin's subset of "technically insoluble problems." It is on this political unit that we will fix our attention.

In America there existed, until very recently, a set of conditions which perhaps made the solution to Hardin's problem subset possible: we lived with the myth that we were "one people, indivisible . . . " This myth postulated that we were the great "melting pot" of the world wherein the diverse cultural ores of Europe were poured into the crucible of the frontier experience to produce a new alloy—an American civilization. This new civilization was presumably united by a common value system that was democratic, equalitarian, and existing under universally enforceable rules contained in the Constitution and the Bill of Rights.

In the United States today, however, there is emerging a new set of behavior patterns which suggest that the myth is either dead or dying. Instead of believing and behaving in accordance with the myth, large sectors of the population are developing life-styles and value hierarchies that give contemporary Americans an appearance more closely analogous to the particularistic, primitive forms of "tribal" organizations living in geographic proximity than to that shining new alloy, the American civilization.

With respect to American politics, for example, it is increasingly evident that the 1960 election was the last election in the United States to be played out according to the rules of pluralistic politics in a two-party system. Certainly 1964 was, even in terms of voting behavior, a contest between the larger tribe that was still committed to the pluralistic model of compromise and accommodation within a winning coalition, and an emerging tribe that is best seen as a millennial revitalization movement directed against mass society—a movement so committed to the revitalization of old values that it would rather lose the election than compromise its values. Under such circumstances former real-life commensurables within the Republican Party suddenly became incommensurable.

In 1968 it was the Democratic Party's turn to suffer the degeneration of commensurables into incommensurables as both the Wallace tribe and the McCarthy tribe refused to play by the old rules of compromise, accommodation, and exchange of interests. Indeed, as one looks back on the 1968 election, there seems to be a common theme in both these camps—a theme of return to more simple and direct participation in decision-making that is only possible in the tribal setting. Yet, despite that similarity, both the Wallaceites and the McCarthyites responded with a value perspective that ruled out compromise and they both demanded a drastic change in the dimension in which politics is played. So firm were the value commitments in both of these tribes that neither (as was the case with the Goldwater forces in 1964) was willing to settle for a modicum of power that could accrue through the processes of compromise with the national party leadership.

Still another dimension of this radical change in behavior is to be seen in the black community where the main trend of the argument seems to be, not in the direction of accommodation, compromise, and integration, but rather in the direction of fragmentation from the larger community, intransigence in the areas where black values and black culture are concerned, and the structuring of a new community of like-minded and like-colored people. But to all appearances even the concept of color is not enough to sustain commensurables in their emerging community as it fragments into religious nationalism, secular nationalism, integrationists, separationists, and so forth. Thus those problems which were commensurable, both interracial and intracial, in the era of integration become incommensurable in the era of Black Nationalism.

Nor can the growth of commensurable views be seen in the contemporary youth movements. On most of the American campuses today there are at least ten tribes involved in "tribal wars" among themselves and against the "imperialistic" powers of those "over 30." Just to tick them off, without any attempt to be comprehensive, there are: the up-tight protectors of the status quo who are looking for middle-class union cards, the revitalization movements of the Young Americans for Freedom, the reformists of pluralism represented by the Young Democrats and the Young Republicans, those committed to New Politics, the Students for a Democratic Society, the Yippies, the Flower Children, the Black Students Union, and the Third World Liberation Front. The critical change in this instance is not the rise of new groups; this is expected within the pluralistic model of politics. What is new are value positions assumed by these groups which lead them to make demands, not as points for bargaining and compromise with the opposition, but rather as points which are "not negotiable." Hence, they consciously set the stage for either confrontation or surrender, but not for rendering incommensurables commensurable.

Moving out of formalized politics and off the campus, we see the remnants of the "hippie" movement which show clear-cut tribal overtones in their commune movements. This movement has, moreover, already fragmented into an urban tribe which can talk of guerrilla warfare against the city fathers, while another tribe finds accommodation to urban life untenable without sacrificing its values and therefore moves out to the "Hog Farm," "Morning Star," or "Big Sur." Both hippie tribes have reduced the commensurables with the dominant WASP tribe to the point at which one of the cities on the Monterey Peninsula felt sufficiently threatened to pass a city ordinance against sleeping in trees, and the city of San Francisco passed a law against sitting on sidewalks.

Even among those who still adhere to the pluralistic middle-class American image, we can observe an increasing demand for a change in the dimension of life and politics that has disrupted the elementary social processes: the demand for neighborhood (tribal?) schools, control over redevelopment projects, and autonomy in the setting and payment of rents to slumlords. All of these trends are more suggestive of tribalism than of the growth of the range of commensurables with respect to the commons.

We are, moreover, rediscovering other kinds of tribes in some very odd ways. For example, in the educational process, we have found that one of our first and best empirical measures in terms both of validity and reproducibility—the I.Q. test—is a much better measure of the existence of different linguistic tribes than it is a measure of "native intellect" (6). In the elementary school, the different languages and different values of these diverse tribal children have even rendered the commensurables that obtained in the educational system suddenly incommensurable.

Nor are the empirical contradictions of the common value myth as new as one might suspect. For example, with respect to the urban environment, at least 7 years ago Scott Greer was arguing that the core city was sick and would remain sick until a basic sociological movement took place in our urban environment that would move all the middle classes to the suburbs and surrender the core city to the " . . . segregated, the insulted, and the injured" (7). This argument by Greer came at a time when most of us were still talking about compromise and accommodation of interests, and was based upon a perception that the life styles, values, and needs of these two groups were so disparate that a healthy, creative restructuring of life in the core city could not take place until pluralism had been replaced by what amounted to geographic or territorial tribalism; only when this occurred would urban incommensurables become commensurable.

Looking at a more recent analysis of the sickness of the core city, Wallace F. Smith has argued that the productive model of the city is no longer viable for the purposes of economic analysis (8). Instead, he develops a model of the city as a site for leisure consumption, and then seems to suggest that the nature of this model is such that the city cannot regain its health because it cannot make decisions, and that it cannot make decisions because the leisure demands are value-based and, hence, do not admit of compromise and accommodation; consequently there is no way of deciding among these various value-oriented demands that are being made on the core city.

In looking for the cause of the erosion of the myth of a common value system, it seems to me that so long as our perceptions and knowledge of other groups were formed largely through the written media of communication, the American myth that we were a giant melting pot of equalitarians could be sustained. In such a perceptual field it is tenable, if not obvious, that men are motivated by interests. Interests can always be compromised and accommodated without undermining our very being by sacrificing values. Under the impact of the electronic media, however, this psychological distance has broken down and we now discover that these people with whom we could formerly compromise on interests are not, after all, really motivated by interests but by values. Their behavior in our very living room betrays a set of values, moreover, that are incompatible with our own, and consequently the compromises that we make are not those of contract but of culture. While the former are acceptable, any form of compromise on the latter is not a form of rational behavior but is rather a clear case of either apostasy or heresy. Thus, we have arrived not at an age of accommodation but one of confrontation. In such an age "incommensurables" remain "incommensurable" in real life.

Erosion of the Myth of the Monopoly of Coercive Force

In the past, those who no longer subscribed to the values of the dominant culture were held in check by the myth that the state possessed a monopoly on coercive force. This myth has undergone continual erosion since the end of World War II owing to the success of the strategy of guerrilla warfare, as first revealed to the French in Indochina, and later conclusively demonstrated in Algeria. Suffering as we do from what Senator Fulbright has called "the arrogance of power," we have been extremely slow to learn the lesson in Vietnam, although we now realize that war is political and cannot be won by military means. It is apparent that the myth of the monopoly of coercive force as it was first qualified in the civil rights conflict in the South, then in our urban ghettos, next on the streets of Chicago, and now on our college campuses has lost its hold over the minds of Americans. The technology of guerrilla warfare has made it evident that, while the state can win battles, it cannot win wars of values. Coercive force which is centered in the modern state cannot be sustained in the face of the active resistance of some 10 percent of its population unless the state is willing to embark on a deliberate policy of genocide directed against the value dissident groups. The factor that sustained the myth of coercive force in the past was the acceptance of a common value system. Whether the latter exists is questionable in the modern nation-state. But, even if most members of the nation-state remain united around a common value system which makes incommensurables for the majority commensurable, that majority is incapable of enforcing its decisions upon the minority in the face of the diminished coercive power of the governing body of the nation-state.

Erosion of the Myth of Administrators of the Commons

Hardin's thesis that the administrative arm of the state is capable of legislating temperance accords with current administrative theory in political science and touches on one of the concerns of that body of theory when he suggests that the " . . . great challenge facing us now is to invent the corrective feedbacks that are needed to keep the custodians honest."

Our best empirical answers to the question—*Quis custodiet ipsos custodes?* —"Who shall watch the watchers themselves?"—have shown fairly conclusively (9) that the decisions, orders, hearings, and press releases of the custodians of the commons, such as the Federal Communications Commission, the Interstate Commerce Commission, the Federal Trade Commission, and even the Bureau of Internal Revenue, give the large but unorganized groups in American society symbolic satisfaction and assurances. Yet, the actual day-to-day decisions and operations of these administrative agencies contribute, foster, aid, and indeed legitimate the special claims of small but highly organized groups to differential access to tangible resources which are extracted from the commons. This has been so well documented in the social sciences that the best answer to the question of who watches over the custodians of the commons is the regulated interests that make incursions on the commons.

Indeed, the process has been so widely commented upon that one writer has postulated a common life cycle for all of the attempts to develop regulatory policies (10). This life cycle is launched by an outcry so widespread and demanding that it generates enough political force to bring about the establishment of a regulatory agency to insure the equitable, just, and rational distribution of the advantages among all holders of interest in the commons. This phase is followed by the symbolic reassurance of the offended as the agency goes into operation, developing a period of political quiescence among the great majority of those who hold a general but unorganized interest in the commons. Once this political quiescence has developed, the highly organized and specifically interested groups who wish to make incursions into the commons bring sufficient pressure to bear through other political processes to convert the agency to the protection and furthering of their interests. In the last phase even staffing of the regulating agency is accomplished by drawing the agency administrators from the ranks of the regulated.

Thus, it would seem that, even with the existence of a common value system accompanied by a viable myth of the monopoly of coercive force, the prospects are very dim for saving the commons from differential exploitation or spoliation by the administrative devices in which Hardin places his hope. This being the case, the natural sciences may absolve themselves of responsibility for meeting the environmental challenges of the contemporary world by relegating those problems for which there are no technical solutions to the political or social realm. This action will, however, make little contribution to the solution of the problem.

Are the Critical Problems of Modern Society Insoluble?

Earlier in this article I agreed that perhaps until very recently, there existed a set of conditions which made the solution of Hardin's problem subset possible; now I suggest that the concession is questionable. There is evidence of structural as well as value problems which make comprehensive solutions impossible and these conditions have been present for some time.

For example, Aaron Wildavsky, in a comprehensive study of the budgetary process, has found that in the absence of a calculus for resolving "intrapersonal comparison of utilities," the governmental budgetary process proceeds by a calculus that is sequential and incremental rather than comprehensive. This being the case " ... if one looks at politics as a process by which the government mobilizes resources to meet pressing problems" (11), the budget is the focus of these problem responses and the responses to problems in contemporary America are not the sort of comprehensive responses required to bring order to a disordered environment. Another example of the operation of this type of rationality is the American involvement in Vietnam; for, what is the policy of escalation but the policy of sequential incrementalism given a new Madison Avenue euphemism? The question facing us all is the question of whether incremental rationality is sufficient to deal with 20th-century problems.

The operational requirements of modern institutions make incremental rationality the only viable form of decision-making, but this only raises the prior question of whether there are solutions to any of the major problems raised in modern society. It may well be that the emerging forms of tribal behavior noted in this article are the last hope of reducing political and social institutions to a level where incommensurables become commensurable in terms of values *and* in terms of comprehensive responses to problems. After all, in the history of man on earth we might well assume that the departure from the tribal experience is a short-run deviant experiment that failed. As we stand "on the eve of destruction," it may well be that the return to the face-to-face life in the small community unmediated by the electronic media is a very functional response in terms of the perpetuation of the species.

There is, I believe, a significant sense in which the human environment is directly in conflict with the source of man's ascendancy among the other species of the earth. Man's evolutionary position hinges, not on specialization, but rather on generalized adaptability. Modern social and political institutions, however, hinge on specialized, sequential, incremental decision-making and not on generalized adaptability. This being the case, life in the nation-state will continue to require a singleness of purpose for success but in a very critical sense this singleness of purpose becomes a straightjacket that makes generalized adaptation impossible. Nowhere is this conflict more evident than in our urban centers where there has been a decline in the livability of the total environment that is almost directly proportionate to the rise of special purpose districts. Nowhere is this conflict between institutional singleness of purpose and the human dimension of the modern environment more evident than in the recent warning of S. Goran Lofroth, chairman of a committee studying pesticides for the Swedish National Research Council, that many breast-fed children ingest from their mother's milk "more than the recommended daily intake of DDT" (12) and should perhaps be switched to cow's milk because cows secrete only 2 to 10 percent of the DDT they ingest.

How Can Science Contribute to the Saving of the Commons?

It would seem that, despite the nearly remorseless working of things, science has some interim contributions to make to the alleviation of those problems of the commons which Hardin has pointed out.

These contributions can come at two levels:

1) Science can concentrate more of its attention on the development of technological responses which at once alleviate those problems and reward those people who no longer desecrate the commons. This approach would seem more likely to be successful than the " . . . fundamental extension in morality . . . " by administrative law; the engagement of interest seems to be a more reliable and consistent motivator of advantage-seeking groups than does administrative wrist-slapping or constituency pressure from the general public.

2) Science can perhaps, by using the widely proposed environmental monitoring systems, use them in such a way as to sustain a high level of "symbolic disassurance" among the holders of generalized interests in the commons—thus sustaining their political interest to a point where they would provide a constituency for the administrator other than those bent on denuding the commons. This latter approach would seem to be a first step toward the " . . . invention of the corrective feedbacks that are needed to keep custodians honest." This would require a major change in the behavior of science, however, for it could no longer rest content with development of the technology of monitoring and with turning the technology over to some new agency. Past administrative experience suggests that the use of technology to sustain a high level of "dis-assurance" among the general population would also require science to take up the role and the responsibility for maintaining, controlling, and disseminating the information.

Neither of these contributions to maintaining a habitable environment will be made by science unless there is a significant break in the insularity of the two scientific tribes. For, if science must, in its own insularity, embark on the independent discovery of "the tragedy of the commons," along with the parameters that produce the tragedy, it may be too slow a process to save us from the total destruction of the planet. Just as important, however, science will, by pursuing such a course, divert its attention from the production of technical tools, information, and solutions which will contribute to the political and social solutions for the problems of the commons.

Because I remain very suspicious of the success of either demands or pleas for fundamental extensions in morality, I would suggest that such a conscious turning by both the social and the natural sciences is, at this time, in their immediate self-interest. As Michael Polanyi has pointed out, " . . . encircled today between the crude utilitarianism of the philistine and the ideological utilitarianism of the modern revolutionary movement, the love of pure science may falter and die" (13). The sciences, both social and natural, can function only in a very special intellectual environment that is neither universal or unchanging, and that environment is in jeopardy. The questions of humanistic relevance raised by the students at M.I.T., Stanford Research Institute, Berkeley, and wherever the headlines may carry us tomorrow, pose serious threats to the maintenance of that intellectual environment. However ill-founded *some* of the questions raised by the new generation may be, it behooves us to be ready with at least some collective, tentative answers—if only to maintain an environment in which both sciences will be allowed and fostered. This will not be accomplished so long as the social sciences continue to defer the most critical problems that face mankind to future technical advances, while the natural sciences continue to defer those same problems which are about to overwhelm all mankind to false expectations in the political realm.

REFERENCES AND NOTES

1. G. Hardin, *Science* 162, 1243 (1968).
2. J. B. Wiesner and H. F. York, *Sci. Amer.* 211 (No. 4), 27 (1964).
3. C. Woodbury, *Amer. J. Public Health* 45, 1 (1955); S. Marquis, *Amer. Behav. Sci.* 11, 11 (1968); W. H. Ferry, *Center Mag.* 2, 2 (1969).
4. C. P. Snow, *The Two Cultures and the Scientific Revolution* (Cambridge Univ. Press, New York, 1959).
5. M. Olson, Jr., *The Logic of Collective Action* (Harvard Univ. Press, Cambridge, Mass., 1965).
6. G. A. Harrison *et al., Human Biology* (Oxford Univ. Press, New York, 1964). p. 292; W. W. Charters, Jr. in *School Children in the Urban Slum* (Free Press, New York, 1967).
7. S. Greer, *Governing the Metropolis* (Wiley, New York, 1962), p. 148.
8. W. F. Smith, "The Class Struggle and the Disquieted City," a paper presented at the 1969 annual meeting of the Western Economic Association, Oregon State University, Corvallis.
9. M. Bernstein, *Regulating Business by Independent Commissions* (Princeton Univ. Press, Princeton, N.J., 1955); E. P. Herring, *Public Administration and the Public Interest* (McGraw-Hill, New York, 1936); E. M. Redford, *Administration of National Economic Control* (Macmillan, New York, 1952).
10. M. Edelman, *The Symbolic Uses of Politics* (Univ. of Illinois Press, Urbana, 1964).
11. A. Wildavsky, *The Politics of the Budgetary Process* (Little Brown, Boston, Mass., 1964).
12. Corvallis *Gazette-Times,* 6 May 1969, p. 6.
13. M. Polanyi, *Personal Knowledge* (Harper & Row, New York, 1964), p. 182.

The Hunting Culture vs
The Agricultural Treadmill
(or Who Can Afford Waste?)

The earth is now on a fossil fuel and photosynthetic energy budget. However, there is a finite supply of fossil fuel. If we turn to nuclear power as our supply dwindles, numerous problems stand in the way of development. Prior to the industrial revolution the life support system was powered almost exclusively by the green plant. How many people could the earth support now on a strictly photosynthetic energy budget?

Agriculture inflated the energy budget of man as a species. Energy budget standards established during nearly two million years of history as a hunter were decidedly raised when agriculture began about 15,000 years ago. While we are examining a depreciated energy budget, one might consider how many people the earth could support on a hunting-only energy budget.

Does man have the wisdom to handle the energy level above that of hunting? Once man got hooked on the inflated agricultural budget and later fossil fuel, there was no turning back. This is the historical background of an expansive economy. Not only does growth promote growth, but more importantly, growth requires more growth. Japan, a crowded nation that has effectively lowered the birthrate, has recently announced the need to increase its population. This nation of 102 million in an area about the size of Montana must increase the number of producers to be economically sound in twenty years or so.

It is likely that in our not too distant past, hunting was a way of life. Abundant rainfall for several seasons in an area produced lush vegetation, an increase in the number of primary consumers and an increase in the number of humans. When drought came, man starved, migrated or began to plant the weeds that followed his campfires. In breaking the ground and reducing the diversity of species in the region, he reduced the total energy moving through the system but increased the energy available to him by growing only plants he cared to eat. Agriculture, a temporary development, became a way of life because food supply is the primary determiner of man's numbers.

The agricultural treadmill moves even faster on a heavily subsidized fossil fuel budget. This fuel which drives our technology has been destroying our biosphere. Can we save ourselves only by de-escalating our numbers to a level that can be supported by a hunting way of life?

An Indian Method of Hunting Buffalo   71

MERIWETHER LEWIS

today we passed on the Stard. side the remains of a vast many mangled carcases of Buffalow which had been driven over a precipice of 120 feet by the Indians and perished; the water appeared to have washed away a part of this immence pile of slaughter and still their remained the fragments of at least a hundred carcases they created a most horrid stench. In this manner the Indians of the Missouri distroy vast herds of buffaloe at a stroke; for this purpose one of the most active and fleet young men is scelected and disguised in a robe of buffaloe skin, having also the skin of the buffaloe's head with the years and horns fastened on his head in form of a cap, thus caparisoned he places himself at a convenient distance between a herd of buffaloe and a precipice proper for the prupose, which happens in many places on this river for miles together; the other indians now surround the herd on the back and flanks and at a signal agreed on all shew themselves at the same time moving forward towards the buffaloe; the disguised indian or decoy has taken care to place himself sufficiently nigh the buffaloe to be noticed by them when they take to flight and runing before them they follow him in full speede to the precipice, the cattle behind driving those in front over and seeing them go do not look or hesitate about following untill the whole are precipitated down the precepice forming one common mass of dead and mangled carcases: the decoy in the mean time has taken care to secure himself in some cranney or crivice of the clift which he had previously prepared for that purpose. the part of the decoy I am informed is extreamly dangerous, if they are not very fleet runers the buffaloe tread them under foot and crush them to death, and sometimes drive them over the precipice also, where they perish in common with the buffaloe.

Food Production in Prehistoric Europe   72

H. T. WATERBOLK

By about 3000 B.C. all the plains south of the Scandinavian mountains were inhabited by people who lived together in villages of a more or less permanent character. These settlers cut the deciduous forest with stone axes, cultivated a variety of crops, and raised cattle, sheep, goats, and pigs. Hunting was of little importance.

The art of pottery was known everywhere. From highly varied shape and ornamentation, archeologists have been able to distinguish a number of cultures of limited geographical and chronological occurrence and various degrees of relation.

How different is the picture if we go back in time another 5000 years, to about 8000 B.C. The last cold spell of the Ice Age was then almost over. Hunting and gathering were the major means of subsistence. Animal domestication and plant cultivation were unknown. Camp sites were relatively impermanent, shifting from one place to another.

From 8000 to 3000 B.C. in southwestern Asia there was a progression from food collecting to urban civilization, through the levels of incipient cultivation and domestication, of primary effective village farming and of developed village farming and town life.

73   The Tehuacan Story

ROBERT CLAIBORNE

The Tehuacan story begins around 10,000 B.C. Then and for some 3000 years thereafter, the valley was occupied by a few families of nomadic hunters, totaling perhaps twenty men, women, and children. Their lives resembled those of today's South African Bushmen. Season by season, each family group wandered from one camp to another, hunting game with stone weapons and collecting the fruits, seeds, and roots of wild plants. Their meat diet came chiefly from small game—jackrabbits, gophers, rats, birds, and turtles. These people were not the "mammoth hunters" whose remains have been found elsewhere in North America. The first Tehuacanos, commented one expert, "probably found one mammoth in a lifetime and—like some archaeologists—never got over talking about it."

Slowly, these primitive people evolved a slightly more complex culture. The valley's population increased, though by 7000 B.C. it still numbered less than 100. Meat was scarcer, perhaps because there were more people, perhaps because the valley, growing drier, had become less hospitable to animal life. When the spring rains came, the families now congregated in somewhat larger bands to gather the briefly burgeoning wild plants. To prepare these increasingly important plant foods, they hammered out a variety of stone scrapers, choppers, and grinding stones. Their diet now included a kind of squash, amaranth, tiny avocadoes with pea-sized pits, and chili peppers—all of which were subsequently cultivated in Mexico, and still are. They wove nets, perhaps for snaring animals, and baskets, as well as colorful blankets of dyed wild cotton.

Along with these richer material goods, they had developed a fairly complex ceremonial and spiritual life. They may have practiced human sacrifice (a motif that crops up repeatedly in Middle American culture) and unquestionably buried their dead elaborately.

Though the Tehuacanos had clearly progressed beyond the bare subsistence level, by Old World standards they were still terribly primitive. Their contemporaries in Mesopotamia and Asia Minor were already full-time farmers, raising grain and vegetables and herding cows, sheep, goats, and pigs.

Sometime around 5500 B.C. these ancestral Mexicans seem to have conceived the notion that if you drop a seed in the ground at the proper time, a plant will grow up. The archaeological record shows that by that date the avocado pits are no longer pea-sized but acorn-sized, presumably as a result of cultivation. A little later, a new type of squash has appeared in the valley—and one that had no wild counterpart there. The prevalence of its seeds leaves little doubt that the "import" was sown and harvested in Tehuacan.

Around 5000 B.C. corn makes its first appearance among the relics. It was far from the corn we know today. Its skinny cobs, most of them less than an inch long, bore some fifty small kernels. These were rather loosely attached to the cob, and, unlike modern corn, were not completely enclosed in a husk, so that at maturity they could be jarred loose by a gust of wind and scattered to reproduce themselves. (Modern corn could not survive if it were not sown by man.) These remnants are true wild corn. Gathering it must have been a rather unprofitable business. The open husk gave free rein to birds and rodents, and the loosely attached kernels could too easily be scattered by a careless harvester.

By 4000 B.C. the Tehuacanos are quite definitely growing two kinds of squash, gourds, beans, and several other food plants. And they are growing corn. But this corn hardly differs from the wild variety. Its cobs are merely a little bigger.

Altogether, these cultivated plants supply only about a quarter of the Tehuacanos' diet. Though the people can now gather in large groups during the growing season, in the dry season they must still hit the foraging trail in small, family bands. The valley's population, in 300 generations, has grown only to about 200. (In Mesopotamia, men are already living in towns and building mud temples; before very long they will invent writing and the wheel.)

Now the pace of progress in Tehuacan begins to speed up a little. As the people harvested their corn patches, they must have selected the larger, more productive ears for next year's seed. Moreover, a new variety of corn makes its appearance. Called "early tripsacoid," it seems to represent a cross between corn and related wild grasses. The hybrid yielded ears considerably larger than those of the original Tehuacan strain; moreover, its kernels were more firmly attached to the cob, making for easier harvesting.

By 2000 B.C., the valley is dotted with half-a-dozen little villages, each surrounded by patches of corn, beans, squash, and pumpkins; dogs scavenge among the refuse heaps (and are doubtless served up as the *piece de resistance* on feast days). The population still raises less than half its food, but it is a considerably bigger population—800 or so. It is also more skilled—its basketry, weaving, and stonework are more sophisticated, and it has learned how to make pottery, albeit still crude and poorly fired.

The corn crop continues to improve. The tripsacoid strain has crossed with the original Tehuacan strain, and some of the crosses are yielding fat ears, three inches or more long, bearing several hundred kernels. The ears are beginning to reach maturity enclosed in tight husks, which help ensure that men, rather than animals, will reap the crop—and which also make corn wholly dependent on man for propagation. It was this strain of corn that eventually replaced its wild ancestor.

By 1500 B.C. Tehuacan's transition toward an agricultural way of life is nearly complete. The population, farmers all, has passed the 2,000 mark, and is grouped in permanent villages of perhaps 200 souls. Before many generations have passed, these villages will begin to group together around small towns, each with its mud or mud-brick temple.

Around 800 B.C.—about the time that Homer was writing the Iliad—the Tehuacanos reach another milestone: they begin to irrigate their fields, constructing earth dams and crude ditches. With this systematic use of water, plus continued improvement in crop strains, the food supply leaps, and with it the population, to perhaps 8,000. The villages are larger, the temples are beginning to be built in stone rather than mud. Moreover, the valley is now in regular contact with other peoples. Chief among these—judging from the new patterns of tools and pottery—are the already-civilized Olmecs, who live several hundred miles to the east along the Gulf of Mexico.

By the time of Christ, other peoples have contributed additional food resources: peanuts, sunflowers, tomatoes, guavas, and turkeys. Agriculture is almost certainly regulated by some sort of calendar. One of the irrigation dams is now a masonry structure 70 feet high and a quarter-mile long. Anticipating the design of the most sophisticated modern dams, it is curved against the pressure of stored water, and has stone breakwaters upstream to protect it from the summer's flash floods. The population has swelled to around 20,000, and some of the villages have grown into sizable hilltop towns.

In the reigns of Charlemagne and Alfred the Great, the Tehuacanos number close to 100,000, supported by an agriculture based on large-scale irrigation. The valley is divided up into four or five little city-states, each consisting of a half-dozen farming villages centered around a city. The states may already be—as they certainly become later—feudal dependencies of the Mixtec Empire. Trade is thriving. Specialist craftsmen produce cotton textiles, pottery, and salt for export.

To coordinate and enforce this complex social structure, other classes of specialists have grown up: professional priest-bureaucrats who keep records in picture writing, professional soldiers of a standing army, and perhaps a god-king or emperor over all. These, in turn, were undoubtedly supported by some system of taxation. Tehuacan has become thoroughly civilized.

Japan: A Crowded Nation Wants   74
To Boost Its Birthrate

PHILIP M. BOFFEY

Japan is the most crowded nation in the world. It has 102 million people—half as many as the United States—all crammed into a string of narrow islands that are smaller in total area than Montana. Moreover, 85 percent of Japan's territory is mountainous—a scenic splendor but ill-suited for habitation—so the huge population is actually squeezed into a series of narrow valleys and coastal plains. Japan far exceeds any other country in population density per inhabitable area. As of 1968, Japan had 1333 inhabitants per square kilometer of cultivable land, compared with 565 for runner-up Holland.

The resulting congestion seems unbelievable to many Westerners. Farmland is so scarce that one finds crops growing everywhere—up the sides of steep hills, in the narrow alleys between adjacent railroad tracks, even at the front stoop, where one ordinary expects to find a lawn. In the cities, and even in rural villages, tiny houses are jammed side by side, with little or no yard space and barely enough room to walk between. Living is so close that privacy is difficult. As one Japanese physician expressed it: "It's a standing joke among us that you can always tell what a neighbor is cooking. If you can't smell it, you can hear the conversation."

Thus it came as a shock to many Westerners last summer when Prime Minister Eisaku Sato publicly advocated an *increase* in Japan's birthrate. Sato's statement, made in a speech to Japanese newspaper editors, seemed to mark a major reversal of Japan's population policy. For the past two decades, Japan has struggled to curb its population growth, and to a large extent it has succeeded. But now, the Prime Minister indicated, the population control effort may have gone too far. Sato noted that Japan's birthrate had fallen below the average for other advanced nations, and he said the government would strive to bring it back up to that average level. Thus, while other world leaders are struggling to curb the widely feared "population explosion," Japan seems to have embarked on a somewhat contrary course.

The Prime Minister's remarks caused great consternation in family planning circles in Japan, for even at the current rate of expansion, Japan's population is expected to rise to 131 million by early next century before starting to decline. Takuma Terao, an economist who is chairman of the Family Planning Federation of Japan, told *Science*: "I am entirely against the idea of raising the birthrate. Japan already has too large a population." Similarly, Minoru Muramatsu, one of Japan's leading authorities on the public health aspects of population growth, said in an interview: "In terms of space, Japan already has too many people. If you live in Tokyo, all you can find is a place to eat and a place to earn money. There is no green, no trees. I don't feel that people are living a very human life."

A High-Level Recommendation

Yet Sato's statement was no irrational, off-the-cuff remark by an uninformed politician. It was based on some cautiously worded recommendations made by the Population Problems Inquiry Council, a cabinet-level advisory group which includes some of Japan's leading demographers. Moreover, the recommendations are aimed at alleviating some potentially serious economic and social problems that are related, at least in part, to Japan's success at curbing its population growth. One such problem is a worsening labor shortage that threatens to undermine Japan's "economic miracle"; another is an increasing number of elderly people who will have to be cared for somehow, particularly now that Japan's traditional descendant family system, in which the younger generations cared for the older, is breaking up.

This article will make no attempt to prescribe what Japan's population policy should be, for the Japanese, one of the world's most highly educated and industrious peoples, are certainly capable of deciding for themselves what sort of future environment they want. But the Japanese situation is worth examining in some detail because the same problems—and the same political and economic pressures —may well arise in this country as the population growth here is brought under tighter control.

Japan has undeniably achieved remarkable success at controlling its birthrate. In the early 1920's, the birthrate stood above 36 per 1000 population, but then it declined moderately and steadily, a phenomenon that usually accompanies the transition from an agricultural to an industrial society. The rate fell as low as 26.6 in the late 1930's before the trend was reversed by the pronatal policy of Japan's military leaders. After the Second World War the rate soared back up as Japan experienced the normal "baby boom" that occurs when soldiers and overseas civilians return home. The birthrate reached 34.3 in 1947 (an intermediate level by world standards) and stayed above 33 in 1948 and 1949, before beginning the precipitous drop that has brought Japan such praise for its "population miracle." By 1957 Japan's birthrate had fallen to 17.2, a historically unprecedented drop of 50 percent in just 10 years. The decline seems especially sharp when measured from the peak of the postway baby boom, but even compared with prewar trends, the reduction is considered significant.

What was the secret of Japan's success? Interestingly enough, many Japanese demographers describe the achievement as largely "spontaneous" in the sense that the Japanese people, faced with near-starvation economic conditions after the war, concluded on their own that they should limit the number of children. The news media and women's magazines issued dire warnings, particularly at the height of the baby boom, about the bleak future faced by a nation with too many mouths and a war-ravaged economy, and the highly literate Japanese population obviously got the message. The national government unquestionably helped the population control effort, chiefly by reversing its pronatal policy of the war period. A national Eugenic Protection Law, passed in 1948 and subsequently amended, removed the previous obstacles to birth control, abortion, and sterilization. But many Japanese experts believe the government was always at least one step behind what the people were already doing. One reason for the Eugenic Protection Law, for example, was that so many women were obtaining illegal abortions that the government decided it should protect their health by legalizing the procedure. "The government had no definite policy to bring about population control," says Toshio Kuroda, chief of the migration research division at the government's Institute for Population Problems. "It just happened under the very extraordinary situation after the war. Ten years later people looked back and said we were successful at controlling our population. But no expert in Japan predicted it would happen."

The chief method for curbing the birthrate was induced abortion. The Japanese do not seem to have the strong religious scruples against "taking a life" that have hobbled efforts to increase the use of abortion in this country. Indeed, during the 18th and 19th centuries Japanese peasants often resorted to infanticide to get rid of unwanted children at times of crop failure. Today, abortions are legally obtainable for a number of health and economic reasons. In practice, they are said to be obtainable almost at will. The vast majority of abortions are preformed by private physicians within the first 3 months of pregnancy, and most of these take place without overnight admission to a hospital or another medical facility. The operations are quite inexpensive, costing an average of $10 to $15, according to one estimate published in 1967. Health insurance benefits often bring the out-of-pocket cost down much faster—sometimes even below $1.

Abortions Declining

The number of officially reported abortions (which is believed to represent about half the total number of abortions) reached a high of 1.17 million in 1955 but has since declined to 757,000 in 1968, largely because of government efforts to encourage contraception as an alternative to abortion. In the early 1950's, according to studies by the Institute for Population Problems, abortion accounted for roughly 70 percent of the decline in Japan's fertility while family planning accounted for 30 percent, but in recent years the percentages have been reversed.

The percentage of couples practicing contraception in Japan seems to be somewhat lower than the figure for comparable populations elsewhere. A 1965 survey indicated that about 67 percent of all Japanese couples either had practiced or were then practicing contraception, compared with perhaps 80 to 90 percent for Great Britain and for the white population of the United States. The most popular contraceptive methods have consistently been the condom and the "safe period" or a combination of both. The Japanese make little use of the "pill" or the intrauterine device (IUD), which are mainstays of the population control effort elsewhere, largely because conservative medical opinion in Japan believes it is not wholesome to introduce foreign materials into a healthy body. The government officially prohibits the insertion of IUD's and the sale of oral contraceptives, and while there are large loopholes in these laws, few Japanese use either of the methods.

Japan's success at curbing its population growth is believed to have contributed significantly to the fantastic economic boom that has propelled Japan's gross national product to third rank in the world. If Japan had not curbed its birthrate so sharply, some analysts say, then a sizable portion of the nations's capital resources would have been used to support new additions to the population and would not have been available for economic recovery and industrial investment. Yet the curbing of population growth has not been an unmixed blessing. As conditions have changed in recent years, industry has increasingly complained about a labor shortage, particularly a shortage of young laborers.

I found considerable disagreement as to whether Japan is really suffering from a labor shortage and, if so, what should be done about it. The age composition of the Japanese population has changed considerably over the past decade or two. There has been a sharp decrease, both absolute and relative, in the population of children below the age of 15, and a sharp increase, both absolute and relative, in the population over 65. Meanwhile, the working age population, from 15 to 64, has continued to increase, but at a slower and slower rate. The average annual increase in the working age population exceeded 1 million for the 1965-70 period, but it will drop to 620,000 for the next 5 years and will become negative by the end of the century. When viewed against the needs of a rapidly expanding economy, the labor pool appears to be shrinking.

"The labor supply has changed rather remarkably from surplus to shortage," says Saburo Okita, director of the Japan Economic Research Center and a member of the Population Problems Inquiry Council. "There is already a shortage of young workers, and while there is still some surplus of middle-aged workers and women, many of us predict there will be a serious labor shortage in the coming years." Some Japanese economists contend that a decline in West Germany's economic growth rate in the late 1950's was caused primarily by a drop in the growth rate for Germany's labor population, and they suggest that Japan's "economic miracle" may be stalled by the same problem.

Seeking Cheap Labor?

Yet Takuma Terao, the economist who heads the Family Planning Federation of Japan, offers a much different analysis. "The industrialists say the labor shortage is very severe," he says. "But I say what is deficient is young labor, which is very cheap. So all we can say is that we lack cheap labor, only that." Terao and most other experts agree that the chief factor behind the shortage of young labor has not been the low birthrates, but rather the great growth in the number of young people who now go on to high school or college instead of beginning work at an early age. Terao believes it would be "rash to raise fertility" simply to assure more laborers. He believes it would be more sensible for Japan to "rationalize" its traditionally inefficient business enterprises so as to gain greater labor productivity. "We already have an abundance of laborers," he says, "but they are not well utilized."

The Population Problems Inquiry Council—the cabinet-level advisory group whose recommendations provided the basis for Prime Minister Sato's remarks—took a middle-of-the-road position. The council which is made up of some 40 public and private members, including academics and business and labor leaders, was asked in April 1967 to study the implications of Japan's low birthrate. Last August a subcommittee of the council issued an interim report on its findings; a final report is due this year [1970]. According to Kuroda, who sat on the council, the interim report represents a "compromise between those who are worried about a labor shortage and those who think Japan is already too populated." The report is said to have been drafted by Minoru Tachi, an eminent demographer who heads the government's Institute of Population Problems. An unofficial English translation was prepared by the U.S. State Department.

The report, if read carefully, does not seem especially earth-shaking. It notes that Japan's population, by some measures, is no longer replacing itself; it warns that this is causing certain problems; and it recommends that Japan seek to achieve a "stationary" population in terms of both total size and age distribution. The reports makes no mention of what the ideal population for Japan should be, and as far as I could tell from talking to two members of the council—namely, Kuroda and Okita—there was little discussion of optimum population size. Instead, the report focused its attention on indicators that measure the changing growth rate and age composition of the Japanese population.

The report expressed particular concern over trends in the net reproduction rate, a measure of the extent to which the female population of child-bearing age is reproducing itself with female babies. If the net reproduction rate is 1, the population will potentially become stationary one generation later. If the rate exceeds 1, the population will continuously increase, and if it falls below 1, the population is expected to begin to decrease one generation later. Japan's rate is currently the lowest in the world except for some East European Communist bloc nations. It has remained slightly below 1 almost every year since 1956, generally ranging between 0.9 and 1.

A Rare Occurrence

The report states that while the rate has occasionally dipped below 1 in other countries, "it is very rare for such a situation to continue for more than ten years." (The net reproduction rate for the United States was 1.2 in 1967 and has not dropped below 1 since the 1930's.) The report suggests that Japan's population reproductivity is now "too low," and while it acknowledges that "a high population increase rate cannot be welcomed," it nevertheless believes it would be "desirable" for the net reproduction rate to return to 1 "in the near future" in order to ease the "severe changes in population composition by age."

But the report is very careful not to suggest any direct intervention by the government, such as subsidies to support additional children. Instead, the report simply urges the government to improve social conditions so that Japanese couples will spontaneously decide to have more children. The report also recommends that Japan improve its old-age welfare system and increase the productivity of its labor system.

The report gives no hint as to how its recommendations would affect the size of Japan's population, but there is no question that the population will continue to rise substantially. Government estimates for Japan's population in the year

2025 range from a minimum of 129 million (if the net reproduction rate remains below 1) to a maximum of 152 million, with the median projection being 140 million.

The report is so cautiously written that even such critics as Muramatsu acknowledge there is "nothing really wrong with it if you read the text very carefully." After all, who can object to the government improving social conditions? But opponents of the report are upset that mass media stressed the need for more births and largely ignored the question of social improvement. Some also feel the government was premature in its announcement, since they believe the net reproduction rate is already heading back toward 1, or even higher, without any encouragement. Other critics fear the government will eventually decide to intervene in a very direct way to encourage more births, and some even fear that the government's action was partly motivated by a desire to grow soldiers for a future large army.

At bottom, the disagreement is one of priorities. Those who regard economic expansion as the greatest good want more bodies to man the assembly lines. Those who are worried about overcrowding are willing to sacrifice some economic growth in return for more living space. The question of how much living space is desirable, however, is a knotty one. My own reaction to Japan was to be appalled at the overcrowding. But there is some evidence that the Japanese have grown accustomed to their close living conditions and actually even like them. Ichiro Kawasaki, a former Japanese diplomat, has written that the massive stone buildings of the West "overwhelm" Japanese travelers, and they soon "begin to miss the light wooden structures and small landscape gardens to which they have so long been accustomed." Similarly, Maramatsu, who spent several years at Johns Hopkins University and who frequently travels abroad, laments that many Japanese have no idea what he is talking about when he extols the "spacious way of living" in other countries. "For generations," he says, "many of our people have been living under the same conditions, so they don't question whether it is wrong or right."

Such differing attitudes toward space needs make it difficult for the experts in one advanced nation to suggest the best population policy for another advanced nation. Such differences also make it difficult to visualize how much of a burden population growth in any one country would really impose on future generations in that country. Perhaps future generations will enjoy living shoulder to shoulder.

The Lesson of Japan's Exerience

Japan's decision to boost its birthrate slightly may have an impact and significance beyond its own borders. Some family planning advocates fear Japan's action may throw a monkey wrench in worldwide efforts to curb population growth by somehow downgrading the importance of birth control. Others fear Japan demonstrates that radical population control can never succeed, for the minute a nation reaches the point where its population is apt to level off and then decline, various pressures—political, economic, and nationalistic—build up to reverse the trend. Both views are probably too apocalyptic, for Japan is merely trying to boost its net reproduction rate by a modest amount until it returns to 1—a level that is considered the desirable goal by planners in many other countries. Some U.S. experts, for example, have called for a stationary population and a zero rate of growth, and that is precisely what Japan is seeking.

The real significance of Japan's experience may be that it underlines the costs involved in achieving population control. Some experts in this country, such as Ansley J. Coale, director of the Office of Population Research at Princeton University, have pointed out that a stationary population and a zero growth rate have unfavorable as well as advantageous effects. Coale suggests, for example, that a stationary population "is not likely to be receptive to change and indeed would have a strong tendency towards nostalgia and conservatism." He also suggests that such a society would no longer offer "a reasonable expectation of advancement in authority with age," since there would be essentially the same number of 50-year-olds as 20-year-olds. Zero growth is unquestionably desirable at some point before crowding becomes painful, but in the current rush to jump on the population control bandwagon, it is well to remember that population control is not an unmixed blessing. There are costs involved, and someone will have to pay them.

The Impending Food Crisis

How soon will the crisis come? What will be the consequences? Will governments topple and anarchy reign? What is it like to starve and how does starvation affect the observer of the starving? How will the United States react to the inevitable catastrophes?

We have time to plan and prepare for some of the predictables, but do we have the foresight and will to do so?

75   On The Balance

... and lo a black horse; and he that sat on him had a pair of balances in his hand. And I heard a voice say, A measure of wheat for a penny, and three measures of barley for a penny; and see thou hurt not the oil and the wine.

Revelation 6:5, 6

76   The Locomotive and the Mudslide

WILLIAM AND PAUL PADDOCK

A locomotive is roaring full throttle down the track. Just around the bend an impenetrable mudslide has oozed across the track. There it lies, inert, static, deadly. Nothing can stop the locomotive in time. Collision is inevitable. Catastrophe is foredoomed. Miles back up the track the locomotive could have been warned and stopped. Years ago the mud-soaked hill could have been shored up to forestall the landslide. Now it is too late.

The locomotive roaring straight at us is the population explosion. The unmovable landslide across the tracks is the stagnant production of food in the undeveloped nations, the nations where the population increases are greatest.

The collision is inevitable. The famines are inevitable.

The Time For Rhetoric Is Over 77

LYNDON B. JOHNSON

State of the Union Message
January 10, 1967

Next to the pursuit of peace, the really greatest challenge to the human family is the race between food supply and population increase. That race tonight is being lost.

The time for rhetoric has clearly passed. The time for concerted action is here and we must get on with the job.

The Starving as a Race Apart 78

JAMES BONNER

We will, I suspect, begin to regard the starving populace of the under-developed nations as a race or species apart, people totally different from us, as indeed they will be. "They are just animals," we will say, "and a serious reservoir of disease." The inevitable culmination of the two cultures will be that one culture will devour the other. I would think that it would turn out that the rich and strong will devour the poor and weak.

The Dual Challenge of Health 79
and Hunger—A Global Crisis

GEORG A. BORGSTROM

In the euphoria over a "Green Revolution" which some scientists and many politicians believe is already in the making, two facts are often overlooked: (1) More, not fewer, people suffer from malnutrition each year, and (2) This circumstance prevails at a time when agricultural technology has already been making impressive strides. In the following paper, adapted from an address to the Eleventh Congress of the Medical Women's International Association in the summer of 1968, Dr. Borgstrom examines the roots and dimensions of the food crisis and warns that our present optimism is undercutting the commitment of brains, agencies and money needed to solve the crisis.

If all food in the world were equally distributed and each human received identical quantities, we would *all* be malnourished. If the entire world's food supply were parcelled out at the U.S. dietary level, it would feed only about one third of the human race. The world as a global household knows of no surpluses, merely enormous deficits. Yet there is in the well-fed nations a great deal of nonsensical talk about abundance.

Already short of food, the world is adding 70 million people to its feeding burden each year—the equivalent of an entire United States every three years. The annual increase is itself growing at a rapid pace; it is outstripping the gains in world food production despite all the triumphs of agriculture and fisheries since World War II.

The Hunger Gap

It is not enough to talk about absolute deficits, however, for the world's food resources are distributed with great unevenness. Over 2 billion of the world's 3.5 billion people live lives dominated by extreme shortages of food and water and by inadequate resources in soils and forests. These billions lack satisfactory shelter, clothing, education and medical care. In sharp contrast to their misery, a Luxury Club of at most 400 million people enjoys a rich and steadily more abundant diet as well as a high standard of living in most other respects. Between these two extremes are hundreds of millions of people who may be designated as fence-straddlers. They manage well enough despite numerous handicaps and limited resources, but their diet, although barely adequate, is monotonous and their life, in general, parsimonious.

The richly endowed are found in the United States and Canada, parts of Western Europe, Australia, New Zealand and the La Plata countries of Latin America. The Russians, East Europeans and Japanese belong to the in-between group. Asia, Africa and most of Latin America, with a combined population of more than 2 billion, are the most critical hunger areas. Their human numbers are increasing more than twice as fast (in percent) as those of the well-fed world.

The widening hunger gap is an ominous feature of our days. It poses the greatest challenge mankind has ever faced, overshadowing atom bombs, continental missiles, microbial toxins and nerve gases.

Despite courageous efforts by devoted groups, this crisis has not yet received the attention it desperately needs. Timid bureaucracies are caught in a striking discrepancy between thought and action. Although mankind is "hitting the ceiling"—reaching the limit in its use of the vital resources of soils, water and forests —it is quite obvious that nowhere in our population control measures have we moved beyond the very limited tactic of family planning. True population control in the sense of a deliberate effort to bring down birth rates has hardly anywhere been adopted. Limiting our efforts to averting "unwanted" children, however, is wholly inadequate. Studies show that even if successful, such a policy would have only marginal effects on world population growth by the year 2000.

The most disquieting aspect of the food issue is the fact that, with few exceptions, the scientific and technical community has been signaling a green light to mankind when a stop sign would have been far more appropriate. Recent statements by leading Western scientists in almost all disciplines reveal a shocking disregard for the abject conditions which enclose almost three-fifths of the human race.

It is indeed macabre to witness the present game of calculating how many people the world *could* nourish—*if.* The figures soar beyond 7 billion to 10 billion and even more. Yet, scandalously, the world has failed to provide satisfactorily for even half the 3.5 billion people alive *now.* To give our current population a minimally sound diet would require the immediate doubling of world food production. Thus, whatever else happens and whatever urgent measures are taken, food is going to be the overriding issue of the next 30 years.

The Great Land Grab

Few undertakings in human history have had a greater impact than the enormous, prolonged effort to Europeanize the world. The psychological investment in this drive may explain both the West's lofty promises of abundance for all men and its complete misjudgment of mankind's true situation. In truth, the white man's experience has been misleading. No group of individuals ever seized a greater booty than did the Europeans who took possession of the vast forests and rich prairie soils of the North American continent. Unassuaged, the white man also grabbed the fertile pampas and most other good soils in Central and South America, the South African veld and the rich highland plateaus of interior Africa. He managed to gain control of an entire continent, Australia, with its valuable satellite, New Zealand. In addition, he secured strongholds all over Asia where he monopolized trade and to a considerable degree controlled agricultural production, making India British and the East Indies Dutch.

The Second World War ostensibly brought an end to this era in geopolitical relations. But as late as 1939, shipload after shipload of groundnuts left starving India to fatten the cows of the British Isles. Hundreds of millions of people in Asia and Africa have since attained independence. Superficially, world food markets have adjusted to this fact. More than 25 million tons of grain are now moving from wealthy areas to feed the hungry—as against the latter part of the 1930s when 11 million tons of cereal grains were dispatched from the hungry world to provide for the well-fed.

The monopoly of the European tribe, however, is still strong in the economic field. While public attention is focused on grain, let us direct the searchlight to other commodities and especially to proteins. Here the West finds no cause for self-congratulations. The almost 3 million tons of grain protein recently contributed to the poor nations by the rich and well-fed have been more than counterbalanced by a flow to the Western world of no less than 4 million tons of *superior* proteins in the form of soybeans, oilseed cakes and fish meal. The West is benefiting from a most deceptive exchange.

Crops for Cash vs Crops for Food

Thus, although it has far greater per capita soil and water resources than the hungry world, the West is tenaciously intruding on the latter's struggle for subsistence. Hundreds of millions of people in the tropics must limit their harvests for domestic consumption in order to raise export crops (groundnuts, cotton, coffee, tea and cacao, etc.) for foreign currency. This situation is further aggravated by the fact that the cash crops now enjoy a high priority with regard to credit, fertilizers and irrigation. Their fortunes in the world market, however, are declining. Since 1952 the developing nations have been delivering about 33 percent more tonnage in cash crops while registering only a 4 percent gain in income. Prices, of course, are largely controlled by the West. These somber facts help explain the collapse of two UNCTAD conferences, both of which ended in solemn pledges by the rich countries to devote a mere one percent of their Gross National Product to the dire circumstances of the needy. Not only have most industrialized countries failed to live up to this meagre commitment, but the percentage of GNP which the United States parcels out as "aid" has actually been declining.

The great good luck of Western man in the lottery of history underlies his profound belief that technology will bestow a universal abundance. Good luck has also made him complacent. He imagines that he is more capable than the poor and the hungry. He blames them for listlessness, apathy, laziness, inefficiency, lethargy, resistance to change, notorious backwardness and wavering creativity. In his self-deception he forgets that the ancestors of today's poor and hungry people created a host of great civilizations which, with an improvidence much like his own, wore out their soils, and forests.

In his imagined superiority, Western man chooses to label this hungry world "underdeveloped." If it were not for his historical oversight, he would find "overdeveloped" a more appropriate term. The overwhelming majority of the underfed live in countries where the soil has been over-cultivated for thousands of years, where forests have been pulled down in the erroneous belief that this act would best provide for ever-growing populations, and where water reserves have been exploited to the utmost.

We should not underrate the ingenuity of Asian, African and Latin American societies which not only survive but slowly advance under these conditions. With the meagre resources available to them, many farmers in India and other parts of the so-called "underdeveloped" world display outstanding efficiency. Throughout Asia and Latin America, one can find an astonishingly thorough use being made of available land.

Hundreds of millions of hungry people live in the tropics, where farm acreages are exceedingly small and constantly fragmented through inheritance. Often it is possible to see original two- to four-acre holdings which have been subdivided into five or more plots. Though large-scale increases in production are difficult even on the poor world's *latifundia,* we naively expect the "mini-plot" farmers of Asia, Africa and Latin America to triple or quadruple their production within three decades—something the Western world has never been able to do with all its immense resources of enriched soil and ample land.

The soils from which the poor nations must feed their people are often far inferior to those of the West's "marginal" lands, which are now being abandoned by agriculture. Water is also a scarce commodity in most regions of the hungry world, and agriculture is subject to many more vagaries of climate than in the temperate regions. Moreover, the farmer in a poor nation usually lacks capital for expanded irrigation, for fertilizers, for better sprays against insects and fungi. The handicaps he faces are so severe that any comparison with farmers in the West is absurd.

Health and Hunger

I could delve at great length into the human consequences of this situation but will limit myself to a few remarks about the relationship between health and hunger. A great many people in this world are hungry or malnourished all of the time or part of the time. How is their working capacity affected? And what does an insufficient diet do to their overall health?

The prime global deficiency is that of protein. Until recently this fact was grossly neglected by experts who measured tonnages and profits but who limited their nutritional considerations to calories. Indeed, 10 to 15 percent of the world *is* short of calories, or "undernourished." But vastly more people—perhaps 1.5 billion—suffer from the calamity of inadequate nutrients, or "malnutrition." A shortage of protein is the number-one problem everywhere in the hungry world. Many other deficiencies related to shortage of fat, minerals (calcium, iodine, etc.) and vitamins (B1, B6, folic acid, vitamin A, etc.) are also quite common, and as the hunger problem broadens, these and other dietary shortcomings will greatly assert themselves.

Today a wealth of documentation confirms the existence of a nutritional crisis. Detailed dietary and health surveys have been made in numerous countries in tropical Africa, Latin America, the Caribbean and other regions of the world. Many medical experts believe the situation is even more grave than these studies indicate, since victims of undernourishment who are already thoroughly sick or dead are seldom taken into account. For each case of malnutrition treated in the hospitals, many others never come under care. It is clear that the nutritional crisis has far greater dimensions than have so far been mapped out.

Some telling examples

Vitamin-A deficiency frequently results in blindness, curtailing productivity. In India alone there are at least one million cases of such blindness. In East Pakistan 50,000 children every year are threatened with a possible lifetime of blindness due to their precariously low vitamin A intake. The blind have limited opportunities to contribute to society and often become a drain on it. Yet, for a few pennies a year, such blindness could easily be prevented.

Deficiency diseases are extremely insidious in that they often sap vitality without causing other easily noticed symptoms; they thus frequently belong to the category of "hidden hunger." Hundreds of millions of people are now short of proteins, minerals and vitamins—not to the degree of manifesting precise symptoms but short enough to suffer from lowered efficiency, alertness, endurance and creativity.

One of the most significant findings of modern nutritional research is that protein hunger may cause devastating brain damage in infants. Since the damage is irreversible, it can lead to a lifetime of mental retardation or to other mental and physical aberrations. Similar effects are traceable to prenatal malnutrition. These findings should be a cause for overwhelming global concern. The recognition that malnourished children may emerge from childhood without the ability to reach their full intellectual potential injects a new and frightening element into development theorizing.

The implications are ominous. For many years we have assumed that, given educational opportunities and environmental advantages, even children born to poverty have every prospect of growing up to be bright and productive. It is now suggested that malnourished children may become permanently retarded. The significance of this can be appreciated when we recognize that as many as two-thirds of the children of most developing countries are now suffering from some degree of malnutrition.

Much earlier it became evident that malnutrition profoundly retards physical growth—and this, too, in a frequently nonreversible way. In many developing countries the average twelve-year-old has the physical stature of an eight-year-old in Western Europe and North America. Indian nutritionists report that four out of five preschool children in certain areas suffer from malnutrition-caused dwarfism. During the months of breast feeding, children from the poorest areas grow at a rate comparable to the best nourished children elsewhere. Usually, after six months of age, when breast milk is no longer a sufficient source of protein, growth is progressively retarded.

The relationship of malnutrition to mental growth dramatizes the issue, but the insidious drain of malnutrition on natural development takes other even more harsh forms. Half the deaths in the developing countries occur among children under six years of age. In parts of Southeast Asia, 40 percent of the children die of disease in their first four years. This is a proportion of deaths not cumulatively reached in the Western world until the age of 60.

Most of these childhood deaths are commonly attributed to infectious diseases. Yet such diseases would be of relatively minor consequence in the West. Among children in poor countries, we now know, the cause of death is often not the infection alone but a combination of the infection and malnutrition. In other words, malnutrition debilitates the body to such a degree that it is incapable of resisting what otherwise would be a passing infection. In a country like Ecuador, child deaths ostensibly due to measles are more than 300 times more frequent (per thousand of population per year) than in North America. Whooping cough is still a major killer in much of the world. Similarly, chicken pox is often fatal because of poor nutrition. Diarrheas cause more deaths than any other infectious diseases through the operation of a vicious spiral: the diarrhea is keenly aggravated or even invited by malnutrition, and the malnutrition is exacerbated by diarrhea.

The world has close to one billion children below the age of 14. A very large number of these children will never reach adulthood. They will die prematurely, largely because of malnutrition. This is the tragedy of hunger in its grimmest perspective. To hundreds of millions of children life is very little more than a vigil of death; it is certainly no banquet.

The true economic costs to the poor world of nutritionally induced disease, inefficiency and death have never been calculated. They must run into many billions of dollars per year. Yet one can still encounter innumerable experts who would give health and dietary measures a very low priority in development programs. We face a gigantic educational task right in our own midst, thanks to a series of false notions and to the fact that most of our technology and much of our agriculture and medicine have lost sight of the ecological dimension.

The bulldozer and the miracle drugs may be chosen as symbols of Western man's simplistic faith that he has become the master of his destiny. Only gradually and painfully is he learning that he cannot go on working *against* nature if he is to endure.

The groundnut fiasco in Tanzania, the collapse of Gambia's big poultry project, the persistent spread of schistosomiasis in China, Egypt and tropical Africa, the resurgence of rodents in Europe and malaria in Southeast Asia, the firm hold of malaria and sleeping sickness in tropical Africa—all are examples of man's ecological malfeasance.

But far more serious is another shortcoming. We of the rich, well-fed world are subject to a gigantic self-deception. There is, for instance, nothing wrong with our impressive dairy development, but we conveniently fail to realize that its high level of performance depends on the influx *from the hungry world* of millions of tons of proteins, partly of high quality. And so with other aspects of Western food production. Europe, for instance, receives through the back door over ten million tons of feed protein and close to one million tons of fish protein. In the postwar period there has been a massive exploitation of the oceans, but only to a very limited extent does its bounty reach the poor. Japan and the Soviet Union have expanded their large-scale catching operations into all oceans—primarily to procure food to fill their own needs. They have been followed in highsea fishing by Eastern and Western Europe. It is true that the most spectacular gains in ocean fishing have been made by a poor country, Peru. The result, however, has been to create a majestic feeding bastion not for Peru or Latin America but for the wealthy world, to which are annually delivered more than one million tons of fishmeal. Postwar developments have therefore seen a steadily growing percentage of ocean catches being earmarked to feed the chickens and hogs of the United States and Europe and to provide cheap margarine for the industrialized populations of Western Europe. The underfed millions remain . . . underfed.

One third of the world, in short, is disposing of two-thirds of the harvests both from the lands and the seas. The West's glib talk of a Green Revolution therefore has implications quite different from those its propagandists like to talk about.

Back to Reality

Facing the world food issue, it is high time we abandoned simplistic notions and came to grips with the complexities. Despite innumerable projects and an almost hypertrophic bureaucracy within WHO, FAO, UNESCO and other specialized agencies, the joint efforts of governmental and international organizations have yet to reflect the magnitude of this issue. There is little awareness that, to avert catastrophe, mankind must mobilize all its available resources in money, material and brainpower.

The most serious fallacy connected with the world food issue is the idea that man's globe is limitless, when it should be evident to everyone that our planet is clearly restricted in its resources of soils and water. Over the centuries, biologically useful forests and pastures have lost far too much ground to the plow; this implement has been pushed by mankind's growing millions into places where it has no business. Despite ingenious irrigation accomplishments, it has helped man convert far larger acreages into deserts than he has managed to transform into productive farmlands.

The self-destructive process continues. One third of the irrigation water of the Nile is already used to remove salt left largely by previous irrigation. Man is fighting a desperate struggle with salt, and he has rarely managed to turn this battle from a losing to a winning one.

Soil erosion is furthermore taking a frightful toll. In critical areas where land should be reverted to forests and grasslands or where grazing pressures should at least be reduced—all with the urgent aim of saving the topsoil—the old hell-for-broke exploitation continues. We here touch upon the basic ecological requirements for life.

Instead of protecting our land at high productivity for future generations, we have contented ourselves with busy-work. Much of this busy-work reflects an almost religious faith in gadgets. We naively seem to assume that by willing the means we attain the goals. If someone in a fire station got the idea that silencing the alarm clock would be a good way of handling fires, we would classify him as a mental case. Yet this is the way we act as a human family in facing malnutrition.

We talk about giving the world adequate amounts of fertilizer, forgetting to analyze water as the major limiting factor. Only one tenth of all fertilizer is currently used by the hungry world and, absurdly enough, not for food but for cash crops. Many times more fertilizer are needed for adequate harvests today and still more to feed the additional billions of people we will have at the end of the century. But is there water enough to accommodate such a massive chemical assault on the soils? Presumably not.

Today we talk about high-yielding strains of wheat and rice, forgetting that their productive capabilities have to be honored with much more water, much more fertilizer, more insecticides and fungicides, greatly expanded storage and processing facilities, and vastly increased amounts of capital. Even assuming all this is possible, we have yet to face up to the ecological consequences. Only in very few instances do we know these new strains will stand up in entirely new environments and under bombardment from insects and fungi to which they are not adapted. Simply by hoping for the best, we will not attain our goals. What is required is a sophisticated strategy and very large-scale measures.

Global Planning Required

Despite the euphoria over various new high-protein foods now emerging from laboratories—spun soybean protein, fish and grain protein concentrates, and so forth—their impact on human nutrition has been insignificant. There is no sign that they will be distributed to the hungry on a massive scale in the foreseeable future. Meanwhile, as the talk goes on and as the gap between words and action grows and grows, the ranks of the hungry increase by millions each year. It is not sufficient, in this crisis, to provide free or low-cost school lunches, to cure infants suffering from kwashiorkor, to help an occasional Indian village, to ship food relief to Colombian *campesinos* or Polynesian islanders, and to set up soup kitchens in the slums of Lima and Sao Paolo. These are all commendable acts, but the world has long ago passed the point where charity sufficed.

In conclusion, I would argue that the hunger crisis reflects man's inability to imagine what he already knows. We are participating in a grand-scale evasion of reality which bears all the signs of insanity. In order to bring health and restore vitality to the whole human species, nothing less is required than a global *will* to act, simple justice, true population control, worldwide food planning, effective execution by the scientists, engineers and public leaders of states and regions—and a massive commitment of funds. Furthermore, the resources of lands and seas must reach the larders of all mankind, not just the wealthy. It is time the West kept faith with the Atlantic Charter, which proclaims that all peoples should have equal access to the harvests of the world.

Resources and Needs

Agricultural Production in the Developing Countries   80

G. F. SPRAGUE

At least half the world's population endures some degree of malnutrition. The gap between food production and world population is constantly widening. It has been estimated that by 1985 this situation could become catastrophic. Two approaches appear obligatory: (i) a substantial decrease in the rate of population growth, and (ii) full utilization of our biological technology to increase food production on all economically arable lands. The utilization of microorganisms, algae, or petrochemicals to produce protein has been suggested by many. These and other possibilities should be actively explored and, where feasible, utilized. However, the total impact of such possible developments cannot greatly lessen the need for an expanded agriculture limited only by the ecological potential.

This article is concerned primarily with the possibilities for increasing agricultural production in the developing countries through improvement in varieties, in fertilization, and in management practices. As background, a brief review of selected examples of progress achieved in the developed countries with the three most important food crops—rice, wheat, and corn—during the past 35 years seems desirable.

Rice Production in Japan

Japan has the highest acre yields of paddy rice among the major rice-producing countries. There is evidence that rice was cultivated in Japan as early as 300 B.C. Through the centuries there has been a gradual expansion in acreage, improvement in varieties, and modification of cultural and production practices.

The major developments, however, have occurred since about 1885, when the national average yield was approximately 1800 kilograms per hectare. Average yields had increased to approximately 4000 kilograms per hectare by 1963. Somewhat greater percentage gains have been achieved in the cool northeast portions of Honshu and in Hokkaido.

As is typically the case, this increase in yield is the result of many factors: improvement in varieties, increased use of fertilizer, modification of cultural and production practices, and better control of disease, insect pests, and weeds.

In the earlier days varietal improvement was limited to selection among the various land-race populations. Later, intensive selection for pure lines was practiced by the National and Prefectural Experiment Stations. Since about 1927 breeding efforts have been centered on crossing of selected parents, followed by the isolation and evaluation of true-breeding types from among the resulting progeny. All the varieties now in use have resulted from this breeding method. In the development of new varieties major attention has been given to short, stiff-strawed types able to make effective use of large quantities of fertilizer.

The first artificial fertilizers to be used extensively were fish-scrap and soybean cake. These were replaced by ammonium sulfate, superphosphate, and other chemical fertilizers. Attention has also been given to soil-dressing, deep plowing, and a more liberal use of iron and other minor elements. Current rates of application of nitrogen, phosphorus, and potassium are higher for Japan than for any other rice-producing country.

With the expansion and intensification of rice production, both disease and insect infestation became increasingly important. Efforts toward disease control have been continuing, use having been made of resistant varieties and of fungicides ranging from Bordeaux mixture to the new mercury and phosphorus compounds. The earlier measures for controlling stem borer and leafhoppers ranged from the burning of refuse to applications of whale oil. Extensive use is now being made of the many organic insecticides.

Wheat Production in the United States

Wheat is the world's second most important food crop. Approximately 15 percent of the total supply is produced within the United States, where five main types are grown: soft red winter, hard red winter, hard red spring, white, and durum. Each of these types has its maximum concentration in a different geographical area, each fills a special commercial need, and each presents unique problems with respect to quality evaluation, resistance to disease and to insect infestation, and hazards of production.

Wheat is not native to the United States. The varieties grown during the colonial period and the era of expansion were direct importations from abroad or selections of deviant types within the imported strains. The scientific approach to the improvement of wheat dates from about 1900. The first efforts were directed toward selection of pure lines within the better adapted strains. The possibilities of improvement under this method were soon exhausted. Increased genetic variability was obtained through hybridization, followed by intensive selection within the segregating populations. This breeding method is responsible for all of our modern varieties of wheat.

Average per-acre yields have doubled in the past 30 years. The impact on the economy has been greater than this rate of increase would suggest. Severe losses from stem rust were experienced in 6 of the 20 years between 1920 and 1940, and measurable losses occurred in many of the remaining years. Rust-resistant types in a continuous succession have been developed, and used extensively for a time, only to be replaced by newer strains in the continuing battle to cope with the ever-changing biotypes of the pathogen. In comparisons involving old and new varieties, in the absence of rust epiphytotics the newer varieties exhibit only moderate superiority, suggesting that the greater selective pressure has been for resistivity to disease.

This situation has been drastically changed in the Pacific Northwest in recent years with the development of new semi-dwarf varieties. These types have a tremendous capacity to respond to improved cultural practices, particularly to increased levels of nitrogen fertilization. Yields of 200 bushels per acre (13,450 kilograms per hectare) have been recorded. Comparative yields for the area and for the nation were 38 and 23 bushels, respectively. Northwestern Europe provides a more favorable climate for wheat, and average yields for the same period would approximate 60 bushels per acre. Unfortunately the semi-dwarf types adapted to the Pacific Northwest do not appear to have the same yield potential in other major wheat-producing areas of the United States. Work is progressing, however, on the development of semi-dwarf types adapted to other geographical areas.

Corn Production in the United States

The development and utilization of hybrid corn has had an important impact on our agricultural economy. In the early 1930's, before hybrid corn was used, the United States produced approximately 2.5 billion bushels of corn per year on roughly 100 million acres. In 1963 we produced over 4 billion bushels on 60 million acres—that is, 70 percent more corn on 40 percent fewer acres. In other words, the average per-acre yield of corn has nearly tripled in the past 30 years. In this same period the percentage of our corn acreage planted to hybrids has increased from 0.1 to more than 95 percent. The pertinent data are presented in Table 1.

I do not mean to imply that the increases in production, just detailed, have resulted solely from genetic improvements. Genetic improvements, however, have been one of the components of what may be described as an agricultural revolution. Other components include the use of increasing quantities of fertilizer; an increase in plant populations; improved means of controlling weeds, insects, and disease; and better timing of all farming operations, made possible by the availability of more efficient machinery. It would be extremely difficult to assign realistic weights to these individual components, inasmuch as their relative importance would vary for different crops.

In the case of corn, however, the development and adoption of hybrids in the major production areas preceded and made economically feasible the utilization or improvement of the other components. Only limited quantities of fertilizer were used on open-pollinated varieties because yield response from such applications was limited. The open-pollinated varieties were susceptible to root-lodging and stalk-breaking, thus mechanical harvesting was both costly and inefficient. Population densities were low, by current standards, because the varieties could not tolerate heavier planting without reductions in yield.

Many farmers felt that the public research agencies had little real knowledge of agricultural problems and were slow to accept new recommendations. This general attitude accounts for the initial reluctance to accept hybrid corn. The superiority of this product was readily apparent, however, and after the first few years the rate of utilization was limited only by the availability of seed. In the Corn Belt the transition from open-pollinated varieties to hybrids was essentially completed in a 10-year period. Hybrid corn and the many other more recent innovations have resulted in a drastic change in the farmer's viewpoint.

Farmers now recognize the value of research, do a considerable amount of experimentation on their own initiative, and tend to adopt new practices before their value has been adequately established. This historical sequence must be kept in mind in any attempt to extrapolate from our highly developed agricultural economy to the agricultural economy of the developing countries.

Most of the developing countries lie outside the latitudes of the United States. Although basic principles know no geographical boundaries, the practices flowing from such research have strong ecological limitations. In general the improved crop varieties grown in the United States are unsuited to the requirements of the developing countries. When grown in Kenya, a hybrid from the Corn Belt may be inferior to a local unimproved variety. A fertilizer regime suited to the southeastern United States may be quite inappropriate in Nigeria. Improved crop varieties and management and cultural practices suitable for the developing countries must be developed through locally conducted research.

International Rice Research Institute

The International Rice Research Institute was established at Los Banos, the Philippines, in 1961. The research program organized possibly represents the most extensive effort yet made, within a developing country, to study all factors affecting production of a single crop. The institute is jointly sponsored by the Ford and Rockefeller foundations and has a senior staff of approximately 20 scientists, representing all major areas which affect production capabilities. These areas include genetics and breeding, physiology, pathology, soil science, agricultural engineering, entomology, crop production, management and rotations, economics, and extension. It became apparent almost immediately that neither the technology nor the varieties developed in Japan or the United States were suited to tropical regions.

Marked progress has been achieved in several areas. Information has been accumulated on growth form, on efficient utilization of sunlight, on short-statured types with erect leaves, and on the minimizing of shading effects. Through the use of insecticides and insect-resistant plant varieties, damage caused by the major insect pests has been materially reduced. In some experimental plantings, control of the stem borer through the use of the insecticide gamma BHC has given yield increases of 150 percent. Extensive screening within the world rice collection, maintained at Los Banos, has revealed types resistant to some virus diseases, to leaf blight, to certain strains of rice blast, and to other important diseases. Resistance is being incorporated into high-yielding types. Striking increases in yield have been achieved through nitrogen fertilization. In some instances the return

TABLE 1: Corn Acreage, Production, Average Yields Per Acre, and Percentage of Acreage Planted to Hybrids for Selected Years During the Period 1933 to 1964. [*Agricultural Statistics* (U.S. Department of Agriculture)].

Year	Acreage harvested (1000 acres)	Total production (1000 bushels)	Average yield (bushels/ acre)	Percent of acreage planted to hybrids
1933	105,918	2,397,593	22.6	0.1
1938	92,160	2,548,753	27.7	14.9
1943	92,060	2,965,980	32.2	52.4
1948	83,778	3,605,078	42.5	76.0
1953	80,459	3,209,896	39.9	86.5
1958	63,549	3,356,205	52.8	93.9
1963	60,549	4,091,785	67.6	95.0+

on investment in fertilizer has been as high as 600 percent, as calculated on the assumption that nitrogen costs about four times as much as paddy rice.

The opportunities for growing two or more crops of rice per year depend upon the availability of water and the growth requirements of the varieties used. The early short-statured varieties are well suited for this purpose. Where water is limiting, sorghum, mung beans, and other short-season crops may follow rice. Some form of multiple cropping appears to offer great promise for increasing total production.

Perhaps the most striking of the short-term developments has been development of the variety IR-8. This short-statured type has many of the characteristics desired, and has given yields of over 10 metric tons of rough rice under conditions in which the tall *Oryza indica* types produced less than 6 tons. Yields of IR-8 have also been high in experimental tests in Pakistan, Thailand, Malaysia, and

India. In some cases yields of IR-8 have been double those of local varieties. Production of seed of IR-8 has been increased, so that additional comparative trials may be made and planting of IR-8 may be started in these countries. At the same time, work on breeding is going forward in an effort to incorporate greater resistance to disease, improved milling characteristics, and improved quality of the rice.

Rockefeller Agricultural Program in Mexico

A research program involving the Rockefeller Foundation and the Mexican Ministry of Agriculture was initiated in 1943. This was a broad-based program, designed to improve the agriculture of Mexico and to provide opportunity for the training of Mexican scientists who would eventually assume leadership of all phases of research. The operation has been so successful that it has served as a model for other assistance programs. Although work was initiated with several crops, here I consider only one phase—wheat research.

In 1943, when the program was initiated, Mexico imported half of the wheat consumed. At present, in spite of the high rate of population increase during the past 20 years, Mexico is a wheat-exporting nation. The progress achieved is shown in Table 2.

This increase in production has been achieved through a combination of research developments in several disciplines: genetics and breeding, soil fertility, irrigation management, plant pathology, entomology, and cereal technology. Stem rust *(Puccinia graminis* var. *tritici)* and stripe rust *(P. glumarum)* were the diseases of primary importance. Extensive use was made of known sources of resistance, and new sources were identified. The first of many improved varieties was released in 1947. A continuing succession of new varieties followed, each superior in productive capacity to those it replaced. The most spectacular developments have been achieved in recent years with the release and rapid adoption of several semi-dwarf varieties.

As is often the case with new varieties, the maximum utilization of genetic potential can be achieved only through a complete reevaluation of production practices. The new semi-dwarf types could make effective use of up to 140 to 160 pounds of nitrogen per acre. Similarly, under the heavy cropping practices followed, applications of 40 pounds of phosphoric acid became profitable. Four irrigations were required where two had previously been adequate. With this combination of improved varieties and modified management practices, yields of 80 to 100 bushels per acre were achieved. This is in contrast to the 7- to 10-bushel yields that were common with the varieties and cultural practices used in 1943.

In addition to the increase in total production which has been achieved in Mexico, this program has made other outstanding contributions.

The new varieties developed in this program are relatively insensitive to day length and therefore exhibit wide adaptability. One strain, designated Mexipak, is currently being grown extensively in Pakistan.

When stem rust is a serious problem, new resistant varieties resist rust for approximately 5 years, after which time a new race of rust, to which the variety is susceptible, becomes predominant. The concept of controlled backcross derivatives (multilineal varieties) was developed, in which each component of the mixture would possess resistance to a different race or constellation of races of rust. Practical results with the method have been satisfactory. Recently, the concept has been extended to include hybrid seed production, when this becomes feasible in wheat.

Techniques for early-generation testing of gluten quality, which should simplify the evaluation of quality, have been developed.

TABLE 2: The Impact of Research on Wheat Production in Mexico.
[N.E. Borlaug, *Phytopathol. 55,* 1088 (1965)].

Year	Cultivated area (1000 hectares)	Yield (kg/ hectare)	Production (1000 metric tons)
1945	500	750	330
1950	625	900	600
1955	790	1,100	850
1960	840	1,417	1,200
1964	846	2,600	2,200

Important as these developments have been, they are probably overshadowed by the extensive training aspects which have been an integral part of the program. In the 20 years from 1943 to 1963, more than 700 young men and women, representing many different countries, received inservice training. Many of these received advanced degrees and are now contributing to agricultural progress in their respective countries.

Maize Improvement in Kenya

The maize-improvement program of Kenya (*maize* is the common term for corn outside the United States) provides a striking illustration of the genetic improvement that is possible when other technological requirements are met. Support for this program is provided by the Kenya Government, the Kenya Maize and Produce Marketing Board, the Ministry of Overseas Development (Great Britain), the Rockefeller Foundation, and the United States AID-ARS Major Cereals in Africa Project. The research staff includes both geneticists and agronomists. Excellent and widespread extension support has been provided by the Kenya Ministry of Agriculture.

This maize-breeding program was initiated in 1958 as a conventional inbreeding-hybridization program based on use of the local variety, Kenya Flat White. By 1963 a double-cross hybrid which gave yield increases of 25 percent had been developed; the percentage increase was roughly equivalent to that achieved in the United States with the first hybrids produced commercially.

TABLE 3: Acreages of Hybrid Maize Grown in Kenya.
["Major Cereals in Africa" Project, Third Annual Report].

Year	Large-scale farms (acres)	Small-scale farms (acres)
1963	300	10
1964	27,000	3,000
1965	52,000	18,000
1966	50,000	50,000
1967*	100,000	350,000

*This projection is based on seed produced and seed orders currently in hand.

During the early stages of this program it became apparent that lack of genetic diversity was limiting progress. Extensive introductions were made from the United States, from Central America, and from northern South America. The great bulk of this introduced material was unadapted and was discarded. A few of the high-altitude types from Central and South America appeared worthy of further evaluation. This exotic material was crossed with the local variety, and the resulting hybrids were evaluated in yield trials. One of these, Kenya Flat White X Ecuador 573, gave yields equal or superior to those of the double-cross hybrid, depending upon altitude and fertility level. As the varietal hybrid possessed the greater potential for yield enhancement, breeding efforts were increasingly directed toward improvement of the two base populations.

Agronomic research had established optimum planting densities and planting dates, as well as efficient fertilization practices. The Ministry of Agriculture established an effective demonstration program, showing the advantages of hybrids over the local variety of maize and the relative importance of the major management practices. The Kenya Seed Company, which had specialized in grass-seed production, was induced to undertake large-scale production and distribution of hybrid maize.

Hybrid seed was first offered under a package plan. Each purchaser of seed was obliged to buy fertilizer of the recommended formulation and amount, and each agreed to follow certain minimum cultural recommendations. The utilization of hybrid seed which has been attained is shown in Table 3.

Each year the acreage of hybrid grown has been limited by shortage of seed rather than by lack of demand. After an initial lag, acceptance by the small-scale native farmer has been as great as acceptance by the large-scale farmer. Because of the procedures followed, the farmers consider hybrid maize to be a new crop, and the saving of seed from the hybrid planting, F_2 seed, has not been a problem.

This program involving use of hybrid seed, proper fertilization, and improved cultural practices has already had an important impact on total production. Further increases appear to be quite feasible. The genetic variance of the two parental varieties has been found to be primarily additive. Simple selection schemes have resulted in yield increases of 10 percent in the parental populations, and this improvement is retained in their F_1 hybrids.

Breeding programs such as the one in Kenya are admirably designed to fulfill both short- and long-range needs. Short-term needs are met by the rapid development and utilization of improved hybrids. Substantial improvement of the parental types is possible through simple selection schemes which pose minimum demands for trained manpower, financial support, or operational facilities. The improvement achieved in the base parental populations increases their potential value as sources of inbred lines, should a conventional inbreeding-hybridization program later become desirable.

Similar programs are feasible in many of the developing countries. Varietal hybrids, superior to the best available double crosses, have been identified in Mexico, India, and Thailand, but, outside of Kenya, little commercial use is being made of such material. This appears to be largely a problem of seed-production capabilities and of status. Because single and double crosses constitute the hybrids of commerce within the United States and other developed countries, the developing countries feel that commercial utilization of heterosis should be deferred until they can market hybrids of similar types. Thus substantial, immediate, and potential progress is being sacrificed to prestige.

These examples of success need not be unique. The improved varieties of rice, wheat, and maize, developed in the programs cited, are being extensively used outside the area of their development. Similar programs could develop new types of these or other crops to satisfy different ecological requirements. A total increase in food production of 50 percent in the developing countries appears to be a completely realistic goal. An increase in wheat yields of this magnitude in India would represent over 6.5 million metric tons.

Requirements for an Effective Assistance Program

A consideration of programs exhibiting varying degrees of success suggests that significant progress requires the fulfillment of certain minimum conditions. (i) A realistic system of research priorities must be developed. Under food-deficit conditions emphasis should be given to one or two of the major food crops of the area. (ii) The program must include research scientists representing several disciplines (genetics, agronomy, plant pathology, entomology, and so on) if the program is to achieve continuing success. The concept of "critical mass" in nuclear physics provides a useful analogy. A vigorous extension program must complement research activities. (iii) The scientific staff must actively participate in the research. Consultative and advisory functions have their place, but an adequate program cannot be developed on the basis of these alone. (iv) Adequate financial support must be provided, and operations in a foreign country are always expensive. (v) Provision must be made for the training of nationals. Such persons must be assigned responsibility as rapidly as their training and aptitude will permit. (vi) Governmental policies must be favorable to agricultural development. Provision must be made for satisfying a wide variety of needs—adequate supplies of fertilizers and other agricultural chemicals, a realistic pricing policy for agricultural produce to make the adoption of improved techniques attractive to farmers, and policies which will permit the development of an effective seed production and distribution industry responsive to local needs, to name only a few.

The importance of the first five requirements is generally recognized. The necessity for the sixth is often overlooked. The achievement of increased agricultural productivity in the developing countries requires more than the improvement of crop plants and associated management practices. Favorable economic, political, and social conditions and policies also are essential.

The food shortage in India has been much in the news and may thus serve as a useful illustration. It should be stressed that the situation in India is not unique. Detailed consideration of governmental policies and priorities lies outside the scope of this article and of my capabilities. It is readily apparent, however, that, had agriculture received a higher priority, the current situation would be much less critical than it is.

India uses about 4 pounds of fertilizer per acre (4 1/2 kilograms per hectare). Local varieties of wheat, rice, and corn have a limited capacity to respond to high levels of fertiliztion. The new varieties of wheat introduced from Mexico, however, are much more responsive to application of fertilizer. Yield increases of at least 50 percent are possible, under adequate management. If all the fertilizer currently available in India were used on such varieties, only a fraction of the wheat acreage could be fertilized at the optimum rate. Similar situations prevail for the new varieties of rice and for corn hybrids. Thus, potential gain in food production has not been realized because of inadequate supplies and the high cost of fertilizers.

India produces some nitrogenous fertilizer and imports more. Importation costs represent a serious drain on the supply of hard currency. Nitrogenous fertilizers could be produced locally from either naphtha or natural gas. The need for a major expansion of this industry has been recognized in the successive 5-year plans, but the goals established fall short of the need, and no decision has yet been reached on the production process to be used.

An effective seed industry is essential to agricultural progress. Historically, government-controlled operations have been unsatisfactory. The quality of seed produced is often inferior, distribution is inadequate, and seed-production goals are relatively insensitive to local needs.

Other instances could be cited, in India and other developing countries, of the effects of low priorities for agricultural development on food-production capabilities.

Conclusion

The following general conclusions appear valid. The developed countries cannot feed the world. On a short-term basis, food must be supplied to developing countries as needs exist. A long-continuing policy of supplying food grains, through donation or by sale, may be self-defeating if this practice tends to limit expansion of local food-production capabilities.

Tremendous possibilities exist for an expansion of food production within the developing countries. The extent to which this potential is realized will depend upon the scope of assistance programs undertaken, and upon the priorities assigned to agriculture by the developing nations. Even though capabilities are fully utilized, the result may still be inadequate if population growth remains unchecked.

Can We Prepare for Famine?

A Social Scientist's View

E. JAMES ARCHER

1. The Death Rate

Most people think that the population explosion is due to an *increased* birth rate, i.e., number of births per 1000 people. This is a gross oversimplification. As Robert Cook, the president of the Population Reference Bureau said, "We've been trying for years to get people interested in death rates, to get people to understand that the 'explosion' is due primarily to falling death rates and not to changing birth rates."

The relationship is quite simple: *Only* live people have babies and live people *do* have babies. The more people you save from death due to typhoid, cholera, diphtheria, smallpox, malaria, and bubonic plague, the more people will be around to have babies.

In many underdeveloped countries the death rate has been cut in half since World War II. The relationship between death rate and population explosion is nicely illustrated by the following observation, "If by 1975 the death rate in Guatemala fell somewhere near the 1950 United States level (9.6)—a not unlikely development—this alone would increase the number of women reaching the beginning of the child-bearing period by 36 percent and the number at the end of the child-bearing period by 85 percent."

2. The Younger Generation

Nearly one-half of all the people in the underdeveloped countries are under the age of 15. Young people marry and married people have babies. One statistical prediction presents the case: by 1975 there will be 60% more marriages formed in Latin America than in 1960. Sixty per cent more marriages formed in 1975 will mean 60% more babies in 1976. Again, it is not the birth rate, i.e., births per 1000 population, which accounts for the explosion, rather there are just more people in the child-bearing ages.

3. The Birth Rate

For many years it was thought that a birth rate of 45 per thousand was the physiological maximum. This figure was based on the observation that of 1000 people 500 will be women. Of that number, 410 were either too old or too young or sterile. Of the remaining 90, we could find another 45 who were pregnant or who just had a child and had not had time to conceive and deliver another child. However, with a shift to a lower average age (Population Dynamic Number Two) we find a few instances of birth rates exceeding the "classical limit" of 45/1000. For example, in 1963, Costa Rica had a birth rate of 50.2/1000.

We also see an interaction of some of these Population Dynamics in that those techniques which lower the death rate generally also improve the health of the individual and people who are both young *and* healthy, are more fertile, have more frequent intercourse, and if a child is conceived, it is more likely to come to full term, i.e., there will be fewer miscarriages and still births.

4. Man's Reproductive System

"Man has been evolving and reproducing for a million years. Those who expect science to be able to find quickly a birth control method which can successfully circumvent this million years of such single-mindedness both overestimate modern science and underestimate the efficiency of the reproductive system which evolution has provided man."

Now the optimists will react with a list of things that will assure themselves that all is well. For example, they might cite the control of population in Japan, but that is a very special case and not applicable to other areas. Specifically, Japan has a literacy rate which is so high that they don't even bother with this measure in their census taking today. In 1948 Japan showed an illiteracy level of 1.1%. In contrast, Africa's is 84% and Latin America's is about 40%. Japan also had legalized abortions in 1948. The impact of this decision is best seen in the following statistics: In 1955 there were 1.2 million abortions performed. Even assuming the higher proportion of males at birth, because these 1.2 million conceptions did not come to full term, Japan will have approximately 0.5 million *fewer* women entering the child-bearing age next year than would have occurred in the absence of the abortions which took place in 1955.

Japan has a large medical profession as compared to the underdeveloped nations. If we look at the number of inhabitants per physician ratio, we see Japan's is 900:1, but Mexico's is twice that ratio. Pakistan has a ratio of 11,000:1 and Ethiopia has 96,000:1. If you think the intrauterine device (the IUD) is the answer, you have another problem. Who will insert it?

The IUD is another false hope of avoiding widespread famine due to the exploding population. Consider these data. The designer of the most widely used IUD claims it can be inserted in 6 minutes. One well trained team even managed to insert 75 IUD's in a 3-hour session—that is one IUD insertion every 2 minutes and 24 seconds. While this sounds good, it must be recognized that 850,000 women entered the child-bearing age in India alone last year and the number will increase in succeeding years. You cannot insert IUD's fast enough.

The hope of the Pill is equally discouraging. Its use requires daily attention plus motivation. Remember also when a woman goes off the Pill, or forgets to take it regularly, her fertility is actually increased. Furthermore, because of the undesirable side-effects, the Pill is not recommended for all women. Until a "morning after" or monthly pill is developed, the Pill as it is now known is only promising and not an answer.

Let me mention a few other hopes which the optimists cite but which also appear to be *false* hopes. We have frequently heard, and the PSAC report emphasizes this point, that what we need to do is to improve the agricultural production of the developing countries. One way to do this is to send them seeds, stock, and fertilizers; then they can raise more food to feed their exploding population and all will be well.

First, many strains of wheat and corn which do very well in the United States either perform poorly or even fail to come to seed in other climates and on other soils. You cannot export seed; you have to develop the appropriate strains and agricultural technology in the field where the grain is to grow. For example, it is estimated that corn production in Mexico has been increased about 200% by the work of the Rockefeller Foundation program. This sounds great and may seem to be the obvious solution, i.e., we export the know-how and all will be saved. There are a few hitches, however. First, half of the increased yield was due to double cropping (but getting in two growing seasons is not always possible). Second, the research program did *not* find just *the* right strain of corn to grow in Mexico. The soils, micro-climates, macro-climates, and irrigation conditions are so different in different areas that about a dozen different strains are needed —each appropriate to its growing conditions. Third, the program took 25 years. We just do not have 25 years.

Look at it this way—in the best of our agricultural research and training institutions, how long does it take you to train one plant pathologist? One geneticist? And remember, he comes from and lives in an environment that financially supports him, offers rewards for successful work, and has a supporting intellectual climate of chemists, biochemists, cell biologists, plant physiologists, biophysicists, and agricultural engineers. Finally, he has the elaborate infra-structure of an agricultural extension system to communicate his work to the point of meaningful effect—the farmer. Even if we had all of the personnel, equipment, and financial resources available, we do not have the time—no matter how many chickens sit on an egg, it still takes 21 days to hatch it. The same principle applies to successive plant breeding tests.

Some of the optimists will feel safe because man will solve his food problems by "harvesting" the sea. Paddock and Paddock point out the special relish with which the word "harvest" is used. Hoping to harvest the sea in time to avoid major famines is truly a false hope. How little we know of the sea is shown in another PSAC publication entitled "The Effective Use of the Sea," which appeared in 1966. We are a long way from ever understanding the processes of turbulence which contribute to the essential stirring of the sea. The sometimes cyclic churning action brings necessary organic material to intermediate depths to provide food for plankton, which becomes food for shrimp, which becomes food for man. We do not even have a satisfactory buoy network technology to enable us to study the microclimate of the seas. If you do not understand the climate on land, you will be a poor farmer and if you don't understand the "climate" in the ocean, you will be at least as poor a harvester of the sea. How long will it take to train an oceanographer? The climate for such personnel development is nowhere comparable to that which exists for training a plant pathologist.

Even if I have not persuaded the optimists that there is cause for concern about the population explosion, I hope I have brought the matter to their attention.

82   Paying The Piper

PAUL R. EHRLICH

The battle to feed humanity is over. Unlike battles of military forces, it is possible to know the results of the population-food conflict while the armies are still "in the field." Sometime between 1970 and 1985 the world will undergo vast famines—hundreds of millions of people are going to starve to death. That is, they will starve to death unless plague, thermo-nuclear war, or some other agent kills them first. And we are not embarking upon any crash programme. These are the harsh realities we face . . .

The trends in both population growth and food production are clear. Only the U.S. will be in a position to donate food to starving countries, and a catastrophic gap will appear soon between her supply and demand. The United States Department of Agriculture has predicted that the curve representing possible exportable U.S. grain surpluses will intersect the curve representing the food aid requirements of 66 developing countries in 1984. In an excellent book *Famine 1975* (Little, Brown; Boston, 1967), William and Paul Paddock argue cogently that the 1984 prediction is optimistic, and that calamity awaits us in the middle of the next decade. In either case it is too late to prevent the famines, and probably too late to do much to decrease their magnitude. . . .

For a moment, let us take the simplistic view that a solution involves only either increasing human food or limiting the human population. First let us look at the problem of increasing food supplies, either from the land or the sea. We rapidly can do away with what I have called the "Food from the sea myth." With very minor exceptions, man hunts the sea, he does not farm it or herd its animals. At the moment he cannot take advantage of its primary productivity, and so must feed at levels in the food chain at which much of the sun's energy bound by photosynthesis has been lost in the inefficient transfers from producer to primary consumer to secondary consumer, and so forth. There already are disturbing signs that our relatively meagre present yield from the sea will be threatened by over-exploitation of fisheries, as the world's protein shortage gets more acute. And what of farming the sea? The insignificant bit that we do now (much less than one-tenth of one percent of the yield) is done along the shoreline and is best viewed as an extension of terrestrial farming. No deep-sea farming is done now, even experimentally—and we lack the technical knowledge even if we wished to start. Some very optimistic people think that with colossal effort and strict international controls, we might conceivably almost double our yield from the sea in the next decade or so. But it should be obvious to all that such effort is not being made, and that such controls are not being developed. And our experience with attempting such controls in the international whaling industry gives us little hope that they would be effective if they were imposed. So from the point of view of the coming crisis, we can relegate the idea of saving mankind by tapping marine food supplies to the same fairyland as using hydroponics, synthesizing food from petroleum, and using desalination plants to make the deserts into vast granaries.

None are practical in the short run—indeed, most would present serious difficulties even if we had a century instead of a decade in which to act. . . .

The United States, as the only world power with a prospect of food surpluses, should take immediate action in two areas. First, it must set an example for the world by establishing a crash programme to limit its own serious "population explosion." Then it must establish tough and realistic policies for dealing with the population crisis at the international level. We can hope that other Western countries will follow suit.

Some biologists feel that compulsory family regulation would be required to stabilize the population of the United States at a reasonable level—say 150 million people. Americans are unlikely to take kindly to the prospect, even though the alternative way of stopping their population growth may be thermonuclear war. I have proposed four less drastic steps which might get the job done, and which would at least make American intentions clear to the rest of the world. The steps are socially unpalatable and politically unrealistic, but, unfortunately, the time when sugar-coated solutions could be effective is now long gone.

The first step would be to establish a Federal Population Commission with a large budget for propaganda—propaganda which encourages reproductive responsibility. This Commission would be charged with making clear the connection between rising population and lowering quality of life. It would also be charged with the evaluation of environmental tinkering by other government agencies—with protecting the U.S. from projects such as the Federal Aviation Agency's supersonic transports.

The second step would be to change American tax laws so that they discourage rather than encourage reproduction. Those who impose the burden of children on society should, whenever they are able, be made to pay for the privilege. The income tax system should eliminate all deductions for children, and replace them with a graduated scale of increases. Luxury taxes should be placed on diapers, baby bottles and baby foods. It must be made clear to the American population that it is socially irresponsible to have large families. Creation of such a climate of opinion has played a large role in Japan's successful dealing with her population problem.

Third, the United States should pass federal laws which make instruction in birth control methods mandatory in all public schools. Federal legislation should also forbid state laws which limit the right of any woman to have an abortion which is approved by her physician.

Fourth, the pattern of federal support of biomedical research should be changed so that the majority of it goes into the broad areas of population regulation, environmental sciences, behavioral sciences and related areas, rather than into shortsighted programmes on death control. It is absurd to be preoccupied with the medical quality of life until and unless the problem of quantity of life is solved. Quantity is the first problem. If that one can be solved perhaps we will buy the time for scientists in fields such as biochemical genetics to solve some of the problems of quality. If the quantity problem is not solved, the quality problem will no longer bother us.

If the United States can attack the problem at home it will then be in a position to bring its prestige and power to bear on the world problem. Perhaps then the time of famines can be shortened. Even more important, perhaps the educational groundwork can be laid which will permit further cycles of outbreak and crash in the human population to be avoided. The United States should:

1. Announce that it will no longer ship food to countries such as India where dispassionate analysis indicates that the unbalance between food and population is hopeless. As suggested by the Paddocks, our insufficient aid should be reserved for those whom it may save.

2. Refuse all foreign aid to any country with an increasing population which we believe is not making a maximum effort to limit its population.

3. Make available to all countries extensive aid in the technology of population control.

4. Make available to all interested countries massive aid for increasing the yield on land already under cultivation. The United States' most important export in this area should not be fertilizers, but teachers who understand not only agronomy, but ecology and sociology as well. Centers should be established in each developing country for the training of technicians who can promote the increase of yield while minimizing environmental deterioration.

5. The United States should use its power and prestige to bring extreme diplomatic and/or economic pressure on any country or organization impeding a solution to the world's most pressing problem. The U.S. has gone against world opinion in other areas—why not in the most important area?

Some Effects of Starvation

83   ## Starvation Patterns

JEAN MAYER

As a nutritionist who has seen famines on three continents, one of them Asia, and as a historian of public health with an interest in famines, I can say flatly that there has never been a famine or a food shortage—whether created by lack of water (droughts, often followed by dust storms and loss of seeds, being the most frequent), by plant disease (such as fungous blights), by large-scale natural disturbances affecting both crops and farmers (such as floods and earthquakes), by disruption of farming operations due to wars and civil disorders, or by blockade or other war measures directly aimed at the food supply—which has not first and overwhelmingly affected the small children.

It is very clear that death from starvation occurs first of all in young children and in the elderly, with adults and adolescents surviving better (pregnant women often abort; lactating mothers cease to have ⁿilk and the babies die). Children under five, who in many parts of the world are often on the verge of kwashiorkor (a protein-deficiency syndrome which often hits children after weaning and until they are old enough to eat "adult" food) and of marasmus (a combination of deficiency of calories and of protein), are the most vulnerable. In addition, a general consequence of famine is a state of social disruption (including panic). People who are starving at home tend to leave, if they can, and march toward the area where it is rumored that food is available. This increases the prevailing chaos. Families are separated and children are lost—and in all likelihood die. Adolescents are particularly threatened by tuberculosis; however, finding themselves on their own, they often band together in foraging gangs, which avoid starvation but create additional disruption. The prolonged and successful practice of banditry makes it difficult to rehabilitate members of these gangs.

Malnutrition, Learning, and Behavior 84

PHILIP H. ABELSON

Children reared in poverty tend to do poorly on tests of intelligence. In part this is due to psychological and cultural factors. To an important extent it is a result of malnutrition early in childhood.

It seems likely that millions of young children in developing countries are experiencing some degree of retardation in learning because of inadequate nutrition, and that this phenomenon may also occur in the United States.

Because of complex social and psychological factors associated with malnutrition, it is not easy to assess the effects of dietary deficiencies in man. However, observations in underdeveloped countries, coupled with studies on animals, provide substantial evidence. In rats and pigs the brain reaches 80 percent of adult size by normal weaning time. At that stage, body weight is 20 percent of that at maturity. During the period of rapid growth the brain is vulnerable to nutritional damage. A relatively short period of undernutrition results in smaller brain size at maturity even if the animals are maintained on a good diet after weaning. Changes in brain size are accompanied by persistent anatomical and biochemical changes.

In humans, the brain of the infant attains 80 percent of adult weight by age 3, when the body weight is about 20 percent of that at maturity. Thus the animal experiments suggest that good nutrition during the first 3 years of life is particularly important.

When the Famines Come

85   What Will We Do?

JAMES BONNER

I stress again that all responsible investigators agree that the tragedy will occur. They differ only as to whether it will take place in ten years or less, or in ten years or a little more. The underdeveloped world is on a collision course with starvation. No technology short of nuclear warfare can be spread with sufficient speed to avert the catastrophe. The only remaining question for the United States and for the nations of the developed world is how to deal with the starving nations, when starvation comes.

86   What Have We Done?

UNITED STATES SENATE CONCURRENT RESOLUTION

Whereas reliable reports indicate that there is a tragic loss of life in the Nigerian civil war, caused by starvation and disease in areas controlled by the Federal Government and under the control of the Biafran authorities; and

Whereas present relief operations are inhibited by poor roads, bad weather, inadequate transport, and the inaccessibility of certain areas to overland supplies; and

Whereas increased shipments of food and medical supplies are needed to reduce the tragic rate of starvation: Now, therefore, be it

Resolved by the Senate (the House of Representatives concurring), That (1) it is the sense of the Congress that the President should act to increase significantly the amount of surplus food stocks, relief moneys, noncombat aircraft, and such other vehicles of transportation as may be necessary for relief purposes; and this relief assistance should be made available to and at the request of the Organization of African Unity, UNICEF, the International Committee of the Red Cross, and such other suitable religious and charitable relief agencies now or hereafter operating in the area with the consent of the responsible authorities; and (2) the Government of the United States should solicit the cooperation of other nations in this humanitarian effort.

Hopes for Delaying the Food Crisis

Viewing proliferating human numbers without alarm, optimists have pointed to a Christmas sack of hopes for averting the food crisis. Some have suggested, for instance, that water for irrigation projects might come from desalinization from dams, and from the importation of water for hundreds and thousands of miles.

While governments urge the development of tropical areas, biologists are not so enthusiastic. The tropics are vast and untapped, to be sure; but careful study reveals that we should not count on large regions of the tropics for substantial food production. Hope in the potential of our oceans remains high, all the while they are being polluted and over-hunted.

Other positive thinkers, unruffled by dwindling reserves of fossil fuel, suggest that there are vast amounts of potential energy yet untapped. Finally, some see a ready solution if we simply change the religious customs and taboos of "backward people."

Some of these alternatives may help delay the inevitable crisis. Others will not.

Irrigation Projects

Desalinization

Dry Lands and Desalted Water

87

GALE YOUNG

> Men spread now, with the whole power of the race to aid them, into every
> available region of the earth. Their cities are no longer tethered to running water
> and the proximity of cultivation . . . they lie out in the former deserts, those
> long-wasted sun baths of the race, they tower amidst eternal snows. . . . One may
> live anywhere.
> —H.G. Wells, *The World Set Free*
> —*A Story of Mankind*(1).

Mounting population and pollution exert pressure on man to enlarge his
living space. At present, the most rapidly growing part of the United States is the
desert of the Southwest, into which the Colorado and Rio Grande rivers have
been largely diverted. Water from the Feather River will shortly be added,
crossing over a mountain range 2000 feet (600 meters) high, by way of conveyance
facilities now under construction.

The building of the Colorado Aqueduct of the Metropolitan Water District
of Southern California was undertaken 40 years ago. Since then, the assessed
valuation of the region served by this water supply has increased by $20 billion,
or by $5 for each 1000 gallons of water that has flowed through the pipes.

These remarks are not intended to impute some exaggerated value to water,
but are made, rather, to point out that people seem to like desert climates (better
than, say, rain forests or frozen tundras) and that they will move into them and
build vigorous societies. Since the water is essential to the welfare of all, whether
they be large direct users or not, the cost of the water in arid areas is often carried
in part as overhead. For example, the Metropolitan Water District derives funds
to meet about half of its costs from water revenues and levies taxes for the balance.

Water-supply projects tend to proceed by large steps. When they are first completed there is an excess of water, and this can be used for agriculture while population and land values build up (2). Later on, the suburban farmland and its water allotments are absorbed in urban growth. This process in now under way around the large cities in our dry Southwest.

A third of the world's land is dry and virtually unoccupied, while half of the world's people are jammed—impoverished and undernourished—into a tenth of the land area. A major part of the coming increase in population will occur in the less-developed countries and, as *Nature* expressed it (3), "this huge army of uneducated, untrained, underfed, underprivileged recruits to humanity is being bred at the very moment when science and technology are rapidly undermining the need for and the status of the unskilled. . . . What stands out most emphatically is in fact the insufficiency of economic factors or motives if the challenge is to be met."

The past decade has seen a quickening of interest in the large-scale desalting of seawater as another means of opening up dry areas of the earth for human occupancy. Thus, Jacob Bronowski writes (4), "let me ask first what is going to be the single greatest technological change in the physical sciences over the next twenty or thirty years. My guess is that desalting of seawater is going to be the most important advance for overall world development. Without this the whole complex program of bringing under-developed countries to an acceptable level of economics, education and political maturity is insoluble." And Charles Lowe writes (5), "The desert is man's future land bank. Fortunately, it is a large one, offering eight million square miles of space for human occupation. It is also fortunate that it is a wondrously rich bank, which may turn green when man someday taps distilled seawater for irrigation. Bridging the gap from sea to desert will be greatly facilitated by the geographical nearness of most of the world's deserts to the oceans. When this occurs it will surely be one of the greatest transformations made by man in his persistent and successful role in changing the face of the planet." As an example, imagine what changes would follow if Baja California were to be opened up for settlement with the help of desalting and power stations. What might another thousand miles of southern California be worth in a few generations?

This process has already begun to take place on a small scale in certain locations. Thus, Kuwait on the Persian Gulf and Shevchenko on the barren eastern shore of the Caspian Sea, where the Russians are building the world's largest desalting unit, are two oil field communities which depend upon desalination for their water supply. As in other locations where desalination would be employed, no cheaper sources of fresh water are available.

In general, desalination will be able to meet the freshwater needs of municipalities and industries located along the ocean shore, or in some interior regions having salty lakes or groundwater. And anywhere that cities go, some agriculture, for fresh fruits and vegetables at least, tends to follow. For example, Kuwait, in one of the most devilishly hot and sandridden environments on earth, has recently ordered acres of enclosed greenhouses at a cost of many thousands of dollars per acre to supply garden produce which will be fresher and reportedly cheaper than imported produce. But it is less clear whether agriculture that depends on desalted water ("desalination agriculture") may someday expand to include substantial production of staple foods as well. Here opinions differ, and, as the saying goes, the less light sometimes generates the more heat.

Water Requirements for Crops

In enclosed agriculture, such as Kuwait will have, so little fresh water escapes that its cost is not important. The situation is quite different in open-field agriculture, since the amount of water lost to the atmosphere in evapotranspiration is generally (6) many times that actually involved in the plant's growth reactions, and the cost of supplying this total by desalination is of prime importance.

Some authors have stated that the cost of desalted water will be for many years "at least one whole order of magnitude greater than the value of the water to agriculture" (7). Other writers have been more optimistic. Thus, the value of distilled water for agriculture in Israel has been estimated by MacAvoy and Peterson (8) to be about 27 cents per 1000 gallons. A generalized study (9, p. 28) indicates that "arid tropical and semitropical regions with year-round growing climates appear potentially capable of growing food at costs in or near the world market import price range, using desalted water at prices like 20 cents per thousand gallons." Estimates have been made of the total (direct plus indirect) benefits of irrigation water in several U.S. locations. There is considerable variation, estimates of losses due to taking water away from crops being 25 to 36 cents per 1000 gallons for the Texas High Plains and 32 to 44 cents for the Imperial Valley (10).

As noted above, the growing of some high-value crops tends to follow the occupation of a dry area, and an economic enterprise would, of course, first seek to saturate the market for this produce. But one is not going to feed the teeming millions on orchids or avocados, so the inquiry turns inevitably to the bulk staple foods. Of the staples, the grains are the most important, and, of the grains, rice is the staple and preferred food of half the human race. Rice, because of this demand, has a value double that of wheat on the world market—but it is not usually talked about in connection with desalination agriculture. Let us, therefore, talk about it.

Rice is indigenous to southern and eastern Asia, where much of the world's starvation occurs. In the monsoon countries, where fields are flooded periodically, the rice plant has the great virtue of being able to conduct oxygen to its roots through a hollow stem, and to flourish where other crops suffocate. Cultivation under such conditions leads to heavy use of water. In Table 1, from a talk by the dean of agriculture of the University of Sydney (11), it may be seen that in Australia, the most favorable of the instances shown, a price for water of 20 cents per 1000 gallons would add 10.6 cents per pound to the cost of rice. This is more than the rice is worth and provides little basis for enthusiasm about desalination.

Table 2 gives data on yield and water use for several other crops which are widely used. The "Rice" row of Table 2 is left blank for the present. The water-use rates were estimated (and checked against measured rates for farms when these were available) for a coastal site in the southeastern Mediterranean area, an irrigation efficiency (the fraction of the applied water which is lost to the atmosphere in evapotranspiration) of 80 percent being assumed. The other 20 percent of the water is that part which evaporates before reaching the crop, or which is carried away by deep percolation below the root zone. With efficient sprinkler or soaker irrigation systems this efficiency can usually be bettered, even without allowing for partial recovery of the deep drainage water. The yields assumed are those obtained regularly today by efficient farmers in production areas specializing in the crops in question. Record yields are considerably higher—more than double in the case of wheat, potato, tomato, and maize and in the case of an assumed yield for rice, discussed below.

Table 1 shows that rice growers typically use several times as much water per pound of grain as is needed for the other grains of Table 2. While some people may have doubted that rice requires this much water, this is the way the picture has stood historically. Just recently, however, results have appeared which do not support the classical view of rice as a water hog. In an experiment with IR 8 rice at India's Central Rice Institute, in Cuttack, a good crop 6350 pounds, 2900 kilograms, per acre as paddy rice was obtained with consumption of only 16.7 inches (42 centimeters) of water, irrigation being applied only when the soil was completely crusted. This work was reviewed and reported by J. S. Kanwar, deputy director general of the Indian Council of Agricultural Research (12). Kanwar states, "The common notion that continuous submergence is essential for paddy is belied." In a corresponding experiment based on the classical practice of continuous submergence, six times as much water (100 inches) was used and the yield was 6 percent higher. Obviously, most of the 100 inches of water was forced into the subsoil by the head of standing water.

If confirmed in subsequent tests and field experience, this finding may turn out to be one of the landmarks in the war against hunger. We add that rice can be grown the year round in warm climates; for example, in the Philippines three crops per year have been grown, yielding a total of 1,800 pounds of rice per acre.

If the results of the Indian experiment are taken at face value, the missing numbers for rice, which can now be added to Table 2, are as follows: yield, 4.2 (10^3 pounds per acre); food value, 16.5 (10^2 Calories per pound); water use—16.7 inches, 108 gallons per pound, 65 gallons per 10^3 Calories. This puts rice right in among the other grains as a user of water. It may be seen that to supply a person a minimum adequate allowance of 2500 Calories per day (13) in this highly intensive and scientifically managed type of agriculture would require an average of 160 gallons of water per day in the case of grain, or half this in the case of potatoes.

Production Cost Estimates for Grain

For any selected price of water, Table 2 enables one to compute the cost of water per pound of product, as illustrated for rice in Table 1. However, water is only one component of the total cost. We have, therefore, made some illustrative estimates of the total production costs for grain for a large, intensively operated farm. These costs are not expected to vary greatly with farm size. The estimates

TABLE 1: Amount of Water Used in Growing Rice in Various Countries.

Location	Pounds of water per pound of paddy rice	Gallons of water used per pound of milled rice
Thailand	10,000	1,800
India	10,000	1,800
Japan	4,900	900
California	3,300	610
Australia	2,900	530

TABLE 2: Relation of Yield to Water Use for Various Crops.

Crop	Yield (10^3 lb/acre)	Food Value (10^2 Cal/lb)	Inches	Gal/lb	Gal/10^3 Cal
		Grain			
Wheat	6.0	14.8	20.0	91	61
Sorghum	8.0	15.1	27.6	94	62
Maize	9.0	15.8	27.6	83	53
Rice					
		Vegetable			
Potato	48	2.79	16.0	9.0	32
Tomato	60	0.95	19.0	8.6	91
		Citrus			
Orange	44	1.31	53.1	33	250

TABLE 3: Estimated Capital Investment.

Item	Dollars per acre
Irrigation and storage-well system	375
Land, land development, and roads	85
Drainage system	110
Water for initial leaching	130
Grain storage	85
Machinery	115
Farm buildings	25
Interest during construction	25
Total	950

TABLE 4: Estimated Overhead Costs.

Item	Dollars per acre per year
Maintenance	14
Pumping power	1
Water losses in storage and canal leakage	12
Experimental station	1
Management and miscellaneous	7
Total	35

TABLE 5: Estimated Direct Costs for Grain Production.*

Item	Dollars per acre per crop
Fertilizer	11
Pumping power	6
Seed	5
Labor	2
Machine operation	2
Storage and marketing	3
Other chemicals	3
Miscellaneous	8
Total	40

289

were made for a farm of 300,000 acres (120,000 hectares) which uses about a billion gallons of water per day.

These estimates are summarized in Tables 3 to 5. Table 3 shows the capital investment per acre, while Table 4 gives annual out-of-pocket costs for items which cannot be allocated directly to specific crops in the year-round rotation. The costs which can be specifically assigned are shown in Table 5.

It should be noted that the water is priced at the farm inlet and that it is supplied to the farm at a rate that is constant throughout the year, except for the time when the desalting plant is shut down for maintenance or other reasons. Thus, because of seasonal variations in the requirement for irrigation water, it is necessary to resort to such measures as (i) making seasonal adjustments in the size of the irrigated area and (ii) storing water in underground aquifers at certain times of the year and pumping it back up at other times (10 percent of the stored water is assumed to be lost in this process). Allowance for such storage has been made in Tables 3 and 4 (14).

An interest rate of 10 percent on the investment shown in Table 3 amounts to $95 per acre per year, and allowance for depreciation and for working-capital needs adds about $10 more. With the overhead costs shown in Table 4, the total fixed charges are thus $140 per acre per year. In regions where a second major crop, of the same or some other product, can be grown in the same year on the same land and share fixed costs with the grain, the cost of an acre crop of grain would be ($140/2) + $40 + cost of water = $110 + cost of water. In some areas, such as parts of India, where it might be possible to grow three crops per year the corresponding cost would be $87 + cost of water.

The resulting costs for milled rice and for wheat are plotted in Fig. 1, along with some representative prices.

In effect, what is here being contemplated is that the high cost of water may be at least partially offset by the opportunity to conduct intensive year-round "food factory" agriculture in favorable growing climates with many conditions under unusually good control. For example, recent observations suggest that very frequent or drip irrigation can cause substantial increases in the crop yield (15). In these experiments the nitrogen fertilizer was applied in the water. There is also speculation that slow release of carbon dioxide beneath the plant canopy might enhance yields. Thus it is entirely possible that future yields may exceed those of Table 2.

Desalination

The newest United States desalting plant, at Key West, Florida, produces 2.5 million gallons of fresh water per day at a cost of about $1 per 1000 gallons. It is anticipated that the larger plants envisaged for future regional water supply will be able to attain lower costs through the economies of scale and the benefits of more advanced technology. A plant producing 8 million gallons per day (16), which will be built around a gas turbine, will have vapor-compressor heat pumps coupled to vertical-tube evaporators and will use the engine-rejected heat in flash evaporators, is expected to produce fresh water at a cost of about half that for the Key West plant (17).

Heat transfer enhancement is currently being introduced into evaporator designs. For example, doubly finned or doubly flutted vertical tubes give several times the heat transfer of plain smooth tubes, and their use can considerably reduce the size and cost of a plant (18). To some degree the heat transfer in the horizontal tubes of a flash evaporator can be similarly augmented. Such advances are now being tried in test units and pilot plants. The preferred large-plant design at present is a combined flash and vertical-tube evaporator with heat transfer enhancement (19).

Economies can be achieved through the design and construction of dual-purpose plants which produce both power and water, as compared to single-purpose plants that produce only water. In terms of 1967 dollars at 10 percent interest (20), the cost of water at a large (billion gallons per day) single-purpose plant, in which most of the steam bypasses the turbine without generating any power, was estimated (9, pp. 3, 4, 19, 20; 21, p. 39) to be 26 to 32 cents per 1000 gallons, while at a dual-purpose station the range for incremental cost of water was 16 to 24 cents. At an interest rate of 9 percent, another study (22) indicated 15 to 26 cents for the dual-purpose cost range. These large-plant studies were based on the use of reactor heat sources, with technology ranging from reactors of the type (light-water) and size being built in the United States today to advanced fast and thermal breeder reactors of the type that will be operational some two decades hence. Since these estimates were made there have been sharp increases in reactor prices, and it may turn out that the costs of water will have to be revised upward by 2 or 3 cents per 1000 gallons (23). On the other hand, advanced evaporator and agricultural technologies appear to be moving ahead more rapidly than had been expected.

The saving effected through dual-purpose operation works the other way as well. Once you have decided to build a single-purpose steam bypass water plant, the incremental cost of producing power also is very low—say, 1.5 mills per kilowatt-hour (21, p. 39) for reactor stations of the largest sizes being constructed today, such as Brown's Ferry (3000 electrical megawatts). This power may be transmitted to a network in some instances, or to adjacent industrial plants in a so-called agro-industrial complex, to help develop and build up the region. A number of industrial processes have been studied in this connection (9, 21, 24), as well as several possible locales (25) and some of the implementation problems (26). One of the large energy consumers is the production of ammonia for fertilizer by way of electrolytic hydrogen, with only air and water used as raw materials. Potassium fertilizer can be produced from the sea, as can other products, such as chlorine, magnesium, salt, and caustic. Hoyle writes (27):

. . . the older established industries of Europe and America . . . grew up around specialized mineral deposits—coal, oil, metallic ores. Without these deposits the older style of industrialization was completely impossible. On the political and economic fronts, the world became divided into "haves" and "have nots," depending whereabouts on the earth's surface these specialized deposits happen to be situated. . . . In the second phase of industrialism, . . . no specialized deposits are needed at all. The key to this second phase lies in the possession of an effectively unlimited source of energy. . . . Low-grade ores can be smelted—and there is an ample supply of such ores to be found everywhere. Carbon can be taken from inorganic compounds, nitrogen from the air, a whole vast range of

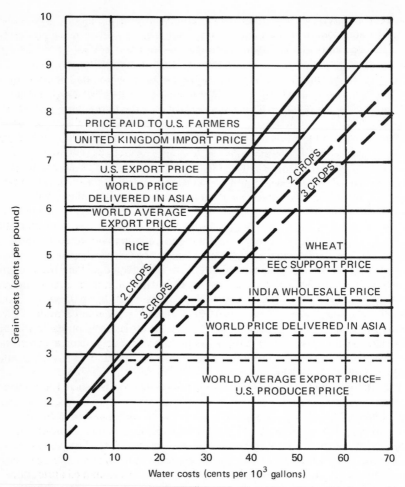

FIGURE 1. The costs of growing grain (sec. 30). [Oak Ridge National Laboratory]

chemicals from seawater. So . . . a phase in which nothing is needed but the commonest materials—water, air and fairly common rocks. This was a phase that can be practiced by anybody, by any nation. . . . This second phase was clearly enormously more effective and powerful than the first.

Summary

The fastest-growing region in our country is the desert of the Southwest. This suggests that the vast, warm, dry areas of the world may be attractive for human occupancy as earth's population soars, if the water and power needs can be met. It may also be that nuclear energy—not tied by any umbilical cord to fossil deposits—will have a significant role in opening up these arid areas and creating usable land for human living space.

Since much arid land lies relatively near the sea and the aggregate length of the coastal deserts nearly equals the circumference of the globe, desalination is a freshwater source of broad potential applicability when cheaper alternative sources are not available. Cities and industries can now spread widely along the ocean shore, bringing with them some agriculture for garden produce.

A more difficult question concerns the extent to which desalination agriculture will be used in newly occupied arid lands for the production of staple foods. Since we cannot predict with any accuracy either the population growth or the increase in food production by various means, let alone the difference between these two large quanities, our knowledge of future food shortages is very poor indeed. It therefore appears prudent to conduct research, development, and pilot planting projects to investigate such potential methods for augmenting food production. These activities should be conducted on a scale sufficient to permit practical evaluation, so that the option of invoking such methods will be open, should circumstances require it. To quote R. R. R. Brooks (28), "The key to (the) . . . future of two-thirds of the human species is rising productivity in agriculture. All political dogmas, party slogans, planning strategies, and models of economic growth shrivel to irrelevance in the face of this fact."

A preliminary and generalized study was conducted at the Oak Ridge National Laboratory with the collaboration of outstanding agricultural and engineering people from other countries and from U.S. government agencies, universities, foundations, and industries. This study considered intensive year-round farming in warm coastal deserts, based on the use of distilled seawater, in association with clustering industries. As indicated in Fig. 1, production costs for rice and wheat appear (29) to fall, for water costs of around 35 and 20 cents per 1000 gallons, respectively, in the general area of recent grain prices. These water prices, in turn, fall (barely) within the estimated future cost range for desalinated water.

The significant conclusion, we believe, is that desalination agriculture is in the realm of practical possibility, rather than being far afield. To our mind this appears of sufficient importance, in view of the population expansion and the interest in opening up new lands and communities, to warrant the development of advanced desalting plants and intensive scientifically managed agriculture. We hope that desert research farms running on distilled water, and controlled-environment agricultural test chambers, may become as well known to you on your TV screen in a few years as starving Biafran babies are today.

REFERENCES AND NOTES

1. H. G. Wells, *The World Set Free—A Story of Mankind* (Dutton, New York, 1914), p. 241.
2. In Los Angeles some strawberry growers use land worth $10,000 per acre and pay city taxes on it.
3. *Nature* 199, 411 (1963).
4. J. Bronowski, *Saturday Rev.* 1969, 45 (5 July 1969).
5. C. H. Lowe, Jr., in A. S. Leopold, *The Desert* (Life Nature Library, New York, 1961), introduction.
6. There are xerophytic plants (such as pineapple) that carry on photosynthesis with closed stomata in the daytime, using stored carbon dioxide absorbed through open stomata at night. They thus transpire much less water per unit of plant matter produced than ordinary crops do.
7. M. Clawson, H. H. Landsberg, L. T. Alexander, *Science* 164, 1141 (1969).
8. P. W. MacAvoy and D. F. Peterson, Jr., *The Engineering Economics of Large-Scale Desalting*

   in the 1970's (Praeger, New York, in press).
9. "Nuclear Energy Centers; Industrial and Agro-Industrial Complexes: Summary Report," *Oak Ridge Nat. Lab. Rep.* ORNL-4291 (1968).
10. C. W. Howe, in *Arid Lands in Perspective,* W. G. McGinnies and B. J. Goldman, Eds. (AAAS, Washington, D.C., 1969), p. 379.
11. J. R. A. McMillan, "Water, Agricultural Production and World Population" (Farrer Oration) (1965).
12. J. S. Kanwar, "From protective to productive irrigation," *Econ. Polit. Weekly Rev. Agr.* (29 March 1969). Data, cited from M. S. Chaudhury and R. G. Pandrey, are given in more detail in an article in *Indian Farming,* in press.
13. R. Revelle, *Proc. Nat. Acad. Sci. U.S.* 56, 328 (1966).
14. If suitable aquifers are not present and an above-ground storage reservoir is constructed in the farming region, there is an increase in cost such that the value $140 in the next paragraph of the text changes to about $150 per acre per year, it being assumed that the reservoir is of a size adequate to supply a farm region with an intake of about 10^9 gallons of water per day.
15. D. Goldberg, B. Gornat, M. Shmueli, "Advances in irrigation in Israel's agriculture," paper presented at the 1st World Congress of Engineers and Architects, Israel (1967). See also D. Goldberg and M. Shmueli, "Drip irrigation—a method used under arid and desert conditions of high water and soil salinity," unpublished.
16. This plant is now in the preliminary planning stage.
17. "Design and Economic Study of a Gas Turbine Powered Vapor Compression Plant for Evaporation of Seawater," *Office Saline Water Res. Develop. Progr. Rep. No. 377* (1968).
18. Such tubes are to be used in the gas turbine unit discussed in the preceding paragraph.
19. "Conceptual Design Study of a 250-Million Gallon per Day Combined Vertical Tube-Flash Evaporator Desalination Plant," *Office Saline Water Res. Develop. Progr. Rep. No. 391* (1968).
20. The cost of desalted water is sensitive to changes in interest rates because, like conventional means of providing new water supplies such as dams and aqueducts, the process requires a large capital outlay.
21. *Oak Ridge Nat. Lab. Rep. No. ORNL-4290* (1968).
22. "Nuclear Power and Water Desalting Plants for Southwest United States and Northwest Mexico" (1968), pp. 113 and 136; this is a preliminary assessment made by a joint United States-Mexico International Atomic Energy Agency study team.
23. This expectation is based on the assumption that combined flash and vertical-tube evaporators are adopted; otherwise, the increase in water costs would be expected to be larger.
24. A. M. Squires, "Steel making in an agro-industrial complex," in *Oak Ridge Nat. Lab. Rep. No. ORNL-4294* (1968); W. E. Lobo, "Acetylene production from naphtha by electric arc and by partial combustion," in *ibid.;* H. E. Goeller, "Tables for computing manufacturing costs of industrial products in an agro-industrial complex," *Oak Ridge Nat. Lab. Rep. No. ORNL-4296* (1969).
25. T. Tamura and W. J. Young, "Data obtained on Several Possible Locales for the Agro—Industrial Complex," *Oak Ridge Nat. Lab. Rep. No. ORNL-4293* (1970).
26. J. A. Ritchey, "Problems in Implementation of an Agro—Industrial Complex," *Oak Ridge Nat. Rep. No. ORNL-4295* (1969); R. L. Meier, *Bull. At. Sci.* 1969, 16 (March 1969); R. D. Sharma, *ibid.* 1969, 31 (November 1969).
27. F. Hoyle, *Ossian's Ride* (Harper, New York, 1959), p. 146.
28. R. R. R. Brooks, *Saturday Rev.* 1969, 14 (9 August 1969).
29. The estimates are based on an interest rate of 10 percent.
30. Figure 1 is based on data and publications as follows. The average price paid the U.S. producer for wheat in the period 1956-65; the average price per pound of milled rice, at 0.65 paddy weight (0.65 pound of milled rice from each pound of paddy), paid the U.S. producer in the period 1950-65; the average price of Siam Patna No. 2 rice imported into the United Kingdom in the period 1955-65; the average wholesale price of wheat in India (the Punjab) in the period 1951-65 *(FAO (Food Agr. Organ. UN) Prod. Yearb. 20 (1966));* the world average export value of wheat in the period 1961-67; the world average export value of rice in the period 1955-67 *(The State of Food and Agriculture: 1968 (Food and Agriculture Organization of the United Nations, Rome, 1968));* the average U.S. export value of rice in the period 1960-65; the European Economic Community's wheat support price *(The World Food Problem* (President's Science Advisory Committee, Washington, D.C., 1967), vol. 2, pp. 145, 149)): recent world prices for wheat and rice delivered in Asia, as given by R. P. Hammond in a paper presented at the International Conference on Water for Peace, Washington, D.C., May 1967.
31. The research discussed here is sponsored by the U.S. Atomic Energy Commission under contract with the Union Carbide Corp.

Importation of Water

Water Importation into Arid Lands   88

JAY M. BAGLEY

What is the philosophic basis for the regional water transfer and how does it differ (or does it differ?) from the philosophy of water resources development within a particular river basin? What are the legal and administrative problems involved in conveying large quantities of water across state boundaries wherever doctrines, principles, and regulations of water rights vary? How are these complicated when sovereign nations are involved? What are the large-scale and long-term physical implications on local water balances and the maintenance of water quality? Can regional growth patterns be regulated by regional water transfer and should they be? What are the ecological implications and can they be predicted? Can existing institutional patterns be adapted to the considerations of large-scale transfers? What institutional changes seem desirable? What are the intrastate, interstate, and international political realities? What are the economic impacts to regions that export and import? If a region has a surplus of water needed by neighboring regions, how can it be determined whether exported water will limit its own future economic growth? How does economic development stemming from regional water transfers compare to alternative investment plans not water-oriented? How can costs and benefits be evaluated and allocated where states and nations are involved? Are there alternatives to large-scale water imports? How can these be evaluated and compared? Will considerations of large-scale water transfer entail a painful reorientation of present philosophy on water resource development? Can this philosophy serve as an instrument for peace between neighboring countries?

The Use of Arid Lands   89

DAEL WOLFLE

The approximately 14 percent of the world's cropped lands that are under irrigation produce a fourth or more of the world's agricultural crops. As the food needs of a too rapidly growing population continue to increase, more and more of the arid and semiarid regions will be cultivated, for much of this land is capable of year-round use, and conditions are more favorable than in humid regions for the control of insects and disease and the advantageous timing of water application. One estimate is that by the year 2000 there will be twice the present 370 million acres under irrigation, even though the cost of new irrigation projects, which now averages almost $400 per acre, is substantially higher than the cost of bringing new land in humid regions under cultivation.

The investment required means that irrigation agriculture can be economically successful only when combined with sophisticated farm technology. Yet too often, over the world, expensive water storage and distribution facilities have been uneconomically coupled with moderately primitive methods of farm operation.

There are a few examples of long-enduring irrigation successes. But they are more than counterbalanced by reminders of how extensively man has unwittingly turned grassland and food-producing areas into wasteland and desert. The Sahara, for example, is still increasing by 40,000 acres a year.

The arid lands experts are uncertain whether the pressure to exploit more of the arid lands would, quite literally, in the long run make the deserts bloom or produce more Saharas.

Dams

90

Dams and Wild Rivers: Looking Beyond the Pork Barrel

LUTHER J. CARTER

In the 1930's, when the U.S. Army Corps of Engineers began changing a considerable part of the American landscape with its program of dam construction, the Corps' role, as it was then understood, was relatively simple. Its mandate, as the nation's largest water development agency, was to prevent floods, produce power, and open up rivers to navigation and, generally, to support economic development. In the Depression years, few people were thinking about leisure, esthetics, or whether the economic benefits from developing a river should be foregone in the interest of keeping the stream wild and free-flowing.

Now, however, the Corps is having to respond to the demands of a different era, and, despite encouragement from its top leadership, the old ways of thinking and doing are not being abruptly abandoned. Bureaucratic inertia and old habits of mind, especially in the field but also at Corps headquarters, combine to resist sudden change. The Corps holds to its traditional bias in favor of meeting water needs by building dams and other structures which it, as an engineering organization, has been chartered to provide. Moreover, in Congress, the "pork barrel" from which senators and representatives dispense water projects for their constituents is a cherished institution that won't be easily given up. The pork barrel is intimately associated with the old helter-skelter way of building dams and navigation projects one by one, often without priorities or any broad assessment of national or even regional needs.

The Corps' dam-building program has been, and is, enormous. Its reservoirs now cover more than 4 million acres and have a shoreline longer than that of the mainland United States. If the Corps achieves its goals for the coming decades, it will flood millions of additional acres and will more than double the storage capacity of its reservoir system. Conflict between water-resource-development objectives and the values involved in keeping some streams in their natural state will, of course, be inevitable.

Aquatic Weeds   91

L. G. HOLM, L. W. WELDON, and R. D. BLACKBURN

In the evolution of the city as a habitat, in the conversion of virgin lands to intensified farming, and in the alteration of watercourses with locks, dams, and reservoirs, man is the interloper. At his behest the natural order of things is set aside. As a result of his activities and their byproducts, new species and numbers of weeds, rodents, insects, and diseases appear where they could not, or did not, exist before. One of our priceless treasures, fresh water, is changed as civilization draws near. Its quality usually becomes poorer; it is seldom improved by man. Communities, planned and unplanned, locate on the water's edge to use navigation routes, irrigate land, and develop power. As a result the watercourses are heated, polluted, and fertilized; the levels fluctuate, and new biological pests are introduced because of man's commerce and mobility.

Several "explosions" of aquatic weeds in the great rivers and lakes of the warm regions of the world have forced us to recognize the power of such infestations. They destroy fisheries, interfere with hydroelectric and irrigation schemes, stop navigation, and bring starvation and disease problems to riverine communities. The rapid growth of weed infestations has been both spectacular and frightening, and the publicity devoted to several of these problems in the past decade has made us aware that something is wrong.

Aquatic weeds obstruct water flow, increase evaporation, cause large losses of water through transpiration, and prevent proper drainage of land. Weeds may interfere with navigation, prevent fishing and recreation, depress real estate values, and present health hazards. In the western United States, Timmons (1) showed that 17 states lost 1,966,000 acre-feet of irrigation water annually because of aquatic and ditchbank weeds. The water, valued conservatively at $20 per acre-foot, is worth $32,230,000 (2). This is enough water to irrigate 132,000 to 315,000 hectares of cropland. In the United States there never has been an evaluation of the total nonagricultural losses due to aquatic weeds. It is certain that this loss, too, would be very high.

The aquatic environment is complex and is of interest to scientists in several disciplines. The management of aquatic vegetation is not a new science, but rather an old field of botany that has been recently revitalized because of increased demand on our fresh waters and the exponential growth in problems caused by aquatic vegetation.

Water Hyacinth

The scourge of some of the world's major rivers is water hyacinth, *Eichhornia crassipes* (Mart.) Solms in the family *Pontederiaceae*. A native of South America, it is now widely distributed over the warm regions of the earth. The plant is free-floating, has very fine roots, and produces stolons and viable seeds. The leaves are 10 to 15 cm across, bright green, shiny, and, because they are upright, serve as sails before the wind. The lovely flowers are pale lilac or mauve with a yellow patch at the center. Because of his admiration for the flowers, man has assisted the spread of this plant by cultivating it in his pools and gardens. His carelessness toward the cleanliness of his commercial and pleasure craft on land and sea has also contributed to the movement of the plant. For example, charcoal is made in the bush in Africa; and holes in the sacks used for transport are sometimes plugged with water hyacinth plants that may survive a very long journey. Large plants are used as cushions for sitting and kneeling in native canoes, to be thrown away at any place where the plant ceases to be useful. The plants catch on the sides and bottoms of river craft and thus move with the commerce of the region. Natural forces and events have also been important in the spread of water hyacinth. From the nurseries in the swamps and backwaters, great islands of the weed are flushed into the mainstream at flood time.

Water hyacinth populations increase rapidly by vegetative reproduction. In one experiment two parent plants produced 30 offspring after 23 days, and 1200 at the end of 4 months. A plant may flower at the age of 26 days and will normally produce viable seeds. Seed production varies from a few to as many as 5000 seeds per plant. The seeds sink to the bottom and may remain viable for at least 15 years. Movement of seeds between watercourses must surely take place in the mud on furbearing animals and on the legs of birds. Recent reports of the long-distance dispersal of seed by waterfowl and shore birds suggest a possibility that has never been taken seriously. These migrating birds can carry seed several thousand kilometers in one season (3). In the face of such vectors, once the seed of a species is on a continent, there may be little that man can do to prevent its spread.

An account of the spread of water hyacinth in the Congo and Nile rivers will illustrate the immensity of the task we face. The species had been introduced at the delta of the Nile and in Natal, South Africa, at the beginning of the century.

Europeans who settled in South Rhodesia in 1937 reported the presence of water hyacinth. It is now generally distributed in Africa. In spite of the losses and human suffering caused by this plant, it was still available in 1965 for purchase as an ornamental in the street markets of Senegal. In the United States, federal law prohibits interstate shipment of water hyacinth, but it is offered for sale in the catalogs of many distributors of water garden plants.

Water hyacinth was first reported in the Congo River in 1952 and in less than 3 years it had spread 1600 kilometers from Leopoldville up to Stanleyville. In 1954 it had already begun to block transportation. Buoys were submerged and navigation channels were hidden. Fish spawning areas were blocked. Many fishing grounds were destroyed by darkness and lack of oxygen as the weed cover became more dense, and, as a result, the riverine communities were denied their principle source of protein. Using herbicides applied from ships, planes, and helicopters, by 1957 Belgian scientists had directed the cleanup of more than 1600 kilometers of the river at a cost of $1,000,000. In spite of this massive effort, Le Brun reports that in the same year water hyacinth was still floating past Leopold- ville on the way to the sea at the rate of 136 metric tons per hour (4). During the turbulent years following independence, the Congo government services could not maintain the weed control program, and the Congo River is again badly infested.

The history of the infestation of the upper White Nile is equally tragic. The first report of the weed in the White Nile was in 1958. Again, the multiplication and spread took place so quickly that even the best efforts of the Sudan govern- ment could not organize a campaign in time to contain the weed. A staff of 200 workers equipped with ships, planes, and land vehicles was organized to keep the river and the harbors open. During the early 1960's, the water hyacinth team of Sudan was able to keep the weed under control in the most critical areas with herbicides. At one time the cost of this operation was $1.5 million per year (5).

In addition to all of the usual hardships caused by the weed, men now began to see the impact of its uncontrolled growth on clogged irrigation pumps and hydroelectric schemes. Some river villages that were regularly supplied with food by boat began to starve because they could not be reached. Insect vectors of human and animal diseases seek harbor in the mats of water hyacinth; so do dangerous snakes and crocodiles. In recent years the political difficulties in the south of the country have prevented workers from spraying many of the nurseries and sources of infestation in the upper White Nile. The region is again in serious difficulty.

The people of Sudan deserve much credit for preventing the spread of water hyacinth from the White to the Blue Nile. The confluence of the two rivers is at Khartoum, and above this point a quarantine system, including many vehicle checkpoints, has been organized and is efficiently administered. By preventing the spread of the weed from the White to the Blue Nile, the Sudanese have protected the great irrigated Gezira cotton scheme.

Water hyacinth is present in the sloughs and backwaters of the Amazon River. It seldom appears to be a problem in the Amazon, perhaps due to lesser demands on utilization of this waterway, or to the presence of natural factors such as insects or plant diseases that limit growth of the weed. It does interfere with man's activities in many lakes, streams, and reservoirs of Central and South America. Many large reservoirs such as Brokopondo in Surinam, Lake Apanas in Nicaragua, and Lake Rio Lempa in El Salvador are threatened with economic disaster if dense stands of water hyacinth are allowed to develop.

The benefit of these reservoirs is dependent upon the amount of available water. However, water hyacinth consumes and wastes tremendous quantities of water through the leaves. The loss of water through evapotranspiration from the leaves has been measured as 3.2 to 3.7 times greater than free evaporation from a surface. This accounted for a loss of more than 6 acre-feet of water in a 6-month period due to a water hyacinth cover. In the dry atmosphere of India, the loss of water through water hyacinth was 7.8 times that of open water (6). Only a partial coverage of water hyacinth on a reservoir can result in the entire river inflow being wasted back into the atmosphere. Thus, the water is not available for hydroelectric power and irrigation.

Water hyacinth is distributed generally in Asia where it may be found in India, throughout the countries of Southeast Asia, and in the Philippine Islands. In East Pakistan some of the farming areas are covered with massive deposits of water hyacinth as the floods come down from the hills in the rainy season. The weed is in Australia and New Zealand as well.

Water hyacinth was reportedly introduced into the United States in 1884 as part of a horticultural exhibit. It spread rapidly and by 1897 was creating enough havoc to navigation to prompt an investigation. Funds for control of the weed became available in 1899. A number of mechanical removal procedures were used initially to control the water hyacinth, but these have largely been replaced with herbicide programs because of the great saving in time and money. Intensive control programs are being conducted by federal, state, and local agencies, drainage districts, and private interests. In spite of this large combined effort water hyacinth caused an annual loss of almost $43,000,000 in Florida, Alabama, Mississippi, and Louisiana in 1956. The types of losses are similar throughout the world (7).

We have indicated some of the navigational problems in Africa. The navigation of rivers and waterways in the southern United States would be just as difficult without proper control of the water hyacinth. Many rivers have to be closed to boat traffic periodically if effective control procedures have not been followed. Fishing camps and marinas are often closed, and many are forced into bankruptcy by inaccessibility.

A cover of water hyacinth on canals with a cross section of 36 to 72 centares may reduce the flow of water by half. The flow in smaller laterals and farm ditches may be almost completely stopped. Many canal systems have to be enlarged 50 percent or more to compensate for retarded flow. An additional problem is the constant accumulation of debris from decaying water hyacinth on the canal bottom. During periods of active growth, the lower leaves and roots of water hyacinth are constantly decaying and being replaced. This debris that falls to the canal bottom may amount to more than 30 centimeters per year. If the extensive water hyacinth cover is not prevented, mechanical removal of the debris becomes necessary—at a cost of $400 to $640 per kilometer. (6, 8).

Salvinia

Some of the man-made lakes constructed in this century are so large that they are included on world maps. Lake Kariba, on the Zambesi River in Southern Africa, is an interesting example of the frustration which comes with massive efforts to arrange great alterations in the environment. The relocation of 50,000 people to make way for this lake caused considerable human suffering. The biological consequence of impounding such a large stream is in part illustrated by the story of the weed problem that later developed.

The Kariba Dam was closed late in 1958. The maximum water level was reached in July 1963, 4-1/2 years later. Lake Kariba now covers more than 4200 square kilometers, has a maximum depth of 115 meters, and extends up to the foot of beautiful Victoria Falls.

In May 1959, floating mats of the water fern, *Salvinia auriculata* Aublet, were reported in the center of the lake. The mats grew in size and moved about with the wind. Before the end of the year a significant portion of the water near the shore was covered with *Salvinia* plants, as they lodged in branches of partially submerged trees and continued to multiply. By this time, *Pistia stratiotes* L. was associating with *Salvinia* in some of the mats. During 1960, less than 2 years after the dam was closed, it was estimated that the rafts of *Salvinia* had covered 420 square kilometers or 10 percent of the surface area (9). By 1965 the infestation had subsided slightly but was still estimated at 8 percent of the lake's surface.

The water fern has floating leaves 3 cm long and submerged leaves so finely divided that they have a feathery appearance. In some areas the plant produces spores when it is crowded, but until 1965 only vegetative reproduction had been observed on Lake Kariba. Before formation of the lake, large infestations of *Salvinia* were present in the Upper Zambesi where they sometimes interfered with the fishing of the local people. The weed was also far up the Chobe River, a tributary which feeds into the Zambesi above Victoria Falls. In 1949, Dr. O. West collected *Salvinia* just a short way above Victoria Falls. Boughey (9) assumed that the weed was already present in that portion of the Zambesi River which was flooded by the lake. The records show that warnings were given about the potential weed problem at the time the lake was being planned. Not until 1960 and 1961 were serious research efforts made toward control measures that would be feasible and safe for the lake (10). As a result of political turmoil in the area, no important measures for control or eradication have ever been taken.

Salvinia auriculata, first described as from Guiana, has spread over a wide area in Central and South America. from Cuba to Argentina. It is known to be in the Cape area of South America, in the Congo River and the Cameroons on the West Coast, and in some of the countries of Southeast Asia. It first "exploded" and became a serious problem in Ceylon in the period before 1955 (11). At that time *Salvinia* had covered an estimated 8800 hectares of rice fields and 800 hectares of canals and other waterways within about 12 years.

Could the disaster at Lake Kariba have been avoided? The infestations of *Salvinia* in Ceylon were well known. Scheduled inspections of the shore line where weeds build up and prompt treatment of early infestations seem the only way to prevent massive explosions of vegetation which may by then be too expensive or too dangerous to treat. When man-made lakes are constructed, vegetation management must be integrated with the work of all bureaus and agencies concerned with maintenance of the watershed, the lake, and the dam. Recently, an infestation of *Salvinia* was found on Lake Naivasha in Kenya, and it was dealt with promptly and effectively with herbicides applied from aircraft and boats. Constant vigilance has kept the weed under control.

Water Lettuce

Lake Volta in Ghana deserves special mention. The dam was closed in 1964. When filling is completed, the lake will cover 8125 square kilometers. It will be the largest man-made lake in the world. By 1965 great rafts of water lettuce, *Pistia stratiotes,* some many kilometers long, could be seen floating on the surface. Extensive fringes of the weed covered scores of kilometers of the lake's edge and filled the inlets of small rivers entering the lake.

Water lettuce, very widely distributed in the world, is one of the free-floating aquatic plants that must be viewed with concern. It has pale green leaves which are broad and softly pubescent on both sides. The leaves occur in rosettes, beneath which are long fibrous roots, and the plants are connected by stolons. There is a tendency to overlook the potential danger from water lettuce on large water bodies such as Lake Volta because, presumably, it cannot tolerate action from large waves.

The most important problem caused by water lettuce is that of disease and the nuisance associated with mosquitoes. Water lettuce serves as a preferred host site for larvae of several species of mosquitoes. One or more of these species of mosquitoes serve as principal vectors of each of several forms of encephalomyelitis and of rural filariasis. The *Mansonia* larvae obtain their oxygen directly from the roots of water lettuce and never surface. The only way to control these mosquitoes is to remove water lettuce (12).

In an interesting experiment in which herbicides were used to destroy a 120-hectare infestation of water lettuce, there was also complete control of *Mansonia* mosquitoes for 4 months. Only an occasional mosquito of this species was trapped in the year following treatment (13). Demonstrations such as this suggest that suitable methods of destroying water lettuce may provide a means of controlling diseases that affect large numbers of people.

All of the foregoing species of plants are free-floating. There are many more, but perhaps the ones that deserve special mention are those of the duckweed family *Lemnaceae L.* A single frond may be the size of a pinhead, and there are no stems or true leaves. Members of this family propagate vegetatively by producing new individuals at the edge of the frond. They can cover the surface of an entire pond in a few weeks. Duckweeds are a nuisance in rice fields and cause trouble in irrigation systems by entering siphon tubes and pumps and by collecting on trashracks.

The free-floating species have drawn much attention if only because massive infestations are spectacular and also frightening when they begin to move. But these are by no means the most difficult of the aquatic weed problems.

Submersed Weeds

Submersed weeds are perhaps the most serious of all aquatic weed problems, because they cannot readily be sprayed with herbicides and do not easily lend themselves to clearance by machines. Herbicidal treatments must be made to the entire volume of water, depending upon sorption of the chemical by the undesirable species to achieve control. It must be obvious that the submersed weeds drastically reduce the rate of water flow. It is as though the water must pass through an infinite series of inverted combs that create friction and turbulence.

Of all aquatics, submersed weeds cause the greatest problems in the United States. The most troublesome in the west and north are the general *Potamogeton* and *Elodea,* and in the east include these genera and *Myriophyllum.* In the south, *Najas* and *Ceratophyllum* are the most common. In addition to these, *Egeria* is widespread throughout the United States. The filamentous and branched algae are almost always present. Also present in the United States, but important on a world basis as well, are members of the genera *Ranunculus, Vallisneria,* and *Utricularia.*

Submersed weeds also have a history of rapid invasion of new sites. Many of the waterways of Europe were blocked by *Elodea canadensis* when it was introduced in the 18th century. One of the most alarming plant invaders is eurasian watermilfoil, *Myriophyllum spicatum* L. The plant, apparently in the United States since the 19th century, has become a problem only during the past 10 years. In that period it has invaded more than 80,000 hectares in the Chesapeake Bay, 2,000 hectares in the Tennessee Valley Authority reservoirs, and 26,800 hectares in Currituck Sound.

The weed causes large losses in commercial fishing, smothers shellfish beds, hinders navigation, depresses real estate values, interferes with recreational use, provides mosquito breeding sites, and clogs water intake systems. This is a perennial submersed plant that spreads very rapidly by vegetative reproduction and probably by seed. The leaves are finely dissected, and the flowering spike, without leaves, may extend 10 centimeters above the water. The plant can tolerate salinities up to as much as one-third that of seawater and can thus invade most fresh and estuarine waters. Large acreages in the TVA reservoirs have been treated with 2,4-D (2,4-dichlorophenoxyacetic acid). The chemical has been safely applied at rates of 22 to 44 kilograms per hectare. The results have varied from excellent control in protected embayments to poor control in moving water in these impoundments. The varied results of this work and the inadequacy of the control methods indicate the lack of knowledge to cope with the problem. The need is for concerned public agencies to contain new troublesome plants wherever they are first reported. In one area of Florida, eurasian watermilfoil spread from 80 to 1200 hectares in 2 years; there was no attempt to control the plant or limit it to the infested area (14).

The story of the invasion by eurasian watermilfoil is still another example of a species that multiplied rapidly after having been in a certain area for a long time. We do not know whether plant material was moved to a more favorable environment, or whether the habitat was altered to make it more suitable for the spread and growth of plants already present.

Submersed weeds are a menace to irrigation systems. Thousands of freshwater reservoirs, large and small, have been constructed throughout the world in the past two decades, and with them have come large new irrigation schemes. Several of these command more than 400,000 hectares. India, for example, the leading producer of three of the world's major crops, has more kilometers of irrigation canals than any other country. As people occupy and farm the land, the effluent from villages, barns, and animal yards, together with the runoff of fertilizers added to the fields, enriches the waters of the canals and reservoirs. Because the distributaries are often shallow, clear, and slow-moving, the added nutrients ensure the growth of weeds. When the weeds enter the system, water can no longer move at the design rate of flow, with the result that the fields most distant from the reservoir cannot be irrigated on schedule. The reduced rate of flow also encourages seepage from canals, and the losses from evaporation are significantly increased. These are matters for serious concern, because they directly affect food production in an already hungry world. The management of aquatic vegetation for an entire irrigation system may be the most complex of all water weed problems. These include reserves of water held in rivers, ponds, and lakes, a network of canals, and a drainage systems. Frequently, the water is used for men, animals, and crops.

It is estimated that over a million additional hectares of arable land will be placed under irrigation before the end of the century. One example may serve to illustrate the futility of planning irrigation systems without, at the same time, making preparations to protect them from aquatic weeds. In one of the countries of Asia, an irrigation scheme with a command area of 560,000 hectares was completed in this decade. One main arm of the canal system is 400 kilometers long and, with its distributaries, totals more than 1600 kilometers. The discharge at the head is equal to that of the Seine River as it flows through Paris. Within 5 years after the system was opened submersed aquatic weeds had cut the flow of water in the main canal by 80 percent.

Man's efforts to increase food production in the United States have resulted in treatment of 105,833 kilometers of irrigation and drainage channels for aquatic weed control in 17 western states (1). This represents about 55 percent of the infested channels and about 45 percent of the total length in use. Greater world pressure for food production will increase the demand for even more efficient control of vegetation which interferes with water flow.

Man's quest for beauty and recreation has brought about some of the most catastrophic of our weed problems. Exotic and beautiful aquarium species are transported throughout the world. *Egeria, Cabomba, Elodea,* and *Hydrilla* are examples of submersed plants that have been carried from one country to another with dire consequences. The problem is twofold. First, in the United States and most other countries there are no limitations on the importation of aquatic plants. Second, most of the aquatic plant dealers grow and harvest the plants in public waters. When a grower desires another species, he simply imports it, places it in several streams or lakes, and then harvests it as it is needed. Many submersed weeds have been introduced in this manner. Failure to restrict their movement has allowed wide distribution of some species.

Emersed Weeds

Emersed aquatic weeds have their roots beneath the water and their stems and leaves above the surface. Many are familiar, including the bulrushes, *Scirpus;* cattails, *Typha;* water lily, *Nymphaea;* spatterdock, *Nuphar;* rushes, *Juncus;* arrowhead, *Sagittaria;* and alligatorweed, *Alternanthera.* Where water levels fluctuate these species may survive for short periods as terrestrial plants. Many are the first to invade newly flooded areas, and they will prosper in the backwater areas which are intermittently wet. Emersed weeds are especially troublesome in irrigation and drainage systems. They choke canals, increase silt deposition, and impede water flow. Frequently, the design rate of flow can never be achieved because of encroachment of plants on the shoreline and the water lost through transpiration.

Phreatophytes

These are the plants that grow at the water's edge or with their roots reaching into the capillary zone overlying the water table. It is as difficult to determine limits for the species which should be in this group as it is to define the shoreline in a swamp. Woody plants, perennial grasses, and broadleaved plants are prominent in this group. There are an estimated 6 million hectares of stream channels, canals, reservoirs, and river flood plains infested with these weeds in the western part of the United States, and they waste 25 million acre-feet of water annually. It would be practical to save 25 percent of this wasted water by maintenance of stream channels and effective weed control (15).

The most common woody plants are salt cedar, *Tamarix pentandra;* willows, *Salix* spp.; cottonwood, *Populus* spp.; baccharis, *Baccharis* spp.; buttonbush, *Cephalanthus occidentalis* L.; velvet mesquite, *Prosopis juliflora;* and grease wood, *Sarcobatus vermiculatis.*

Floating Island Weeds

In accord with many natural growth cycles, large masses of floating dead aquatic vegetation may support progressively larger types of vegetation. As these enter the final phase of this ecological succession, woody species become established. Large islands bearing trees several feet in circumference are impossible to cope with when they lodge in the channels of main streams, for example.

One of the most dangerous and dreaded weeds of the African waterways is papyrus, *Cyperus papyrus* L., of the sedge family *Cyperaceae.* It is feared because it may encroach on open water by extending from the banks. It is one of the principal plants in the formation of sudd which is a mass of free-floating vegetation. The plant grows upright to a height of 4 to 5 meters. The rhizomes by which it spreads vegetatively are woody and strong and may reach far out into open water or may quickly travel over weed mats or penetrate through them and thus knit them together. These massive and sturdy floating islands of vegetation, when loosed on a river at any season, can be a menace to navigation. Sudd formation in two of Africa's largest swamps, the Okavango in Botswana and the great swamp in the White Nile above Malakal, are dominated by papyrus. A study of the papyrus sudd of the White Nile revealed that 50 percent of the water entering the river was lost through evaporation and transpiration as a result of the activity of this weed and its associated vegetation.

Vossia cuspidata (Roxb.) W. Griff., a robust member of the grass family *Gramineae* is frequently mixed with the islands of associated plants. The weed is sometimes called hippo grass, because it is grazed by the hippopotamus as well as by cattle. It can have floating or submersed stalks which grow rapidly for considerable distances under favorable conditions. The aerial portion of the stem is strong and erect and may reach a height of 2 meters. The grass is widely distributed in Africa and Asia. The irrigation canals of the Gezira cotton scheme along the Blue Nile are sorely troubled with this grass because it impedes the flow of water.

Chemical Control

Many selective herbicides have been developed to combat aquatic weeds. Some have such a narrow range of specificity that one species of a genus may be controlled without affecting other species of the same genus. Thus certain problem species can be controlled without adversely affecting the desirable flora and fauna in a waterway. Formerly, large quantities of toxic chemicals, such as sodium arsenite, were used indiscriminately; but today the herbicides used in our waters must pass rigid tests of efficacy, toxicity to fauna and flora in and near the waterway, residues in irrigated crops, and many other hazards.

Chemical control of several floating weeds is possible. Water hyacinth is "managed" and kept under control in the United States with 2,4-D (2,4-dichlorophenoxyacetic acid). At one time the infestations of this weed on the White Nile and the Congo rivers in Africa were controlled with the same herbicide, but now political turmoil and economic problems have made it impossible to continue the control operations.

If sensitive crops are grown in agricultural areas adjacent to infested waterways, some herbicides may not be used because of the danger from volatility and spray drift. Recent development of invert emulsion (water in oil) formulations of 2,4-D, water thickening agents, and new innovations in spraying equipment (such as the microfoil boom) give the applicator new tools to control placement of the chemical. Diquat (6,7-dihydrodipyrido (1,2-α:2', 1'-c)pyrazidiinuim dibromide) has proven effective on water hyacinth at 1.7 kilograms per hectare and can be used with greater safety around ornamentals and crop plants that are very sensitive to 2,4-D. Two applications of diquat usually give about the same control of this weed as would be expected from four treatments with 2,4-D. In Australia, amitrole-T (3-amino-1,2,4-trazole + ammonium thiocyanate) has been used effectively on water hyacinth (16).

Diquat is also effectively used to control water lettuce at the same rates as it is used to control water hyacinth. As these two plants often grow together, a single application of diquat can be used to control both species.

The chemical control of submersed weeds, much more difficult, is achieved through the use of chemicals with several different modes of action. Large quantities of emulsified xylene and other aromatic solvents are used for contact control of vegetation in irrigation canals. The xylene is usually released into the flowing canal, over a 30-minute period, at 6 to 10 gallons per cubic foot per second of flow. As the chemical moves down the canal, the plants absorb lethal doses, the treated portion of the water is spilled into a waste area, and the untreated flowing water is then available for immediate use. The treatment kills the vegetation back to the bottom mud, but regrowth may occur in a few weeks.

Acrolein (acrylaldehyde) is applied in flowing water in the same manner as aromatic solvents (17). In static water sites such as lakes, acrolein (7 parts per million by volume) is injected directly into the water. *Hydrilla* has been controlled with this method for 8 to 16 weeks in both the United States and Australia. Generally two to four treatments are required per year for satisfactory weed control.

Knowledge of the plant cycle has an important bearing on the control of submersed weeds. Sago pondweed, *Potamogeton pectinatus,* and *Hydrilla* produce hydrosoil propagules. In canals that can be dewatered, fenac (2,3,6-trichlorophenylacetic acid) and dichlobenil (2,6-dichlorobenzonitrile) can be applied to the dry canal bottom. The chemical is then leached into the surface soil and released into the water as growth begins. *Hydrilla* also produces large numbers of hydrosoil turions that sprout as soon as the topgrowth is killed. In areas that cannot be dewatered, successive treatments with fatty acid amine salts of endothall (3,6-endoxohexahydrophthalic acid) and diquat reduce the number of these propagules to the point where regrowth is minimum (18).

Foliar treatments with dalapon (2,2-dichloropropionic acid), at 5.6 to 22.4 kilograms per hectare, will afford quite satisfactory control of most aquatic grasses, cattails, and rushes. Often two or more treatments are required in a growing season.

Amitrole-T is another selective herbicide that is effective on grasses. The response of shore weeds to these two herbicides provides us with an example of the interrelation of stage of development and herbicidal activity. Dalapon is most effective on cattails before they flower, while amitrole-T is more effective in the fall, after flowering. A combination or mixture of these two herbicides is often used as a single application that may be effective for several months and which may cover a broader spectrum of weeds. A mixture of dalapon and 2,4-D is sometimes used where control of both grass and broad-leaved species is necessary (19).

There are still many troublesome species for which there are no mechanical, chemical, or biological controls. For most of these we lack information on the physiology and the stages of growth and development. The pace has quickened in the search for ideas, chemicals, and methods for the selective control of aquatic vegetation. Modern herbicides may also be used safely to keep our waterways productive and useful. However, application of most herbicides to potable water is restricted. Some are toxic to fish. Information is needed on the disposition and effects of herbicides in water, in crops irrigated with treated water, and in fish. Because the cost is generally only 10 to 20 percent of other control methods, there is frequently no other practical way to manage the vegetation in a stream, a lake, or a power system.

We do not know whether we shall be able to restore our water resources. It is certain that we shall continue to use them, and many of them are destined to be misused for some time to come. Some types of aquatic vegetation will flourish; we shall find it disagreeable, and sometimes we shall be overwhelmed by its luxuriant growth. Until we have become wise enough to appreciate our water, and until we have come to respect it as one of the most precious of all the gifts of nature, aquatic herbicides will be needed—for they will be one of the few tools that we can afford in the selective management of the vegetation in our waterways. In many places in the world there will be no other choice.

Biocontrol

Natural forces affect aquatic plant growths. These forces are used by man in his biological control programs (biocontrol). Biocontrol, which turns nature against herself, may be the most economical method for the control of portions of this perplexing world problem. Biocontrol has certain advantages, for example, relatively low program costs, ready supply sources, ease of application of techniques which often require no special equipment, minimal training of unskilled personnel, and relative permanence of treatments because of the ability to resist weed reinfestations (20). In this age of emphasis on chemical and mechanical control of aquatic weeds, most people are unaware of the progress being made in biocontrol. Emphasis on this area of weed control has increased rapidly during the last decade.

Biocontrol works best with agents of foreign origin. Scientists have traveled to the native homes of certain species of aquatic plants to collect various organisms that attack the plants. Frequently, in its native habitat, the plant never presents the problem that it does in other parts of the world. The reason for this is that certain natural agents, such as insects, diseases, and the chemistry of the water, have controlled the plant. For this reason the biocontrol of aquatic vegetation should not be confused with the aquatic plant eradication. The plant and the biocontrol agent are part of the aquatic ecosystem.

In nature, a balance is maintained in the aquatic flora through plant-feeding insects, diseases, nematodes, fungi, bacteria, viruses, fish, snails, and mammals. When a biocontrol agent is selected it must be thoroughly investigated before introduction into a new area. It must not be released if it will attack desirable plants or other organisms.

A large freshwater snail *Marisa cornuarietis* has freed small ponds in the southern United States and Puerto Rico of submersed weeds. *Marisa* carries no diseases of man and has been used as food in Puerto Rico. The indiscriminate feeding habits of *Marisa* have also made it a biocontrol agent for disease-carrying snails. A major disadvantage is its sensitivity to temperatures below 6°C. It may feed upon certain desirable plants such as rice, watercress, and water chestnuts which are growing in the water. A second freshwater snail, *Pomacea australis,* shows promise as a biocontrol for submersed and floating aquatic weeds. This large ampullarid is widely distributed in Brazil (21).

Mammals with aquatic weed-cleaning ability are rare, but the sea cow or manatee, *Trichechus manatus latirostris,* has shown its taste for many types of aquatic weeds. Unofficial reports collected from all areas of the world indicate that this mythological mermaid has no peer in the biological world for the volume of aquatic weeds which can be consumed by one animal. There is only limited use of the manatee because of the scarcity of animals, and an increase in population is uncertain because of the lack of knowledge about its reproduction (22).

In contrast to the indiscriminate feeding of snails and manatees is the fastidious taste of the alligatorweed beetle, *Agasicles* sp. In nature this small beetle feeds only on alligatorweed and will starve in its absence. No control technique could be simpler than the release of a handful of beetles into an infestation of alligatorweed. Recent laboratory research has also shown that *Salvinia* may be controlled by a wingless aquatic grasshopper *Paulinia acriminate. Paulinia* is now being evaluated in field trials at Lake Kariba. Investigations are also underway to search for natural enemies of the water hyacinth in its native South American home (23).

Certain freshwater fish consume large quantities of aquatic vegetation. The common carp, *Cyprinus carpio;* Chinese grass carp or white amur, *Ctenopharyngodon idella;* tilapia, *Tilapia* sp.; and silver dollar fish, *Metynnia* sp., are used for control of aquatic vegetation in many areas of the world. Many of these species are sensitive to cold weather and, in colder climates, must be over-wintered in temperature-control tanks. The most promising of this group is the white amur. Ponds choked with *Hydrilla* in India were cleared of the weed in 2 months after they were stocked with 350 white amur per hectare (24). Russia, Poland, Czechoslovakia, China, and other countries have used the white amur as a biocontrol for aquatic weeds.

Ducks, geese, and swans can remove small amounts of vegetation, and they are especially effective in small ponds for the control of duckweed. Controlled grazing of cows, horses, and goats may be used to hold down vegetation along lake shorelines and canal banks (25).

Diseases, viruses, fungi, bacteria, and nematodes have received very little attention in aquatic weed biocontrol research. Two diseases are considered to be the cause of the decrease in eurasian watermilfoil in the United States (26). The diseases have not been identified and may be only an indirect cause of the decline in the milfoil. A disease was the direct cause of the decline of eel grass along the Atlantic Coast of the United States in the 1930s.

Low-growing species of aquatic plants, several centimeters in height, have been planted in canals to compete with the more undesirable species that may attain lengths of several meters. Removal of nutrients from the water environment by partitioning agents is also being considered as a biocontrol agent. Some success has been obtained in controlling submersed aquatic weeds with selective dyes or black plastic that filter out all, or selective portions of, the sunlight in water.

The employment of biocontrol agents in our aquatic weed programs offers a new approach to the solution of an old and aggravating problem. Combinations of biocontrol agents with chemical and mechanical methods of control may someday be the answer to aquatic vegetation management.

Mechanical Removal

The first effort to control aquatic weeds was with hand tools. Since 1900, many machines have been designed to perform such work, and some are so large that several barges are required for flotation. In the United States today there are still many canals and drainage systems maintained by power shovels and draglines, but these machines work slowly and maintenance costs are high. Emersed weeds are sometimes controlled with the use of underwater mowing machines (27). All of these types of mechanical equipment can bring temporary relief from weed infestations and sometimes provide channels through portions of an otherwise inaccessible waterway. When water is used for human or animal consumption, or when valuable crops are in the immediate area, there may be no practical way to control aquatic weeds except by mechanical removal. The ratio of costs for these methods as compared to approved herbicidal methods may be on the order of ten to one (8).

Because large quantities of nutrients accumulate in the tissues of some aquatic weeds, the removal of a heavy stand may be beneficial to the waterway. The yield of such massive quantities of green vegetation raises the question of its value for food, for food amendments, or for improvement of soils. But such questions have already been raised, again and again, as to unwanted terrestrial plants (such as woody species that might be used for lumber and wood products) or as to perennial grasses that might be used for pasture. There are many reports of analytical work on water hyacinth and several other aquatic weeds (28). There is no shortage of information on percent dry matter, crude fiber and protein content, or carotene and other special constituents of these plants. Why, then, have aquatic weeds not been more widely used? The answer is that we lack economical ways of harvesting and processing large masses of plants with a very high water content. In certain countries the weed nurseries and other important sources of infestation are almost inaccessible. Add to this the probable cost of transport of a finished product over long distances and it becomes easy to see why public and private agencies have not accepted these risks.

Summary

The great focal points of civilization placed their roots along streams and in sheltered harbors because man needed to be near water for navigation and housekeeping and because it provided protection. There was little thought of caring for the bountiful supplies of water which seemed endlessly renewable. Within living memory the supplies of fresh water in the beautiful streams and lakes of North America were legendary. But suddenly in the 20th century we have at last begun to sense that both the water and soil of the earth are limited. We now realize that we cannot run off to a clean new place each time we have fouled our nest. We shall have to learn to manage our affairs and our immediate environment. We are sickened by the spectacle of the trash and refuse of our own activity. We become uncomfortable in our role as stewards of this wonderful resource, for we do not understand how we may both use and protect it.

While we have been engaged elsewhere, the rampant growth of aquatic weeds has come to be one of the symptoms of our failure to manage our resources. We assign values to the depreciation of property, to the pollution of municipal water supplies, to the loss of navigable streams, and to the failure of irrigation and power systems because of aquatic weeds. But we must also judge the worth of clean water for man in other, quite different ways. Some of the loveliest places on earth are at the water's edge. These may be the sites of our dwellings or the places that we choose for rest and renewal. As we spoil these, one by one, we shall know that we have surrendered a great part of our humanness, and we shall be anxious because we cannot trust ourselves.

Now we must abandon our view that streams and lakes are great self-cleansing reservoirs that can receive our wastes forever and return to us always as cool, clear water. Many of the watercourses of Asia and Africa, and of Wisconsin and Florida, are now so fertile and so well innoculated with aquatic weeds that they can no longer correct themselves. In many of these places, it is now too late to talk about an equilibrium or the balance of nature. Human activity and neglect have driven the equation far to the right. Within the combinations of mechanical, biological, and chemical methods of aquatic weed control we can find the tools to help with their restoration. We can keep the waterways open so that they can be useful to man and so that he may enjoy them. We can buy the time we need to learn to manage not only the vegetation but each of the resources in an entire watershed.

REFERENCES AND NOTES

1. F. L. Timmons, *U.S. Dep. of Agr. ARS-34-14* (1960).
2. N. Wollman *et al.*, *The Value of Water in Alternative Uses* (Univ. of New Mexico Press, Albuquerque, 1962).
3. C. A. Evans, *New Sci.* 19, 666 (1963); L. J. Mathews, *Pest Art. News Abstr.* 13, 7 (1967); V. Proctor, *Science* 160, 321 (1968).
4. J. Lebrun, *Bull. Agr. Congo* 50, 251 (1959).
5. E. T. Heinen and Salah el Din Hassan Ahmed, *Publication of the Information Production Center* (Dept. of Agriculture, Khartoum, Sudan, 1964).
6. C. E. Timmer and L. W. Weldon, *Hyacinth Contr. J.* 6, 34 (1967); W. T. Penfound and T. T. Earle, *Ecol. Monogr* 18, 447 (1948); R. R. Das, *Proc. Indian Sci. Congr.* 6, 445 (1969).
7. W. E. Wunderlich, *Hyacinth Contr. J.* 1, 14 (1962); *U.S. House of Representatives, Document No. 91, Water Hyacinth Obstructions* (55th Congress, Third Session, 1899); *U.S. House of Representatives, Document No. 37, Water Hyacinth Obstructions in the Waters of the Gulf and South Atlantic States* (85th Congress, First Session, 1957).
8. D. B. Bogart, *Proc. Soil Sci. Soc. Fla.* 9, 32 (1948); J. C. Stephens, R. D. Blackburn, D. E. Seaman, L. W. Weldon, *Proc. Amer. Soc. Civil Eng. J. Irrig. Drainage Div.* 89, 31 (1963).
9. A. S. Boughey, *Adansonia* 3, 49 (1963).
10. E. R. Hattingh, *Weed Res.* 1, 303 (1961).
11. R. H. Williams, *Trop. Agr.* 33, 145 (1956).
12. J. A. Mulrennan, *Mansonia Mosquitoes,* mineographed report (Div. of Entomology, Florida State Board of Health, Tallahassee); R. W. Chamberlain, W. D. Sudia, J. D. Gillett, *Amer. J. Hyg.* 70, 221 (1959); M. W. Provost, *Mansonia Studies in Leesburg in 1949* (Div. of Entomology, Florida State Board of Health, Tallahassee, 1949); W. D. Sudia and R. W. Chamberlain, personal

communication; E. L. Seabrook, *Rep. Annu. Meet. Fla. Antimosquito Ass.* 21, 1 (1950); C. Chow, *Preliminary Note on Herbicides for Pistia Clearance as a Rural Filariasis Control Measure in Ceylon* (World Health Organization, Geneva, 1953).
13. L. W. Weldon and R. D. Blackburn, *Weeds* 15(1), 5 (1967).
14. G. F. Beaven, *Summary of the 1962 Interagency Research Meeting on Eurasian Watermilfoil* (Natural Resources Institute, Univ. of Maryland, 1962); T. E. Crowell, J. H. Steenis, J. L. Sincock, *Proc. S. Weed Conf.* 20, 348 (1967); G. E. Smith, *ibid.* 15, 258 (1962); L. W. Weldon, R. D. Blackburn, D. S. Harrison, *U.S. Dep. Agr. Agr. Handb. No. 352* (1969); R. D. Blackburn and L. W. Weldon, *Hyacinth Contr. J.* 6, 15 (1967).
15. H. C. Fletcher and H. B. Elmendorf, *Yearbook of Agriculture 1955* (U.S. Government Printing Office, Washington, D.C., 1955), pp. 423-429; F. L. Timmons and D. C. Klingman, in *Water and Agriculture*, R. D. Hockensmith, Ed. (AAAS, Washington, D.C., 1960), p. 157.
16. L. W. Weldon, R. D. Blackburn, H. T. DeRigo, R. T. Mellen, *Hyacinth Contr. J.* 5, 12 (1966); D. S. Harrison, R. D. Blackburn, L. W. Weldon, J. R. Orsenigo, G. F. Ryan, *Univ. Fla. Agr. Ext. Serv. Circ. No. 219B* (1966); W. T. Parsons, *U.S. Dep. Agr. Vermin Noxious Weeds Destruction Board Bull. No. 3a* (1967).
17. R. D. Comes, R. R. Yeo, B. F. Bruns, J. M. Hodgson, F. L. Timmons, L. W. Weldon, T. R. Bartley, W. D. Boyle, N. E. Otto, D. D. Suggs, *U.S. Dep. Agr. ARS 34-57* (1963); V. F. Bruns, R. R. Yeo, H. F. Arle, *U.S. Dep. Agr. Tech. Bull. No. 1299* (1964); F. L. Timmons, *Proc. Tex. Annu. Indust. Weed Contr. Conf.* 2, 1 (1967).
18. P. A. Frank, *J. Exp. Bot.* 17, 546 (1966); ———, R. H. Hodgson, R. D. Comes, *Weeds* 11, 124 (1963); R. D. Blackburn, L. E. Bitting, L. W. Weldon, *Hyacinth Contrl J.* 5, 36 (1966).
19. F. L. Timmons, L. W. Weldon, W. O. Lee, *Weeds* 6, 406 (1958); J. M. Hodgson, V. F. Bruns, F. L. Timmons, W. O. Lee, L. W. Weldon, R. R. Yeo, *U.S. Dep. Agr. Prod. Res. Rep. No. 60* (1962); F. L. Timmons, V. F. Bruns, W. O. Lee, R. R. Yeo, J. M. Hodgson, L. W. Weldon, R. D. Comes, *U.S. Dep. Agr. Tech. Bull. No. 1286* (1963).
20. J. B. Butler and F. F. Ferguson, *Proc. S. Weed Conf.* 21, 304 (1968).
21. R. D. Blackburn and T. M. Taylor, *Abstr. Weed Sci. Soc. Amer.* (1968), p. 51; F. F. Ferguson and J. R. Palmer, *Amer. J. Trop. Med. Hyg.* 7, 640 (1958); F. F. Ferguson, J. Oliver-Gonzales, J. R. Palmer, *ibid.*, p. 491; Anonymous, *Agr. Res.* 16, 8 (1968).
22. W. H. L. Allsopp, *Nature* 188, 762 (1960); G. C. L. Bertram and C. K. R. Bertram, *ibid.* 196, 1329 (1962); P. L. Sguros, T. Monkus, C. Phillips, *Proc. S. Weed Conf.* 18, 588 (1965).
23. L. A. Andres, *Abstr. Weed Sci. Soc. Amer.* (1968), p. 51; F. D. Bennett, *Proc. S. Weed Conf.* 19, 497 (1966); *Pest Art. News Sum. Sec. C* 13, 304 (1967).
24. J. W. Avault, *Proc. S. Weed Conf.* 18, 145 (1965); M. T. Philipose, *Indian Livestock* 1(2), 20, 34 (1963).
25. J. Levett, *World Crops* 12, 58 (1960).
26. S. Bayley, H. Rabin, C. H. Southwick, *Chesapeake Sci.* 9(3), 173 (1968).
27. W. E. Wunderlich, *Hyacinth Contr. J.* 1, 14 (1962); C. F. Zeiger, *Ibid.*, p. 16; M. E. Grinwald, *Ibid.* 7, 31 (1968); W. D. Boyle and D. D. Suggs, *U.S. Dep. Interior Reg. I Bur. of Reclam. Misc. Publ.* (1960); G. C. Klingman, *Weed Control: As a Science* (Wiley, New York, 1961), pp. 323-324.
28. E. Little, *Publication No. PL:CP/20* (Crops Protection Branch, Food and Agricultural Organization of the United Nations, Rome, 1968).
29. Contribution from Department of Horticulture, University of Wisconsin, Madison; and cooperative investigations of the Crops Research Division, Agricultural Research Service, U.S. Department of Agriculture; the Central and Southern Florida Flood Control District; and the University of Florida Agricultural Experiment Station, Fort Lauderdale. Journal Series 3262.

The following, cheerfully presented tongue-in-cheek call for escalation of large dam building projects came at a time when conservationists were passionately attacking the proposed new dams at Bridge Canyon situated 80 miles below the famous Grand Canyon National Park, and at Marble Gorge about 12 miles above the park. Then Secretary of the Interior Stewart L. Udall, a conservationist himself, argued in favor of both dams by saying that the 91 miles of river within the park would remain undisturbed and that electric power could be sold to repay the federal investment.

Think Big   92

BRUCE STEWART

An Open Letter to the Secretary of the Interior

Dear Mr. Secretary:

The Bureau of Reclamation in your department is to be commended with faint praise for its recent accomplishments in the southwestern United States. True, it has completed the Glen Canyon Dam (authorized 1955) and 193 other dams without a failure, thus contributing to flood control, irrigation, and power development. Also it is agitating vigorously for dams at Marble Gorge and Bridge Canyon. But these are piddling enterprises. You must learn to think BIG if you hope to leave your mark indelibly written on the face of America. And what bigger project could you choose than to dam the Colorado River, right across Grand Canyon? Think of it. A waterfall one mile high! A lake one mile deep! A solid wall of concrete from the south rim to the north!

If such a dam were constructed, a few of its benefits can be dimly foreseen. First there would be the opportunities for power development. A Grand Canyon Dam would make the generating facilities at Hoover (1936) or Glen Canyon look like a lightning bug on a summer's evening. My rough calculations indicate that you could expect to produce enough electricity to light up not only Grand Canyon Lake area (hereafter called Lake Udall) but Bryce, Zion, the Petrified Forest, and Painted Desert, with enough left over to decorate 1,742,651 evergreens with Christmas lights.

The Grand Canyon Dam would also have great uses for irrigation and flood control. The Colorado River would be permanently tamed. Experts have assured me that with the waters from Lake Udall we could irrigate a maximum of 2,165,000 acres of dry land. Thus we could look forward to wheat fields in the Painted Desert, flower gardens around Sunset Crater, and the Petrified Forest no longer petrified but rather filled with thousands of living trees — orange, grapefruit, fig.

A third, fast-growing use of Grand Canyon waters would be for recreation. With the construction of a few fish hatcheries in southern Utah and northern Arizona, the lake could be kept stocked with fish, and a lake one mile deep and twenty miles wide would accommodate some monsters! Think of sturgeon, muskellunge, pike, ten- or twenty-pound trout. . . . Have you considered the fact that boating is the wave of the future? The steady increase in number of boats, in size, draft, and horsepower will soon make most small lakes obsolete. Putting the family boat of 1980 on one of these old lakes will be like trying to float the Queen Elizabeth in a teacup. Also the family submarine about the year 2000 will require depth beyond anything now present in the government lake system. Viewing the scenery of Grand Canyon underwater would be a thousand time more thrilling than seeing it from the distant north or south rim.

We come to the last but by no means the least of the great advantages of a mile-high Grand Canyon Dam—the magnitude of the economic enterprise. It would require at least twenty years and employ some 100,000 men, benefiting nearly a half-million people directly. Indirectly the economic benefits pyramid almost astronomically. The dam would contain at a conservative estimate some 17,659,873,151.85 cubic yards of steel, copper, rubber, generators, and all the thousands of items required by this great project.

There will of course be carping critics of a Grand Canyon Dam . . . do-gooders, conservationists, starry-eyed liberals and wild-lifers. They will wax lyrical about the beauties of nature, the awe-inspiring depths of great, lonely canyons, the history—white and Indian—to be buried by the waters of Lake Udall. Indeed they are already attacking those two small-time proposals, Marble and Bridge Canyon Dams, just because these will back up a little water into Grand Canyon National Park. Sooner or later, however, every foot of every big river in America must be backed up behind a retaining wall. This is our ultimate goal, and since it is, let up take a giant stride toward that goal by constructing a dam across the Grand Canyon—a marvel of engineering which will put to shame all the Pyramids, the Great Walls, bridges, and dams which have ever been built in the past.

"There is the mighty Colorado River flowing down to the sea. Dam it!"

The Myth of Fertility Dooms Development Plans　　93

DARRYL G. COLE

Not long ago Adrian Alfaro came to our home to tell us that his wife had been in labor for a week and could not give birth to her baby. Adrian owns a small farm near our coffee plantation at Canas Gordas in southwestern Costa Rica. A young man, he had been married a little more than a year. Now he was haggard and distraught. His wife was dying, he said.

My wife and I went to Adrian's farm and found Mrs. Alfaro resting on a bed of boards in a hut with a dirt floor and walls fashioned of split saplings. A white flour sack had been spread on the floor by an elderly midwife to receive the baby. We carried Mrs. Alfaro on a stretcher to our pickup truck. Adrian, two brothers, and his father held the stretcher in the back of the truck to ease the jolting of travel, and we began the trip to the regional medical station at San Vito de Jaba. It was in the middle of the wet season, a light rain was falling, and Adrian covered Mrs. Alfaro with a large sheet of plastic. The road to San Vito, 13 miles distant, was in bad condition. With heavy chains on its tires, and with a front-mounted winch, our truck would get through the mud. But as the rain fell over the soggy land, and the truck churned on, I felt immeasurably depressed.

Great Expectations

My family and I had come to Canas Gordas 13 years earlier. It was a frontier settlement then, emergent in the highland rain forest. We proposed to establish a diversified farm, employing the latest techniques of modern agriculture. Over the years my parents and my wife and I devoted a considerable amount of money and effort to the project. But our venture has yielded only a small measure of the rewards we expected. The emergency involving Adrian Alfaro and his wife underscored for me how mistaken those early expectations were.

I am frequently dismayed by articles appearing in the Costa Rican press asserting that agriculture in this country must be diversified and that the rich bounty and natural fertility of new land must be harvested. Such assertions seem to be made with all of the best intentions and with an eagerness from their writers suggesting that with this or another government program, with a loan or technical assistance, with the right attitude on the part of farmers, the new lands would yield prodigiously. Well-being and even prosperity would follow. I would like to submit that such hopes have not been realized in the Canas Gordas-San Vito area, that they are not being realized in other areas of Costa Rica, and that, on the basis of our present knowledge of tropical agriculture, they will not be realized in similar new lands in underdeveloped nations.

The Myth Persists

The myth of the fertility of these virgin lands has been too long in dying. It has long been dead for the farmers like Adrian Alfaro, whose subservience to a meager soil leaves them few illusions about the "untapped riches" of virgin lands. But the myth persists, and even thrives, among sectors of government and the public where misinformation has been accepted as fact.

When we came to Canas Gordas we purchased a tract of rain forest in an area widely acclaimed at that time as a future center of farming progress and development. An Italian colony had been started two years earlier in San Vito de Jaba, a project eventually involving the investment of about $2,000,000. We looked at the rain forest on our land, at the moist, dark soil supporting it, and concluded that anything would grow in soil so apparently fertile.

Fertility Restricted to Forest

We felled the forest, cleared the land, and planted the first crops. They were a failure from the beginning. We weren't discouraged; we began experimenting —using fertilizers, lime, manure, insecticides, fungicides, varieties of seed, cover crops, various methods of tillage. We consulted agronomists, farm-research and extension agencies, and farmers' publications, and called upon the experience that had enabled us to farm successfully in the United States. We discovered that other settlers in our area were making similar efforts with equally unsatisfactory results.

Finally, we learned what we might have been told at the beginning, had we been less adamant about our ability to succeed where others had demonstrated no remarkable success. We learned that the fertility of these virgin lands is mostly in the forest and in the thin layer of humus carpeting the forest floor.

The soil nutrients needed to sustain plant life are circulated from the soil through plant tissues. Drawn from the humus and top soil by the roots of the forest vegetation, the nutrients return to the soil in falling leaves and dead branches. At any given time the forest itself is a storehouse of soil fertility.

Cut down, the forest ceases to hold nutrients in suspension; violent rains drive over the land, leaching nutrients below root levels; sunlight invades shade-loving retreats; and, unwittingly, the farmer, by tilling and exposing the soil to the sun and rain, outrages its microbiotic order. Fertility vanishes in a sudden, stunning conflagration.

Diversity Is No Solution

Much can be done, of course, to supplement soil fertility with fertilizers. However, where rain drives month after month through loose, permeable soil,

where terrain is hilly and erosion carries soil away, where sunlight burns fiercely
into the land, it requires an art beyond the ability of most farmers to grow crops
well over sustained periods, even with fertilizers and modern techniques. What
is more to the point, such methods applied to soils divested of their original forest
cover are seldom profitable.

There is a good deal of discussion today in Costa Rica about agriculture
diversification. Hardly a week goes by without a pronouncement by someone on
the important subject. It is evident that the traditional mainstays of the Costa
Rican economy—coffee, cacao, bananas, sugar, which are embroiled in market
surpluses or in rising production costs—cannot be relied upon.

What to do? The solution, most frequently advanced, to diversify, is little
better than a restatement of the problem. It too frequently ignores the harshness
of the land.

Farmers whose livelihood is dependent upon a monoculture crippled by the
woes of international overproduction do not continue to rely upon that monoculture by choice; their dependence on the economic loser is largely the product of
conditions that at no time have offered any significant measure of flexibility.
Planners and economists, serving up the latest potpourri of diversification, might
well consider that, where agriculture has seized upon one or two successful crops
over a period of years, diversification has probably been tried and been found to
be competitively impractical.

The basis of our planning from the beginning of our work here in Canas
Gordas has been to develop a diversified farm. Yet, after 13 years, we have been
reduced to dependence upon a monoculture, the production of coffee. It is true
that the soil here will produce other crops: pasture grass, vegetables, corn, beans,
fruits. But given the conditions of climate, soil, and topography, they cannot be
produced and marketed competitively.

Enthusiasm Fades

The enthusiasm and confidence that characterized the beginning steps in
development in the Canas Gordas-San Vito area have languished. They have been
replaced by a lean skepticism, more closely defined by a need to survive than by
a will to succeed. Under the circumstances of these latter years success has
become merely the ability to subsist. Yet, what is more disturbing are the repeated
assertions made publicly purporting that the limitations of this area either do not
exist or can be eliminated with relatively simple measures.

Such arguments abet a form of social irresponsibility. They suggest that
solutions to basic problems hinge on but a few steps that, if taken, would lead
shortly to sweeping remedies.

Too often the standard of living in more-developed nations is used as an
example of what can be accomplished by pursuing this or that technique. This
point of view ignores the basic differences between the ingredients of agriculture
in the developed nation and those in the nation seeking development. It would
be preferable in underdeveloped nations to work within the limits of the environment and recognize that the blessings of fertility and productivity are not everywhere evenly distributed.

Mrs. Alfaro returned to her home not long ago with a baby boy, Adrian Alberto. I would like to believe that when Adrian Alberto goes to school he will follow a road no longer beset with the quagmires that made his arrival in the world the subject of an emergency, that as a man with a family he would enjoy the benefits his father has been denied. I would like to believe this, but 13 years of work in Canas Gordas have left me doubtful.

94 Will the Amazon Basin Become a Desert?

WILLIAM E. MORAN, JR.

Few areas of the world have provoked greater agricultural fantasies than the Amazon Basin, which is itself larger than any other Latin American country. Various schemes have been advanced to turn this steaming jungle into a "breadbasket" for the continent. Few of these master-plans have adequately taken into account the fragile ecosystem of the tropical rain forest, which supports a profusion of plant and animal species but which erodes with stunning suddenness under the slash-and-burn cultivation that is now so tragically on the increase. While scientists have not yet defined the precise relationship between mycorrhizal fungi and tree roots which enables the jungle to thrive on very poor laterite soil, they do agree on one vital point: this incredibly lush jungle, where the rainfall averages over 80 inches a year, is ecologically only a few steps removed from a wasteland. If the forest vegetation were to be cleared, says Colombian geologist Carlos Eduardo Acosta, the Amazon Basin would become "a desert like the Sahara."

The Oceans

Human Food from Ocean and Land

K. O. EMERY
C. O'D. ISELIN

During recent years many claims have been made about the importance of the ocean to man's future well-being. Some of these claims appear to us to be reasonable, whereas others have an Alice-in-Wonderland quality.

The difference in the former productivity of the ocean and the land is so great as to suggest that an enormous effort will be required before the production of the ocean can be comparable with that of the land.

A sort of genetic classification of food resources was used to compare the present stages of technology in the ocean and on the land. For plants, the primitive stage is that of gathering wild plants (on land—berries, nuts, mushrooms, herbs); the next stage is farming (whereby seed are planted and the plants are tended and then harvested). For animals, the primitive stage is that of hunting wild animals for food (on land—deer, rabbits, quail); the next stage is herding (whereby selected breeding, culling of young, and controlled slaughter are practiced along with the nondestructive taking of by-products such as eggs, milk, and wool). This terminology, gathering and farming of plants, and hunting and herding of animals, is also applied to the ocean in a strict sense. For example, we consider that only algae or bacteria can be farmed, and that oysters, clams, and fish can be herded (not farmed) as an improvement over catching them in their wild state. Note that nonedible materials such as lumber, whale oil, shells, pearls, wool, hides, and fertilizer are not included in this study.

Since farming is far closer to the energy source on the complex and inefficient food pyramid than is herding, one should expect greater rewards from farming than from herding. However, farming of the ocean (for plants) has as its major obstacle the difficulty of harvesting. Most of the bulk of plants that live in the ocean are microscopic in size and they are distributed in three dimensions. The cost (energy) of harvesting them exceeds the value (energy) that is recovered by eating (or burning) the crop. Near shore in clear water larger attached algae can be grown, but most of them are not particularly tasty and few are used directly as food. We do not know of a single experimental project in the United States that is designed to farm the ocean! Many projects investigate laboratory aspects of photosynthesis, plant physiology, and biochemistry, but none appear to be making direct tests of planting and harvesting in the ocean. One answer is that "we must understand the processes before they can be utilized," but we may ask in return "how well did early man understand photosynthesis and biochemistry when he improved and adapted to farming the primitive corn and other wild plants that he had encountered in his gathering stage of economy?"

1. Photosynthetic production in the ocean is comparable to that on the land, although great regional variations in productivity exist in both environments. Since the area of the ocean is nearly three times that of the land, the potential harvest is proportionally large, even without equivalent agricultural practices.

2. The old concept of the freedom of the seas, which developed because the ocean was considered nearly worthless except for cheap transportation and defense, is diametrically opposed to wise utilization of the seas.

3. Fishermen prefer to sell fresh fish because the price is much higher than for the so-called "trash" fish, which are being increasingly processed into fish meal as an additive for chicken and cattle food. Fish flour, a more refined product that is fit for human consumption, is just coming onto the market; it is an efficient source of cheap protein for the human diet.

4. Fishermen are likely to remain hunters rather than herders or farmers unless responsibility is clearly defined for management of the biological resources available in the saltwater envelope that covers so much of the world. For some resources national agencies can be adequate, but for others some international agency is needed.

Untapped Resources

Milk Production of Cows on Protein-Free Feed 96

ARTTURI I. VIRTANEN

The synthesis of bacterial protein in the rumen of lactating cows fed on purified carbohydrates, with urea and ammonium salts as the sole sources of nitrogen, can be increased, through feed adaptation, to a level adequate not only for maintenance of the cow but also for a relatively high milk production. The best annual milk yield per cow on the experimental feed has, so far, been 4217 kilograms, calculated as standard milk (684 kilocalories per kilogram of milk). The composition of the test milk is similar to that of normal fat- and protein-rich milk. Fractionation of casein and serum proteins of test milk and normal milk by different methods demonstrated the similarity of the proteins of the two milks. The normal or higher concentrations of the water-soluble vitamins in test milk show that the biosynthesis of these vitamins in the rumen is vigorous. The flavor of the two milks is very similar—proof that biosynthesis of the effective flavor compounds of milk occurs in the body of the cow. The only component of test milk whose composition, when small amounts of vegetable oil have been fed, has differed from that of normal milk is the fat.

The studies of milk production on the experimental feed have opened up new possibilities for investigating the biosynthesis of different milk components. The studies are also of practical importance: Since the vigorous biosynthesis of proteins from simple nitrogen compounds in the rumen of test-feed-adapted cows has been demonstrated, there are greater possibilities for studying the replacement of protein by urea. In countries where there are plenty of forests, part of the feed of cows can be made up of certain wood products—for instance, hemicellulose and cellulose of low quality. The new findings may also be of value in the dry areas of the globe, where milk would be of vital significance for improving the nutrition of the population.

97

Religion and Energy Flow

HOWARD T. ODUM

An example of a primitive agricultural system of man and nature is provided by the system of rice and cattle in India and in other monsoon climates where the severity of the dry season essentially forces all systems of vegetation, whether controlled by man or not, to recommence each year. There is a flow of energy through rice and some grass, man, and the sacred cattle (work animals) with loopback circuits of work control. Harris[1] opposes those who state that the sacred animals on the intensified, nonsubsidized farms are superfluous. He mentions that they glean from a different plant base than man, serve as a source of critical protein, and especially facilitate mineral cycling and work on the plots necessary for a fast start on crop production when the wet monsoon begins. Those who advocate removal of the sacred cows needed under the present agricultural system refer to the simple principle of shortening the food chain to save energy. In this case, a little knowledge about one process without understanding the complete system may be producing recommendations that endanger millions by upsetting a self-supporting system. Harris cites Gandhi's comment that cows are sacred because they are necessary. The more general principle may be that religion is the program of energy control necessary for survival encoded in behavioral language.

1. Harris, Marvin. 1965. *The Myth of the Sacred Cow.* Pp 217-228. *In:* Leeds, Anthony and Andrew P. Vayda. *Man, Culture, and Animals.* Publ. No. 78 of the Amer. Assoc. Advancement of Sci., Washington, D. C. 304 pp.

4B00042